AMERICA'S
TICKING
BANKRUPTCY
BOMB

AMERICA'S TICKING BANKRUPTCY BOMB

HOW THE LOOMING DEBT CRISIS THREATENS THE AMERICAN DREAM— AND HOW WE CAN TURN THE TIDE BEFORE IT'S TOO LATE

PETER FERRARA

BROADSIDE BOOKS
An Imprint of HarperCollins*Publishers*
www.broadsidebooks.net

HarperCollins books may be purchased for educational, business, or sales promotional use. For information, please write: Special Markets Department, Harper-Collins Publishers, 10 East 53rd Street, New York, NY 10022.

Broadside Books™ and the Broadside logo are trademarks of HarperCollins Publishers.

FIRST EDITION

Designed by William Ruoto

Library of Congress Cataloging-in-Publication Data

Ferrara, Peter J.
    America's ticking bankruptcy bomb : how the looming debt crisis threatens the American dream—and how we can turn the tide before it's too late / Peter Ferrara.—1st ed.
        p. cm.
    Summary: "The federal government is about to go bankrupt. This is THE hot-button issue in America from now through the next presidential election in 2012"—Provided by publisher.
    ISBN 978-0-06-202577-7 (hardback)
        1. Government spending policy—United States. 2. Debts, Public—United States. 3. Budget deficits—United States. 4. American Dream. 5. United States—Economic conditions—2009- I. Title.
    HJ7537.F47 2011
    336.3'40973—dc22

                                                                2011006811

11 12 13 14 15   OV/RRD   10 9 8 7 6 5 4 3 2 1

For my son, Peter,
and all the young patriots of his generation
who will raise up a new vision of freedom
and prosperity for America
and the world.

CONTENTS

AMERICA'S
TICKING
BANKRUPTCY
BOMB

CHAPTER 1

LIGHTING THE FUSE

How We Started Down the Road to National Insolvency

The failures of federal, state, and local officials of both major parties, over many years, have primed a ticking bankruptcy bomb for America that will explode the American Dream if we do not disarm it. But it is not too late to reverse course and avert the coming bankruptcy of America. That will require fundamental structural reforms of all levels of government, and our most politically sensitive entitlement programs. If we do this right, thoroughly modernized entitlements will serve the poor and most vulnerable among us far better, and a new economic boom will restore America's traditional world-leading prosperity. How to achieve those goals is explained in this book.

By the end of President George W. Bush's eight years in office, America had abandoned every one of the four major planks of Reaganomics, as explained in Chapter 6. While in his recent book, *Decision Points*,[1] Bush insists that federal spending on average during his two terms was lower than for previous presidents, a lower average for eight years of spending trending up may not be a better record than a higher average for eight years of spending trending down. During Bush's eight years as president, the federal government grew by one-seventh relative to the economy, after the Republican Congress under former Speaker Newt Gingrich had so promisingly reduced it by that much from 1994 to 2000.

But when President Barack Obama got behind the steering wheel in 2009, he accelerated into hyperdrive even more so in all the wrong directions, doggedly pursuing the opposite of Reaganomics in every detail, as also explained in Chapter 6. Federal spending has already soared by another fourth relative to the economy, to the highest in history except during World War II. The national debt, now rocketing toward $20 trillion by 2020, is already the highest in history as a percent of gross domestic product (GDP) except for World War II, and on its current course will soar well past that record. Indeed, the national debt has been rising so fast that under current policies more debt will be run up in one term under President Obama than under all other presidents in history—from George Washington to George W. Bush—combined.

On our current course, indeed, our national debt as a percent of GDP will exceed even the level that triggered bankruptcy for Greece, when the financial markets refused to lend the government enough money to cover its enormous annual deficit. The European Union tried to end that crisis with a trillion-dollar bailout financed by its taxpayers. But who will bail out America? Who even could?

Even worse, the national debt does not nearly encompass everything the federal government owes, or on which it is subject to liability or further financial losses. According to official U.S. government reports, the long-term unfunded liability of Social Security is $15 trillion. If we add in all of Medicare, Parts A, B, C, and D, the total unfunded liabilities for these programs alone climbs to over $100 trillion, or about seven times today's entire economy.

Usually overlooked are the unfunded liabilities of federal military pensions, estimated at $3.7 trillion.[2] Another unfunded liability of $1.5 trillion is for veterans' benefits compensating for disability or death connected to active service.[3] Unfunded liabilities for federal civil service retirees are estimated at an additional $2.1 trillion.[4]

The Federal Deposit Insurance Corporation (FDIC) reports a negative reserve for deposit insurance coverage for $5.4 trillion in insured deposits.[5] The Federal Housing Authority (FHA) bears responsibility for another $1 trillion in home mortgage insurance guarantees.[6] Total federal loan guarantees in 2010 reached close to $2 trillion.[7] The National Flood Insurance Program has $1.3 trillion in outstanding coverage, with little or nothing of note to back it up.[8]

Then there are trillions more in mortgage-backed securities and federal guarantees of those securities held by the Federal Reserve, Fannie Mae, Freddie Mac, the FHA, and the U.S. Treasury. These were the toxic securities at the root of the financial crisis. The federal government has already spent $150 billion on the bailout of Fannie Mae and Freddie Mac, and expects that tab to rise to half a trillion.

Somehow, President Obama insisted that it was a good idea to add all of the entitlement promises of Obamacare on top of these obligations. The Obamacare legislation added a costly new entitlement program to provide federal welfare subsidies for health insurance for families making as much as $88,000 per year to start, climbing to over $100,000 within a couple of years. In addition, woefully overpromised Medicaid was sharply expanded by 24 million new beneficiaries by 2015, covering nearly 100 million Americans by 2021 according to CBO,[9] with what was supposed to be a health care program for the poor. While President Obama won enactment of Obamacare on the promise that it would reduce deficits, as explained in Chapter 4 it will add another $4–6 trillion to the nation's deficits and debt over the first twenty years alone. As with so much else, with Obamacare President Obama forcefully drove America pell-mell in exactly the wrong direction.

State and local governments are adding even further to the problem. When people use the term "failed state," they mean something like Somalia, with its disintegrated government. But on our current course, the term may increasingly be applied to California, New York, Michigan, and Illinois, with their out-of-control state budgets and deficits, runaway public employee pension burdens, dysfunctional education bureaucracies, and increasingly belligerent public sector unions winning bloated workforces and runaway bureaucrat salaries and pensions at taxpayer expense.

These states resemble Greece, with our federal government already bailing them out at taxpayer expense. That started in President Obama's first stimulus bill in February 2009 and has continued since then with additional federal funding. State and local government debt has been soaring in recent years, particularly at the municipal level, climbing to $3.2 trillion, or an additional 22% of GDP, in 2010.[10] That is projected to climb to nearly $4 trillion, or 24% of GDP, by 2012.[11] The municipal bond market alone is nearly $3 trillion.[12]

The unfunded liabilities of state and local pensions total $3.8 trillion, using the same standards as applied to evaluate corporate pensions.

State and local promises to pay retired employee health benefits are completely unfunded without any reserves, adding another $1.4 trillion in unfunded liabilities.

Adding still more to these troubles is the extended weakness and instability of the economy. The average recession since World War II has lasted ten months. The longest previously was sixteen months. Yet three years after the latest recession started in December 2007, unemployment was still rising, stuck at over 9.5% for a year and a half, the longest duration of such unemployment since World War II.

The extension of the Bush tax cuts to 2012 allowed some scope for real recovery, and for unemployment to start to fall. But that extension did not involve any new rate cuts; it merely extended the existing tax rates that had already been in place for ten years. President Obama still pledged to allow those cuts to expire in 2013. Along with the tax increases from Obamacare going into effect, tax rates would then shoot up for every major federal tax on the nation's employers and investors (which is the English translation of the term "the rich").

With the specter of that still hanging over the economy, President Obama has been racing ahead with expensive new regulatory burdens. The Environmental Protection Agency's "global warming" carbon dioxide regulations threatened to impose trillions in new costs on the economy in higher energy costs and lost jobs and output. Interior Secretary Ken Salazar has been shutting down oil drilling in most of the Gulf of Mexico and elsewhere, and other excessive regulation has restricted natural gas, coal, and nuclear production. This is constraining reliable energy supplies, further raising energy costs and sacrificing jobs and GDP, at a time when the price of oil is already climbing over a hundred dollars a barrel. Obamacare's employer mandate beckons to raise the cost of employment, which could only sacrifice still more jobs.

Meanwhile, the Fed's easy-money policy ("quantitative easing") was raising the specter of renewed inflation, heralded by soaring commodity prices at the end of 2010. When the Fed decides it has to reverse course to avoid an inflation explosion, that will cause interest rates to spike from the historically low levels of the last three years.

If all these factors came together to cause a double-dip recession, what would happen to deficits and the national debt then? With the national debt already slated to soar past the records of World War II even without continued war, or further recession, even our ability to finance our national defense in case of extended military conflict would be imperiled. Would that financial weakness invite war?

THE END OF THE AMERICAN DREAM?

From the end of World War II until 2008, a period of more than sixty years, federal spending as a percent of GDP hovered around a stable average of 20%. But over the first two years under President Obama it soared by one-fourth, to 25%. President Obama increased welfare spending alone by one-third in his first two years. This wasn't just a short-term, recession-related phenomenon. Federal, state, and local welfare spending is now projected to total $10.3 trillion over the next ten years. While welfare was originally the province of the states, the federal government now sponsors 185 means-tested welfare programs. Obamacare spending doesn't even start in earnest until 2014.

Under current policies, federal spending will rocket to 40% of GDP by 2040,[13] nearly double the long-run historical average. Balancing the budget then would require basically doubling all federal taxes, or cutting all federal spending in half. Adding state and local spending to federal spending would leave total government spending in America over 50% of GDP by 2040.

This would fundamentally transform America into a static, low-growth, socialist European state. America's traditional world-leading prosperity and opportunity, the American Dream, would be gone.

By 2080, federal spending under current policies will explode to 75% of GDP,[14] nearing four times the historical average. Total government spending would eat up virtually our entire economy, like the old-fashioned, now-defunct communist states of the last century.

This all assumes no spike in interest rates or inflation, no further recessions, no negative economic effect from the burden of federal spending, taxes, deficits, and debt. Those inevitable results would reduce GDP and raise federal spending even more, increasing government spending as a percent of GDP even further.

RESTORING THE AMERICAN DREAM

All of the above, from the increasingly damning numbers to the possible bankruptcy of America, is like a visit from the Ghost of Christmas Future—shadows of what will be, but does not have to be, if we will change. This book is not just about the problems, and their possible magnitude. It is also about solutions, and the way out for America. It is about restoring the American Dream.

We can avoid the coming bankruptcy of America, and the loss of our American heritage of world-leading prosperity. But to achieve that, we must think anew regarding all aspects of our federal, state, and local governments. In particular, we must think outside the box of current long-standing policies, and the special interests that now mandate those policies, to achieve the rebirth of America.

I don't believe in human suffering. I fully accept the "liberal" premise that prosperity and opportunity must be available to all Americans. A booming economy that benefits just a few at the top is no success. The American Dream must be for all, or it is inoperative. What we need is a rising tide that lifts all boats, in Kennedy's phraseology, along with a comprehensive safety net to catch any that may fall under it.

We can and must adopt the economic policies to achieve that. But success requires an intellectual commitment to hard analysis, and the reality of experience, rather than a stale ideological romanticism for the socialist struggles of the late 19th and early 20th centuries. Too many of America's intellectuals, journalists, and political activists remain trapped in the web of that outdated ideological romanticism. It is long past time to move on to the 21st century.

We know, in fact, how to create another twenty-five-year, generation-long economic boom in America. President Reagan showed us the way. A booming economy is the foundation, and the first priority, for averting bankruptcy for America.

We must begin by first adopting those proven and logical policies to restore long-term economic growth and prosperity, starting with a tax system thoroughly reformed to maximize such growth. Then we must resize our government spending and obligations to fit within those policies. Even some European countries, such as Great Britain, France, and socialist Sweden, have begun to show the way, as have some U.S. states.

Indeed, this book will explain in detail how to balance the budget, not just over the short run, but permanently, over the long run. That requires not some brain-dead budget deal increasing taxes to kill the economy in return for cutting Grandpa's retirement benefits and Grandma's health benefits. It requires terminating outdated programs, agencies, bureaucracies, even whole cabinet departments that are actually counterproductive in our modern, 21st century economy. Then it requires putting the remaining government on a diet consistent with the long-term economic growth needs of the economy. For the long run, it requires fundamental, structural, modernizing entitlement reforms.

But a true concern to end human suffering requires more than a booming economy, though that would go a long way to achieving the goal (which is not nearly adequately understood). It does require as well a new, modern social safety net ensuring that the essential needs of the poor and vulnerable regarding income support, health care, housing, and nutrition are met. But a central theme of this book is that such a truly modernized social safety net, based on highly effective market incentives rather than 19th century tax and redistribution programs, would achieve all the liberal social safety net goals far better, at just a fraction of the cost of the current, outdated, counterproductive entitlement programs. The new social safety net's programs would reinforce and further economic growth, rather than counterproductively hold it back.

America's current entitlement programs are all based on old-fashioned tax and redistribution models dating back to late 19th century Europe. Rather than trying to address the entitlement crisis by raising taxes and cutting benefits, we need to think outside the box with fundamental, structural reforms that would transform the programs to rely primarily on modern capital and labor markets, with positive, pro-growth incentives. What is involved here is an extension of supply-side analysis to the incentives of essential social safety nets and how to structure those to maximize effectiveness, growth, and prosperity.

For Social Security, as discussed in detail in Chapter 3, workers should be allowed the freedom to choose to save and invest some and eventually all of their payroll taxes in personal savings, investment, and insurance accounts that would ultimately finance all of the benefits currently financed by the payroll tax. This would replace large, growing, and ultimately impoverishing payroll taxes with a personal store of savings and wealth for each and every working family, involving a personal ownership stake in America's business and industry. With real, long-term market investment returns, workers would actually enjoy higher benefits than Social Security even promises today, at lower costs. The accounts would provide wave after wave of new savings to fuel new capital investment, contributing to a booming economy. This system has been proved by real-world models already in existence at home and abroad.

For health care, as discussed in Chapter 4, we should repeal and replace Obamacare with a true health care safety net that ensures access to essential health care for all Americans, for a fraction of the cost of Obamacare, by focusing assistance on the truly needy who cannot afford health insurance on their own. Health care costs can be reduced by introducing real market incentives and competition in health care and insurance.

For welfare, as discussed in detail in Chapter 5, we can finally and ultimately truly win the war on poverty with an entirely new welfare safety net system building on the enormously successful but mostly overlooked welfare reforms of 1996. This book will show how to build that system, based on real incentives to work and to maintain stable families, while still providing essential assistance for those in need, ultimately eliminating poverty in America. That would involve sending the remaining 184 federal means-tested welfare programs back to the states on the model of the enormously successful 1996 reforms of the old Aid to Families with Dependent Children (AFDC) program. Instead of taxpayers subsidizing the bottom 20% of the income distribution not to work, those on the dole today who are able-bodied would join the workforce and thereby further contribute to the booming economy, to the benefit of all.

This book will consequently present a vision for a true, modernized social safety net that would actually serve those in need far better, with far less in government power, control, taxes, and spending. That truly "liberal" safety net would greatly expand the freedom, prosperity, and power of those in need and of working people. Such sweeping fundamental reforms would solve the looming intractable entitlement crisis

while allowing future tax *reductions* to the benefit of all, especially working people, rather than tax increases. Sweeping future tax reductions,
in fact, are possible because over the long term all the reforms in this
book would ultimately reduce federal spending by roughly half (though
admittedly that would take decades to fully play out), while a booming
economy generates consistently surging revenues.

However, another key theme of this book is that going beyond such
safety net policies, to tax and spend to achieve more equal incomes,
wealth, and equality of results, is counterproductive and ultimately dis-
empowering for working people, the poor, and society as a whole. It is
fundamentally irreconcilable with economic freedom and the American
Dream of booming prosperity and opportunity for all. Consequently,
as discussed in detail in Chapter 9, such equality of results should not
be a goal of American public policy. The equality of freedom is equality
under the law, meaning equal rules not equal results.

As indicated above, this book will also explain in full detail in Chapters 6 and 7 how to create another generational economic boom, which I
watched President Reagan and his senior economic advisors accomplish
when I was a very young man, from my modest perch in the Reagan
White House Office of Policy Development. Such booming economic
growth is much more beneficial for working people and the poor than
counterproductive socialist redistribution to achieve equality of results.
A booming market economy produces a much higher standard of living
precisely for working people and the poor, as we will see in this book.
This is especially so when policies are structured to channel the flows
of booming economic growth through working people and the poor, as
through the safety net reforms further explained below. Economic experience, theory, and logic show that, by contrast, outdated, throwback
socialist redistribution inevitably leads to lower standards of living, and
to stagnation and decline.

Indeed, the safety net reforms and the rest of the economic liberation agenda outlined in this book would produce much greater freedom,
prosperity, and power for working people and the poor across the board.
On issue after issue, that agenda involves shifting power away from centralized, big bureaucracies based on coercion and over to the average
working man and woman, and to students, retirees, families, the poor,

African-Americans, Hispanics, and other minorities. In short, this book presents a true vision of power to the people, which was the ultimate liberal goal.

I will also provide a specific agenda for the states on tax reform, pension reform, and how to balance their budgets in Chapter 8. The book ultimately serves as a policy guide and agenda not only for America, but for all countries throughout the world.

Sadly, instead of reforms taking America to this future of personal empowerment and economic liberation and prosperity, President Obama is taking us backward, seeking to steer the entire country into a national version of the Chicago urban political machine. We thought he would be a modern, forward-looking president advancing a new agenda of progress. Instead we got the failed Keynesian economics and make-work policies of the New Deal, and the stagnation economics of the 1970s. Instead of freeing us to go forward, President Obama and his allies are desperate to take us back, to the socialized medicine they are so certain we should have had seventy-five years ago, to the union-run economy that farsighted thinkers thought was in our future in the 1930s, to the central planning bureaucracy that was the cutting-edge dream of turn-of-the-century progressives (that would be the turn of the last century). It is all so retro.

What we need instead is to move forward with a freedom and prosperity vision for the American economy of the 21st century.

CHAPTER 2

AMERICA'S COMING BANKRUPTCY

The Overwhelming Swirl of Deficits, Debt,
and Unfunded Liabilities

What would bankruptcy for America look like?

Even President Obama's own budget projected that by 2012 the national debt held by the public will have doubled in only four years, to $11.9 trillion from 5.8 trillion in 2008. That alone means that in one term of office, President Obama will have accumulated more national debt than all prior presidents combined, from George Washington to George W. Bush. By 2021 the national debt held by the public will have more than tripled since 2008 to $19 trillion, again under President Obama's own projections.

By the end of last year, the national debt had already reached 62% of GDP, higher than at any time in our history except for World War II and shortly thereafter.[1] By 2023, the Congressional Budget Office (CBO) projects, under current policies the national debt held by the public will grow past 100% of GDP,[2] which means the federal government will owe more by then than what our entire economy produces in a year. These projections all assume that the stimulus spending instituted in 2009 is not continued, and consequently that federal spending outside of entitlements and debt interest is cut permanently by 16% as a percent of GDP.[3] The U.S. Government Accountability Office (GAO) presents an alternative fiscal simulation, based on the best work of the government's own actuaries, that projects that by 2020 the national debt held by the public will exceed even the World War II historical peak of 109% of GDP.[4]

But it gets worse. Even President Obama's budget projects that the federal government's gross federal debt, which includes such items as the debt held in the Social Security trust funds (real debt that will have to be paid in the future), would be over $26.3 trillion by 2021, or 110% of GDP. The Bank for International Settlements (BIS) estimates that this gross debt will accelerate faster, hitting 200% of GDP by 2022, and 300% by 2030.[5] The federal debt ceiling, or debt limit, we often hear about in the news applies to this gross federal debt, which was $13.7 trillion as of September 30, 2010,[6] rising rapidly at the start of 2011 to the then federal debt limit of $14.3 trillion.

Under current policies, CBO projects that even the smaller national debt held by the public, as opposed to the gross federal debt, would rocket to 185% by 2035,[7] and to 200% by 2037,[8] twice as large as our entire economy. This national debt would explode further to unprecedented levels of 233% of GDP by 2040, and to 854% by 2080.[9] As Erskine Bowles, cochairman of President Obama's Deficit and Debt Commission and White House chief of staff under President Clinton, has said, "This debt is like a cancer that will destroy the country from within."

An international study for the National Bureau of Economic Research by Kenneth Rogoff of Harvard and Carmen Reinhart of the Peterson Institute for International Economics, covering the experience of forty-four countries over two hundred years, found that economic growth slows substantially when national debt climbs over 90% of GDP.[10] In 2009 the national debt of Greece reached 115% of GDP. Within a year, the international markets refused to lend the Greek government any more money by buying its government bonds. That meant that Greece could not borrow the money to finance its budget deficit, sparking the Greek/euro crisis. That resulted in a trillion-dollar bailout from the European Union (EU), financed by EU taxpayers.

But as indicated in Chapter 1, the national debt is just the starting point for toting up everything the government owes, or may owe. The unfunded liabilities of Social Security and Medicare together run up to over $100 trillion, according to the government's own actuaries.[11] The so-called trust funds for Social Security and Medicare provide exactly zero help in financing those long-term liabilities. The Social Security trust funds are reported to hold close to $3 trillion in assets. But those assets are all special-issue government bonds that just represent still more government debt, more accurately viewed as internal federal IOUs.

The federal government has no cash or other assets to back up those trust fund bonds. As discussed in Chapter 3, Social Security operates on a pay-as-you-go basis, meaning current benefits are financed with current revenues, and there is no actual savings and investment anywhere in the system. When Social Security needs money from the trust funds to pay promised benefits, which has already started to happen, the special-issue government bonds, or internal federal IOUs, will be turned in to the Treasury to get the cash. But the Treasury has no cash lying around to pay that debt. The Treasury can get the money only from the taxpayers, by raising taxes, in addition to all the payroll taxes we will continue to pay for the program, or effectively from the Chinese, by borrowing still more in the debt markets. That is why all the "assets" in the Social Security trust funds are actually included in the federal government's gross federal debt, subject to the debt limit.

In reality, and as a matter of federal law, the Social Security trust funds are nothing more than a statement of the legal authority that Social Security has to draw from general revenues, meaning ultimately you the taxpayer, when the money is needed to pay benefits. The estimate by the government's own Social Security actuaries of the unfunded liabilities of Social Security fully accounts for these "trust funds." All of this is also true of the Medicare trust funds.

In addition, there are the further unfunded liabilities for federal military pensions, promised veterans benefits, and the retirement benefits for federal civil service workers. The FDIC is responsible for trillions in guarantees of government-insured deposits, the FHA is liable for another trillion dollars of home mortgage insurance guarantees, and the National Flood Insurance Program is responsible for over a trillion in outstanding coverage, with nothing of significance to back it up.

Then there are all the guarantees piled up by the Troubled Assets Relief Program (TARP) and other bailouts over the past few years. As of September 30, 2010, the Treasury still held close to $200 billion in outstanding direct loans and stock investments due to the TARP bailouts.[12] Altogether the Treasury held nearly $1 trillion in net loans receivable and stock equity interests, including 33% of the stock of General Motors,[13] 10% of the stock in Chrysler,[14] $42 billion (80–90%) of AIG stock,[15] and over $100 billion in the stock of Fannie Mae and Freddie Mac.[16] Fannie

Mae and Freddie Mac alone hold $4.4 trillion in mortgage-backed securities (MBSs), and owe another $1.4 trillion in debt not counted in the national debt.[17] The Federal Reserve, the FHA, and the U.S. Treasury hold trillions more in MBSs, and federal guarantees of those toxic securities that were at the root of the financial crisis.[18] The federal bailout of Fannie Mae and Freddie Mac has already cost $150 billion, projected to rise ultimately to half a trillion.[19]

Total federal loan guarantees have now climbed close to $2 trillion. The face value of federal loans outstanding in 2010, including education, agriculture, housing, and other loans, reached over $700 billion.[20] With long-term near-double-digit unemployment, those education loans are now particularly risky. The federal government is also responsible for an estimated $320 billion in environmental cleanup costs for federal properties required under current law.[21] All these liabilities are in addition to the national debt discussed above. Thoroughly wrongheaded Obamacare just adds further trillions to all these liabilities, as discussed below and in Chapter 4.

The additional unfunded liabilities of state and local governments are also on top of the national debt discussed above. That includes over $3 trillion in municipal bond and state-level debt, close to $4 trillion in unfunded state and local pension liabilities, and over $1 trillion more in completely unfunded retirement health benefits promised to state and local employees. In the last two years state and local governments have spent nearly half a trillion more than they have collected in taxes, due to federal stimulus spending and their own effectively uncovered deficits.[22] At the beginning of 2011, they faced at least $110–150 billion in additional deficits for the year.

President Obama himself projected the federal deficit for 2011 at $1.645 trillion, the highest in world history. That came after unprecedented trillion-dollar deficits of $1.3 trillion in 2010 and $1.4 trillion in 2009, adding $4.35 trillion to the national debt in just three years. For context, the highest deficit in history previously was $458 billion in 2008, President Bush's last year. The highest deficit during the Reagan years, when there was so much yelling and screaming over it, was $221 billion.

In President Obama's 2011 budget, for every dollar spent, 43 cents will be borrowed. Spending for Social Security, Medicare, Medicaid, and the income-security programs (mostly welfare) will consume 95% of all federal revenues. What is left will not even be enough to pay interest on the national debt, equal to 10% of federal revenues, leaving half of that to be borrowed. All the money for everything else the federal government does, including all of national defense, law enforcement, transportation, agriculture, indeed, for *every* cabinet department outside of spending for the above entitlements, all will have to be borrowed. All of Obamacare will now be on top of that, including the vast expansion of Medicaid to nearly 100 million Americans by 2021, and an entirely new entitlement program providing health insurance subsidies for families earning over $100,000 a year.

Then, members of the post–World War II baby boom generation start to retire on Medicare this year, and on Social Security next year. Obamacare on top of Social Security and Medicare just made America even more dangerously vulnerable to two very debilitating long-term trends. First is the aging of the population due to the retirement of the baby boom generation coupled with the baby bust they left behind (the result of a low fertility rate in the baby boomers' young adult years). Second is rapidly rising health costs, soon raising the costs of Medicare, Medicaid, and Obamacare, as well as general health care burdens on the economy, as explained further in Chapter 4.[23]

But even this is not a fully accurate picture of the federal budget. That budget is reported in official documents, echoed in the national media, on a cash accounting basis, the most simpleminded form of accounting. But the U.S. Treasury Department's annual Financial Report of the United States Government presents the federal budget each year using the same generally accepted accounting standards as apply to private corporations. In particular, costs are recognized when they become owed, not when they are paid. For 2010, the actual federal budget deficit calculated this way was $2.1 trillion, an all-time record,[24] as compared to the cash accounting deficit for that year reported as $1.3 trillion. That deficit had soared two-thirds from the year before, further revealing the profligacy of the Obama administration.[25] Net federal spending by this measure had rocketed upward by 25% in one year to $4.3 trillion for 2010,[26] compared to $3.5 trillion reported by the traditional, cash accounting budget measure for 2010.[27]

For most of the last fifty years, annual Social Security surpluses have been masking the full scope of the federal deficit, as those surpluses were lumped in with the gross federal deficits in the unified federal budget accounting. But no more. Those annual surpluses are now gone. In 2010, for the first time since President Reagan saved the program in the early 1980s, Social Security ran a cash flow deficit. That deficit will now widen over the next twenty-five years, when the Social Security trust funds, such as they are, will run out completely. During that time, paying all promised benefits will require an additional $7.3 trillion in taxes or debt for the American people, on top of all the payroll taxes they will have to continue to pay, to cash in the Social Security trust fund bonds.[28]

Once the trust funds run out, paying all promised Social Security benefits will require raising Social Security payroll taxes most likely by nearly 60% by 2030, from a combined employee/employer total of 12.4% of taxable wages to 19%, under the projections that may be most realistic as discussed in Chapter 3. By 2065, when many of today's young workers will still be in retirement, the total Social Security payroll tax rate will likely have to increase to 23% to pay all promised benefits under these projections, nearly double the current rate. Counting Medicare Part A alone along with Social Security, paying all promised benefits by the time today's young workers retire would most likely require raising the total payroll tax rate from 15.3% today to 44%, nearly three times current levels, on its way eventually to 52% by 2085, again all as discussed in detail in Chapter 3.

President Obama barnstormed the country telling us Obamacare would reduce the deficit, citing CBO's score to back him up. But he never told us the basis for that score, which was revealed in the 2010 Annual Report of the Medicare Board of Trustees and the 2010 Financial Report of the United States Government. Those documents show that Obamacare policies will cut future payments to doctors, hospitals, and other health care providers for health care services and treatment for America's seniors by $15 trillion. But as the Medicare actuaries have been trying to warn us, that would leave seniors without the critical care they need when they are sickest and most vulnerable. It would be an early death sentence for millions. That is why several federal financial reports suggest that the cuts are intractable and likely to be reversed. But if they are reversed, the deficits caused by Obamacare will soar. All of this is discussed in detail in Chapter 4.

The broadest possible measure of our shorter-term debt vulnerabilities is provided by another measure—gross federal borrowing needs. The average maturity of the Treasury bonds, notes, and bills that compose our national debt is less than five years, with over 20% maturing in less than a year. That means we have to borrow much more each year than the amount of our deficit, because so much of the outstanding federal debt has to be rolled over during the year. As a result of this and other factors, total new federal borrowings from the public in 2010 weighed in at $8.5 trillion.[29] That was 57% of GDP for the year, second worst in the entire world only to Japan, which has suffered a lost economy for the last twenty years (lost in the Keynesian woods).[30] That was nearly three times the gross national borrowings of Greece at 21.5%, Spain at 20.7%, and Portugal at 21.8%, derisively known as the PIGS, an acronym derived from the first letter of the country names (including Italy), because of their long histories of national fiscal irresponsibility.[31]

Last summer, the International Monetary Fund (IMF) issued a report on its latest regular consultation with the United States.[32] As with every country, the report covered the economic, fiscal, and financial outlook for America. The shocking conclusion of the report was, in technical terms, that the U.S. fiscal gap, defined as the difference between all future federal revenues and all future federal expenditures, is 14% of GDP. That means that bringing the government's finances into long-term fiscal balance would require some combination of tax increases and spending cuts equal to 14% of GDP.

Among the reasons that was shocking is that Greece's long-term fiscal gap is comparatively much less at 11.5% of GDP. Another reason it was shocking is that, again, over the long run, total federal spending has averaged about 20% of GDP and federal taxes have averaged about 18% of GDP since World War II, sixty-five years ago. Moreover, at the time, federal revenues, due to the effects of the recession, were actually about 15% of GDP. This means closing the long-term gap would require either cutting federal spending by two-thirds. Or nearly doubling every federal tax, individual income taxes, corporate income taxes, capital gains taxes, and payroll taxes. Or some combination of each.

TAX THE RICH

Can't we just solve all of these government financial problems by raising taxes on "the rich," so they pay their fair share?

Official IRS data shows that by 2007 the top 1% of income earners already paid more in income taxes than the bottom 95% combined, as the Tax Foundation has accurately reported.[33] That is before all the dramatic, sweeping tax rate increases President Obama wants to impose on upper-income earners.

Those tax increases will produce far less revenue than currently projected, because of the offsetting, negative economic effects, as we discuss in detail in Chapter 6. This means current projections of deficits and debt assuming those tax increases are too low, and the grim reality will be even higher deficits and debt. Indeed, if those tax increases produce a double-dip recession, the result will be much less revenue overall, rather than more. Moreover, even without a recession, over the last forty years, every time the capital gains tax rate has been increased, capital gains revenues have declined (and every time the tax rate has been cut, capital gains revenues have increased). The same would be true for taxation of corporate dividends.

In fact, in the past sixty years, total federal tax revenues as a percent of GDP have stubbornly persisted at no higher than around 19% of GDP, no matter what federal tax rates have been. That same result prevailed with the top income tax rate at 92% in 1952–53, and as low as 28% in 1988–90. This statistical maxim is known by economists as Hauser's Law.[34]

So don't expect higher taxes on "the rich" to bail us out from this deficit and debt crisis. Trying to increase taxes on the rich still further is more likely to result in less revenue rather than more, as has already happened in several states that tried to raise taxes on "the rich" (as we will see in Chapter 8).

THE ROSY SCENARIO

All of the above projections assume stable interest rates, with no sustained long-term increase in rates due to all the record-smashing federal borrowing and national debt, and only modest increases from record-low rates in the short term.[35] But even with that assumption, under current policy trends federal spending for debt interest alone would climb to roughly a trillion dollars for the year in 2020, and consume close to 50% of all federal revenues by 2035.[36]

Yet Moody's credit-rating service has indicated that federal interest spending exceeding about 14% of federal revenues would probably end the U.S. government's AAA credit rating.[37] Under current policy trends, that level would be reached by 2014. Losing that credit rating alone would mean an increase in interest rates. That would increase federal interest spending further, meaning still higher deficits and debt.

Moreover, President Obama's budget projections discussed above already assume that federal taxes will increase from 15% of GDP in 2010 to 20% in 2020, about 11% higher than the long-run postwar historical average of about 18%, which has prevailed for the prior sixty or so years in America. In fact, those budget projections assume that President Obama's tsunami of tax increases goes into effect in 2013, increasing the top tax rates for virtually every federal tax—income taxes, capital gains taxes, taxes on corporate dividends, payroll taxes, death taxes, as discussed further below.

Yet Obama's budget still projects a deficit of $774 billion in 2021, even with trillions in phony, fairy-tale budget cuts over the next ten years, and inflated growth assumptions. That shows that our nation's fiscal problems are not due to inadequate taxes but excessive, runaway spending. Brian Riedl of the Heritage Foundation calculates that under more realistic assumptions regarding federal tax increases and spending, following recent policy trends, the federal deficit by 2021 will actually total $1.9 trillion, with the national debt held by the public at nearly $25 trillion ($24.9 trillion). Federal revenues at 18.4% of GDP would still be slightly above their long-term average, but the enormous nearly $2 trillion deficit would still result because federal spending would total 26.4% of GDP, the highest ever except for World War II.

Both President Obama's and the CBO's projections assume no negative economic effects from those tax increases.[38] Indeed, all of the above projections assume no further recessions, but, rather, sustained, consistent economic growth for the next seventy years. But another—inevitable—recession would mean still higher deficits and debt. Higher interest rates and taxes would result in just such another recession sooner rather than later.

In fact, President Obama's budget numbers assume a sharply improving economy in the short term, with real growth after inflation leaping from 2.1% in 2011 to 3.6% in 2012 to 4.4% in 2013, followed by another stellar year of growth at 4.3% in 2014.[39] It assumes that unemployment will plummet to 6.6% in 2013, and 5% thereafter.[40] It further assumes that despite the Fed's run-up in the money supply and soaring commodity prices at the end of 2010, inflation will stay more than behaved, with the Consumer Price Index at 1.0% in 2011, stabilizing at around 2% thereafter.[41]

But if President Obama pursues his original tax and regulatory agendas, that's not going to happen. His campaign pledge in 2008 to allow the Bush tax cuts to expire at the end of 2010 for couples making over $250,000 per year, and singles making over $200,000, along with the tax increases in the Obamacare health policy legislation, would have resulted in raising the rates of every major federal tax on the nation's employers and investors. The top two income tax rates would increase nearly 20%, counting the phaseout of deductions and exemptions. The top capital gains tax rate would soar by nearly 60%, counting the application of Obamacare's new 3.8% tax on investment income. The tax rate on dividends would nearly triple, from 15% to 43.4%, counting the new Obamacare tax as well. The Obamacare legislation also increased the Medicare HI (hospital insurance) payroll tax rate by 62% on the same top income earners. The death tax would also be restored with a 55% top rate.

Tax *rate* increases are particularly deadly for the economy because they reduce the return to producers, investors, and businesses, or what they are allowed to keep out of what they produce. The less they are allowed to keep, the less they will save, invest, work, expand businesses or start new ones, create jobs, or take on the risks and burdens of entrepreneurship. The less they are allowed to keep the more likely they will freeze hiring, lay off workers, take more vacations, or shut down altogether. Focusing the tax rate increases on the upper-income earners making $200,000–250,000 per year and above, or those who are working and investing in the hope of making that much, focuses the counterproductive incentives precisely on the nation's investors and employers—in other words, the people responsible for your job.

In early 2010, economist Arthur Laffer argued that these sweeping, across-the-board tax rate increases would throw the weak economy, struggling to climb out of recession, back into a devastating double-dip downturn. By December 2010, President Obama's own senior economics advisor, Larry Summers, was saying the same thing, but President Obama only agreed to delay his tax-hike tsunami by two years. By early 2011, he was still vowing to bring those tax increases back in 2013.

While extending the Bush tax cuts for two years gave the economy a reprieve to finally allow real recovery to flower, that extension only temporarily continues tax rates that have already been in place for nearly ten years, so there is nothing new to inspire revived economic growth there. But recovery was already long overdue by the end of 2010, since, as mentioned earlier, the average recession post–World War II has lasted ten months, and the longest previously in that era was sixteen months. Since the recession began in December 2007, the end of 2010 represented a three-year wait for robust recovery. For this reason alone, a more robust cyclical rebound could be expected in 2011 given the extension of the Bush tax rates, all the more so as recoveries are historically stronger the deeper the recession. But President Obama's tax policy is to impose his sweeping tax rate increases at the start of 2013, along with his Obamacare tax-rate increases—all of this, in fact, is already scheduled under current law. That threatens renewed recession in 2013.

Economic recovery is further undermined by the regulatory onslaught the Obama administration is heedlessly pursuing as well. Economist David Kreutzer of the Heritage Foundation estimated that the congressional cap-and-trade emissions bill would nearly double electricity prices, and the higher energy costs would destroy 300,000 jobs in 2012, rising to nearly 1.5 million lost jobs in 2035. Yet even the Obama administration admits that the global warming regulations now pursued by the EPA will be even more economically destructive than cap-and-trade.

Moreover, the Obama administration imposed an oil moratorium last year in most of the Gulf of Mexico, which persisted despite repeated court rulings striking it down. The administration even shut down promising oil drilling under already issued leases off the coast of Alaska.

The same has happened to hundreds of already existing oil and gas leases throughout the country. More recently, the administration has withdrawn authorization for development of promising oil production from shale rock in Colorado, Utah, and Wyoming, which the U.S. Geologic Survey estimates may hold six times the proven oil reserves of Saudi Arabia, enough to satisfy U.S. oil needs for two centuries. As a result, U.S. oil production has declined by around 15% under Obama, with both direct and indirect economically destructive consequences. Direct jobs in the industry are consequently lost, and the economy overall loses reliable supplies of low-cost energy, while the price of oil climbs over a hundred dollars a barrel, which historically has meant trouble for the U.S. economy. If the price of gasoline climbs over four and even five dollars a gallon—as some now even cheer for—that will further stunt the recovery, and contribute even to renewed recession. Similar regulatory moves from the administration now threaten the coal industry as well, with similar economic results to come.

As the Obamacare regulations and mandates further tighten the economic noose, and actually raise rather than lower health costs, the recovery will be pulled down further. The employer mandate in Obamacare will kill substantial numbers of jobs for all employers not currently providing health insurance, by effectively sharply raising the costs of employment. But because it will raise rather than lower health insurance costs, for all of the reasons discussed in Chapter 4, it will sharply raise employment costs for all employers currently providing health insurance as well, killing many more jobs. Indeed, those increased costs will effectively be a further tax increase on all Americans, imposed by the individual mandate as well as the employer mandate.

Contributing further to the prospect of short-term recession is the inevitable rise in interest rates. The Fed has kept interest rates historically low, indeed at rock bottom with real, short-term rates essentially at zero for three years now. From here interest rates can only go up. Indeed, even the Fed publicly admits that it must eventually reverse the incredibly loose monetary policy it has pursued for the last three years, or else the result will be soaring inflation. But tightening monetary policy means much higher interest rates. All the federal borrowing, deficits, and debt will add further to rising rates.

But rising interest rates make capital investment more expensive for business, which reduces that investment. That translates into fewer jobs and lower wages than otherwise, contributing to recession.

The Fed's monetary policy is itself problematic for the economic outlook within a year or two. In 2009, the Fed began buying up government bonds, and Fannie Mae and Freddie Mac securities, adding about a trillion dollars' worth to its balance sheet. In the process, it more than doubled the adjusted monetary base at the foundation of the money supply, from $800 billion to about $2 trillion. In late 2010, it renewed its commitment to stimulative expansionary policy, suggesting it would even reignite inflation to reduce real interest rates below zero. Commodity prices, including oil and gold, began to soar as a result, heralding eventual inflation.

This creates a troubling conundrum for Fed monetary policy. If the Fed persists with such expansionary policies, will inflation soar out of control? Reversing course to a contractionary policy to avoid that, or in response to that, will of course be recessionary. And have the Fed's loose monetary policies created further bubbles in the past couple of years that will quickly pop if the Fed reverses course, further fueling recessionary trends? This same troubling conundrum is what produced the worsening cycle of inflation and recession from 1969 to 1982. Sharply rising oil prices, itself recessionary, created havoc in the economy during that period.

Worst of all is the potential timing of the impact of any such Fed policy reversal to counter galloping inflation. As Milton Friedman taught us, monetary policy operates with long lead times of a year to eighteen months. If galloping inflation over the next year forces the Fed to act to shut it down, the contractionary effect of such a policy may hit with full force in 2013, just when President Obama's sweeping tax hikes would be going into effect. This is a recipe for a horrific renewed recession.

With the deficit already at $1.645 trillion, what happens if we suffer another serious recession soon, the dreaded double dip? How high will the deficit go then?

When a recession occurs, spending goes up because even more people apply for unemployment benefits and welfare assistance. But far more important, in a recession tax receipts fall off the table, as business profits decline sharply, wage and income increases slow or halt, and tax revenues are lost for every unemployed worker or business that goes under.

So another recession in the near term means that even the cash accounting federal deficit would soar further to well over $2 trillion per year. Moreover, as so much of the outstanding national debt is rolled over every year, the rising interest rates, which will soar if the Fed has to pursue contractionary policies to counter inflation, will have further accelerated government spending for debt interest, as trillions in debt will have to be reissued at the higher rates. Moreover, what happens to all the guarantees left over from the 2008 financial crisis, and all the bank and other bailout loans, in a double-dip recession, as securities and bank and corporate balance sheets turn sour again? How much further will all of that run up the deficit?

In the next recession, as the United States goes into world debt markets to raise well over $2 trillion for its deficit, and much more on a gross basis, the still worse trouble is the fact that we won't be alone. All the other countries in the world with their deficits and national debt will be looking to borrow trillions altogether as well. The total, explicit, sovereign debt of governments the world over is nearly $40 trillion.[42] All these governments will be in global capital markets together trying desperately to outbid each other for the available funds with higher and higher interest rates. Those that fail to raise the necessary debt in the markets, and that are consequently left unable to cover their deficits, will effectively be in bankruptcy, like Greece. If that happens to America, the biggest debt market hog in the world by far, we will have effectively reached the point of bankruptcy. This is how vulnerable America is right now to another recession, with its wildly irresponsible deficits.

PEACE THROUGH STRENGTH VERSUS WAR
THROUGH WEAKNESS

America financed World War II to defeat Nazi Germany and Imperial Japan by borrowing and running the national debt to a record 109% of GDP. But we are already on course to race past that record. If a double-dip recession further explodes our $1.645 trillion deficit to new unprecedented heights, where will we get the money to fight a major protracted military conflict if that becomes necessary? Will China lend us the money? Or will they be allied with our enemies?

President Reagan followed a policy of "Peace Through Strength," which won the Cold War without firing a shot. Will our debt and economic vulnerability lead to War Through Weakness by effectively inviting an attack on us or our allies?

Where would we get the money to even respond to such an attack over the longer run? Would not such longer-term vulnerability encourage us to respond with harsher, quick retaliation in the hope of avoiding more costly long-term conflict? Does that heighten the prospect of nuclear war?

You can see how our continued fiscal and economic vulnerabilities can quickly and suddenly lead America to unravel.

BACK TO THE FUTURE

All of this adds up to long-term economic stagnation and decline for America, if not worse. In short order, we are headed back to the 1970s, if not the 1930s (which is where we would be with a sharp double-dip recession). President Obama was elected on the notion that he had a progressive, forward-looking vision for America that would lead us into the future. But instead he is taking us backward with a Rip van Winkle vengeance, implying that nothing has happened since 1980—or anything that has happened must be forgotten down the memory hole.

But vigorously pursuing the opposite of every plank of Reaganomics, as we discuss in Chapter 6, will achieve just the opposite results, as Art Laffer has argued. Increasing every major federal tax rate nullifies incentives to produce, save, invest, work, start new businesses, expand existing businesses, create jobs, and take on the risks and burdens of entrepreneurship. Record-breaking government spending, deficits, and debt drain the essential funds for private sector job creation, business start-up and expansion, and economic growth. That ultimately drives up interest rates as well as future tax rates. The Obama administration's across-the-board reregulation of the economy further contributes to economic downturn by raising the costs of production.

Even before that, we face the undertow of the Fed's conundrum. The Fed has perpetuated an incredibly loose monetary policy for almost three years now, with interest rates near zero, similar to the policies that were at the root of the 2008 financial crisis, as we will see in Chapter 6. The Fed itself well knows this can't continue forever. But those addicted to heroin know that their abuse can't continue forever, either. The question is how to get off.

The Fed's plan is to back off and tighten up as the economy recovers. But colliding with any real recovery and the record spending, deficits, and debt, any such tightening will produce spiking interest rates, short-circuiting recovery. If the Fed waits too long to tighten up, however, it will lay the groundwork for explosive inflation.

Such inflation, along with spiking U.S. tax rates, impaling U.S. investment competitiveness, will cause the world's investors to flee the dollar. That translates into still more inflation, as demand for the dollar collapses in the face of record supply. Rising inflation and tax rates combined with a declining dollar translates further into capital flight from America. That contributes still more to unemployment, double-dip recession, and worse. We may well end up seeing other governments and international financial markets turn away from the dollar as the world's reserve currency, to the great detriment of America.

Contributing further to this economic death spiral is President Obama's high energy cost policy, as discussed in Chapter 6. The energy in traditional fossil fuels such as oil, gas, and coal, as well as in nuclear power, is intensely concentrated as compared to wind, sun rays, switchgrass, and other forms of alternative energy. That is why alternative energy is inherently much more expensive. It stems from the basic science.

This is clearly revealed in the nuts and bolts of President Obama's energy policy. The whole point of cap-and-trade is to make traditional fossil fuels much more expensive, so much so that their use will be dramatically reduced. But making alternative fuels competitively cheaper in large enough amounts to fuel the economy still requires hundreds of billions in annual subsidies, which amounts to further economic cost.

Forcing higher energy costs on America will be another major drag on the economy. It is both inflationary, driving the costs of everything up, and recessionary, raising the costs of doing business, particularly in energy-intensive manufacturing, thus ultimately killing millions of jobs and businesses. Adding to the problem is that alternative sources like wind and solar are unreliable. They go off when the wind stops or the sun goes down. That requires expensive maintenance of traditional fuel backups, adding further to costs.

The notion that "green energy" jobs producing the alternatives will be a source of future prosperity is a snare and a delusion. Switching the economy to high-cost, unreliable energy will kill far more jobs overall. That has been the experience in European countries where this uneconomic propaganda has prevailed and these delusional policies have been tried even for just a few years.

All of these policies portend an ultimate radical decline in America's standard of living. Low-cost, reliable energy powers all the modern products of our advanced lifestyle, from personal and laptop computers, to cell phones morphing into handheld Internet portals, to big-screen, high-definition, 3-D TVs, to our powerful, roomy, luxurious automobiles. The most advanced health care in the world, with widespread availability of the latest medical technology and treatments, is another component of that high standard of living, now threatened by Obamacare as discussed in Chapter 4. Bigger, better, more beautiful and luxurious homes were spreading further and further through American society, but the housing industry now remains hamstrung.

The dollar losing its status as the world's reserve currency will further reduce America's standard of living. Every time Americans want to buy something from abroad, they will have to buy another currency, or medium of exchange, to do it. That will make added costs from a declining dollar more acute. America's much lower tax burden than Europe's was another component of our higher standard of living.

The end result of going back to the economic policies of the 1970s, or the 1930s, will be the same economic morass of those decades. That portends double-digit unemployment, double-digit inflation, and double-digit interest rates, and maybe worse. By the end of 2010, unemployment was still rising, thirty-six months after the recession began, a period more than twice as long as the previous longest recession since World

War II. While historically the harsher the downturn the stronger the recovery, recovery from the recession sputtered along at less than half the growth that should be expected. Yet before recovery has firmly settled in, already the possibility of another double-dip recession has arisen. The 1970s saw repeated worsening recessions, from 1969–70, to 1973–75, to 1980, to 1981–82. On our current course, the high interest rates and perhaps even the monstrous inflation of that period will return as well.

The persistent near-double-digit unemployment and potentially developing double-dip recession suggest perhaps even a return to the unremitting stagnation and decline of the 1930s. But even in the 1970s and 1930s, America did not suffer the entitlement and debt bomb we face today. That is why the ticking sound so particular to our own era is the coming bankruptcy of America.

CHAPTER 3

THE BABY BOOM'S RETIREMENT BOMB

Personal Account Prosperity for All

The government's own official reports show that Social Security is going bankrupt. These reports are produced by the nonpartisan career actuaries of the Social Security Administration. They have been publishing reports showing this developing bankruptcy for many years now.

THE COMING BANKRUPTCY OF SOCIAL SECURITY

Since President Reagan's Social Security reforms saved the program from financial collapse in 1983, Social Security had run cash surpluses of tax revenues over expenditures every year, sometimes running to tens of billions of dollars. Until last year, when the 2010 Annual Report of the Board of Trustees for Social Security showed these long-term surpluses were gone. Last year the program as a whole ran a net cash deficit of $41.4 billion.[1] Another cash deficit will occur in 2011.

From now on, paying all promised Social Security benefits will require dipping into the Social Security trust funds, now totaling $2.7 trillion, to cover ongoing cash deficits.[2] But that is not $2.7 trillion in cash or other real assets.

During all the years of annual surpluses, starting in 1937, Social Security's surplus money was not saved and invested to pay the future benefits of workers and their families. Instead the federal government followed the policy of raiding the Social Security trust funds to spend the surplus money on the rest of the federal budget, from foreign aid to "bridges to nowhere." Whatever surplus cash came into Social Security during the year was lent to the federal government for such spending. Social Security received in return an internal federal IOU promising to pay the money back if it was ever needed to pay promised benefits. The IOUs supposedly earned interest every year. But that interest was paid with still more IOUs.

The entire $2.7 trillion in the Social Security trust funds is composed of these internal federal IOUs. To get the money to continue to pay all promised benefits when Social Security is running cash deficits, the Social Security Administration will have to turn in those IOUs to the U.S. Treasury for cash.

And where does the U.S. Treasury plan to get that cash? Actually, from you. The truth is that the Social Security trust fund "assets" are not assets at all, but debt owed by you, which you will have to pay for retirees to continue to get all their promised Social Security benefits, in addition to the hundreds of billions you and other taxpayers pay in payroll taxes each year. The Social Security trust fund "assets," indeed, are rightly included in the gross national debt owed by the federal government, on behalf of the nation's taxpayers. When Social Security comes to the Treasury to turn in the trust fund IOUs to get the cash to pay promised benefits, the Treasury will get that cash either by raising your taxes or by borrowing still more and running even bigger deficits.

This will continue until the Social Security trust funds run out of such IOUs in 2037.[3] From 2010, when the deficits started, until that trust fund exhaustion in 2037, the American people will have to come up with a grand total of roughly $7.3 *trillion* to cover all of the IOUs in the Social Security trust funds.[4] *This, again, is in addition to the trillions they will have to pay in Social Security payroll taxes over those years.* That is because the trust fund bonds will continue to earn interest all those years, until all the bonds are exhausted, and the taxpayers will have to make good on that interest as well.

After 2037, paying all promised Social Security benefits will require sharp increases in payroll taxes. The current total Social Security payroll tax rate of 12.4% will have to jump by close to 40% to start, to about 17% at least, climbing still further in the following years.[5]

But the Social Security actuaries admit it could be even worse than that. That projection is based on an intermediate set of assumptions the Social Security actuaries use regarding various economic and de-mographic factors that affect Social Security financing. But they also make projections under a so-called pessimistic set of assumptions that are quite plausible, if not more realistic. In the past, the supposedly pessimistic projections have often turned out to be closer to reality than the intermediate projections.

For example, one critical factor for long-term Social Security financing is life expectancy. The longer people live, the more years they will collect Social Security benefits, increasing long-term Social Security deficits. Over the nearly seventy-year period from 1940 to 2009, the life expectancy of males born in the U.S. increased 14.2 years, from 61.4 to 75.6.[6] Yet under the intermediate assumptions for Social Security financing, life expectancy for males over the fifty-year period 2010 to 2059 is assumed to grow only 5.4 years, just over a third of the experience over the previous fifty years.[7] Even under the so-called pessimistic assumptions, life expectancy for males over the next fifty years is assumed to grow by 8.4 years, only 60% of the experience over the previous fifty years.[8]

For females born in the United States, life expectancy grew 14.6 years from 1940 to 2009, climbing from 65.7 years to 80.3 years.[9] Yet under the intermediate assumptions for Social Security financing, life expectancy for females over the following fifty years is assumed to grow 4.4 years, only 30% as much as in the previous fifty years.[10] Under the pessimistic assumptions, female life expectancy is assumed to grow 7.1 years, less than half the experience over the previous fifty years.[11]

Yet we are in a high-tech medical-science boom that promises astounding breakthroughs in the coming years. Some talk of curing cancer and Alzheimer's disease over the next twenty-five years. Heart disease and stroke would likely be even more greatly reduced than they have been. Then there are the enormous potential breakthroughs based on modern genetics, from gene therapy to treatments based on personal gene analysis to growing new organs. Yes, the human body may resist further extensions at older and older ages. But given the magnitude of developing modern scientific advances, if anything life expectancy could well grow even more over the next fifty years than over the last fifty.

Inflation increases Social Security benefit obligations because they are indexed to grow with inflation. It also retards economic growth, which results in lower wage growth and hence lower growth in payroll tax revenues. Inflation was modest in the 1960s, but boomed in the 1970s. From 1960 to 1982, inflation averaged 5.4% a year. But the anti-inflation policies of President Reagan and then–Fed chairman Paul Volcker slayed rapid inflation growth and seemed to establish a new era. From 1983 to 2006, inflation averaged just over 3% a year.[12]

But the intermediate assumptions for Social Security still assume long-term inflation of even less than that, at 2.8% a year. The pessimistic assumptions put inflation at 3.8% per year. Over the entire period 1960 to 2006, inflation grew at 4.2% per year.[13] The monetary policies of the current Fed under Obamanomics may well bring back the roaring inflation of the pre-Reagan years, leaving these inflation assumptions woefully inadequate.

Unemployment reduces payroll tax revenues, since fewer workers pay into the system. Since 1960, unemployment has averaged about 5.9%.[14] But the intermediate assumptions put unemployment at 5.5% over the long term. For the pessimistic assumptions, it is 6.5%.[15]

Under the so-called pessimistic assumptions, the Social Security trust funds run out in 2029.[16] Paying all promised benefits in 2030 would require raising the total Social Security payroll tax rate from 12.4% today to 19%, an increase of almost 60%.[17] By 2065, when those entering the workforce today will still be in retirement, paying all promised benefits would require a payroll tax rate of nearly 23%, close to double the current rate.[18] Eventually Social Security payroll taxes would have to grow to 26% to pay all promised benefits.[19]

But even this does not include the whole problem. The hospital insurance (HI) portion of Medicare, Medicare Part A, is financed by the HI payroll tax, which is currently 2.9% of all payroll with no maximum taxable income, split between employer and employee. The HI program is already in deficit, with the trust fund projected to run out of funds to pay promised benefits by 2017. Counting HI along with Social Security, paying all promised benefits to today's young workers in retirement would require raising the total payroll tax rate from 15.3% today to 27%, on its way eventually to 30%, under the intermediate assumptions.[20] Under the pessimistic assumptions, paying all promised benefits to today's young workers would require raising the payroll tax rate to 44%, three times current levels, on its way to 52%.[21]

Payroll tax rates in these ranges will cause soaring unemployment, which in turn will mean less revenue than expected, which will require still higher tax rates. This gives a bracing new meaning to the term "death spiral."

The root cause of this long-term fiscal disaster is the fundamental structure of Social Security financing. As mentioned earlier, Social Security operates on a "pay-as-you-go" basis. That means the tax money paid by workers today is not saved and invested for their future retirement. The great majority of that money is instead immediately paid out to finance current benefits. The future benefits of today's workers would then be paid not out of the savings and investment of their past tax payments, but out of the future taxes to be paid by future workers when today's workers are retired.

With almost all of the money coming into the program immediately going out to finance current benefits, there is little margin for error when adverse developments threaten the financing balance. With a fully funded savings and investment system, by contrast, a huge accumulation of reserves provides a much greater margin of safety.

Major adverse developments have greatly scrambled Social Security's pay-as-you-go balance. First there was the birth of the baby boom generation after World War II. The fertility rate, or lifetime births per woman, had soared to over 3 by 1947, on its way to a peak of 3.68 in 1957. The rate remained over 3.6 until 1960, and was still 3.3 in 1963.[22] Those born in 1947 are sixty-four years old today, and over the next twenty years this huge baby boom generation is going to retire, massively increasing the benefit obligations Social Security must pay.

But to make matters worse, this baby boom generation was quickly followed by a baby bust. The new public availability of the Pill and swiftly changing social mores in the 1960s caused the nation's demographics to turn virtually on a dime. Fertility collapsed to 2.88 in 1965, 2.42 in 1969, and 2.25 in 1971.[23] Just maintaining a stable population requires a fertility rate of 2.1. But in 1972 the rate collapsed all the way to 1.99, down 1.31, or 40%, in just nine years.[24] Fertility continued to decline, reaching a bottom of 1.74 in 1976.[25] It stayed near that level until starting an increase in 1987 toward a level of 2.0 in 1989. It has remained near that level since then.[26]

This fertility double whammy is disastrous for a pay-as-you-go system. Just when the huge baby boom generation is retiring and causing benefit expenditures to soar, the generation behind them paying taxes to support their benefits is much smaller than expected, causing a sharp drop in expected tax revenues.

But there is still more. Life expectancy in America has long been rising, which you would think would be good news for everyone. But not for Social Security. As indicated above, in 1940 life expectancy was 61.4 for males and 65.7 for females. Social Security adopted in 1935 with a retirement age of 65 would consequently not be seen as such a great financial burden then. But again, since then life expectancy has grown 14.2 years for males, to 75.6 years, and 14.6 years for females, to 80.3 years. And of course, it is expected to increase even more over the coming decades, as discussed above.

This will make the huge cost of benefits for the baby boom generation so much greater, because they will be living so much longer in retirement. For Social Security today to be an equivalent burden to what it seemed to be in the 1930s, the retirement age would have to be 79, due to the increased life expectancy alone, even before counting the huge increase in numbers of the baby boom generation.

It is these powerful demographic factors that have caused the collapsing number of workers financing each retiree, financial death for a pay-as-you-go system. In 1945, there were 42 workers paying into Social Security for every retiree drawing benefits out.[27] In 1950, there were still 16.5 workers per beneficiary.[28] But the gyrating fertility rate starting over sixty years ago and the increased life expectancy have radically revised these ratios. Today there are 3.3 workers per covered beneficiary.[29] By 2032, under the intermediate projections, there will only be 2.1, on the way down to 1.9.[30] Under the pessimistic projections, by 2033 there will be 1.9 workers per beneficiary, on the way down to 1.4.[31]

In a pay-as-you-go system, where current workers pay the taxes to support the current retirees directly, without investment and accumulating returns, a steep decline in the ratio of taxpayers to beneficiaries means a steep increase in taxes per worker to finance the benefits per retiree. This is reflected in the long-term projections of Social Security finances discussed above.

STEALING THE PATRIMONY OF WORKING PEOPLE

Now let's engage in a fantasy and assume that all promised Social Security benefits could somehow be paid. In other words, let's just assume away the entire financial crisis we just discussed. The sad truth is that even if Social Security could somehow pay all the benefits promised under current law, those benefits would represent a poor deal in return for all the past years of work and tax payments.

To evaluate Social Security, start by taking the actuarial value of all of the program's benefits—retirement benefits, survivors benefits, and disability benefits. Then compare that to the actuarial value of the program's taxes. An earlier study[32] examined a hypothetical family where the husband works and earns the average income for full-time male workers each year and the wife works and earns the average income for full-time female workers each year. They have two children, and each spouse entered the workforce in 1985 at age twenty-two, right after they graduated from college.

Even if all their promised Social Security benefits were somehow paid, those benefits would represent an annual real rate of return of less than 1% (0.78%) on the taxes paid by these two workers and their employers over their working careers. Almost all hypothetical two-earner couples examined in the study would receive a real return right around this 0.78%. Single workers get an even worse deal. A full-time average-income single worker would receive a real return through the system of around 0% (0.31%). Overall, for most young workers today, even if the program could somehow pay all of its promised benefits, Social Security would pay a real return of 1.5% or less.

Many above-average-income workers would actually receive a negative real return from the system, again even assuming all promised benefits are somehow paid. A negative real return is like depositing your money in the bank, and instead of the bank paying you interest, you pay the bank interest on your deposit. This is what Social Security already is for a lot of people today. There are workers today who, along with their employers, are paying over $10,000 a year, each and every year, into Social Security, but instead of getting any real interest on that money at all, they are effectively losing money on it every year with a negative real rate of return from the system. This is counting the value of all promised benefits from the program on an actuarial basis, survivors and disability benefits as well as retirement benefits.

Worst of all, this is where Social Security is heading for all workers in the future. For if the government raises taxes or cuts benefits, or does both, to eliminate the long-term deficits of Social Security, then the effective rate of return under Social Security will decline further for all workers across the board. Eventually, virtually all workers under Social Security would be driven down into the range of negative effective real returns.

Now let's look at standard, long-term market returns workers would earn in a savings and investment system. Jeremy Siegel, in his definitive book *Stocks for the Long Run,* documents that the real annual compound rate of return on corporate stocks in America over the period 1802 to 2001 was 6.9%.[33] It was the same 6.9% over the period 1926 to 2001, which included the Great Depression, World War II, the Korean War, the Vietnam War, and the Great Inflation of the 1970s.[34]

From 1926 to 2009, the real rate of return on large-cap stocks, representing the larger companies in America, was 8.64%. The real rate of return on small-cap stocks, representing smaller, midsize firms, was 13.17%. A sophisticated, diversified portfolio of 90% large-cap and 10% small-cap stocks earned a 9.1% real return over that period. *This period covers the 2008–9 financial crisis.*

Moreover, over the entire post–World War II era, corporate bonds have averaged a real return of 4%.[35] Harvard professor Martin Feldstein, chairman of the National Bureau of Economic Research, and his associate Andrew Samwick calculated in 1997 that a portfolio of 60% stocks and 40% bonds would have generated a real return of 5.5% since 1946, and the same return over the period going back to 1926.[36]

Compounding these much higher returns over a lifetime adds up to an enormous difference as compared to the much lower returns offered by Social Security's pay-as-you-go, tax and redistribution system. Let's go back to our average-income two-earner couple. Suppose they can save and invest the taxes—counting both the employee and employer shares of the payroll tax—that would otherwise go into Social Security in their own family personal account over their entire lives. Suppose funds are set aside each year to buy private life and disability insurance that would pay at least the same survivors and disability benefits as Social Security promises. The rest of their funds are saved and invested each year in a diversified portfolio of half stocks and half bonds, earning a conservative real return on average of 5%, after paying for all administrative costs to manage the account.

This average-income family would reach retirement with a personal account fund of $1,223,602 in today's dollars, after adjusting for inflation. That fund would be able to pay out of the continuing investment returns alone just about *twice* what Social Security promises to pay them under current law, *while still allowing them to leave the $1.2 million fund to their children.* Or they could use the fund to buy themselves an annuity that would pay them over four times what Social Security currently promises, let alone what it can pay.

All workers across the board, of all income levels and family combinations, would now get much higher benefits saving and investing in the market through personal accounts than the benefits Social Security even promises today, which the program cannot pay. Two low-income spouses somehow earning little more than the minimum wage over their entire careers would reach retirement with well over half a million in their personal accounts in today's dollars, as discussed further in Chapter 11. That fund would be sufficient to pay them over three times what Social Security promises them, but cannot pay.

Just think about what sweeping changes in our society would result if workers at all income levels were accumulating several hundred thousand dollars in their own personal accounts by retirement. All workers would be accumulating a substantial direct ownership stake in America's business and industry. And all workers would consequently prosper along with the American economy. This would be a historic breakthrough in the personal prosperity of working people.

In 1862, the Homestead Act opened land ownership to working people. The law said that if you got your family out to open land, settled on the land in a new home, fenced it in, and worked it to produce crops or raise cattle, the land would be yours. Many people of little means did just that, and built a family legacy of prosperity that succeeded them in following generations. Land ownership in America became widespread as a result.

In the 1900s, the Federal Housing Administration and later similar agencies opened easy mortgages and home ownership to average-income working people. With a reasonably manageable down payment and hard, consistent work to meet the monthly payments, moderate-income families could own their own homes and prosper with such real estate ownership along with the rest of the market. Today close to 70% of Americans own their own homes.

Now, in the early 2000s, the next great breakthrough in the personal prosperity of working people would be personal accounts for Social Security. Even the lowest-income workers would be able to provide their children with a major financial boost with the substantial funds accumulated in their personal accounts by retirement. As a result, new private sector capital would flow into the inner city and other poor communities across the nation. This would provide a financial foundation for higher education, start-up small businesses, the launching of professional careers, the construction of new housing, and other signposts on the road to the middle class.

Across America, new savings and investment would flow through the personal accounts, increasing economic growth. The personal accounts over time would transform the payroll tax into a wealth-building asset owned within each family, and this effective tax relief would further spur the economy. The result would be new jobs and higher wages and family income for working people. Martin Feldstein estimates that the present value of the future economic gains from shifting from pay-as-you-go Social Security to a fully funded savings and investment system like personal accounts is $10–20 trillion.[37]

But why the enormous gulf between what can be earned through Social Security as compared to private savings and investment? That stems again from the fundamental pay-as-you-go financing of Social Security. Because of that financing structure, there is no actual savings and investment at all anywhere in the Social Security system. The great majority of the money paid into Social Security is immediately paid out to finance current benefits. Any money left over is lent to the federal government and immediately paid out for other government spending, in return for the federal IOUs we found in the Social Security trust funds above. So that money is spent and not saved as well.

As a result, Social Security is not a savings and investment system. It is a tax and redistribution system, where the money is taken from one group of people through taxes and just redistributed to other people in benefits and other government spending.

What are the implications of this current system for Social Security? Well, the program was in fact a good deal for those who got into it at the beginning, just as with any Ponzi scheme. Money was pouring into Social Security with no justified claims on it due to past tax payments. The money was not to be saved and invested for the future benefits of the taxpayers at the time. So the money could be used to pay generous benefits to those then just retiring. These early retirees had paid very little into the program in the past, because it was in effect for just a few years before their retirement. So the benefits they got represented a very high return on whatever they had paid in.

The classic example is the very first Social Security recipient, Ida M. Fuller of Vermont. She and her employer had paid a total of $44 into Social Security before she retired in 1940. She went on to live for another 35 years, passing away at age 100 in 1975. During that time she collected close to $20,000 in benefits, an enormous return on an investment of $44.

But over time, this all reverses. As the years go by, workers pay higher and higher taxes for more and more of their working years. As late as 1949, the maximum annual Social Security tax was still only $60. By 1957, the tax had tripled, but it was still only $189. Twenty years after the Social Security tax had begun, that was all that had to be paid for all of Social Security's promises to each worker. No wonder the program was so popular then.

But by 1966 the tax had almost tripled again to $554. By 1974 it had almost tripled again to $1,544. By 1980, just six years later, the tax was $3,175. By then the total payroll tax rate was 12.26% on the first $25,900 of wages for the year. By 1990 the total payroll tax was 15.3% on the first

$51,300 of wages, resulting in a maximum tax of $7,848 for the year, close to tripling again from 1980.

For 2007, the payroll tax of 15.3% applied to the first $97,500 of wage income, for a total tax of $14,917. But 2.9 percentage points of the tax, the portion that goes to Medicare, applies to all wage income without limit. So even this $14,917 is no longer the maximum tax for the year.

Eventually the system reaches a point where workers are retiring who have paid these high taxes for their entire careers. Then even the benefits *promised* to them by the system are not a good deal in return. With no savings and investment in the system, these workers are losing the accumulating and compounding returns that would be earned each year by real savings and investment. They get any return at all from the pay-as-you-go, tax and redistribution system only to the extent that total tax revenues to the system can be raised faster and faster over time. Such a system could never remotely keep up with the full market returns that would be earned by a savings and investment system.

The full social gain in switching from a purely redistributive pay-as-you-go system like Social Security to a fully funded, real savings and investment system like personal accounts is measured not by the rate of return on stock investments, or by the market returns on various bonds, but by the before-tax real rate of return to capital. Professor Feldstein understood this all the way back in the 1970s, but too many self-satisfied academics have since been lost in confusion over this critical point. The before-tax real rate of return to capital measures the full value of the increased production resulting from increased savings and investment. That is actually higher than long-term stock returns, because those stock returns are partially after-tax returns left after the multiple taxation of capital at the corporate and business level.[38]

Workers can gain the advantages of such a savings and investment system through personal accounts, without giving up the social safety net provided by Social Security today and exposing workers to excessive risks. There is no reason why workers with personal accounts cannot be provided the same government guarantee as Social Security now provides. As included in the personal accounts bill introduced in Congress discussed below, the government can guarantee that all workers with personal accounts would receive at least as much in benefits as promised by Social Security under current law. This is possible because market capital investment returns are so much higher than what the pay-as-you-go, noninvestment, purely redistributive Social Security system can even promise today, let alone what it can pay. So few, if any, workers can be expected to fall into this continuing safety net, resulting in little cost to the taxpayers.

This is especially so since, as discussed further below, workers would choose investments for their personal accounts through a structured framework that would be easy for unsophisticated investors. Workers would choose highly diversified investment funds sponsored by experienced private sector investment fund managers approved and regulated by the federal government for safety and soundness. So average workers would not have to be experts in picking and choosing individual stocks and bonds. They need choose only an investment fund from a list of options approved by government regulators, which would include simple stock index funds with no discretionary investment management. Through this process, the government would also be able to control and limit the risks that could be taken with personal account investments.

With these protections, personal accounts are not actually displacing Social Security. Instead they are expanding and modernizing the Social Security framework to rely centrally on real savings and capital investment, rather than counterproductive tax and redistribution. That is the key to transforming Social Security into a prosperity system for working people.

WHAT ABOUT THE FINANCIAL CRISIS?

But what about the financial crisis America just suffered through? Didn't that prove that capital investment, and stocks in particular, are too risky and unreliable to rely on for retirement financing? Didn't we just see, in President Obama's words, "the wealth [that] people worked a lifetime to earn wiped out in a matter of days"?[39]

To address that issue, I produced a study last year for both the Jefferson Institute and the Social Security Institute, coauthored with William G. Shipman, formerly a senior official with State Street Global Advisors, one of the largest pension investment management firms in the world, with the results published in the *Wall Street Journal*.[40] We examined a hypothetical case of a couple, Joe the Plumber and his wife, Mary, who entered the workforce at the start of 1965, each at the age of twenty-one. They both work, with Joe earning the average income each year for full-time male workers, and Mary earning the average income each year for full-time female workers.

Suppose back then they had the freedom to choose personal accounts to finance all of their retirement benefits, and they made that choice. Each year, the same amounts that they and their employers would otherwise pay in Social Security taxes[41] are saved and invested in their personal account instead. Suppose also, being young and rash, they choose to invest all of it in stocks. And they never change that decision, all the way through to their retirement forty-five years later, at the end of 2009, about a year and a half after the financial crisis hit. This consequently provides a maximum-risk example directly testing President Obama's taunts about risking your retirement money in the stock market.

Suppose as well that their funds are invested for them over the years by an experienced major investment firm handling millions of personal accounts, a choice the couple made out of dozens of alternative options, with the firm regulated by the federal government for safety and soundness. In accordance with their expressed investment preferences, the firm invests their money in an indexed portfolio of 90% large-cap stocks and 10% small-cap stocks.[42] Assume that they earn the same actual market stock returns that were actually earned on these investments for each year in the past through to their retirement.[43]

The study showed that this average-income couple would have reached retirement at the end of 2009 with accumulated account funds, after administrative costs, of $855,175, almost millionaires. Indeed, they were millionaires for a while, but the financial crisis caused them to lose 37% of their accumulated account funds the year before they retired. This can be considered, in fact, effectively a worst-case scenario, as the couple retired just one year after the worst ten-year stock market performance—from 1999 to 2008—going all the way back to 1926 (the first year of the easily accessible data).

In retirement, the study assumed that the couple switched to a diversified investment portfolio of government and high-grade corporate bonds earning on average a real return of just 3%. This would avoid the risk of short-term market ups and downs affecting their monthly income. But in fact, if the couple used their funds to purchase an annuity promising a specified monthly income for life, the insurance company selling them the annuity could continue to invest part of its reserve pool in stocks, which would support higher monthly benefits.

With that investment return in retirement, the accumulated account funds would be sufficient to pay them about 75% more than Social Security would pay them under current law, adjusted annually for inflation just like Social Security.[44]

These differences would be even more stark in the future, because as discussed above, Social Security promises most young workers today real returns of 1.5% or less, counting the actuarial value of all promised benefits, with promised returns zero or even negative for many. Again, if taxes are raised or benefits cut to close Social Security's long-term financial gap, these returns would be even lower. In contrast, the real stock returns for Joseph and Mary from 1965 through the financial crisis to the end of 2009 were 8.64% for large-cap stocks and 13.17% for small-cap stocks.

This is why, despite the financial crisis, every state and local government pension fund, every corporate pension plan, the federal employee retirement plans, and the successful Social Security reform in Chile discussed below continue to be based precisely on capital investment to finance the expected retirement benefits. President Obama's admonition against "tying your benefits to the whims of Wall Street traders and the ups and downs of the stock market," and his pledge to "stop those who would gamble your Social Security on Wall Street," suggest that the unfunded liability pension crisis can be solved immediately, with the notion that capital investment to finance retirement benefits is actually not a good idea after all. But it is simply mathematical fact that the least expensive way to provide for an almost certain future liability is to save and invest in capital markets prior to the onset of the liability. That is why doing so is so common, and is considered basic, sound practice, including with all insurance reserves as well as retirement and pension finance.

Note, however, that personal accounts as proposed later in this chapter are just an option that all workers are individually free to accept or reject. Moreover, no one is required to invest any personal account funds in stocks at all. So no one is going to force you "to gamble your Social Security on Wall Street." Finally, in that proposal, the Social Security safety net remains in the personal account system, so even in those extreme cases where the government mistakenly trashes the financial markets, as in the 2008–2009 financial crisis (as discussed in Chapter 6), or as in the Great Depression (as discussed in Amity Shlaes's brilliant history, *The Forgotten Man*,[45] and elsewhere), retirees would not in any event be lost without sufficient income.

A PROVEN SUCCESS

Personal savings and investment accounts for basic retirement benefits have been tried and have succeeded spectacularly in many contexts around the world.

Chile

The best model of a true personal account option for Social Security was adopted in the South American nation of Chile over twenty-five years ago. Chile was actually the first nation in the Western Hemisphere to adopt a traditional Social Security system, doing so in 1925, ten years before the United States. But by 1980, their old Social Security system was suffering from many of the same problems as the U.S. system today. Payroll tax rates were 26% or higher, yet the system was still running deficits that were only projected to grow larger. The promised benefits were inadequate and represented a poor deal on the huge tax payments that were then required for the system.

To address these problems, Chile adopted a new personal account system that became effective on May 1, 1981. There was no change of any sort for those who were already retired. Those in the workforce were free to choose either the new personal accounts or to stay in the old Social Security system. Workers who chose the personal accounts paid, in place of the old Social Security taxes, 10% of wages each month into a personal account directly and personally owned by the worker.

The worker is free to choose to contribute up to an additional 10% to his account each month, which he may do if he wants to accumulate more funds faster to retire early.

All payments into the account are tax-deductible, with investment returns accumulating tax-free. The worker pays taxes on the income he takes from the account in retirement.

For investment of the individual account funds, the worker chooses from among twenty or so alternative investment funds approved and regulated by the government for this purpose.[46] These funds are each managed by a major, private sector, experienced investment management company, called an AFP (Administradora de Fondos de Pensiones). These have included major American financial firms, such as Chase Manhattan Bank (renamed just "Chase" today) and State Street Global Advisors, and firms affiliated with Chilean labor unions.[47] These companies choose the particular stocks, bonds, and other investments for their funds, creating a highly diversified and sophisticated portfolio, subject to government regulation mandating diversification and excluding high-risk investments.

Each investment company is required by law to pay at least a minimum return on the personal account investments set as a percentage of the average return earned by all twenty AFPs for the year. Workers can change investment companies on short notice. This creates intense competition among the investment firms to provide higher returns and better service.[48]

As a result, workers do not need to be experienced investors to participate in the personal account system. They need only to pick one of the twenty investment funds, and the investment company will choose the individual stocks, bonds, and other investments for the worker. At this very moment, there are workers walking around in the mountains of Chile, wearing serapes and pulling along burros on ropes, who have Chase investing their money all around the world, earning consistently high returns.

In retirement, workers can use some or all of the funds in their accounts to purchase an annuity from their chosen investment management company (the AFP) or any other financial institution offering such products. The annuity guarantees the worker a specified monthly income for life, indexed to inflation. The annuity would also pay a specified survivors benefit for the worker's spouse or other dependents after the worker dies.

Or the worker can forgo any annuity and just choose to live off regular withdrawals from the personal account, subject to restrictions based on the life expectancy of the worker and of any dependents eligible for benefits. Any funds remaining in the personal account at death would go to the worker's family and/or other designated heirs.

The government in Chile backs up the accounts with a guarantee that all workers will get at least a minimum benefit in retirement equal to about 40% of average wages. This is about what the U.S. Social Security system pays to average-income workers. If the benefits payable through a worker's personal account by retirement are not enough to pay at least this minimum benefit, the government provides whatever additional funding is necessary out of general revenues to finance the minimum benefit. After thirty years of experience under this system in Chile, the government has never had to make a payment under this guarantee, including during the recent worldwide financial crisis.

The investment companies, or AFPs, are legally separate entities from the personal account funds they manage.[49] So if an AFP itself should ever suffer financial difficulties, there would be no losses to the personal accounts of the workers. If necessary, government regulators would take over an AFP's personal accounts and redistribute them among other AFPs of the worker's choosing. Yet again, in the thirty years since the Chilean personal account system has been adopted, that has never happened, even during the recent worldwide financial crisis.[50]

The retirement age for the Chilean personal account system is sixty-five for men and sixty for women, as compared to the U.S. Social Security system with a retirement age heading to sixty-seven under current law. Workers can retire earlier if they accumulate enough funds in their accounts to pay at least a minimum level of benefits throughout their longer retirements. Making extra contributions to the accounts during working years can help workers achieve an early retirement goal. Workers can also continue to work after the retirement ages, and no longer have to pay into their accounts at that point.

Workers also contribute an additional 2.3% of wages for the purchase of group life and disability insurance through their AFP, taking the place of the pre-age-sixty-five survivors and disability benefits of the old system.[51] All of the benefits paid by the new personal account system, including all the assets in the accounts, are automatically indexed for inflation. This means the chosen investment management companies have to pay annual adjustments into the accounts and to the payable benefits to keep everything stable in real terms, after inflation. This reflects history in Chile, where the population has suffered through brutal bouts of inflation in the past.[52]

Workers who were already in the workforce for several years when the reform was adopted, and chose the personal accounts, were given recognition bonds to be held in their accounts in return for the taxes they had already paid into the old system. The amount of the bonds was set so that with specified interest they would equal the accrued benefits that these workers had earned from their past payments into the old system.

Within eighteen months of the reform, 93% of workers chose to switch to the new personal account system, 25% in the first month.[53] José Piñera, the Chilean minister of labor at the time and who spearheaded the reform, says, "They moved faster than Germans going from East to West after the fall of the Berlin Wall."[54] By 2004, after twenty-three years under the reform, the real rate of return on personal account investments averaged a shocking 10.2%.[55] Pensions equal to 70% of pre-retirement income can be financed with a real return of less than half that, at 4%, which is what reform advocates had expected.[56] With just half the taxes of the old system, the personal accounts even by 1997 were paying retirees nearly 80% of their average income in the last ten years before retirement.[57] This is about double the rate that the U.S. Social Security system pays to average-income workers. As workers retire having invested in the accounts for most of their careers, their benefits should rise relative to their preretirement incomes even further.

After twenty years under the reforms, the enormous savings in the personal accounts totaled 70% of GDP.[58] Piñera adds, "Chile's private pension system has been the main factor in increasing the savings rate to the level of an Asian tiger. Our [annual rate of savings] is 26 percent of GNP, compared to about 15 percent in Latin America. The Asian tigers are at 30 percent."[59] Because of these accounts, the average Chilean worker probably now has more savings than the average American worker, even though American workers earn seven times as much as Chilean workers. Within a few years after the reform was adopted, annual economic growth soared to 7%, double the country's historic rate, while unemployment fell to 5%.[60] The higher savings and lower taxes resulting from the personal account reforms are recognized as major contributors to that.[61] In fact, Chile is well on its way to becoming a fully developed, first-world country.

In 2005, John Tierney, a columnist for the *New York Times*, wrote about some personal experience he had with the Chilean personal account system:

> I made a pilgrimage to Santiago seeking to resolve the Social Security debate with a simple question: What would Pablo Serra do?
>
> I wanted to compare our pensions to see the results of an accidental experiment that began in 1961, when he and I were friends in second grade at a school in Chile. He remained in Chile and became the test subject; I returned to America as the control group.[62]

Tierney explained, "By the time we finished college, both of our countries' pension systems were going broke." But Chile adopted the personal accounts in 1981, while "America rescued its traditional system in the early 1980s by cutting benefits and raising taxes, with the promise that the extra money would go into a trust to finance the baby boomers' retirement."

Tierney noted that both countries "required our employers to set aside roughly the same portion of our income, a little over 12 percent, which pays for disability insurance as well as the pension program. It also covers, in Pablo's case, the fees charged by the mutual-fund company managing his money."

Pablo had grown up to become an economist teaching at the University of Chile. Working together, they extrapolated what would have happened if Tierney had put his money into Pablo's mutual fund, one of Chile's most popular retirement fund options, instead of U.S. Social Security. They came up with three options that Tierney would have had under the Chilean personal account system:

(1) Retire in 10 years, at age 62, with an annual pension of $55,000. That would be more than triple the $18,000 I can expect from Social Security at that age.

(2) Retire at age 65 with an annual pension of $70,000. That would be almost triple the $25,000 pension promised by Social Security starting a year later, at age 66.

(3) Retire at age 65 with an annual pension of $53,000 [still more than Social Security promised Tierney, let alone what it can pay] and a one-time cash payment of $223,000.

Tierney noted further that the Chilean personal accounts are backed up by a minimum safety net guarantee that, "relative to the median salary, is actually more generous than the median Social Security check."

In his next column, Tierney further explained his prospects under Social Security: "By the time I am in my 70's, the Social Security shortfall will force Congress to find new taxes or make spending cuts that are half the size of the Pentagon's budget. If I make it to age 88, there will be no more i.o.u.'s left in the trust fund, so everyone's benefits would have to be cut by 27 percent." Tierney added,

I can't protect my pension against political risk, but Pablo can help protect his against the risks of the stock market. As he approaches retirement, he can gradually shift his money out of stocks and into bonds, like the ones that financed the private road between Santiago and the port city of Valparaiso, which will be paid off by tolls. The Chilean pension system has billboards along the road proclaiming, "Your savings are financing this highway, and this highway is financing your retirement."

Investment performance naturally sank in the financial crisis, reflecting worldwide troubles. But the Chilean personal accounts sailed on, without the loss of a single AFP financial manager. The system, of course, is subject to financial risk. But with diversification and the long-term horizon of retirement account investments, the financial crisis shows that the risk is manageable even among the worst of circumstances, without even the need to draw on the safety net guarantee.

In Chile, even those on the left now see the personal account reforms as providing enormous gains for working people. Widespread personal ownership of capital is recognized as a liberating force for the working class, and the foundation for long-term prosperity. Chilean labor union leader Eduardo Aguilera reflects the views of unionists across the board in that country in having initially opposed the reform, but now saying, "The bottom line is that the private pension system has been an enormous advancement for the Chilean workers." Piñera explains:

> Every Chilean worker knows that he is the owner of an individual pension account. . . . The Chilean worker is an owner, a capitalist. There is no more powerful way to stabilize a free market economy and to get the support of the workers than to link them directly to the benefits of the market economy. When Chile grows at 7 percent or when the stock market doubles . . . Chilean workers benefit directly, not only through higher wages, not only through more employment, but through additional capital in their individual pension accounts.
>
> Private pensions are undoubtedly creating cultural change. When workers feel that they own a fraction of a country, not through the party bosses, not through a politburo (like the Russians thought), but through ownership of part of the financial assets of the country, they are much more attached to the free market, a free society, and democracy.[63]

Chile's reform has been seen as such a success that seven other nations in Latin America have acted to adopt similar reforms. These included Peru in 1993, Argentina and Colombia in 1994, Mexico, Bolivia, and El Salvador in 1997, and now Uruguay as well.[64] The reforms have often been compromised from the original Chilean model, and governments have not always been stellar in implementation. But the result from the essential elements of reform that have been adopted has again been huge benefits. The reform enacted in El Salvador has been closest to the Chilean model. Similar reforms have now flowered as well in Great Britain, Australia,[65] Hungary, Poland,[66] and elsewhere.[67]

The Galveston Plan

But we don't have to go all over the world to find models for personal accounts. We have a highly successful example right here in America.

In 1981, workers for Galveston County, Texas, voted to opt out of Social Security into a new defined contribution plan under a provision of federal law that allowed state and local government workers to make this choice. In 1982, local government workers in Matagorda and Brazoria counties next door voted to join them. The opt-out provision for public employees was repealed in 1983 because more and more state and local government units were deciding that they could provide a better deal than Social Security, and the federal government did not want to lose so many taxpayers.

Under the Galveston Plan, close to 10% (9.737%) of the worker's salary is contributed to the defined contribution account each year. The money goes to a bank, First Financial Benefits of Houston, which then lends the money long-term to top-rated financial institutions for a guaranteed interest rate. That rate has averaged 7.5% to 8%. Those financial institutions make their own investments with the funds and use the earnings to pay the guaranteed interest rate. The risk to workers is consequently greatly reduced. Their investment returns do not go up and down with the stock market. The workers also do not have to make investment decisions. The bank does that for them.

Just as in Chile, workers in this real savings and investment plan have enjoyed documented benefits much higher than even promised by Social Security, two to three times as much, with higher survivors and disability benefits as well.[68] Investment performance again naturally sank during the financial crisis, falling to 3.75% at the lowest point, and varying between that and 6% in the past couple of difficult years. But again, the system survived without real trouble, and the covered workers will prosper going forward along with the recovering economy.

The Federal Thrift Savings Plan

Finally, there is another example from America, the Thrift Savings Plan (TSP) for federal employees. This plan is provided to federal employees on top of Social Security, not in place of it. But it has been so successful and so popular that it serves as a model for how a real personal account system can work.

This TSP system has 3.5 million investors with a total of $158 billion in investments. The maximum federal contribution to the account is 5% of salary, which would be matched by 5% from the worker, for a total of 10%. For investment, the workers choose among six fund options with different mixes of investments among stocks and bonds, and can choose to shift among these funds at any time. At retirement, workers can use some or all of the assets in their accounts to purchase an annuity guaranteeing a specified monthly income for the rest of the worker's life. With 10% of the worker's salary going into this system each year, over an entire career at standard market investment returns this system alone would end up paying much more than Social Security even promises, let alone what it can pay.

Investment returns declined in 2008 due to the financial crisis, with three of the funds suffering sharp losses. But those funds have since rebounded sharply, recovering prior losses. But none of the funds went "bankrupt," or lost all of the workers' money. This shows again the savings and investment system weathering virtually a worst-case scenario.

Clearly, federal employees have developed a good deal for themselves. What about the rest of us?

A CONCRETE PROPOSAL

In 2005, fully comprehensive legislation providing for personal accounts for Social Security was introduced in Congress. Representative Paul Ryan (R-WI), now chairman of the U.S. House Committee of the Budget, was the lead sponsor in the House and Senator John Sununu (R-NH) was the lead sponsor in the Senate.

I was centrally involved in developing this legislation, meeting extensively with the chief actuary of Social Security, Stephen Goss, in developing a "score" for the bill. A score is an official assessment of the impacts of the bill. During those meetings, Goss provided considerable input regarding how to make the proposal workable. I also worked closely with legislative counsel in developing the exact language for the bill.

The bill also incorporated the pathbreaking work of William G. Shipman, formerly a principal at State Street Global Advisors, one of the largest pension fund investment managers in the world. Shipman developed an administrative framework for personal accounts that would make them workable for the investment fund companies as well, and minimize the costs of administration.[69]

Just completing and introducing this comprehensive, practical legislation was a huge accomplishment, providing a model for the future.

The Ryan-Sununu Bill

Here's how the Ryan-Sununu bill worked.

First, there would be no changes of any sort for those already retired. They would continue to receive all of their promised Social Security benefits in full without any change from current law.

Workers up to age fifty-five, however, would be free to choose to shift on average roughly the employee share of the payroll tax to their personal accounts.[70] Lower-income workers would be able to contribute a slightly higher percentage of the tax, and higher-income workers a slightly lower percentage. This is done so all workers would achieve roughly the same percentage net gain in benefits from the accounts. On average, workers would be able to contribute 6.4% of taxable wages to the accounts, while the employee share of the tax is 6.2%.

Workers choose investments by picking a fund managed by a major private investment firm, from a list of firms officially approved for this purpose and regulated for safety and soundness. Companies that wanted to offer investment funds on this list would apply to the U.S. Treasury Department for approval of their companies, and for the particular investment funds they wanted to offer. Only major, well-established companies with substantial expertise and experience would be approved. The investment funds would have to be highly diversified for investment safety, but could be invested in a broad range of stocks and bonds and other investments to maximize returns and benefits for workers. The personal account investments would be kept strictly separate from the rest of the company, as in

Chile, so any financial troubles the company might experience would have no effect on the personal account investments.

This framework would make investment easy for unsophisticated investors, who would not have to pick particular stocks and bonds. They would just pick an investment fund, like a mutual fund, managed by highly experienced professional investment fund managers, who would choose the particular stocks and bonds and other investments, and when to buy and when to sell each of them. Workers would be free to change the investment fund they have chosen each year. This would be very much like the highly successful investment systems used in Chile, Galveston, and in the federal employees' Thrift Savings Plan.

Labor unions, or social organizations like the NAACP, La Raza, or AARP, could team up with investment firms to offer investment funds to their members. While they would have to obtain the same federal approvals and be subject to the same regulations as all other investment fund options in the system, they would be able to tailor investment options to the actuarial characteristics of different subgroups in the population. For example, since African-Americans have lower life expectancy, the NAACP could develop annuities for these members that would pay higher benefits because on average they will live fewer years in retirement to collect these benefits. Mining unions could focus on developing early retirement options for their members, who are unlikely to be able to work in the mines all the way until their late sixties.

In retirement, benefits payable from the personal accounts would substitute for a portion of Social Security benefits based on the degree to which workers exercised the account option over their careers, and shifted payroll taxes from Social Security to the accounts. Workers currently in the workforce exercising the personal accounts would continue to receive a portion of Social Security retirement benefits under the current system based on the past taxes they have already paid into the program, just like with the recognition bonds under the Chilean system. Workers would then also receive the benefits payable through the personal accounts.

Take someone in high school today who chooses the personal account option when he enters the workforce. In retirement, the benefits from the personal account would substitute for all of the worker's Social

Security retirement benefits promised under the current system. With standard, long-term market investment returns, this worker would receive substantially higher benefits than under the current system, as discussed further below.

Now let's take someone who is around forty when he first exercises the personal account option. In retirement, the benefits from the personal account would substitute for about half of his Social Security retirement benefits. In other words, the worker would get all of the benefits payable through the personal account, plus still get from the old Social Security framework about half the benefits promised under current law. Again, with standard, long-term market investment returns on the account, the benefits from the personal account would be substantially higher than the proportion of Social Security benefits they replace. This worker, however, would not gain as much as the younger worker who is able to take advantage of the higher market investment returns over his entire life.

Now let's look at someone who is fifty-five when the new system becomes effective. He decides to opt for the personal account during his remaining working years. He shifts basically the employee share of the tax to the account each year until his retirement. His personal account funds would have fewer years to earn and accumulate returns. But that is taken into account in the actuarial formula that determines what proportion of Social Security benefits the personal account benefits would replace. For this older worker, the personal account would replace about 10–15% of his Social Security benefits under current law. In other words, the worker would get all benefits paid by the personal account, and 85–90% of the promised Social Security benefits under current law. The worker would consequently gain substantially as well, though not as much as workers who start the personal accounts at younger ages.

The option is explicitly designed so that all workers will gain the advantage of the higher market investment returns available through personal accounts for their remaining years of work before retirement. As a result, all workers of all ages and all income levels would gain higher benefits through the personal accounts.

The retirement benefits payable through the accounts would be tax-free. The current taxation of Social Security benefits should be eliminated as well. Of course, the accumulating investment returns in the accounts would also be tax-free. Workers would also be free to choose to leave their remaining account funds at death to their families, without any inheritance tax, more popularly known as the death tax.

The bill would also maintain the current Social Security safety net in full with a federal guarantee that all workers with personal accounts would receive through their personal account and continuing Social Security benefits at least as much as promised by Social Security under current law. If the total benefit for a retiree with a personal account fell below currently promised Social Security benefits, the federal government would send the retiree a check each month to make up the difference.

This works because again market investment returns are so much higher than what Social Security even promises, let alone what it can pay. So it is very unlikely that after forty-five years or more of real capital market investment, with any short-term market declines averaged out by market rebounds and booms, workers with personal accounts would end up with less than what Social Security promises financed by their accounts. The system is designed so that these workers would instead end up with a lot more. That also means it is unlikely the guarantee would result in significant costs to the government.

This is all the more so because of the carefully structured investment system described above, with workers choosing among professionally managed investment funds approved and regulated for this purpose. Through that system, the government can fully limit and control the risks workers can take on with their personal accounts. Again, this system has worked well in a range of other contexts, with no losses or need for any bailouts after decades of operation.

Workers would be completely free to choose to stay in Social Security as is without exercising the personal account option at all. There would be no benefit cuts or tax increases for these workers, either. They would continue to get all the benefits promised by Social Security under current law. This works because, as the chief actuary of Social Security concluded, the personal accounts would be such a good deal that over time all workers would choose them. That is indicated in his official score for the Ryan-Sununu bill. This in turn would eliminate the long-term deficits of Social Security, without benefit cuts or tax increases, as discussed further below.

This Ryan-Sununu proposal would consequently maintain for everyone at the very least all the current benefits promised under current law (though ultimately financed through private savings and investment rather than through taxes and redistribution). Almost all other proposals would reduce those benefits in some way, and even include tax increases in some cases. By maintaining the full current safety net with a federal guarantee and a social structure for investment options and benefit payments, the proposal actually expands the current Social Security framework so that workers can gain the enormous advantages of market savings and investment.

The Chief Actuary's Score

The chief actuary of Social Security thoroughly analyzed this Ryan-Sununu bill and published a comprehensive official score estimating the effects of the legislation. That score is still available on the official Web site of the Social Security Administration at www.ssa.gov, under solvency memoranda.[71]

First, the chief actuary found that the personal accounts in the Ryan-Sununu bill would achieve full solvency for Social Security, completely eliminating Social Security deficits over time without any benefit cuts or tax increases. The chief actuary stated, "The Social Security program would be expected to be solvent and to meet its benefit obligations throughout the long-range period 2003 through 2077 and beyond."[72] This is because so much of Social Security's benefit obligations are ultimately shifted to the accounts, while the employer share of the tax remains in place.

Indeed, over several decades, virtually 100% of Social Security retirement benefits would be shifted to the personal accounts, since, as the chief actuary concluded, the accounts proposed in the bill would be so beneficial for workers that all workers would eventually choose the accounts. (By the way, this would be the largest reduction in government spending in world history.) With the employer share of the tax remaining in place until it is phased down as unnecessary, the resulting surpluses are so huge that they would eliminate the long-term deficits of the disability insurance program as well, even though the reform plan does not otherwise provide for any changes in that program.

The accounts achieve this without benefit cuts or tax increases in Social Security. Over time, in fact, the accounts would lead to major payroll tax *cuts*, as well as substantially *higher* benefits. The Ryan-Sununu bill included a payroll tax cut trigger providing that when the Social Security surpluses get too large, the payroll tax rate will be reduced automatically. The chief actuary's score shows that eventually the personal accounts would reduce the total Social Security payroll tax rate from 12.4% today to 4.2%, which is enough to finance all remaining survivors and disability benefits. (This would be the largest tax cut in world history.) On our present course, by contrast, paying all promised Social Security benefits would require raising the total payroll tax rate to close to 20%—or more, quite possibly much more. The Ryan-Sununu bill provides for workers to put only half the total Social Security payroll tax into the accounts. That is because private market investment is so productive that with only half as much paid in, workers would still get much better benefits, as we saw in Chile.

I calculated how much better in a study for the Institute for Policy Innovation.[73] With personal accounts of this size, at standard, long-term market investment returns, an account invested consistently half in corporate bonds and half in stocks would provide workers with roughly two-thirds more in benefits than Social Security promises but cannot pay. An account invested two-thirds in stocks and one-third in bonds would pay workers over twice what Social Security promises today. With the rest of the payroll tax money, Ryan-Sununu then allows for the long-term tax cuts.

Ryan-Sununu would also eliminate the unfunded liability of Social Security, currently officially estimated at $15.1 trillion. This results because over time, pay-as-you-go, noninvested, purely redistributive Social Security is transformed into the fully funded savings- and investment-based personal accounts. (This would be the largest reduction in government debt in world history.)

Workers would also directly own and control the funds in the personal accounts, just as much as the funds in their individual retirement accounts

(IRAs) or 401(k)s. After just the first fifteen years with the Ryan-Sununu personal accounts, workers would have accumulated in the accounts $7.8 trillion in today's dollars, after adjusting for inflation. This is as large as the entire mutual fund industry today. After just the first twenty-five years, workers would have accumulated $16 trillion in today's dollars.

Workers would be free to choose to leave some portion of these funds to their families at death. What a boost that would be to future generations to have such a foundation for their own future prosperity. Imagine an economy with low-, moderate-, and middle-income families leaving some substantial portion of these accounts to their children, along with a home of substantial value. That would be a financial foundation for higher education, or starting a new small business or a professional practice. Or pursuing some other dream.

With such personal accounts, working people across the board, at all income levels, would each hold a substantial ownership stake in America's business and industry. No other reform would do so much to promote equality of wealth among the American people. Indeed, a study by Harvard professor Martin Feldstein concluded that if Social Security was shifted to a fully funded system like personal accounts, the concentration of wealth in America would be reduced by half.[74] Other approaches to such equality are usually based on redistribution punishing the successful, and thereby creating counterproductive incentives that drag down the economy. But these personal accounts achieve more equality by creating vast realms of new wealth broadly owned throughout the population. This reinforces and strengthens the economy, expanding economic growth.

The personal accounts funnel new rivers of savings and investment into the economy. Higher savings and capital investment translates into higher productivity and increased wages for working people. It creates new jobs and new opportunities. The bottom line is increased economic growth. Increased capital will feed the more rapid development and innovation of our booming modern technology, increasing economic growth even more.

Moreover, when workers start paying the employee share of the payroll tax into their own personal accounts, which they own and control, in order to finance their own future benefits, then as a matter of economics, that portion of the payroll tax is no longer a tax. The workers are no longer paying that money to the government to finance the benefits of others. They are keeping that money as their own property and all accumulated investment returns are theirs as well. Through the personal accounts, the payroll tax is being transformed into a personal wealth engine for workers and their families rather than a tax.

This has virtually the same positive effect on the economy as eliminating the employee share of the payroll tax. It would again cause wages, employment, and overall economic growth to expand more rapidly. A booming economy right now in which to work is another enormous benefit for working people.

Finally, with personal accounts, workers would each be free to choose their own retirement age. Moreover, they would have full market incentives to delay their retirement age as long as possible, because the longer they delay, the more their accounts geometrically accumulate to higher and higher amounts. Consequently, those with less physically demanding jobs who can remain productive may decide to delay their retirement age well past 70, which would otherwise be politically intractable to require by law. Others with more physically demanding jobs may most benefit from retirement at 62, or even 60. Those with such jobs would also have incentives to train for and transition to less physically demanding jobs, where they could remain productive as they age. Or they could save more during their working years knowing they will have to retire from their physically demanding profession earlier than others. Isn't this individual flexibility based on individual choice and market incentives the ideal solution to the question of the retirement age?

Financing the Transition

Any plan for personal accounts for Social Security involves a transition financing issue. That arises because Social Security again operates on a pay-as-you-go basis, with almost all of the money coming in immediately going out to pay current benefits. If half of the money coming in goes for savings and investment in personal accounts instead, additional funds will have to come from somewhere else to continue paying all promised benefits to today's retirees.

The need for this transition financing phases out over time as workers retire and rely on their personal accounts instead. But in the interim the money to continue paying all promised benefits in full needs to come from somewhere.

This is a cash flow financing issue, not a matter of transition *costs*. What the reform involves is moving from a tax and redistribution, pay-as-you-go system, with no real savings and investment anywhere in the system, to a fully funded, savings and investment system. When you save $1,000 in your savings account, you don't think *That cost me $1,000*. It doesn't *cost* you anything, because you still have the money in your savings account. Of course, because you can't have your cake and eat it, too, you can't spend the $1,000 you are saving, or else you wouldn't be saving it. That may create a cash flow issue for you, depending on your personal finances. But it is not a matter of the savings *costing* you $1,000.

The transition financing money is effectively financing the savings going into the personal accounts of working people across America, growing with earned returns to $7.8 trillion over the first ten years, and $16 trillion over the first twenty-five years. That accumulated savings and investment is not a cost to the economy—it is a mighty, productive contributor to the economy. The working people seeing that money growing in their own personal accounts would certainly recognize that it is not a cost, but in fact an asset. Overall, what the transition is really financing is the increased savings and investment involved in shifting from a pay-as-you-go system to a fully funded system, just as with eliminating the unfunded liabilities of any underfunded pension plan.[75]

The savings from the other reforms described in this book would provide sufficient funds to finance this transition, effectively by reducing other government spending. How this can work is shown by the Roadmap for America's Future, additional comprehensive legislation introduced by Representative Ryan, now chairman of the House Budget Committee. That legislation includes personal accounts for Social Security, fundamental reform of Medicare and Medicaid, general health care reform, tax reform, and other budget reforms. The Congressional Budget Office (CBO) has officially scored the Roadmap as achieving full solvency for Social Security and for Medicare, and balancing the federal budget indefinitely into the future, completely eliminating all long-term federal deficits, with no tax increases. In the process, the transition to the personal accounts for Social Security is fully paid for, effectively by the spending reductions.

The reforms advocated in this book are not the same as in the Ryan Roadmap. But they are similar. The CBO score of the Ryan Roadmap shows that financing the transition to personal accounts through the reduced government spending from such reforms is plausible and feasible. Some federal borrowing would likely be needed in the early years of the reforms, as the savings from all the changes phase in. But all such borrowing can be segregated in a separate government account slated to be paid off out of the future surpluses generated by the reforms. The chief actuary's score of Ryan-Sununu shows that is feasible as well.

Moreover, another factor, one unfortunately not well understood, is that even such shorter-term borrowing is just *borrowing back some of the trillions in increased savings flowing into the personal accounts.* If workers save $300 billion in personal accounts in year one, and $200 billion is borrowed to finance the transition in that first year, the economy is actually gaining net savings of $100 billion. So this borrowing does not have the negative economic effects of deficit spending in crowding out the savings and capital for private investment, and possibly increasing interest rates. To the contrary, it is enabling a $100 billion increase in savings and capital for private investment, and possibly reducing interest rates. Over time, as the broader transition financing savings kicks in, and the longer-term benefits of the reform grow, the increased savings and investment would skyrocket.[76]

Financing the personal account transition through reduced government spending is the most economically beneficial way to finance the transition. The personal account money would then go right into increased savings and investment, benefitting the overall economy without any counterproductive economic effects such as would result from increased taxes.

But in fact, through the Ryan-Sununu reform plan, the majority of the transition is financed by the continuing and even increased revenues resulting from the reform itself. The employer share of the tax is continued to pay effectively half of the transition financing burden, to be phased out after the transition is complete. In addition, the increased savings and investment through the personal accounts generates increased revenues from the corporate income tax and other taxes on corporate income. The increased savings in the personal accounts would be invested in corporations, generating increased corporate income as a result, which means increased revenues from the taxation of that corporate income.[77] The score of Ryan-Sununu by the chief actuary of Social Security reflects this effect as well, and gives an indication of its magnitude, based on the work of Harvard economics professor Martin Feldstein.

Further revenues would be generated by the increased economic growth resulting from the reform in the ways discussed above.[78]

A Vision for the Future

The personal accounts do not need to start at a level as large as in Ryan-Sununu. They can start at a level half as large, or at whatever level seems feasible at the start. But the vision should be to eventually expand the accounts to the full Ryan-Sununu level, and solve all of the problems of Social Security that way, without tax increases or benefit cuts.

After that, the personal accounts can be expanded further to a larger proportion of the payroll tax to provide for the purchase of life insurance to take over full responsibility for survivors benefits, and the purchase of disability insurance to take over responsibility for disability benefits, as in Chile. Such further reform would again provide far better coverage and benefits than Social Security even promises today, let alone what it can deliver.

The personal accounts can then be expanded to the Medicare portion of the payroll tax, with the benefits to be used in retirement to buy private health insurance, as discussed further in Chapter 4. Ultimately, the personal accounts would replace the entire payroll tax, transforming that burdensome tax, the largest that working people pay, into a wealth-producing engine for working families, embodied in the personal accounts.

This would establish a new foundation of prosperity for working people in America.

How Bush Lost Personal Accounts

When George Bush ran for president in 2000, he explicitly campaigned on empowering workers with the freedom to choose personal accounts for Social Security. His campaign employed all the positive, populist themes originally envisioned for the reform effort. He emphasized the personal ownership and control workers would enjoy through the accounts, the better returns on investment and consequently higher benefits, the accumulated family funds that could be left as an inheritance to children or other heirs, and the full solvency for Social Security that would be achieved without raising taxes or cutting benefits. He specifically contrasted personal accounts with the unpopular alternatives of raising taxes or cutting benefits. He explained that with the personal accounts, he was modernizing Social Security for a better future.[79]

In a major address on Social Security in Rancho Cucamonga, California, on May 15, 2000, Bush said,

> Personal accounts build on the promise of Social Security—they strengthen it, making it more valuable for young workers. Senator Moynihan, Democrat, says that personal accounts take the system to its "logical completion." They give people the security of ownership. They allow even low-income workers to build wealth, which they will use for their own retirement and pass on to their children.
>
> Senator [Bob] Kerrey, also a Democrat, recently said: "It's very important, especially for those of us who have already accumulated wealth, to write laws to enable other people to accumulate it, and arrive where we are." Ownership in our society should not be an exclusive club. Independence should not be a gated community. Everyone should be a part owner in the American Dream.
>
> Yet, without reform, younger workers face a great risk—a lifetime of paying taxes for benefits they may never receive. The reforms I have in mind will actually increase their retirement income.
>
> Within the framework of these principles, we can keep Social

Security strong and stable. We can keep our commitments. We can avoid tax increases. And millions of Americans will have an asset to call their own. This is the best thing about personal accounts. They are not just a program, they are your property. And no politician can take them away.[80]

Regarding possible payroll tax increases, Bush added,

Third, the payroll tax must not be raised. We cannot tax our way to reform.[81]

On September 18, 2000, the Cato Institute reported on how candidate Bush was doing with his Social Security personal accounts proposal:

Social Security has traditionally been a Democratic strong suit but not this year. Whereas polls in the past showed Democrats with a 20-point or more advantage on the question of which party would best handle Social Security, now the parties are running close to even. More important, when voters are asked whether they support Bush's proposal to allow workers to divert a portion of their Social Security taxes to individually owned, privately invested accounts, they strongly endorse the proposal. In the latest Washington Post–ABC News Poll, 59% of voters supported the Bush proposal; 37% were opposed. Vital swing voters are even more supportive of individual accounts. According to a Zogby International poll, 72% of independent voters support individual accounts.[82]

In other words, Bush's positive, populist approach of focusing on the personal accounts alone and emphasizing all of their benefits for the common man was working. Cato also applauded Bush's strategy of contrasting the personal accounts with the unpopular alternatives of cutting benefits and raising taxes:

It was Bill Clinton who best explained the options available to fix Social Security. There are only three: raise taxes, cut benefits, or increase the rate of return by investing Social Security funds. Clinton proposed to do the latter by allowing the government to invest a portion of the Social Security Trust Fund, a dangerous idea that has wisely not seen the light of day. George Bush proposes to do it by allowing workers to invest for themselves. Al Gore rejects both approaches, opposing any investment of Social Security funds. With investment and higher returns off the table, that leaves Gore with only two alternatives; either he raises taxes or cuts benefits. Bush should simply turn to Gore in debate and ask him which of those he plans to do.[83]

Larry Kudlow, who was a senior official in the Reagan administration, also commented in *National Review Online* regarding the brilliance and effectiveness of George Bush's campaign for personal accounts in 2000. Kudlow noted in particular the focus on personal accounts and all of their advantages, in contrast to benefit cuts:

Way back in time, during the early months of the Reagan Administration, a number of the Gipper's more libertarian economic advisers wanted to trash the New Deal—especially Social Security—by severely rolling back benefits in order to shrink government and curb the budget deficit. Wisely, President Reagan always rejected this approach. Time and again, he reminded his staff that he himself voted for FDR four times and went on to vote for Truman. Throughout the budget arguments, Reagan insisted on invoking and preserving the so-called social safety net.

Yes, he intended to radically transform the economic landscape by slashing marginal tax rates and putting an end to double-digit inflation. And yes, he worked hard to slow domestic spending. But he steadfastly refused to rip large holes through the New Deal/Great Society safety net, believing that these programs were an integral part of the fabric of American life. What's so interesting to me about George W. Bush's freshly minted Social Security reform plan that provides for individual-retirement-account-investing in the stock market—set forth in a speech today in California—is that he makes it clear that he intends to strengthen and save Social Security, not to destroy it. This is smart Reagan-style politics. . . .

Give him credit. Enormous credit. This is 21st Century break-through stuff.[84]

Perhaps even more surprising than Bush's politically aggressive, pathbreaking embrace of personal accounts for Social Security during the 2000 campaign was what we didn't hear from his opponent in that race, Vice President Al Gore. You would think from the way the Washington establishment talks about the current Social Security system in such hallowed terms, Gore would have been pounding away at Bush on this issue in massive ad campaigns and through other means.

But Gore didn't. Gore did criticize Bush, and there were some ads against the personal accounts, especially late in the campaign. But Gore never came close to developing his attack into a major issue of the campaign. The reason for this is that the Democrats saw in their own internal polls what Bush already knew: freedom to choose personal accounts for at least part of Social Security was a very popular, even populist, idea at the grass roots. Polls at the time were consistently showing that 60–70% of the public generally supported personal accounts. Moreover, strong majorities of base Democrat constituencies supported the idea: African-Americans, Hispanics, blue-collar workers. These constituencies viewed personal accounts as their only real chance to start accumulating some personal and family wealth.

Attacking Bush over the issue would at best spread the word that Bush was for the popular accounts. At worst, it would identify Gore as on the wrong side of the issue. Gore, in fact, spent more time on a watered-down me-tooism than in attacking Bush on personal accounts. Gore proposed an add-on account to Social Security, where workers could save and invest additional money on top of what they pay into Social Security. But many Democrat core voters do not have the discretionary funds for substantial savings on top of Social Security. Moreover, we already have a lot of such add-on accounts, for example IRAs and 401(k)s.

Bush, of course, went on to a narrow victory in 2000, with many arguing that personal accounts provided a net gain for him. The proposal did not stop him from winning the senior vote in Florida, and without that he would not have been president.

But Bush was not the only candidate who won on personal accounts.

In the late 1990s, congressional Republican candidates started running on the idea as part of their platforms. They consistently won. The big breakthrough came in 2002, when the Democrats tried to make personal accounts a pivotal issue in the midterm congressional elections. Top pollster John Zogby summed up the results: "in every campaign where personal accounts were a major issue, the candidate in favor of personal accounts won, and the candidate opposing them lost."

All of these candidates campaigned for personal accounts the way Bush did. They emphasized that the accounts provided a better deal for workers, that benefits for future retirees would go up not down, that Social Security would be strengthened, and that there would be no tax increases. They did not say they would cut future promised retirement benefits by monkeying with the basic Social Security benefit formula (a proposal called "price indexing," which we will see more of below), delaying the retirement age, raising the cap on the maximum taxable income for Social Security, or otherwise increasing payroll taxes.

In 2004, Bush pledged again to adopt personal accounts for Social Security as a top priority for his second term. His opponent, Senator John Kerry, was even quieter about it than Gore had been. He talked again at times about add-on accounts. If Kerry's internal polls had shown that Bush was vulnerable over personal accounts, Kerry and the Democrats would have ripped his throat out over it. But again the dog did not bark.

At the start of 2005, Bush had just decisively won reelection while for the second time advocating personal accounts for Social Security. Strong polling majorities favored the idea. The Republicans had substantial majorities in both houses of Congress, including fifty-five senators. Comprehensive personal account legislation had been introduced in both the House and the Senate. And the chief actuary of Social Security had scored that legislation as achieving full solvency for the program.

Everything was poised for fundamental, sweeping, historic Social Security reform through personal accounts. But it never happened.

Bush's White House staff in charge of the Social Security reform effort never understood the politics or policy of personal accounts, and proved ineducable on the subject. They were stuck inside the Washington establishment box that insisted that Social Security reform was all about some combination of tax increases and benefit cuts. In deference to the president's campaign proposals, they lumped personal accounts on top of their tax increase/benefit cut conception of what Social Security reform was all about.

As a result, by 2005 there was little evidence of the pathbreaking, populist themes and rhetoric that the president had so brilliantly and successfully used in arguing for personal accounts during his 2000 campaign in particular. Gone was the discussion of a better deal and better benefits from personal accounts. We barely heard anything anymore about ownership, building personal wealth, and leaving an inheritance to children and family.

Instead, the focus of discussion had moved to a huge cut in future promised Social Security benefits under the label of "price indexing." As for tax increases, while the president proclaimed during the campaign that no tax increases was one of his seven principles of reform, and that we could not "tax our way to reform," tax increases were now "on the table."

Indeed, the mantra came to be that "everything was on the table," every brutally unpopular idea, such as delaying the retirement age, or means testing, along with the one politically successful and transforming idea of personal accounts. This crowded tabletop just buried all the positives of personal accounts and at best confused the public. Were future benefits going to rise under personal accounts, or fall under price indexing? The public soon was lost.

Under the new White House conception of Social Security reform, personal accounts were "the dessert" to make palatable the "spinach" of benefit reductions.[85] Even White House criticism of those calling for tax increases was short-circuited. The president had been steered away from the positive, personal empowerment approach of the 2000 campaign, which had proved so successful in transforming Social Security from the third rail of American politics to a populist issue on which Republican after Republican was winning elections.

The White House Social Security policy team convinced President Bush and the senior White House staff that congressional Democrat support for Social Security reform including personal accounts would be won if the president would just publicly announce support for the notion of "price indexing" as well. Price indexing involves changing the fundamental Social Security benefit formula for calculating the future benefits that workers would receive at retirement (not the postretirement Social Security cost-of-living adjustment, or COLA). Instead of growing over time with wages, which keeps Social Security benefits stable as a percentage of preretirement income, under price indexing the benefits to be paid at retirement grow during the worker's career with prices. Since prices grow slower than wages each year, this would result in a growing reduction in Social Security benefits over time from currently promised levels, about a 40% cut in the future benefits Social Security would pay under current law for today's young workers.

This worked directly contrary to the natural political appeal of personal accounts to young workers. It also begged a response from liberals that tax increases would have to be included in any reform package if benefit cuts were.

With personal accounts, such price indexing was completely unnecessary, as workers over time would be *replacing* the promised wage-indexed benefits, which Social Security admittedly cannot finance, with the fully funded personal account benefits financed by real savings and investment. But the White House Social Security policy team was impenetrable on this point.

In the fall of 2005, the president himself went on national television in a highly confusing and forgettable appearance to endorse price indexing. The public had no idea what he was talking about. The response from congressional Democrats was crickets chirping. Despite White House staff fantasies, not one elected Democrat rose to endorse personal accounts in return. Indeed, not one elected Democrat rose to endorse price indexing in any form. How, in fact, could anyone have ever expected Democrats to support personal accounts in return for a 40% cut in future promised Social Security benefits?

No wonder that the more President Bush talked about Social Security reform and personal accounts, the more his support dropped on the issue. By the time the president was done trying to promote Social Security reform in late 2005, the polls still showed 50–60% of the public supporting personal accounts, down only about 10 points. But when asked if they supported "the President's plan" on Social Security, the public's support dropped by half, to the range of 25–30%. This was the direct result of the touted work by the White House Social Security policy staff in switching the administration's conception of reform from the positive, populist model focusing entirely on personal accounts that the president originally supported, to a Pain Caucus model focusing on a package of benefit cuts and tax increases with personal accounts as the dessert.

As a result, the legacy of sweeping, fundamental Social Security reform would belong to some future president.

CHAPTER 4

OBAMACARE: DEATH AND TAXES

Repeal and Replace with Patient Power

National health care costs have been growing faster than the economy for close to a hundred years. But that cost growth accelerated over the past fifty years, soaring from 5% of GDP in 1960 to 10% in 1985 to 17% in 2009.[1] Close to one-fifth of everything we produce today is spent on health care.

That is the highest proportion of output devoted to health care of any country in the world, by far. Second is France at 11.2% of GDP, followed by Switzerland at 10.7%. Germany spends 10.4%, with the United Kingdom only at 8.7%.[2] The average among countries in the Organisation for Economic Co-operation and Development (OECD), basically the major Western industrialized nations, is 9%.

Since we still have the biggest economy in the world by far, that means we spend far more on health care than any other country in the world. U.S. health costs totaled $2.5 trillion in 2009, larger than the entire economies of every other country in the world except China, Japan, Germany, and France.[3] Per person, we spent $7,538 on health care in 2008, again higher than any other country by far. That was 50% more than the second-ranked, Norway, at $5,003, with Switzerland in third at $4,627.[4] Germany only spent half as much, at $3,737 per person, and the United Kingdom less than half at $3,129. The OECD average was less than half as well, at $3,060.

These trends are expected to continue. CBO projects that on our current course, by 2040 health care costs would consume close to one-third of GDP.[5] By 2080, as much as half of everything produced in the United States would go to cover health costs, according to CBO projections.

Close to half of all health care spending today is paid for through federal programs, primarily Medicare, Medicaid, and the Children's Health Insurance Program (CHIP). So rising health costs have enormous implications for federal taxes and spending.

Let's examine the finances of Medicare under the 2009 Annual Report of the Medicare Board of Trustees. (We will discuss below the additional challenges of the 2010 Annual Report.) The largest component of Medicare is Part A, the hospital insurance (HI) program, which pays for hospital expenses for America's senior citizens. Part A is already running annual deficits, which will continue until the HI trust fund is entirely exhausted in 2017. By the next year, 2018, just this part of Medicare alone would be running an *annual* deficit of nearly $100 billion, under the intermediate assumptions.[6] Under the so-called pessimistic assumptions, which, as discussed in Chapter 3 in regard to Social Security, may be more realistic, the Medicare Part A deficit by 2018, just seven years from now, would be $225 billion.[7]

Paying all promised Part A (HI) benefits to those entering the workforce today would require raising today's total HI payroll tax rate from 2.9% to 10%, under the intermediate assumptions.[8] Under the so-called pessimistic assumptions, that payroll tax would have to be raised to close to 18%.[9]

Medicare Part B pays for the doctors' expenses of America's seniors. Premiums paid by seniors themselves cover about one-fourth of this program's expenses. Three-fourths of Part B costs are paid by the taxpayers through general revenues. By 2018, Medicare Part B alone will be costing taxpayers $268.3 billion in general revenues under the intermediate assumptions, and $352.8 billion under the alleged pessimistic assumptions.[10]

Then there's Medicare Part D, the prescription drug benefit. Premiums from seniors themselves cover only a little over 10% of the costs of this program, with the rest from general revenues. Some of those general revenues come from state governments, but that money ultimately comes from the same taxpayers as federal revenues. By 2018, Medicare Part D will require $123 billion from the taxpayers under the intermediate assumptions, and $160.2 billion under the supposed pessimistic assumptions.

Counting Parts A, B, and D altogether, Medicare alone will be costing taxpayers nearly $500 billion in general revenues by 2018 under the intermediate assumptions, and nearly $750 billion under the "pessimistic" assumptions, in addition to Medicare payroll taxes and the premiums paid by seniors.

Even with all that taxpayer financing, Medicare premiums will not be any walk in the park for seniors, either. The monthly premiums for Part B and Part D will be nearly $200 per senior, or nearly $400 per couple, by 2018, under the intermediate projections alone.[11] In addition, seniors would be liable for a deductible of nearly $1,600 for hospital stays by 2018 under the intermediate projections.[12] For longer hospital stays, seniors will be liable for an additional $400 per day after the first 60 days, and $800 per day after 90 days. While President Obama insisted it was so important to eliminate all lifetime caps on benefits under all private insurance plans, Medicare hospital coverage itself has a lifetime cap equal to 90 days for each spell of illness, plus 60 additional lifetime reserve days that can only be used once.

This is why most seniors buy private Medigap coverage in addition to Medicare, bearing still another premium. In fact, despite the enormous spending under Medicare, seniors spend as much out of pocket today on health care as they did before Medicare was adopted!

Medicare spending is projected to total over $1 trillion per year by 2020, just under the intermediate projections. That would involve close to $20,000 in spending per Medicare beneficiary for that year alone. You can imagine then, as the baby boom completes its retirement, how Medicare spending will explode further. Paying all promised Medicare benefits to those entering the workforce today will ultimately require more than 10% of GDP per year, just under the intermediate assumptions.[13] The general revenues consumed by Medicare alone would eat up 40% of all individual and corporate income taxes.[14]

This all adds up to an unfunded liability for just Medicare Part A of $36.4 trillion.[15] That is the amount of funds that would have to be saved and invested right now to finance future promised benefits as under a private or state and local government pension plan. Despite the supposed Medicare Part A trust fund, which is as phony as explained in Chapter 3 for the Social Security trust funds, the total amount actually saved right now is zero. The total economy for 2010 was $14.6 trillion, so the shortfall measured this way is two and a half years of everything America produces today. Again just for Medicare Part A.

In addition, the present value of future general revenue requirements for Medicare Part B is $37 trillion.[16] The present value of future general revenue requirements for Medicare Part D is $15.5 trillion. So total present unfunded liabilities of Medicare today may be calculated as $89 trillion, or over six years of everything America produces today.

On top of all this spending for Medicare is Medicaid, which is the federal program to pay for medical care for the poor. Even before passage of the Patient Protection and Affordable Health Care Act of 2010, President Obama's government takeover of health care, which we explain in detail below, Medicaid already cost federal taxpayers alone $275 billion in 2010, projected to rise to $451 billion by 2018.[17] But the states pay for 40% of Medicaid costs in addition, and that money comes from the same taxpayers as bear the federal burden. The states spent another $150 billion on Medicaid in 2010,[18] bringing the Medicaid total to $425 billion for the year. By 2018, total Medicaid spending was already projected to reach $800 billion, costing overall $6.2 trillion over the ten years from 2010 to 2019.

Congress has adopted and expanded as well since 1997 the Children's Health Insurance Program (CHIP), which pays for health insurance for children whose families earn too much to qualify for Medicaid. That was originally supposed to be a limited, low-cost program helping out a few modest-income families, with enrollment of 660,000 children in 1998.[19] But expanding it broadly became a crusade of Nancy Pelosi, Speaker of the U.S. House from 2007 to 2011, with coverage under the program exploding to 7.7 million children by 2009.[20] CHIP is consequently now projected to cost an additional $200 billion from 2010 to 2019.[21]

OBAMACARE: POURING OIL ON THE FIRE

President Obama surveyed all these entitlement spending burdens we have discussed so far, and decided that what we needed was still more. So Obamacare added or sharply expanded three entitlement programs.

First, Obamacare expanded eligibility for Medicaid to families beyond poverty, to those earning up to 138% of the poverty level. Moreover, previous eligibility for Medicaid was limited to families with children and to low-income seniors, especially those who needed but couldn't afford nursing home care. But Obamacare expanded eligibility to all childless couples and singles of all ages who meet the income requirements. The result will be to increase Medicaid enrollment by 24 million additional beneficiaries by 2015, resulting in over 100 million Americans dependent on Medicaid and CHIP by 2021.[22] This will add another $674 billion in further federal costs for these programs over the next decade alone.[23]

But that was just a start. Obamacare added a whole new federal entitlement program providing subsidies, through refundable tax credits, for the purchase of health insurance for families earning up to four times the poverty level, or $88,000 for a family of four. The eligibility thresholds, moreover, are indexed to grow over time. By 2014, this new program will be providing $3,000 in taxpayer funds to families making $95,000 for the year.[24] By 2018, almost $5,000 will be going to families making $102,000.[25]

CBO estimates that these subsidies will cost taxpayers an additional $523 billion over the first ten years alone.[26] The chief actuary of Medicare estimates the total cost of this new entitlement will reach over $500 billion over the first six years, through 2019. This is only the beginning, as this program will ultimately cost far more than is now projected, as we will explore in more detail below.

This new entitlement is a massive increase in welfare extended to middle- and even upper-income families, irresponsibly added on top of the runaway, financially intractable entitlement promises the federal government has already made.

But Obamacare was not done. It created still another entitlement program, the Community Living Assistance Services and Support Act, known as CLASS. This program will pay for in-home caretaker and/or adult day services for seniors and the disabled who are incapable of taking care of themselves, measured by being unable to perform two of six activities of daily living, such as getting dressed, bathing, cooking, going to the bathroom, cleaning the house, or shopping for essential groceries. For those who qualify for the benefits, the program will pay $50 or more per day *directly to the senior citizen or disabled individual, not the service provider.* Fifty bucks a day adds up to $18,250 a year.

Here is one trick behind this boondoggle that most commentators have missed. For most seniors who need help with these activities of daily living, the help is provided by family members, friends, and neighbors. For example, for many senior citizens who can no longer cook, drive to the grocery store, or clean the house, their spouses, adult children—especially those they live with—or roommates perform these services for them, at no charge. But in these cases, the senior citizen himself will now receive close to $20,000 a year or more in cash benefits.

The program is to be financed by premiums paid by workers, expected to cost between $150 and $240 per month to start.[27] That totals $1,800 to nearly $3,000 per year. For employers who choose to participate, workers will be automatically enrolled in the program, though they may opt out and forgo the premium payments, at least for now. To qualify for the benefits, workers need only pay the premiums for five years, though they have to be working for three of those five years. What that means is that seniors can qualify for the benefits by signing up just five years before retirement, or maybe just three if they continue to pay the premiums for two more years in retirement.

Consequently, the program will be collecting premiums during its first five years, but not paying any benefits. Benefit payments won't start until the sixth year, and then only for the tiny proportion of the population that was working during the previous five years but then became unable to take care of themselves in the sixth year. During its first ten years, the program will accumulate further only the beneficiaries who become so functionally disabled in the last four years of the period.

But it was these first ten years that were counted in determining the impact of the Obamacare legislation on the deficit. Counting ten years of premium payments but only five years of negligible start-up benefits, CBO estimated that the CLASS component of Obamacare would contribute $70 billion in deficit reduction during the ten-year budget window considered by Congress. None of that net $70 billion in excess premium payments in the first ten years will be saved to pay future CLASS program benefits. Just like with the Social Security and Medicare trust funds, it will all be taken by the federal government to be spent on other programs.

The second ten years, however, will involve ten years of growing benefit payments, likely throwing the CLASS program into deficit, unless the premium payments are raised. But if they are raised, more workers will likely opt out, perpetuating the deficit. The overall result is likely to be perpetual and growing deficits under the program. This is why the CBO concluded, "We have grave concerns that the real effect of [the CLASS Act] would be to create a new federal entitlement program with large, long term spending increases that far exceed revenues."[28] Even one of the supporters of Obamacare who actually voted for the bill, Senator Kent Conrad (D-ND), called the CLASS Act "a Ponzi scheme of the first order, the kind of thing that Bernie Madoff would have been proud of."[29] Too bad he and so many other Democrats nevertheless voted to pass the bill.

Health Cost Napalm

President Obama promised while barnstorming for his health care takeover legislation that it would reduce the "growth of health care costs for our families, our businesses, and our government."[30] While campaigning for president, he promised repeatedly that his health plan would reduce the cost of health insurance by $2,500 per family. But the Patient Protection and Affordable Health Care Act as passed will have exactly the opposite effect, causing health care costs to soar further for families, businesses, and government.

We have already seen how this will be so for the federal government, with the adoption or expansion in Obamacare of three entitlement programs. But that is just the beginning.

Obamacare includes an employer mandate that requires employers to provide the health insurance for their workers that the government specifies they must buy. For those workers who don't get health insurance from their employers, Obamacare includes an individual mandate that requires workers to pay for the health insurance the government says they must buy.

That mandated insurance will include costly required benefits. President Obama repeatedly touted that these required benefits will include "free" preventive care. They will also include the elimination of all lifetime limits and caps on health insurance benefits. They will include as well coverage for alcohol and drug rehabilitation, mental health, and obesity treatments and counseling. Newt Gingrich points out, "if you are a single male with no children, the legislation still requires you to have maternity benefits and well-baby and well-child care."[31] Same for women well past childbearing years. You may want lower-cost insurance with a high deductible focusing on essential catastrophic health care for life-threatening diseases, knowing you have your own resources to cover more routine expenses, which, as discussed below, is a powerful means of reducing health costs. But the government will limit your choice of deductibles, as well as co-payments. Some employers may have had success in controlling costs with particular plan designs, but now under Obamacare the government will decide what insurance they must provide.

Other costly mandates will be added through the political process as well. Over two thousand benefit mandates have been adopted among the fifty states due to the political pressures from coalitions of service providers and their patients to add their treatments and services to the list of required benefits. These include such basics as hairpieces, acupuncture, and chiropractic services. These mandates account for as much as one-quarter of the cost of health insurance today. This political process will now bloom at the federal level as well, as the same special interests begin their campaigns to have their services and treatments added to the federally mandated required health insurance as well.

You will be forced under the law to buy insurance with all of these required benefits whether you want them or not. Since these required benefits must be paid for, they will increase health insurance costs substantially, just so health insurers will have the money to pay for all of the promised benefits in their health insurance plans. President Obama, congressional Democrats, and professional liberals have howled that the resulting health insurance premium increases are the fault of evil, greedy health insurance companies. But this is childish, immature politics. The resulting health insurance cost increases are the result of foreseeable math, not the evil and greed of insurers. Opponents of Obamacare told President Obama and congressional Democrats that the Obamacare legislation would increase rather than reduce health insurance costs. And already it is doing precisely that, before it is even fully implemented.

Health insurance costs will further increase under Obamacare due to the regulatory burdens involved in the legislation's mandated requirements of guaranteed issue and community rating. What are those? Obamacare requires all insurers to cover all preexisting conditions and issue health insurance to everyone that applies, no matter how sick they are when they first apply or how costly they may be to cover. This is known as guaranteed issue. The Act also prohibits insurers from varying their rates based on the medical condition or illnesses of applicants. Insurers can only vary rates within a limited range for age, geographic location, and family size. This regulatory requirement is known as modified community rating.

Guaranteed issue and community rating have been proved to raise insurance premiums sharply at the state level every time they have been tried.[32] That should be no surprise. They are like requiring fire insurers to grant coverage to applicants who call after their house is on fire. Then the insurers can charge no more to such applicants than to anyone else. Under such requirements, no one would ever get fire insurance until their house caught fire. Fire insurers would then have a "risk" pool of all burned-down houses, which would naturally require very high premiums to cover.

This is exactly what happens in health insurance. Younger and healthier people delay buying insurance, knowing they are guaranteed coverage at standard rates after they become sick. Sick people apply with very costly illnesses such as cancer and heart disease, which the insurer must then cover and pay for. This means the covered risk pool includes more costly sick people and fewer less costly healthy people, so the costs per person covered soar. The insurer then has to raise rates sharply just to be sure to have enough money to pay all of the policy's benefits.

The Act's proponents believe the legislation will avoid this problem through the individual and employer mandates requiring everyone to be covered at all times. But the tax penalties for failing to buy the insurance are not strong enough to make this work. Individuals who violate the mandate are required to pay $695 per family member, up to a maximum of $2,085 per family. The penalty for employers is $2,000–3,000 per worker. But qualifying health insurance coverage will cost $15,000 per year by 2016, much more even than the $12,000 or more per year that is a typical cost for employer-provided coverage today.

Workers and employers can save too much by just forgoing the coverage and paying the penalty, if they are caught and forced to pay it. Moreover, the Act expressly states that criminal penalties will not apply for failing to pay the fine, and it cannot be enforced by imposing liens on the taxpayer's property, so the penalties are not even enforceable. But such individuals can still buy insurance after they or a member of their family gets sick.[33]

The price-raising effects of all the requirements of the Act were documented a few months before its adoption in a study by the accounting firm of PricewaterhouseCoopers, which examined the actual cost and accounting data of major health insurance firms. The study concluded that under the Act an average family health insurance policy costing $12,300 today will rise to $17,200 by 2013, $21,300 by 2016, and $25,900 by 2019.[34] Another study, conducted by WellPoint, which utilized its own cost and claims data, showed health insurance premiums for the young and healthy would *triple* in some states. Average middle-class families will see their premiums more than double.[35] For example, the premium for a healthy 25-year-old in Ohio would increase from $52 per month to $157, a 199% increase. A 40-year-old husband and wife with two kids would suffer a premium increase from $332 per month to $737, a 122% jump. A small business with eight employees in Franklin County, Ohio, would suffer an 86% premium increase. An earlier study in 2009 by the Council for Affordable Health Insurance similarly concluded that the regulatory requirements of the Act would cause premiums in the individual market to nearly double.[36] Both CBO[37] and the federal government's Centers for Medicare & Medicaid Services[38] confirm that health insurance premiums will rise under the Act, rather than fall as President Obama has repeatedly promised.

Further confirmation that health insurance costs will rise due to these effects is shown by the experience of Massachusetts, which adopted legislation similar to the Act in 2006. The Massachusetts reforms were also based on guaranteed issue and community rating, individual and employer mandates enforced by a penalty of over $1,000 a year per resident,[39] expanded Medicaid, extensive subsidies for the nonpoor to purchase health insurance, and an exchange called Health Connector.

Health insurance for a family of four in Massachusetts cost nearly

$17,000 by 2010, 33% more than the national average,[40] with premiums increasing at nearly double the national average since the reform.[41] The state's costs for health programs soared by 42% in less than three years under the reform,[42] one-third more than projected when the reforms were adopted.[43] And that is with the federal government heavily subsidizing the reform with $21.2 billion in the first three years, $3,000 per Massachusetts resident.[44] Employers who were induced to support the reform with the promise of lower health insurance costs have seen those costs increase by $500 million, with more expected.[45] In the first two years under the reform, premiums for employer-provided insurance grew 21–46% faster than the national average.[46] Despite claims that the reforms would reduce health insurance costs in the individual market by 25–40%,[47] the same claims echoed by President Obama in the 2008 presidential campaign, the opposite has been true.

Just over half of the previously uninsured say their health costs have gone up under the reform as well, with just 14% saying their costs have gone down.[48] Just 22% of the previously uninsured say the law has helped them, with 60% saying it has hurt them.[49] Since the reform was passed, per capita health spending in the state has increased by 23%.[50]

Clearly, the individual and employer mandates did not prevent cost increases resulting from the reform, with what has been apparently considerable gaming to evade the mandates. Harvard Pilgrim, one of the top insurers in the state, reported that between April 2008 and March 2009, about 40% of its new enrollees dropped their coverage in less than five months, but incurred about $2,400 in monthly medical expenses, about 600% higher than normal.[51] This indicates that many in the state are waiting until they need expensive medical care to buy insurance, then dropping it after the insurer pays the costs, knowing they can always get coverage later when they need further expensive care. Grace Marie Turner writes, "There is growing evidence that many people are gaming the system by purchasing health insurance when they need surgery or other expensive medical care, then dropping it a few months later."[52]

Public policies do need to ensure access to essential health care for those with preexisting conditions or who become sick with serious illnesses while uninsured. But as we will see at the end of this chapter in regard to alternative reforms, there are far better means of ensuring this essential access to care.

Further sharp health cost increases will result from the effects of Obamacare on the supply and demand for health care. Obamacare will increase the demand for health care by covering the low-income uninsured through expanded Medicaid, subsidizing middle- and upper-income families to buy extensive health insurance with enriched benefits, and requiring that employers and individuals purchase extensive health insurance with those enriched benefits as well. With everyone covered or potentially covered by comprehensively mandated insurance, the perverse incentives of the third-party payment problem at the root of soaring health costs, explained below, will be maximized.

At the same time, Obamacare will sharply constrict the supply of health care, as also discussed below. Rising demand with declining supply is a perfect storm for soaring prices, and hence costs, for health care overall. That means health insurance costs will go up as well, for families and for businesses.

The price of private health insurance will be further increased due to greater cost shifting by doctors and hospitals from Medicaid and Medicare patients. The Act's expansion of Medicaid means eventually 35 million additional people will be covered by Medicaid, which so badly underpays doctors and hospitals that they must increase fees paid by privately insured persons to make up the losses. The expansion of Medicaid will increase the volume of this cost shifting. Moreover, the policies of Obamacare provide for a shocking $15 trillion in future cuts to doctors and hospitals for the services and treatments they provide to seniors under Medicare. That will sharply increase cost shifting, too, as doctors and hospitals scramble to try to recoup as much of that as possible from the fees they charge patients with private insurance.

A study conducted by one of the nation's top actuarial firms, Milliman, Inc., concluded that cost shifting to private insurance due to the low compensation paid to doctors and hospitals by Medicaid and Medicare raised the cost of private health insurance by $88.5 billion per year, or $1,788 for an average family of four.[53] And that was before passage of Obamacare greatly increasing these effects. If even a small proportion of the increased losses to doctors and hospitals from adding 35 million new dependents to Medicaid and from the $15 trillion in future Medicare cuts is successfully cost shifted, the cost of private health insurance will soar further.

New taxes on health insurance imposed by the Act will further increase the cost of buying health insurance. The Act imposes a so-called Cadillac tax on higher-cost insurance plans, projected to raise $32 billion in new tax revenues over the first ten years. That tax equals 40% of the cost above $10,200 for individuals and $27,500 for families. Those thresholds are indexed to grow only with general inflation after 2020, not health costs, so over time more and more health plans will be subject to the tax, ultimately including standard, average health plans.

The Act imposes an additional tax on the health insurance premiums paid to all insurers, calculated by dividing the total tax to be collected among insurers based on the proportion of total health insurance premiums collected by each. This tax will further increase health insurance costs by $60 billion over the first ten years alone.[54]

Further health cost increases will result from Obamacare's new $27 billion tax on prescription drugs, and the new $26 billion tax on medical devices, which will raise the prices of these drugs and devices for consumers, either directly or through their insurance.

Finally, the employer mandate will directly raise health costs for business. For businesses that do not currently provide employee health insurance, the mandate will, of course, be a large new additional cost. But even for businesses that do currently provide employee health insurance, the mandate combined with all of the above effects of Obamacare in increasing costs will mean sharply higher costs even for these businesses.

As CBO director Douglas Elmendorf testified before Congress in the summer of 2009 regarding the then pending legislation,

> In the legislation that has been reported we do not see the sort of fundamental changes that would be necessary to reduce the trajectory of federal health spending by a significant amount. On the contrary, the legislation significantly expands the federal responsibility for health care costs.[55]

Gingrich adds in his 2010 book, *To Save America*, "Sadly, little changed in the final product that was signed into law."[56]

The Obamacare Spending Explosion

With large Democrat majorities in both houses of Congress last year, CBO was a Democrat-controlled institution. But even CBO admitted that Obamacare involves close to $1 trillion in increased federal spending.[57] The latest projections indicate close to $1.4 trillion in increased costs over the next ten years.[58] That results primarily from the sharp increase in Medicaid, and in the new entitlement subsidies for the purchase of health insurance, subsidizing incomes approaching $100,000 a year and more in the near future.

But this is just the beginning of the likely costs. When Medicare was adopted in 1965, the official government estimates projected the program would cost only $12 billion by 1990. The actual costs of the program by that year were $109.7 billion, nine times greater.[59]

Congressional rules require CBO scores for ten years for pending legislation. But the spending under the Act mostly does not get under way until 2014. So the initial CBO score included only six years of full spending in its ten-year estimate. Over the first full ten years of implementation, 2014 to 2023, the Act involves $2.4 trillion in increased spending based on the CBO estimates.[60] Over 2010 to 2029, which is basically the first full fifteen years of implementation, the Act involves $5.3 trillion in increased costs.[61]

But even these numbers don't take into account all the effects of the legislation in increasing government spending. Not included is any increased state spending for the expanded Medicaid program. Moreover, costs for the new entitlement subsidies for health insurance will be a multiple of projections, as explained below. Nor do the spending projections take into account most of the ways Obamacare will actually increase health costs, as discussed above. The cost of newly mandated benefits is not adequately accounted for. The spending impacts of guaranteed issue and community rating are not remotely sufficiently considered, nor are the effects of the increased cost shifting, or the impact of the effects on supply and demand.

The Obamacare Tax Explosion

When he was asking for our vote in 2008, then-candidate Barack Obama famously promised the American people, "I can make a firm pledge. Under my plan no family making less than $250,000 a year will see any form of tax increase. Not your income tax, not your payroll tax, not your capital gains taxes, not any of your taxes."[62] Candidate Obama didn't just make that pledge once or twice. He promised it to the American people over and over, making it the centerpiece of his campaign. Little surprise, then, that in postelection polls voters thought Obama was more likely than his Republican opponent, Senator John McCain, to cut taxes or keep taxes low. That was an amazing achievement for a senator with the most liberal voting record in the entire U.S. Senate.

The Patient Protection and Affordable Care Act violates Obama's pledge, not just once but many times. If you do not obtain the health insurance that the Act requires, either through your employer or by direct purchase yourself, then you must pay a new 2.5% income tax, or a minimum of $695 per person up to $2,085 per family. This applies to everyone, including those making less than $250,000 per year.

The mandate to buy insurance is itself indistinguishable from a tax. Even with the budget-crushing new entitlement subsidies in the Act, the total health insurance costs under Obamacare will be quite expensive, ranging from up to 2% of income for people at 133% of poverty to 9.5% of income for people at 400% of poverty. That is like a new payroll tax. Indeed, soon after Obamacare was passed, the president's lawyers were in court arguing that the individual mandate was constitutional precisely because it is just another tax.

Moreover, candidate Obama first issued his above-quoted pledge in a speech right after he attacked McCain for proposing to tax the so-called Cadillac health plans of all workers, including those making less than $250,000 per year. Obama said then, "The better your health care plan, the harder you fought for your good benefits, the higher the taxes you'll pay under John McCain's plan,"[63] an attack he repeated in several commercials. But the Act that President Obama signed taxes precisely those health plans regardless of the income of workers who have them, albeit not until after 2018.

President Obama owes John McCain an apology, and he owes one to Hillary Clinton, too. During the Democrat primary battle, Obama attacked Hillary for supporting an individual mandate forcing people to buy the health insurance the government specifies. But the Act he signed includes precisely such a mandate.

In addition, Obamacare's other tax on health insurance, the tax on prescription drugs, the tax on medical devices, the tax on tanning salons, and other tax increases in the Act will be paid directly or effectively by those making less than $250,000 per year, not just those making more than $250,000.

The last time a president so blatantly violated a similar pledge was during the administration of the first President Bush. After campaigning and winning in 1988 on a pledge of "Read my lips, no new taxes," he broke that pledge in agreeing to the 1990 budget deal. The public rightly voted him out of office in the next election, because if a candidate once elected can so blatantly violate what he campaigned on, then we have lost our democracy, as there is then no way to express the will of the people among different policy choices.

The employer mandate embodies a further additional tax. Obamacare requires that employers who have fifty or more employees, and who do not provide the mandated insurance as specified by the government, pay a nondeductible tax of $2,000 for every uninsured full-time employee above thirty employees. If any employee receives the federal subsidies for insurance purchased on his own, the employer penalty for that worker increases to $3,000. Moreover, even employers that provide the mandated insurance to their workers will be subject to a tax penalty if even one employee receives the federal subsidy for buying health insurance on his own.

But just as with the individual mandate, the employer mandate itself is a costly additional tax. It is a costly new tax for all employers that do not provide health insurance today. But even for employers who do provide insurance, the impact of Obamacare in increasing the cost of health insurance makes the mandate effectively a burdensome tax increase.

The fact that employers pay these mandate taxes, rather than employees, will not insulate workers from the cost. To the extent that employers do not take the employer mandate tax increases out of the wages they would otherwise pay workers, workers will suffer the impact in reduced jobs and opportunities.

Then there are the Obamacare tax increases on high-income workers: singles earning over $200,000 a year and families earning over $250,000. These workers will pay a new 3.8% tax on investment income, such as capital gains, dividends, interest, rents, royalties, and annuities, projected to raise $123 billion over seven years. President Obama tried to justify applying the payroll tax to investment income by saying these high-income investors are going to need Medicare in their future as well. But besides the fact that such investors already overpay for Medicare, as compared to others, through the tax on their wage income, *the Obamacare legislation provides that the revenues from applying the Medicare HI payroll tax to investment income do not go into the Medicare trust fund to finance Medicare!* As the Medicare chief actuary states in his official report on behalf of the federal government's own Centers for Medicare & Medicaid Services, "Despite the title of this tax, this provision is unrelated to Medicare; in particular, the revenues generated by the tax on unearned income are not allocated to the Medicare trust funds." [64]

Obamacare also raises the Medicare HI payroll tax for these same higher-income workers by 62%, to raise $86.8 billion over seven years. Moreover, the income thresholds of $200,000 for singles and $250,000 for couples for these tax increases are not indexed to inflation, so over time more and more taxpayers will be subject to the tax increases.

The total for these tax increases over the first ten years is $500 billion, not counting the individual or employer mandates themselves as a tax.

Piling on the Deficits

President Obama promised the nation over and over that he would "not sign a plan that adds one dime to our deficits." [65] This seemed to be confirmed by CBO projections that the Act would actually reduce the deficit by $143 billion in the first ten years, and by over $1 trillion in the second ten years. But this was based on misrepresentations, double counting, budget tricks, fallacies, and radically unworkable assumptions.

Correcting for these leaves Obamacare causing massive increases in deficits and debt.

First, the deficit projection for the first ten years includes ten years of tax increases but only six years of spending increases. For the second ten years, the intractable Medicare cuts for that period discussed below become dominant.

Second, the deficit projection includes $29 billion in increased Social Security revenues, which are actually all devoted under current law to financing Social Security, not any of the Act's new entitlements. (Those increased revenues result because CBO assumes that employers will actually drop coverage for millions of workers on net due to the costs of Obamacare, and will pay higher wages subject to taxation by the payroll tax in place of the formerly tax-exempt health insurance expenses.)

Moreover, the new CLASS entitlement program starts collecting premiums during the first ten years, and the projected $70 billion in resulting net revenues are similarly counted as reducing the Act's deficit over those years, even though the funds are raised to pay the longer-term benefits of that program. Counting these revenues as reducing the deficit is the exact same accounting that Bernie Madoff used to scam his investors.

The deficit projection also includes $63 billion of the increased Medicare payroll taxes on the wages of higher-income workers, which taxes are actually devoted under the law to financing Medicare, not the Act's spending.[66]

Yet the CBO deficit projections do not include $115 billion in increased discretionary spending that will be necessary over the first ten years alone to finance Obamacare's administrative costs and 159 new boards, agencies, commissions, and bureaucracies, an estimate that CBO did not produce until after the Obamacare legislation was enacted.[67] However, the projections do include $19 billion in supposed savings that would result from the completely unrelated government takeover of student loans that was included in the Act.

But these miscalculations, budget tricks, and misrepresentations do not even scratch the surface compared to the big fallacies that will blow up Obamacare deficits. Digging into the detailed data in the Annual Report of the Medicare Board of Trustees for 2010, and the supplemental tables accompanying the Annual Report of the Social Security Board of

Trustees, one finds the full extent of the year-by-year Medicare cuts enacted in the Obamacare legislation.

Medicare's own Office of the Actuary was careful to explain in its own unprecedented accompanying report that the Medicare payment rates for the doctors and hospitals serving seniors will be cut by 30% over the next three years.[68] By 2019, those Medicare payment rates will be lower than under Medicaid.[69] The chief actuary for Medicare reports that ultimately under Obamacare, Medicare payment rates will be only one-third of what will be paid by private insurance and only half of what is paid by Medicaid, which already doesn't pay enough for the poor to find regular access to essential care.[70]

Still further Medicare cuts adopted in the Obamacare legislation add up to $818 billion over the first ten years of full implementation, 2014–23, and $3.223 trillion over the first twenty years, 2014–33, *for Medicare Part A (HI) alone!* Adding in the cuts for Medicare Part B brings the total to $1.048 trillion over the first ten full years, and $4.95 trillion over the first twenty full years. That is for today's seniors already retired, not future retirees years in the future, who can plan for alternative ways to pay for their care.

Ultimately, by the end of the projection period, Medicare Part A is cut by 60% for the year. Part B is cut by 43%. These again are all basically cuts in Medicare payments for the doctors, hospitals, and other health care providers that serve America's seniors. These draconian Medicare cuts were the primary basis for the CBO score repeatedly cited by President Obama that Obamacare would actually reduce the deficit by $143 billion over the first ten years and over a trillion dollars over the second ten years, while expanding or adopting three entitlement programs. Too bad the president never disclosed that.

Full confirmation of these draconian cuts comes from the 2010 Financial Report of the United States Government: "The 2010 projection is lower than the 2009 projection in every year of the projection period almost entirely as a result of the Affordable Care Act (ACA), which is projected to significantly lower Medicare spending and raise receipts."[71] Later the report repeatedly indicates the full present value of Obamacare's future cuts in payments to doctors and hospitals under Medicare—*$15 trillion.*[72]

Such draconian Medicare cuts will create chaos in health care for seniors. Doctors, hospitals, surgeons, and specialists providing critical care to the elderly—such as surgery for hip and knee replacements, sophisticated diagnostics through MRIs and CT scans, and even treatment for cancer and heart disease—will shut down and disappear in much of the country, and others will stop serving Medicare patients. If the government is not going to pay, then seniors are not going to get the health services, treatment, and care they expect.

Indeed, Medicare's Office of the Actuary reports that even before these cuts, already two-thirds of hospitals were losing money on Medicare patients.[73] Health providers will either have to withdraw from serving Medicare patients, or eventually go into bankruptcy. The severe effect of these Medicare cuts is why the U.S. Government Accountability Office issued a disclaimer of opinion on the Statement of Social Insurance component of the federal government's 2010 Financial Report,[74] saying, "Unless providers could reduce their cost per service correspondingly, through productivity improvements, or other steps, they would eventually become unwilling or unable to treat Medicare beneficiaries."[75]

Imagine a national defense budget savings policy based on not paying the manufacturers of the air force's planes, the navy's ships, the army's tanks and artillery, all the bullets, bombs, and guns. How long would our national defense function under that policy? Medicare will function about as well as that under the misguided cuts in compensation to doctors and hospitals for the health care they provide to the nation's seniors.

Apparently, President Obama's concept of spreading the wealth includes sacking the Medicare system on which America's seniors have come to rely for highly beneficial medical care, in favor of others the president's progressive vision deems more worthy. By 2030, under Obamacare, Medicare will have been cut by 20%, while Medicaid will have been increased by 20%.[76]

As discussed at the outset of this chapter, Medicare suffers dramatic long-term deficits and unfunded liabilities. Of course, no progress will be made against America's coming bankruptcy by cutting one massive entitlement by 20% to increase another by 20%, while adding still more entitlement promises at the same time.

But more fundamentally, effectively refusing to pay the doctors and hospitals that provide the medical care Medicare promises to seniors is no way to solve Medicare's financing problems. Not only would it leave doctors, clinics, specialists, and hospitals with uneconomic practices for seniors, practices they entered into in good faith on the promise of payment from the government, but it would leave seniors without the health care they have been promised and have come to rely on as a result.

Think of it this way. You wouldn't try to balance your own family budget by just refusing to pay your bills, particularly for goods and services you planned to continue to consume. You would recognize that is really just stealing, and impractical. Instead you would either cut back on your purchases or find ways to increase your income. Too many conservatives have been too reluctant to criticize these draconian Medicare cuts under Obámacare, because they know that sweeping changes in the program are going to be financially necessary. But they along with President Obama and the Democrats are failing to grasp the moral and practical reality of what these cuts involve. The fundamental structural reforms discussed at the end of this chapter would serve seniors, workers, and the nation far better. Conservatives as well as liberals need to study and understand those true reform alternatives.

As a practical matter, if Obamacare's Medicare cuts are not reversed, then Medicare will have effectively been gutted by Obamacare and become dysfunctional. While establishment Washington expects that reversal sooner or later, the Obama administration has continued to tout the supposed budget savings in Medicare resulting from Obamacare.[77] But if the Medicare cuts are reversed, then Obamacare will increase future federal deficits and debt by $15 trillion on these grounds alone. Because all of these Medicare cuts are included in the 2010 Annual Medicare Trustees Report, that report is worthless as a projection of the future financial liabilities of Medicare.

A second big deficit miscalculation results from the gross underestimation of the costs of the new Obamacare health insurance subsidies. The health insurance subsidies go only to those who buy insurance on their own individually through state-based health insurance exchanges set up by the legislation. Those who receive employer-provided coverage are not eligible for them. CBO assumed that only 30 million workers will obtain their health insurance through the exchanges, with 162 million still receiving employer-provided coverage.[78] Of those 30 million, CBO estimates that 19 million will receive subsidies at a cost of $450 billion over the first ten years, or actually the first six years of implementation under the Act.[79] But with the mandated insurance likely to cost $15,000 or more by 2016,[80] employers will have powerful incentives to dump their employee coverage and pay the $2,000-per-worker fine that applies to such termination of coverage.

Employers are all the more likely to do this and pay their workers higher wages in place of the health coverage precisely because the workers would then be able to get the huge subsidies for purchasing their insurance through the exchanges. Douglas Holtz-Eakin explains:

> For example, a family earning about $59,000 a year in 2014 would receive a premium subsidy of about $7,200. A family making $71,000 would receive about $5,200; and even a family earning about $95,000 would receive a subsidy of almost $3,000. By 2018, . . . a family earning about $64,000 would receive a subsidy of over $10,000, a family earning $77,000 would receive a subsidy of $7,800 and families earning $102,000 would receive a subsidy of almost $5,000.[81]

In fact, in the exchanges, low- and moderate-income workers can even get subsidies covering their out-of-pocket expenses. Holtz-Eakin calculates that employers could gain the enormous savings from dropping the coverage and just paying the $2,000 penalty, while giving their employees a net pay raise because of these enormous subsidies, for all workers making roughly $60,000 per year or less.[82] That means it would make sense for employers to drop their coverage for 43 million workers who would then receive the subsidies for obtaining their insurance through the exchange.[83] That alone would triple the $450 billion in estimated costs for the health insurance subsidies of Obamacare under the first six full years, adding nearly a trillion dollars to the costs and deficits of Obamacare during that time alone. In future years, that added cost contributing to still higher deficits would soar further.

A third major factor dramatically increasing the resulting deficits under Obamacare is that the tax increases won't raise nearly the revenue projected. Considering as well President Obama's general tax increases now scheduled for 2013, the capital gains tax rate would increase by close to 60% that year, with the expiration of the Bush tax cuts and the Medicare payroll tax soon applying to capital gains as well. But over the last forty years, every time the capital gains tax rate has been increased, revenues have declined.[84]

Similarly, the tax rate on dividends would nearly triple in 2013, due again to the expiration of the Bush tax cuts and the application of the Medicare payroll tax to dividends as well. The last time dividend taxes were that high, corporate dividend payments were greatly reduced. Corporations just kept the money internally for corporate investment. Corporate earnings are already subject to the 35% corporate income tax rate. So revenues from the tax on dividends will decline sharply as well, exactly the opposite of what happened when President Bush cut the tax rate on dividends in 2003.

Moreover, as employers drop employee coverage under Obamacare, revenues from the new taxes on health insurance will fall short as well. Expect companies to cut back on high-value, "Cadillac" health insurance plans in particular. To the extent that employers respond to the employer mandate by reduced hiring, or even laying off existing workers, that will cause a loss of income tax and payroll tax revenues, further adding to the deficit. Indeed, the employer mandate seems to have had such an effect even before it has become effective.

Finally, all of the additional ways in which Obamacare will increase health costs and spending beyond projections as discussed above will further increase deficits. Former CBO director Holtz-Eakin has estimated that Obamacare would actually increase the deficit by $554 billion in the first ten years, and $1.4 trillion in the second ten years.[85] But counting all of the above effects, with the Medicare cuts reversed, the resulting deficit would be two to three times as large, or $1–1.5 trillion in the first ten years, and $3–4.5 trillion in the second ten years.

THE ROOT OF THE HEALTH COST PROBLEM

America's explosive health cost problem owes much of its existence to modern medical technology. In the words of the CBO:

A crucial factor underlying the rise in per capita spending for health care in recent decades has been the emergence, adoption, and widespread diffusion of new medical technologies and services. Major advances in medical science allow providers to diagnose and treat illnesses in ways that previously were impossible. Many of those innovations rely on costly new drugs, equipment, and skills. Other innovations are relatively inexpensive, but their costs add up quickly as growing numbers of providers and patients make use of them.[86]

Another important factor for future projections is demographics and the aging of the population, since older people tend to be sicker on average and need more medical care. Rising incomes over time also tend to add to health costs, since those with higher incomes tend to choose to spend more on health care.

But the root of the entire problem is really economic. It all stems ultimately from what is known as the third-party payment problem. The great majority of health costs in America are not paid by the patients themselves. There is almost always some third party paying the bills, either an insurance company, an HMO, or the government through programs such as Medicare and Medicaid. Indeed, in 2008, 84% of health expenses were paid for by private health insurance, Medicare, Medicaid, CHIP, or other public spending.[87]

The fundamental economic problem should be readily apparent. The consumer is making the choice of what health care to buy, on the advice of his chosen doctors, who get paid for what they provide, but someone else is paying the bill.

Try this thought experiment. Consider sending your teenage daughter to the mall on a Saturday with a debit card for a bank account with $1,000 in it. Tell her that what she doesn't spend today she can keep for the future, with interest, to spend later. Then consider sending her to the mall with Uncle Sam's credit card. Tell her you effectively have already paid for whatever she might charge through your income taxes. How do you think the magnitude of what she purchases would differ in these two scenarios?

The fundamental problem, of course, is that with a third party paying the bills, the consumer, or the patient, has no incentive to control costs. In formal terms, the consumer has an incentive to spend until the marginal benefit of additional spending, or additional health care, is zero, which is much different from an efficient market, where consumers spend until the marginal benefit is equal to the marginal cost. In more colloquial terms, this means consumers have the incentive to spend on health care until it hurts.

To make matters worse, consumers lack expertise in health care, and make their health care purchases on the advice of their chosen doctors and specialists, who not only also have no incentive to control costs, they actually have instead a direct financial interest in spending more.

Because the consumer doesn't even have an incentive to shop for the lowest-cost care for what he does decide to consume, health care providers for their part have no incentive to compete to reduce costs, since consumers and patients are not making their health care decisions on the basis of costs. They are making their decisions on the basis of primarily quality, and secondarily convenience. That is why the American health care system produces far and away the highest-quality health care in the world, resulting from highly effective capitalist competition and traditional Yankee ingenuity in producing the latest and best innovations.

This also explains why new medical technology increases costs, while in every other field new technology drives down costs. Since in American health care there is competition only to maximize quality, regardless of costs, developers and innovators of new medical technology are focused primarily on increasing quality regardless of cost.

The only solution to this problem is to unite the decision over what health care to purchase and consume with the economic responsibility to pay the costs, so costs can be weighed against benefits in health care consumption. There are two alternative ways to do that. Either the third-party payer is given the power to decide what health care the consumer or patient is allowed to consume, in which case the third-party payer weighs the costs of the patient's health care against the benefits to the patient from that health care. Or the patient is given market incentives to consider the full costs of the health care they choose to consume, in which case the patient weighs the personal benefits of his or her health care against the costs of that care.

THE GOVERNMENT POWER SOLUTION

Most countries have chosen the former alternative. With the government taking primary responsibility for paying health expenses through its taxpayer-financed health programs, the government takes primary responsibility for deciding what health care its citizens are allowed to consume and when. The government then decides to what extent each individual's health care is worth the costs.

This solution introduces some of its own perverse incentives. Call them the political logic of socialized medicine. At any point in time, only a relatively small number of people are sick with serious, life-threatening or disabling illnesses, such as cancer or heart disease. Moreover, their illness disables them from effective political activism. In addition, the great majority lacks the expertise to know what health care modern science could actually provide them, or what some government bureaucrat or central government regulation or dictate might be denying them. Indeed, no one can really know what a fully free-market health care system might have been able to provide them to save their lives or ease their suffering. Often they are soon gone, taking their story, their vote, and their costs to their grave.

Moreover, providing what the latest science possibly could do to rescue these people from ill health or even death would be very costly. Consequently, political logic dictates minimizing the expenditure of available resources on these sickest portions of the population most in need of health care but least capable of providing political reward in return.

It's far better politically to maximize the expenditure of available resources on the vast majority who are healthy at any point in time. They will think as a result that the system works great and will be there for them when they get sick. Moreover, it costs relatively little to satisfy them because their good health requires relatively little in health costs. This strategic approach to the politics of health care provides the maximum political payoff per dollar spent. But it sacrifices the sickest and those most in need of health care.

Moreover, in such an environment, private sector incentives for the investment of human capital, in terms of scientific expertise, or physical capital, in terms of investment dollars, for development of medical innovations or breakthroughs to treat the sickest are minimized. With government policy focused on expenditures for the healthy rather than the sick, investment in caring for the sick is unlikely to be adequately rewarded.

Finally, this system raises troubling moral issues, with the government effectively deciding in place of citizens whether their health care is worth the costs, and consequently who should live and who should die. Do we really want the government making such decisions, especially as there is no objective basis for it to do so? To my moral compass, such government power is the essence of fascism.

Experience with such government-run health care systems bears this analysis out.

The National Institute for Health and Clinical Excellence is the national health care rationing board used in Great Britain, with the Orwellian acronym NICE. In 2006, NICE proved so nice that it ruled that elderly patients with macular degeneration could not get a costly new drug to save their sight until they went blind in one eye.[88] There are no guidelines for elderly patients who go blind in both eyes at the same time. To decide who gets what health care services, NICE uses a formula that divides the cost of the treatment by the number of years the patient would likely live and receive the benefits of that treatment.[89] This greatly disadvantages senior citizens in getting health care, as compared to younger people who on average have longer to live.

The Council for Affordable Health Insurance adds,

In Great Britain's National Health Service [NHS], breast cancer patients have been denied access to widely used cancer drugs, and lack of access to dentists has led patients to pulling out their own teeth. In Canada, 12% of the Ontario population can't get a family physician, and Nova Scotia resorted to a lottery so people could get a doctor's appointment.[90]

Britain's own Rarer Cancers Forum concluded that twenty thousand Britons had died prematurely after NICE denied them cancer medications available elsewhere in Europe.[91] A question that begs further investigation is whether NICE and the NHS have killed more British subjects than the Nazi Wehrmacht.

In Canada, the median average wait for treatment after referral to a specialist was 18.3 weeks in 2007.[92] Patients in Saskatchewan waited the longest—27.2 weeks—followed by New Brunswick (25.2 weeks) and Nova Scotia (24.8 weeks). Britain's National Health Service has more than one million people on waiting lists for care. The cumulative waiting time expected by all Britons already in the queue for medical treatment exceeds *one million years*.[93]

The number of physicians per capita is nearly 50% higher in the United States than in Britain and Canada.[94] Moreover, out of these available doctors, only 11% in the States are general practitioners, while in Canada and Great Britain nearly half are, which means American patients have much greater access to specialists.[95] American patients also have much greater access to the latest medical technology. American patients receive 83.2 MRI exams per 1,000 people versus 25.5 for Canadian patients and 19.0 for British patients.[96] American patients also receive 172.5 CT scans per 1,000 people versus 87.3 for Canadian patients and 43.0 for British patients.[97]

Long queues and limited access to specialists and the latest medical equipment in countries with government-run health care result in health outcomes that are inferior to those of the United States. For example, one-quarter of those diagnosed with breast cancer in the United States die of it, while the comparable figure is 35% in France and 46% in Britain and New Zealand.[98] Moreover, about 19% of American men die from prostate cancer once diagnosed. The comparable figures are 30% in New Zealand, 35% in Australia, 49% in France, and 57% in Britain.[99]

Nadeem Esmail, director of health system performance studies at the Fraser Institute in Canada, provides some real-world examples from the Canadian system:

In Ontario, Lindsay McCreith was suffering from headaches and seizures yet faced a four and a half month wait for an MRI scan. . . . [H]e went south, and paid for an MRI scan across the border in Buffalo [New York]. The MRI revealed a malignant brain tumor. Ontario's government system still refused to provide timely treatment, offering instead a months-long wait for surgery. In the end, McCreith returned to Buffalo and paid for surgery that may have saved his life.[100]

Esmail offers another example:

In March of 2005, [Ontario resident Shona] Holmes began losing her vision and experienced headaches, anxiety attacks, extreme fatigue, and weight gain. Despite an MRI scan showing a brain tumor, Ms. Holmes was told she would have to wait months to see a specialist. In June, her vision deteriorating rapidly, Ms. Holmes went to the Mayo Clinic in Arizona, where she found that immediate surgery was required to prevent permanent vision loss and potentially death. Again, the government system in Ontario required more appointments and more tests, along with more wait times. Ms. Holmes returned to the Mayo Clinic and paid for her surgery.[101]

And another example:

[Alberta resident] Bill Murray waited in pain for more than a year to see a specialist for his arthritic hip. The specialist recommended a "Birmingham" hip resurfacing surgery [a state-of-the-art procedure that gives better results than basic hip replacement]. But government bureaucrats determined that Mr. Murray, who was 57, was "too old" to enjoy the benefits of this procedure and said no. In the end, he was also denied the opportunity to pay for the procedure himself. He's heading to court claiming a violation of constitutional rights.[102]

President Obama's Government-Run Health Care

President Obama's Patient Protection and Affordable Health Care Act, passed in 2010, commits America to follow this government-power solution alternative. Despite the political rhetoric to the contrary, the Act provides for a thorough government takeover of health care. It creates 159 new bureaucracies, boards, agencies, commissions, and programs to govern American health care.[103] Included among them are the Health Choices Administration, the Health Benefits Advisory Committee, the Medicare Independent Payment Advisory Board, the Bureau of Health Information, the National Priorities for Performance Improvement office, the Interagency Working Group on Health Care Quality, the National Health Care Workforce Commission, the Patient-Centered Outcomes Research Institute, the National Center for Health Workforce Analysis, state-based reinsurance programs, etc. This does not include the Federal Coordinating Council for Comparative Effectiveness Research, which was created by the 2009 stimulus bill.

These government authorities will now be involved in telling doctors and hospitals what are the "best practices" in health care, what "works" in health care and what doesn't, what health care is "comparatively effective" or "cost effective," and what is and is not "quality health care."[104] Doctors, specialists, surgeons, and hospitals will also be told how their medical practices should be structured, and what they will be paid and when.

In addition, under the Act, the government further dictates to insurance companies what benefits and coverage they must provide,[105] whom they must cover,[106] what they can charge,[107] and what deductibles, copays, and other out-of-pocket expenses their plans can include.[108] The government even redistributes premium income among insurance companies through "reinsurance" and "risk adjustment."[109] This is government taking over and running health insurance, contrary to President Obama's repeated statements to the contrary.

As already discussed, the Act includes an individual mandate dictating that you must buy health insurance with the specific benefits that the government decides you must have, whether you want those benefits or not.[110] It also includes a mandate requiring employers to provide health insurance with the specific, costly, politically correct benefits the government decides they must provide.[111]

It was precisely because President Obama and the Democrats recognized that this mandated health insurance will be expensive that the

Act provides for extensive subsidies for the purchase of health insurance for families making up to four times the poverty level, which will soon mean families making over $100,000 a year. The Act also provides for a health insurance "exchange" to be established in each state, where individuals can go to buy health insurance, similar to eHealthInsurance .org.[112] But the Act specifies in great detail exactly what insurers must offer on the exchanges, including benefit plans in four categories, designated as Bronze, Silver, Gold, and Platinum.[113] The new health insurance entitlement subsidies are available only for insurance purchased on the exchanges, which effectively gives the government even greater power to run health insurance in America, buying the public off with their own taxpayer funds.

There is actually no aspect of essential health care that the Act leaves beyond government control. As a result, the Act also takes America toward the health care rationing we see in other countries with government-run health care.

That begins with the huge Medicare cuts that begin to starve the system of the resources needed to maintain current levels of care. Such draconian cuts again will leave health care for seniors dysfunctional. Doctors, specialists, clinics, and hospitals heavily serving seniors will have to migrate to focus their practices on serving others, or go bankrupt. Seniors will lose access to the health care they have come to expect and rely on. Former House Speaker Newt Gingrich, since founder of the Center for Health Transformation, writes,

> Clearly, you cannot cut Medicare by more than half a trillion dollars and not jeopardize seniors' access to care. Medicare access is already declining. The Mayo Clinic announced that on January 1, 2010, its Arizona facilities would stop seeing Medicare beneficiaries because the federal government does not pay the clinic enough to even cover its costs. According to Lynn Closway, spokeswoman for Mayo, the clinic lost $840 million in 2008 treating Medicare patients. And that's before the Democrats' half a trillion in cuts.[114]

The Act, moreover, provides for even more future Medicare cuts. It creates a Medicare Independent Payment Advisory Board, an unelected, appointed body with the power to adopt further Medicare cuts it deems necessary. These cuts would become effective without further congressional action. The report of the chief actuary of Medicare states, "The Secretary of HHS is required to implement the Board's recommendations unless the statutory process is overridden by new legislation."[115]

Then there are the additional cuts to Medicare Advantage, the private option to Medicare that close to one-fourth of all seniors have chosen for their coverage under the program because it gives them a better deal. Medicare's chief actuary estimates that 50% of all seniors with Medicare Advantage will lose their plan because of these cuts. President Obama's pledge that under his health care takeover scheme, "If you like your health plan, you will be able to keep it," clearly does not apply to America's seniors.

Moreover, even before passage of the Act, the Obama administration started rationing health care for seniors on Medicare. The new Medicare payment rules for 2010 imposed an 11% overall cut on cardiology and a 19% cut on radiation oncology (cancer treatment). Payments for basic tools and treatments for heart disease, such as stress tests and catheterization, were slashed by 42% and 24% respectively. Payments for diagnostic imaging services such as MRIs and CT scans that help identify cancer early were cut by 24%. Payments for antitumor radiation therapy were cut by 44%.[116] Ultimately the payment practices adopted by Medicare will be adopted by insurance in the private sector as well, backed by government policy.

Incentives to Ration Care

Several provisions of the Act give doctors and hospitals incentives to deny health care to their patients, contrary to the patients' interests. Free market health policy guru John Goodman points out the incentives for insurers created by guaranteed issue and community rating, where insurers cannot refuse coverage or charge more for applicants who are sick with costly illnesses.[117] Insurers will affiliate with preferred provider networks not well equipped to provide essential care for the sickest and most costly, and seek reputations for serving well the young and healthy instead. The last thing they would want is to be affiliated with specialists, surgeons, or institutions known for successfully serving patients with cancer, heart disease, or other costly conditions. The hope would be that the sickest and most costly would choose other insurers instead. Goodman explains, "The easiest way [for insurers] to keep costs down is to enroll only the healthy. And the easiest way to do that is not to have the doctors and facilities sick people want."[118] Similarly, Alain Enthoven writes, "A good way to avoid enrolling diabetics is to have no endocrinologists on staff. . . . A good way to avoid cancer patients is to have a poor oncology department."[119]

Goodman elaborates with a more formal economic analysis:

> In free markets, competition tends to cause the price to change until it equals average cost. . . . Yet, because community-rated premiums are constrained to be the same for all members, competition will cause cost to change until it equals price. . . . [I]f the premiums are artificially constrained, the plans will compete the cost of care down to the level of the artificial premium. . . . This means that health plans [under guaranteed issue and community rating] have a strong financial self-interest in underproviding services to the sick and overproviding services to the healthy.[120]

Scott Gottlieb, a former official at the federal government's Centers for Medicare & Medicaid Services, explains that health providers and insurers are already beginning to consolidate so they will have the market power to implement just such practices.[121] Doctor Lloyd Krieger adds, "Obamacare . . . has already yielded profound destructive changes. . . . The most significant change is a wave of frantic consolidation in the health industry.[122] Insurers face growing political pressures to avoid premium increases, with the threat of overt legal restrictions on those increases. To meet these cost pressures, insurers will turn to rationing for the sickest and most expensive to reduce their costs. Gottlieb explains:

> One of the few remaining ways to manage expenses is to reduce the actual cost of the products. In health care, this means pushing providers to accept lower fees and reduce their use of costly services like radiology or other diagnostic testing. To implement this

strategy, companies need to be able to exert more control over doctors. So insurers are trying to buy up medical clinics and doctor practices. Where they can't own providers outright, they'll maintain smaller networks of physicians that they will contract with so they can manage doctors more closely.[123]

This is why we are seeing now the increasingly rapid decline of private, independent practices. Sally Pipes reports that while in 2005 at least two-thirds of doctors' practices were private, independent operations, less than half are today, with that expected to fall below 40% by the end of this year.[124] Krieger adds, "Six years ago, doctors owned more than two-thirds of U.S. medical practices. . . . By next year, nearly two-thirds will be salaried employees of larger institutions."[125]

Gottlieb explains further that this means less and lower-quality care for patients: "Consolidated practices and salaried doctors will leave fewer options for patients and longer waiting times for routine appointments."[126] Salaried doctors subject to corporate oversight will have primary allegiance to their corporate finance departments and paymasters, rather than to sick patients requiring expensive treatments and surgeries to stay alive. When the doctors come to tell you or a loved one that there is nothing more that they can do, usually you won't even know what you are missing. You won't really know whether that is due to medical science or to corporate financial policies and practices.

These incentives would have an even more powerful effect on HMOs, which have even more control over the medical facilities with which they are affiliated. They have every incentive under Obamacare to feature facilities and programs that appeal to the young and healthy, such as gyms, dancing lessons, sports contests, etc., and to avoid facilities best suited for treating patients with cancer or heart disease. They would gain the most if they got reputations as not serving those sickest patients well, so those patients would go elsewhere.

Because HMOs would have the most power to control their costs in this way, we may find other insurers phasing out over time, leaving patients with less real choice and power regarding their health care. Moreover, new regulatory requirements under the Act greatly disfavor new insurance competitors, by limiting what can be spent on marketing and administration for such things as monitoring costs and stopping fraud. Selling a new insurance product requires higher marketing costs to penetrate the market. With the Act's new restrictions on such costs, few new competitors are likely to even try.[127] Indeed, because all health insurance must conform to the Act's specifications regarding benefits, deductibles, and co-pays, there is less scope for new insurers to compete with new products serving different consumer preferences.

All the new costly burdens of the Act on insurers favor consolidation into an oligopoly of a few, large health insurers that are better able to absorb these costs than smaller firms or start-ups, and have more market power to shift those costs to consumers or health providers.[128] To defend against the market power of this emerging health insurance oligopoly, hospitals will consolidate into an oligopoly of a few large chains as well.[129] The Act shuts off the emerging competition of physician-owned hospitals, contributing to this trend, on the simpleminded view that they inherently represent a conflict of interest. The Act provides further incentives for doctors to consolidate into a few oligopolistic large chains as well.[130]

The few—and large—insurers and hospital and clinic chains that remain will have greater power to implement rationing and comply with government policies favoring such rationing, leaving consumers with little choice or power of their own. As top health insurance expert Merrill Matthews Jr. explains, "Although Democrats claimed their reform would bring competition to the health care system, in fact the system will rapidly move to a bevy of oligopolies where a handful of large players will survive, and maybe even thrive. The losers will be competition, innovation, and . . . patients."[131] Krieger further explains, "There is little mystery how the government will exercise its power. Choices will be limited. Pathways to expensive specialist care such as advanced radiology and surgery will decline. Cutting-edge devices and medicines will come into the system much more slowly and be used much less frequently."[132] Sounds just like the practices in Canada and Great Britain discussed above.

An ominous move pushing these developments toward more overt rationing came just before Christmas in 2010. U.S. Secretary of Health and Human Services Kathleen Sebelius claimed authority buried deep within the vague language of the Obamacare Act to impose federal price controls on health insurance companies, issuing a 136-page regulation providing for that power.[133] Most states have long regulated insurance premiums, knowing from long experience that they have to make sure the insurance company has the money to pay the promised benefits. State health insurance regulation is consequently a simple matter of mathematics. There is nothing for the feds to add to it that is helpful.

But what is emerging from the federal regulation is a policy of denying resources to the insurers, so they will have to deny resources to the doctors and hospitals, so they will have no choice but to ration and deny care. The consolidation process discussed above creates the framework to make this possible. This process is further along in the Massachusetts health reform forerunner of Obamacare, where policy makers are now openly discussing going to even more overt rationing through a "global budget." That means the state would place a total limit on the resources going to hospitals and doctors, and they would then do triage among patients to decide whom they have the money to save and whom they should let die. As Sally Pipes explains, "In other words, give hospitals and doctors a pool of money and tell them to make do. Change the incentive from providing the best possible care to the best care the bureaucrats can possibly afford."[134]

Sebelius's federal price controls are just a more sneaky way of achieving this same end. And if the insurers turn out not to have the power to constrain the resources going to doctors and hospitals for care in response to the federal price controls, then they can just go out of business, and the left will have their "public option" and overt socialized medicine after all. This is why the insurers, doctors, and hospitals are all consolidating, and why it all portends rationing and denial of care particularly for the sickest of patients.

Other incentives for health care providers to cut back on and deny care are provided in pilot projects established by the Obamacare Act that can later be expanded throughout the health care system. These include the "medical home" model,[135] and Accountable Care Organizations (ACOs), which are just new forms of the HMOs that consumers have long disfavored.

Comparative Effectiveness

We saw the beginnings of more overt health care rationing in 2009 when the U.S. Task Force on Community Preventive Services abruptly reversed its long-standing recommendations that women over forty should get mammograms to test for breast cancer every year. Now it recommends no more mammograms for women under fifty or over seventy-four, and only every other year for the ages in between. Under the prior practice, breast cancer death rates fell by 30% over the past twenty years.[136] Dara Richardson-Heron, CEO of New York Susan G. Komen for the Cure, recounted in the *New York Post* how her breast cancer was discovered, and her life saved, by a mammogram at age thirty-four.[137] But the government panel indicated that it takes 42% more mammogram tests to save a life for women in their forties compared to those in their fifties,[138] so saving those lives before fifty is apparently not worth the costs of the tests anymore.

The task force's recommendation of no mammograms for women over seventy-four says if you have breast cancer at that age, the bureaucrats who will ultimately be in charge of access to health care services don't even want to know about it. Under the Obamacare Act, this same task force is empowered to determine your coverage for preventive services.

This is an example of the concept of "comparative effectiveness" in government health care policy. Comparative effectiveness means analyzing which alternative health care treatment is comparatively more effective than another. This is what doctors do all the time. It is central to the practice of medicine. But when a faraway, centralized government bureaucracy that doesn't even know you tries to take over this function, it is a counterproductive perversion of medical care that empowers the government to ration and deny your health care under the cover of this concept.

According to the Obamacare Act, the Federal Coordinating Council for Comparative Effectiveness Research is empowered to tell, but not yet dictate to, doctors and hospitals what are the "best practices" in medicine, "what works in health care and what doesn't," and what treatment, practice, or care is comparatively more effective than another.[139] A centralized government bureaucracy will make such determinations on the basis of trials and observational data that are known to have serious shortcomings.

This movement toward "one size fits all" medicine is made necessary when a government agency operating under budgetary constraints must decide what health care services to cover and not to cover. But a bureaucracy cannot know better than your own doctors what will work best for you, an individual patient. Making such judgments for your particular case is exactly what you hire your doctors to do. Indeed, the most advanced practices are trending toward "personalized medicine" involving increasingly possible gene therapies based on your personal genetic makeup, and such advances as "molecular analysis" of the particular cancer a patient may suffer.[140]

Gingrich further explains the problem:

Let's say a government uses comparative effectiveness to determine the efficacy of new drug treatments. The research reveals drug A works 70% of the time and drug B works 50% of the time. The government would then decide to cover drug A. But what if, as so often happens in medicine, 30% of the people who did not respond to drug A did respond to drug B? Or what about the even smaller groups that may have responded best to drug X, Y or Z? Not wanting to cover less effective drugs, the government may simply decree those people are out of luck.[141]

In addition, comparative effectiveness research (CER) will always be behind the curve of the latest scientific advances, knowledge, and practice. Careful, independent, controlled studies are expensive and time consuming. By the time they are completed, the science and the data have raced on. As Dr. Leonard A. Zwelling, professor of medicine and pharmacology at the University of Texas M. D. Anderson Cancer Center, has written recently, "while carefully controlled, independently monitored clinical trials are the gold standard of CER, they are very expensive, time consuming and do not guarantee that the one best therapy will be identified. In the case of prostate cancer progress is so rapid that the use of historical data for definitive answers is not a worthy expenditure of time or money."[142] Zwelling adds:

Since CER uses analyses of older, previously completed studies or collections of clinical data from disparate hospital records, CER is unlikely to help the individual with a newly diagnosed cancer in 2010. That patient may choose among therapeutic options that were unavailable even a few years ago.[143]

Even more troubling is that the concept of comparative effectiveness can be stretched to include the question of what is comparatively more effective *given the cost of the care.*[144] A centralized government bureaucracy assigned to determine comparative effectiveness could then determine whether the essential health care needed to cure your illness, ease your pain, or save your life is worth the cost. Gingrich writes:

> Consider this: what happens when one drug is more effective than another but costs three times as much? Do you want government to decide that relieving your pain and suffering isn't worth the cost? That's what happens in Britain. Government approves and government decides—not patients and doctors. Here is what Britain's National Health Service (NHS) tells its citizens: . . . "If the local NHS decides not to fund a drug or treatment you and your doctor feel would be right for you, *they will explain that decision to you.*"[145] (emphasis in original)

Gingrich explains that Obamacare "has put comparative effectiveness research in the United States on the same path as in Britain: toward becoming a bureaucratic cost control measure. The United Kingdom, which has a nationalized, single-payer health system, explicitly uses comparative effectiveness to ration medical care. Government uses this research to decide, sometimes with devastating consequences, which treatments its citizens can get."[146]

Betsy McCaughey points out that under another troubling section of the Act, health insurers can pay only doctors who follow the regulations the secretary of health and human services imposes under the Act to improve health care "quality."[147] McCaughey explains that quality is a very broad term that can cover everything in medicine. Regulations under this authority can provide that new innovations and technologies do not yet qualify as quality medicine, effectively delaying their implementation to control costs. Quality can also be defined as not involving health care the government deems "wasteful," or not sufficiently effective, or not yet warranted, contrary to what your doctor says. Health care may also be deemed not "quality" if it doesn't follow the conclusions of the Federal Coordinating Council for Comparative Effectiveness Research regarding what health care is comparatively more effective than another in treating particular illnesses and conditions.

Numerous provisions in the Act grant the newly created bureaucracies broad powers to control "quality," which takes power and control over health care away from patients and the doctors and hospitals they choose for their care. Under the rubric of "quality," the government can effectively delay, ration, or deny care to reduce costs or otherwise suit government policy preferences. The decisions of all these bureaucracies can be enforced through the payment system by using concepts such as "pay for performance" and "accountable care."

An often-overlooked report of the President's Council of Economic Advisors issued in 2009 foreshadowed the use of these methods to hold down costs.[148] That report stated that 30% of American health care is waste that can be identified and cut out by wise, centralized government bureaucracies. The now-enacted legislation creates the bureaucracies with the power to do precisely this.

Investment Incentives

The final component of the rationing framework ultimately leaving us with Potemkin Village health care is the effect of the Act on incentives for investment in health care. Investors are not going to finance acquisition of the latest, most advanced equipment and technologies if the government slashes compensation for the services such technologies provide. HMOs and insurers' preferred provider networks would have every incentive to be slow in adopting such technologies, innovations, and breakthroughs for the sickest and most costly, preferring a reputation for being behind the times that would cause the sickest and most costly to go elsewhere.

Investors won't finance new or expanded hospital facilities or clinics, or even the full maintenance of existing ones. This is how the long wait-ing lines for diagnostics, surgery, and other referrals begin to develop in countries with socialized health care. It is why hospitals and other medi-cal facilities in those countries are often old and deteriorating.

We are already starting to see some of these results. Because of the incentive effects and costly new regulatory burdens of the new legis-lation, plans for sixty new doctor-owned hospitals across the country have already been scuttled.[149] The Act also slashes compensation under Medicare for MRI and CT scan facilities in doctors' offices. Such facilities ease burdens on patients, who don't have to struggle to get appointments and sit in waiting rooms elsewhere, and improves health by accelerat-ing diagnosis.[150] But with the compensation to doctors for such services slashed, patients will increasingly lose this convenience and superior health care.

Incentives for medical research, innovation, and development of the next generation of medical technology would be decimated as well. Low reimbursement levels, and the bias of the new bureaucracies against such new developments and their costs, would destroy incentives for in-vestors to put their money into research and development to discover the next generation of advanced, high-tech medical care. Vast new op-portunities for innovative health services and care pioneered by modern science, such as gene therapies and biotechnology, would freeze up, un-derutilized. Drug companies would ultimately cut back on investment in cutting-edge, curative, pain-relieving, and lifesaving miracle drugs. Some major drug companies have already announced plans to invest in marketing existing drugs in other countries rather than bring new drugs to market in the United States.[151] Just when the rapid advancement of science and technology is revealing new vistas to counter disease, suf-fering, and death, self-congratulatory politicians and bureaucrats are stomping in and drawing the curtain. Many people will suffer or die unnecessarily as a result.

Investment in *human* capital would also be negatively affected. Un-derpaid doctors, surgeons, and specialists would choose less demanding and perhaps more remunerative fields. Some would see fewer patients, devote more time to their families, and take more vacations. Others would simply retire earlier than planned. Survey evidence reveals that, thanks to underpayment from Medicaid and Medicare, this is already starting to happen.[152] With less investment in technology and facilities and lower pay in the future, some of the bright young students who would have pursued careers in medicine and health care will choose other professions instead.

A smaller supply of health professionals will exacerbate the problems of longer lines, waiting times, and less health care. Combined with the effects of greater demand for health services from millions of people wanting their "free" health care and from the formerly uninsured, the severity of inadequate supply of health care will become even more acute.

Indeed, these incentive effects indicate a reduced supply of health care overall, which means even further increases in prices and costs. Colliding with the increased demand for such health care described above, the result is what Milton Friedman called "the black hole of socialized medicine," with everyone paying more and more for less and less.[153]

Bad Advice

President Obama surrounded himself with advisors who openly promoted and even celebrated the concept of government control of health care decisions to reduce costs. Former Senate majority leader Tom Daschle was Obama's first pick for secretary of health and human services, and when a tax scandal denied him that post, he remained a central advisor to Obama on health care. In his 2008 book, *Critical: What We Can Do About the Health Care Crisis*, Daschle explicitly advances the British model of extreme government health care rationing for the United States.[154] He advocates a U.S. Federal Health Board explicitly modeled on Britain's NICE, and using the concept of comparative effectiveness for the government to decide who gets what health care, to control costs.[155] He advocates an enforcement mechanism for doing this that is very similar to what is advocated in the 2009 report by the Council of Economic Advisors. Writes Daschle:

> The federal government could exert tremendous leverage with its decisions on covered benefits and payment incentives. In choosing what it will cover and how much it will pay, it could steer provid-

ers to the services that are the most clinically valuable and cost-effective. . . .[156]

That is, clinically valuable and cost-effective as decided by a faraway government bureaucracy, not your doctor.

Similarly, President Obama's head of the Centers for Medicare & Medicaid Services, Dr. Donald Berwick, says, "I am a romantic about the NHS. All I need to do to rediscover the romance is to look at the health care of my own country," which he calls "crazy" and "immoral."[157] He is also romantic about NICE, the bureaucracy in charge of rationing and denial of health care for the British people.[158] Berwick says, "NICE is extremely effective and a conscientious, valuable, and—importantly—knowledge-building system."[159]

Ezekiel Emanuel, brother of former White House chief of staff Rahm Emanuel, served as a top White House health care policy advisor to President Obama. Ezekiel Emanuel has made a career of calling for government control of health care to control costs by rationing and denying care. He has written several articles in top medical journals promoting government health care rationing based on cost-effectiveness rationalizations. Betsy McCaughey explained his thinking in an article in the *New York Post*:

> Emanuel wants doctors to look beyond the needs of their patients and consider social justice, such as whether the money could be better spent on somebody else. . . . He says medical care should be reserved for the non-disabled, not given to those "who are irreversibly prevented from being or becoming participating citizens. . . . An obvious example is not guaranteeing health services to patients with dementia." . . . Translation: Don't give much care to a grandmother with Parkinson's or a child with cerebral palsy.

Another top White House health policy advisor, Dr. David Blumenthal, agrees with Emanuel. McCaughey explains:

> He recommends slowing medical innovation to control health spending. Blumenthal has long advocated government health

spending controls, though he concedes they're "associated with longer waits" and "reduced availability of new and expensive treatments and devices." (New England Journal of Medicine, March 8, 2001) But he calls it "debatable" whether the timely care Americans get is worth the cost. (Ask a cancer patient, and you'll get a different answer. Delay lowers your chance of survival.)

Former Office of Management and Budget head Peter Orszag expressed the same views in saying, "Future increases in spending could be moderated if costly new medical services were adopted more selectively in the future than they have been in the past, and if the diffusion of existing costly services was slowed."[160] Prominent Obamacare booster Paul Krugman expressed these same views in a November 14, 2010, broadcast of ABC's *This Week*, explaining his view of the ultimate solution for the coming bankruptcy of America: "Some years down the pike, we're going to get the real solution, which is going to be a combination of death panels and sales taxes."[161]

President Obama himself indicated his sympathy for such health care rationing during a national broadcast by ABC News of his own White House town hall discussion. A woman rose to ask him whether under his health plan there would be any room for taking into account "spirit of life" as exemplified by her own mother, now age 105. At age 100, her mother needed a pacemaker to survive. Doctors at first declined to conduct the operation on someone so old. But the daughter persisted, asking that they talk to her mother to see firsthand her continued vivaciousness and "spirit of life." When the doctors did so and realized the mother was still very much alive, they conducted the operation, and the mother was still alive five years later.

Obama answered by saying that "spirit of life" was too vague a concept for a national health plan to consider. He launched into bureaucrat-speak, saying that "end of life" care involved difficult decisions for everyone, and that many times the best decision is just to give the patient a painkiller and send him or her home. Translation: No, under his cost-effective vision of social justice, he would not have allowed the woman's mother a pacemaker, and so she would be dead today. He failed to notice that in the mother's case, the pacemaker was not end of life care.

President Obama, of course, shares the central-government-control, rationing views of all of his advisors, or else he would not have chosen them to surround him. His Obamacare Act provides the foundation for implementing those views in American health care policy. Consequently, at the heart of Obamacare is a cruel perversion. The Act labors mightily to expand insurance coverage to everyone (though it actually fails, with over 23 million, and likely more, still to be uninsured). But then it empowers bureaucracy and institutes incentives to deprive you of the very health care that you may need to save your life, or the life of a loved one, or to cure you of disease or ease your pain. Berwick summed up the true health policy views of President Obama and his health policy advisors when he famously said, "The decision is not whether or not we will ration care—the decision is whether we will ration with our eyes open."[162] They believe that because they don't understand that there is another alternative, as we will see.

BEST HEALTH CARE IN THE WORLD

Danny Williams lived in the progressive health care paradise of "single payer," national health insurance in Canada, as the premier of the province of Newfoundland and Labrador. When he himself needed heart surgery at age sixty, however, he snuck into the United States to get it. Williams told reporters after his surgery, "This was my heart, my choice, and my health. I did not sign away my right to get the best possible health care for myself when I entered politics."[163] That best possible health care was at Mount Sinai Medical Center—in Miami, Florida.

Why Williams felt he had to come to America was further illuminated by the heart surgery of former president Bill Clinton. As Dr. Marc Siegel explained in the *New York Post*:

Clinton, of course, got the best of care—a cardiac stent (a tiny metal cylinder) coated with a drug to help keep his artery open. Recent studies in the *New England Journal of Medicine* and elsewhere have shown that these drug-eluting stents are more effective than bare metal ones. But they cost two-to-four times more—and the

technology is relatively new. That combination has left government run health-care systems slow to adopt them. . . . Per capita,
our neighbors to the north receive only half as many coronary
[operations]. And only 30% of the stents placed in Canada are
drug-eluting, compared to a whopping 80% in the United States.
So a Canadian cardiac patient is less than a quarter as likely as
an American to be outfitted with the kind of state-of-the-art stent
that Clinton had. In Canada, land of single payer health insurance,
you're also less likely to get the stent as soon as the need is clear.[164]

When their own lives are at risk, suddenly political leaders can understand it quite well. America has enjoyed until today the best, most
advanced health care in the world. That is why so many come here from
all those countries with national health insurance, or "universal" health
care, to get their essential care. That is why America produces far superior results for those afflicted with such deadly illnesses as cancer and
heart disease.

At this moment in history, modern science is already producing great
leaps forward in modern medicine. As Dr. David Gratzer recently ob-
served, half of all medical treatments in use today were invented in the
last twenty-five years.[165] Among those modern miracles is a pacemaker that
enables doctors to monitor your heart while online. They can actually call
their patients in the morning now and tell them to go to the hospital because they are going to have a heart attack today. That is a world of difference from the first pacemakers thirty-five years ago, which were backpacks
with short battery lives. Today, pacemakers are small enough to fit in the
rib cage muscle wall, with a battery life of more than seven years.

Those modern pacemakers are also equipped with technology that
will jolt a stopped heart back to life while the patient is on the way to the
hospital. In one case, an elderly man with such modern technology in his
chest awoke one morning not feeling right. His wife called his doctor,
who checked him out online. His doctor's orders: get to a hospital now.
As his wife drove him to the hospital, four times his heart stopped, and
he slumped over, dying. Four times his pacemaker jolted his heart back
to life. As of this writing, he has lived to enjoy several more Christmases
with his family.

At the other end of the age spectrum, only America enjoys the wide-spread technology today to rescue the lives of premature babies born smaller than your hand. These preemies grow up to live normal lives, and have children and grandchildren of their own. These people and their growing tribes of progeny are a testament to the moral disgrace of phony, misleading statistics regarding infant mortality in America, cooked up for political gain and to shore up hopelessly outdated ideologies.

In another case, a three-year-old boy was diagnosed with a rare and aggressive soft tissue cancer in his bladder. Because he was so young, radiation would prevent his pelvic bones and hips from growing properly, and his bladder would remain the size of a three-year-old's for his entire life. Another option was radical surgery to remove his bladder, prostate, and portions of his rectum. That would leave him impotent, using a colostomy bag for life, and urinating through a bag in his abdomen (if the surgery was successful).

But a third option was the new technology of proton beam therapy, which would target the radiation dose so it would not cripple him for life. Thanks to that new technology, the boy is now growing up cancer-free, and his body functions normally. But in 2009 the *New York Times* offered the increased use of this expensive technology as an example of how our health system is "hard-wired to be bloated and inefficient," a malady to be corrected by President Obama's health care overhaul.

Thanks to exploding modern medical science, today you can avoid invasive exploratory surgery by taking a pill with a camera inside that transmits fifteen high-quality color pictures a second of the inside of your digestive track. Recent advances have also enabled much smaller MRI and CT scan machines to migrate out to doctors' offices, where easy, efficient access enables earlier detection of serious illnesses such as lung cancer. If lung cancer is detected and treated before it spreads, the five-year survival rate is over 70%. But only 16% of those diagnosed with the disease survive past five years, because it usually goes undetected for so long. Obamacare, however, changed the Medicare reimbursement formula to force this advanced imaging equipment out of doctors' offices because it supposedly involves a conflict of interest, thus forcing seniors to go to hospitals to get the examination.

Since 1960, the U.S. age-adjusted death rate for heart disease has declined by 54%, due to advancing technology. New drugs for blood pressure and cholesterol account for 33–50% of the reduction in heart attack mortality. New drugs now arriving on the market cure once-lethal leukemia. Now on the horizon are vaccines to prevent other types of cancer.

As Sally Pipes reports,[166] deaths from breast cancer have dropped steadily in the United States since 1990. Pipes cites the American Cancer Society's most recent numbers: "[P]atients with stage 4 breast cancer, widely seen as 'incurable,' now have a 20 percent 5-year survival rate, while those with stage 1 breast cancer have a 100 percent 5-year survival rate."[167]

More miracles are on the way with advances now being produced with such cutting-edge science as the human genome project. It is increasingly possible to treat patients with individualized medical breakthroughs based on the particulars of their own body, their own genes, and the particular contours of the disease that may threaten their life. Modern gene therapy offers the prospect of altering an individual's genes even before disease strikes.

These are the fruits of the best, most advanced health care system in the world, which is a central component of the high standard of living the American people enjoy and expect to continue. The American people do not want to give this up. What they want is just the opposite: even more of this lifesaving, health-improving, pain-slaying modern science and medicine.

But this is exactly what will be lost under the incentives, central economic decision making, payment compensation policies, and ultimately the rationing of Obamacare. Fortunately, there is a better alternative.

THE PATIENT POWER SOLUTION

The alternative solution to solving the health cost problem is to unite in the patient the decision over what health care to purchase and consume with the full market incentives to control costs. This alternative solution provides a complete replacement for the Obamacare Act, which should be repealed for all the reasons discussed above. The trailblazer in this approach has been John Goodman, founder and president of the National Center for Policy Analysis, located in Dallas. Goodman inaugurated a new era in health policy with the publication of his pathbreaking book *Patient Power* in 1991.

Health Savings Accounts

Since most patients can't pay for much health care out of their own pockets, making this approach work requires some creativity. And Goodman provided that creativity with development of the concept of Health Savings Accounts (HSAs) in the early 1980s.

The concept behind HSAs is to start with an insurance policy with a high annual deductible, in the range of $2,000–6,000 in today's products (the higher the better). The insight that Goodman had was that such high deductibles reduce the cost of the insurance so much that the savings would mostly cover the deductible in the first year. After one healthy year with little or no medical expenses, the patient by the second year would have more than enough in the account to cover all expenses below the deductible.

The HSA funds would earn interest tax-free and roll over year after year, to be used for health expenses in later years. Any HSA funds used for health care expenses are also tax-free. In retirement, remaining HSA funds could be withdrawn for any purpose, subject to ordinary tax if not used for health care. This mirrors the tax treatment provided for employer-provided health insurance, equalizing the playing field for HSAs.

This transforms the incentives of third-party payment. For all but catastrophic health expenses, the patient is essentially using his own money for health care. Whatever he doesn't spend he can keep. He can use it for other health expenses later, or for anything in retirement. So the patient will try to avoid unnecessary care, and look for less expensive care and alternatives for what he does need.

In turn, since patients would now be concerned about controlling costs, doctors, hospitals, and other health providers would now compete to control costs, as well as maximize quality, as in all normal markets. (This competition would become more intense and effective the more widespread HSAs become.) These incentives would flow all the way through to the developers of new technologies. Since both patients and health providers are now concerned with costs, technology innovators will now have incentives to develop technologies that reduce costs as well as improve quality.

Goodman also had the insight that the patient can and should enjoy complete freedom in deciding what health care to spend his money on from the HSA. The money can be used for regular checkups, any preventive care or diagnostics, dental care, vision care, and any alternative medicine the patient desires, even if the health insurance above the deductible would not pay for any of this. This makes HSAs very empowering and liberating for patients. Goodman consequently invented the term "patient power" as the theme for free market health reform.

A sophisticated RAND Corporation study conducted in the early 1980s demonstrated that when patients pay for health care out of pocket, as with an HSA, they do reduce their health spending substantially.[168] Yet they are judicious in how they do it, with no apparent negative effects on health. Indeed, studies show that patients with HSAs actually spend more on preventive care than others, perhaps because they have economic incentives to preserve their future HSA funds as well as their future health.[169]

Federal legislation providing for HSAs was adopted by the Republican congressional majorities in the 1990s, and improved over the years. These HSAs and similar high-deductible plans have been proved to reduce costs. Premiums for HSA plans in 2009 for those ages 30–54 in the individual market averaged $2,465 a year for singles and $5,335 for a family.[170] In the group market, family premiums averaged nearly 25% less than the standard charge of over $12,000 per family, with average premiums for singles at $3,691 in the large-group market and $3,944 in the small-group market.[171] Growth in health costs for companies with at least half of their workforce enrolled in such plans has been cut by more than 50%.[172] Similar results were found for federal employees choosing HSAs over standard coverage. WellPoint and Cigna report no increase in costs for their HSA plans from 2007 to 2008. Similar programs offered by the American Postal Workers Union and the Government Employees Health Association experienced no increase in premiums for four years running.

Similar to HSAs are the health reimbursement arrangements (HRAs) offered by some employers. The employer contributes all of the money to an HRA and retains control over it, but the employee is free to use the money in the account for the health care he or she wants.

Participation in such high-deductible coverage plans (HSAs and HRAs) has been soaring in recent years.[173] The number of Americans with an HSA or similar high-deductible plan increased by 43% from 2006 to 2007, 35% from 2007 to 2008, and 31% from 2008 to 2009.[174] The latest numbers show another increase of 25% from January 2009 to January 2010.[175] Coverage in the large-group market rose by 33% from 2009 to 2010, and in the small-group market by 22%.[176] Overall, the National Health Interview Survey (NHIS), conducted by the federal government's Centers for Disease Control and Prevention, found that in 2009 about 23% of the privately insured population was covered by HSAs, HRAs, or similar high-deductible health plans,[177] which may have exceeded HMO enrollment that year.[178] Almost 50% of those with private insurance obtained outside their employment were covered by such high-deductible plans.[179] Funds held in HSA accounts totaled more than $9.2 billion in 2009, and were projected to grow to over $16 billion by the end of 2010.[180]

Patient power reform ultimately involves making such HSAs more attractive and accessible for everyone. Consumers should be allowed complete freedom to choose their deductible on the high end, since the higher the deductible, the more effective the HSAs will be in reducing health costs. They and their employers should be free to contribute to HSAs up to the full amount of the annual deductibles, with such contributions tax-deductible.

Moreover, the cost reduction incentives of HSAs are maximized to the extent the patient can pay himself a reward at the end of the year, without special penalty, out of whatever HSA funds he doesn't spend during the year on health care, for then the money will be most like his own. He would then be making a complete trade-off between spending on health care and on other goods and services, resulting in full market incentives to control costs. Any withdrawals not spent on health care, however, would be treated as fully taxable income.

Professional critics of individual liberty have argued that HSAs are good for the wealthy and the healthy, but not for the poor and the sick. But just the opposite is true. They benefit the poor and the sick the most.

The poor most need the cost savings from HSAs. They are a lower-cost form of essential health insurance, which is why 30% of HSAs are purchased by the formerly uninsured.[181] Moreover, the poor and lower-income most need the savings they can generate in their HSAs by saving on wasteful, unnecessary, and overly expensive health costs. In addition, with HSAs they have the money in their accounts to finance routine checkups and preventive care, and other often uncovered essentials such as eyeglasses, hearing aids, and dental care. Before Obamacare, they could even use the money for over-the-counter drugs as well as all pre-scription drugs. That can be restored by repealing Obamacare.

The critics *always* fail to consider the savings in the HSA available to pay for health costs below the deductible. But after just one healthy year, the accumulated HSA funds are always more than the deductible, leaving the poor at no risk of net loss from health costs. Moreover, even should they deplete their HSA savings accounts due to sickness in the first year, their net out-of-pocket exposure for that year will still not be more than in a standard traditional insurance plan.

For the sick, the maximized freedom of choice and flexibility of HSAs is most valuable. They are free to use HSA funds to pursue whatever health care they think would be most effective, on the advice of their chosen doctor, with no role for the insurance company. Moreover, they have the ready funds in the account to pay for whatever regular tests and preventive care they may need.

With some more creativity, we can extend these market incentives even to catastrophic care, particularly high health expenditures in the last year of life, which many people find wasteful (until it is themselves or a member of their family threatened with death). Consider this inno-vation. Why not allow insurance companies to offer to pay the money to the insured to forgo care they are entitled to under their policies?

For example, assume a patient has a deadly cancer that would cost a million dollars to treat, with a substantial probability of failure neverthe-less. Why not allow the insurer to offer the patient to split the savings if the patient will choose to forgo the care? Patients may decide they would rather leave the half-million dollars to their families than spend it on heroic medicine, which may entail a lot of physical pain and suffering, with highly compromised quality of life on the other end at best. The insurer should be free to offer the patient as much of the savings as possible.

The patient must be completely free to make this decision, with no power in the insurance company to force it. Any compromise of this absolute patient freedom would be fascism. But empowering the patient to weigh the costs against the benefits and make this decision about their own health care would be morally unobjectionable. Indeed, only the patient can morally make this decision for himself or herself, not some third-party government or insurance company bureaucracy. And fundamental economic logic tells you that somebody should be making this decision. The resulting cost savings for the system as a whole would likely be quite substantial. About a third of Medicare expenditures are incurred in the last year of life.[182]

A Health Care Safety Net

Besides addressing the problem of rising health costs, the patient power alternative addresses fully the issue of the uninsured and ensuring access to health care for all. As stated at the outset, I do not believe in human suffering, and that principle is most salient in regard to essential health care, where true pain and suffering, and actual death, may be involved. No one in our society should suffer deteriorating health, disease, pain, or worse because of lack of essential health care.

Perhaps the greatest tragedy of Obamacare is that virtually all of it—the 159 new boards, agencies, commissions, and programs, the three new or expanded entitlements, the trillions in new spending, taxes, and deficits, the intractable Medicare cuts, the individual and employer man-dates, the overall government takeover of health care—was not neces-sary to solve this problem. What is needed instead is a true and complete health care safety net ensuring that no one will suffer because of lack of essential health care, and that everyone can get such care when they need it. Doing that the right way, drawing on modern markets and their incentives, can mean less in government burdens, spending, and taxes, not more.

Such a safety net policy starts with a focus on the truly needy—the poor and the sick—who do need help to get essential care. With that focus, the problem of the uninsured starts to get a lot smaller. While we were constantly told that 46 million Americans are uninsured, 12 million of them are already eligible for current programs like Medicaid, CHIP, or Medicare, but are not enrolled.[183] They immediately become enrolled and insured when they enter a hospital for care. Another 6 million are already eligible for employer-provided insurance, but again have not enrolled.[184] Another 10 million earn over $75,000 per year, well above average incomes, and must take responsibility for paying for their own insurance.[185] About 10 million of the uninsured are foreign noncitizens, whether here legally or illegally, and they are not part of the problem of uninsured *Americans*.[186] American taxpayers cannot be asked to take the responsibility of paying for the health care of everyone in the world.

That leaves less than 10 million uninsured who really can't afford health insurance. At least half of these are young adults, ages 18–34, whose essential health expenses will not be costly to cover in any event, whether through insurance or directly through government assistance, because of their youth.[187] Many, if not most, of the remainder are only temporarily uninsured for a few months, and would not be costly to assist, either. Three-quarters of the uninsured regain coverage within twelve months.[188]

The policies recommended below would provide a true health care safety net for all Americans. The point here is to understand why that does not need to be costly. The primary reason is that we already have the huge Medicaid entitlement paying close to half a trillion dollars a year for health care for the poor, and more soon enough. If we just focus on providing the additional assistance needed by those who truly can't afford to pay the whole cost of health insurance themselves, the cost will be quite manageable. Indeed, that added cost would quite likely be more than offset by other efficiencies and cost savings of the reforms.

MEDICAID REFORM

Providing that additional assistance for the truly needy can be achieved by reforming the Medicaid program, which is central to the entitlement problem threatening to bankrupt America. Such Medicaid reform should be based on the enormously successful 1996 reform of the old Aid to Families with Dependent Children (AFDC) welfare program, discussed in detail in the next chapter.

That reform sent the federal share of spending for the program back to each state in a finite block grant, with each state then to create a new welfare program based on required work for the able-bodied. Under the old program's matching-funds formula, the federal government sent states more money the more they spent on the program, effectively paying states to enroll more and more people in AFDC, which they did quite assiduously. The states each saw the resulting runaway enrollment as "bringing more federal money to our state." In 1996, that matching-funds formula was replaced with a fixed federal block grant to each state that did not vary with the amount of state spending. If costs for the program rose in a state, the state would have to pay for the added costs itself. If the state saved money through innovation and finding work for those on welfare, the state could keep the savings.

While this reform included important new incentives for the welfare recipients themselves, arising from a work requirement, even more important were the transformed incentives for the state bureaucrats running the programs. Together these rationalized incentives produced spectacular results. Within a few years, the rolls of the old AFDC program were reduced by two-thirds, with recipients earning paychecks in place of welfare checks. Spending on the program remained flat for a dozen years, which saved huge sums over where spending would have been under the old system. Indeed, with two-thirds leaving the program for work, spending on the program could and should have been reduced by over half.

Medicaid reform should follow that model. The current federal matching-funds formula for that program should be replaced with finite block grants, adjusted each year under some formula accounting for health care inflation, to be used for a completely redesigned Medicaid program in each state. The states would each have broad discretion in how to design the program in their respective jurisdictions. But states would best serve the poor by using the program to provide vouchers that would help to pay for the private health insurance of their choice in the marketplace. Among those choices would be the Health Savings Accounts discussed above. Like modernized AFDC, Medicaid vouchers should be subject to a work requirement for the able-bodied. CHIP should be rolled into the Medicaid block grants as well.

Each state's voters would be free to decide how much assistance for the purchase of health insurance they wanted to provide at what income levels. That would differ with varying cost of living, income levels, and health costs from state to state. Reforms that would increase the quality of care while lowering costs, which state lawmakers and bureaucrats currently have little incentive to consider, could finally get the attention they deserve.[189] Indeed, state lawmakers would have powerful incentives to adopt further reforms that would drive down the cost of health insurance, reducing the cost of the necessary assistance to help the poor buy health insurance. Through this reform, the poor would be assured of enough assistance to purchase at least basic health insurance, so no one would have to go uninsured because they didn't have enough money to buy it.

This would greatly benefit low-income families, freeing them to escape the low-quality coverage and care of the current Medicaid ghetto, which underpays doctors and hospitals so severely for the services they provide to the poor that nationally one-third do not accept any Medicaid patients, and many of the rest limit the number they will treat.[190] This leaves the poor on Medicaid often suffering disabling difficulties in obtaining essential health care, with documented worse health outcomes as a result. For example, a 2006 study published in the *Annals of Internal Medicine* found that patients on Medicaid were more likely to fail to recover from a heart attack than patients with either private insurance or Medicare.[191] Similar results were reported in 2009 in the journal *Psychiatric Services* for those requiring medication for mental illness.[192]

Under this patient power reform, the poor would enjoy the power and control to choose their own health coverage among the full range of options in the marketplace. They would consequently enjoy the same health care as the middle class, because they would have the same health insurance as the middle class, a huge improvement over Medicaid. This would help the middle class as well, given the current shifting of costs to their insurance coverage because Medicaid so badly underpays doctors and hospitals.

This reform is not going to reduce the Medicaid rolls by two-thirds like the AFDC reforms, in part because about 30% of Medicaid spending goes for residents of nursing homes, who are never going to work.[193] Paying doctors and hospitals market rates through private insurance will add to costs, as will transforming the program into a reliable safety net for all. But this new, reformed Medicaid is a replacement for all of the costs of the current Medicaid and CHIP programs, as well as of Obamacare and all of its costs. The broad discretion, flexibility, and incentives given to the states by the block grants would reduce administrative and other program costs. Moreover, this new Medicaid would operate in the context of the broader transformation of the entire welfare system discussed in the next chapter, with all of the current, counterproductive, perverse incentives of that system transformed into positive, pro-growth incentives, leading a major portion of the American population off public dependency and into productive work.

If the net result is to stop government spending on health care entitlements for the poor from growing faster than GDP, we will have accomplished what is necessary in this area to avert the coming bankruptcy of America. But the net result would likely be to reduce government spending on this function by much more as a percentage of GDP, as will be made more clear in Chapter 5.

STATE HIGH-RISK POOLS

The above component of the health care safety net focuses on the poor uninsured. But a complete safety net needs a second component, focusing on the sick uninsured, those without health insurance who have become too sick with costly illnesses like cancer or heart disease to be able to get new coverage in a private insurance market, like the caller asking for fire insurance for his house that is already on fire.

This would involve the concept of state high-risk pools. The majority of states already have such risk pools, and they have worked well for the most part.[194] Those who cannot obtain health insurance because of their health condition would be eligible for coverage through the state's risk pool and charged premiums based on their ability to pay, with remaining risk pool costs subsidized by general tax revenues. Relatively few people become completely uninsurable because of a preexisting health condition. But trying to force those who do into the same insurance market as everyone else, through such regulations as guaranteed issue and community rating, just ruins health insurance for the general public, making it too expensive and thereby sharply increasing the number of people who choose to go without insurance. Providing for the uninsurable separately through their own pool is a much better policy.

High-risk pools would also address the problem of individuals being able to obtain health insurance but finding that a preexisting condition is excluded. Most insurers limit coverage for preexisting conditions for only a few months. Each state's high-risk pool could provide coverage for preexisting conditions during those excluded months, or for however long is necessary to get coverage for that condition.

The Obamacare Act in fact provides for setting up such a risk pool in every state in 2011,[195] recognizing to a degree the desirability of the idea, which has been a patient power reform for at least twenty years. But the president's legislation would then eliminate these pools in 2014, folding everyone into the state exchanges instead.

But the risk pools should be permanent, with the states each free to design and run them as they prefer, without the unnecessary federal control in the Act. The federal role instead should be to ensure that the state risk pools are adequately funded to serve to cement a true health care safety net for every American. States should consequently be free to use Medicaid block grant funds for this purpose. Policy makers should recognize that these risk pools would work in conjunction with Medicaid in providing such a safety net, so those without funds to pay high-risk pool premiums would receive Medicaid vouchers to do so. This would provide a much lower-cost solution to the problems of preexisting conditions and the uninsurable who have not previously obtained coverage.

Newt Gingrich has proposed complementing high-risk pools with health plans that specialize in managing care for the sick with costly chronic diseases. Such special needs plans actively compete in Medicare Advantage to cover the sickest Medicare beneficiaries.[196] Instead of eviscerating Medicare Advantage, as the Obamacare Act does, the role of these plans should be expanded in Medicare, Medicaid, and in employer and individual coverage.

CONSUMER PROTECTIONS

A final component of a comprehensive health care safety net involves what is usually called consumer protection, but is actually only sound, fundamental principles of contract law. In a town hall meeting in New Hampshire in 2009, President Obama said that under his health plan,

> [I]nsurance companies . . . will not be able to drop your coverage if you get sick. They will not be able to water down your coverage when you need it. Your health insurance should be there for you when it counts—not just when you're paying premiums, but when you actually get sick. And it will be when we pass this plan.[197]

But dropping or watering down your health insurance coverage after you get sick has long been illegal in America, and well it should be. Health insurance that can be cut off after you get sick is, again, like fire insurance that can be cut off after your house catches fire. That is not health insurance; it is fraud.

The prohibition against this fraud was nationalized in the landmark bipartisan Health Insurance Portability and Accountability Act legislation, enacted in 1996. That legislation even provided that if you lose employer-provided health insurance coverage for any reason (changing jobs, layoff, employer goes out of business, divorce), any private insurer you apply to within two months must take you, regardless of health condition. That is workable because such individuals are not trying to game the system, waiting until they are sick before they buy guaranteed coverage, but are actually trying to responsibly maintain continuous coverage.

Before Obamacare, the law did allow insurers to cancel coverage if the insured lied about his or her medical condition or history during the application process, which would involve fraud on the part of the applicant. But the alternative safety net discussed here would still cover those in this situation, through the state high-risk pools and the Medicaid health insurance vouchers.

The law in America has also long provided for what has been termed guaranteed renewability, which means that as long as you continue to pay your premiums, the insurance company cannot cut you off because you get sick, nor can it impose premium increases any greater than for anyone else in your original risk pool.

There may have been some loopholes in the employer group market in regard to these consumer protections that should have been closed.

But in making the above argument, President Obama was trying to take credit for solving a problem that had already been basically solved and did not require the massive government takeover of health care that he imposed on the country.

These consumer protections should be included in the patient power alternatives that should replace the Obamacare Act. These safety net provisions together ensure that every American will have access to essential health care when needed. If you have health insurance, you will be able to keep it no matter how sick you get. If you are too poor to pay for it, you will get assistance to help you pay for it. And if you still don't get coverage and then you become too sick to buy it for the first time, you will still be able to get essential coverage and care through the high-risk pools.

The Consumer Choice Tax Credit

Obamacare's tax credits for the purchase of health insurance should be replaced with the Consumer Choice Tax Credit, as provided in Representative Ryan's Roadmap for America's Future. The refundable credit would equal $2,300 for individuals and $5,700 for families for the purchase of health insurance. This would not pay for all of the costs of typical health insurance, but it would be enough to make insurance affordable for those without employer coverage, considering the additional Medicaid vouchers for the poor, and the risk pools available for the uninsured already sick with costly illnesses.

True to patient power, workers would then be free to choose the health insurance coverage they each prefer, rather than being stuck with the insurance chosen for them by their employer. That insurance would be the property of each worker, and therefore completely portable, so the worker would not lose health coverage if he changed or lost his job. Workers would then shop for and choose the lowest-cost health plans in a competitive market.

The credit would be financed on a revenue-neutral basis by including the value of employer-provided health insurance in taxable income, but the credit would offset any additional net tax for everyone except those higher-income workers with the most expensive, "Cadillac" health plans (discouraging the purchase of such cost-increasing plans). This would result in enormous net savings to taxpayers equal to the entire cost of the Obamacare health insurance subsidies the credit would replace, at least $500 billion for the first six years, and probably more than $1 trillion based on the analysis above.

Medicare Reform

Patient power reforms can and should also be extended to fundamental reform of Medicare, which is one of the biggest problems threatening the bankruptcy of America. That begins first by extending the personal account option for Social Security to the Medicare payroll tax as well. Every worker below a certain age would be free to choose to save and invest the employer and employee share of the Medicare payroll tax (HI) in a personal account operating under the same framework as for the Social Security reform discussed earlier. In retirement, the accumulated saved funds would finance a monthly annuity that the retiree could use to help purchase the private health insurance of his choice. Among those insurance choices would be Health Savings Accounts.

Payroll taxes finance only about half of overall Medicare expenses. General revenues finance the rest. Under this reform, those general revenues would be used to provide supplemental means-tested vouchers to lower-income seniors to further help them purchase private health insurance, ensuring that all could afford the essential health coverage. But the amount of such total general revenue spending would be limited to grow no faster than the rate of growth of GDP. That would ensure that Medicare spending burdens would no longer threaten to overwhelm our economy and bankrupt America. Yet it would maintain the same level of commitment to Medicare that is obligated today, holding Medicare spending to the same percent of GDP. Obviously, we cannot maintain a commitment to Medicare spending that is perpetually growing faster than GDP. Otherwise, as a matter of mathematics, it will ultimately consume all of GDP, meaning, precisely, bankruptcy for America.

Based on the calculations for the Social Security reform discussed above, saving and investing over a lifetime the 2.9% HI payroll tax in the personal accounts would produce an income stream in retirement roughly three times as large as the uninvested, tax-and-spend, purely redistributive, pay-as-you-go Medicare payroll tax today. That means the equivalent in retirement available for the purchase of private insurance of the revenues that would be produced by a 9% payroll tax. Seniors could also contribute to such insurance the equivalent of what they are spending today for Medicare Part B premiums, Medicare Part D prescription drug coverage premiums, and Medigap premiums. They would also enjoy the cost savings from the incentives of HSAs. With the supplemental vouchers from general revenues, this should be sufficient to finance future health care for seniors without any additional drain on government or national resources.[198]

In any event, public resources through the general revenues would be focused on protecting lower- and moderate-income seniors from any additional costs. If higher-income seniors have to spend a little more in the future to purchase their health insurance, that is fair and economically reasonable.

Overall such reform would result in a large reduction in federal spending. That is because all of the taxes and spending generated by the Medicare payroll tax would be shifted to the private sector. Moreover, limiting the general-revenue-financed portion of Medicare to growing no faster than the rate of growth of GDP will produce huge savings from where Medicare spending would otherwise be.

For doctors and hospitals, the shift of Medicare to private insurance would mean that they would be paid market rates for their services, and their compensation would no longer be a political football for demagogues. But seniors would be the ultimate beneficiaries of this, as it would ensure their continued access to the highest-quality health care. Younger people would benefit as well, as they would no longer be subject to bearing the burden of cost shifting from Medicare.

Rather than the draconian, arbitrary, unworkable Medicare cuts in Obamacare, this Medicare reform is far superior, far better for seniors, taxpayers, and America.

Further Patient Power Reforms

Additional reforms would provide for complete patient power. These would include allowing the interstate sale of health insurance, maximizing consumer choice, and competition, which would further reduce costs. Regulations that unnecessarily increase costs should be repealed. These include the thousands of state benefit mandates, guaranteed issue, and community rating, as well as regulations that unnecessarily prevent new health providers from entering markets and increasing competition, such as mandating a showing of need for the services first.

Businesses of all sizes and consumers should be allowed to establish their own private exchanges to replace the Obamacare government exchanges, allowing a broad choice of different health plans in each exchange to all workers in the group. Employers can offer each worker a defined contribution amount toward the purchase of any of the exchange options, encouraging and enabling more employers to offer health coverage.

Medical malpractice liability reform should be based on restoring traditional tort standards to the law, holding doctors and hospitals responsible only for damages for which they were the proximate cause. Punitive damages should apply only in criminal proceedings, not civil trials.

Patient Power and Health Insurance

Some defenders of the Obamacare vision argue that private health insurers ration and deny health care just as socialized medicine systems do. So Berwick is right that the issue is not whether we ration health care or not, but whether we do so with our eyes open. It is important to realize just how thoroughly the patient power perspective rejects this view.

Again, most fundamentally, patient power solves the third-party payment problem by uniting in the patients themselves the decision over what health care to purchase, with market incentives to control costs. Each patient then ultimately decides to what extent health care choices and their benefits are worth the costs. Neither the government nor the insurance companies can usurp this role and decide what health care the patient can have and what he can't.

Insurance companies should be allowed only a much more limited power: to challenge a health care expense as not supported by medical science, since ratepayers don't benefit from having their costs run up by quackery. But the insurer must bear the burden of proving any such case, with penalties if they fail to carry that burden. Otherwise the role of private health insurance is to pay the bill at reasonable and customary market rates for whatever a patient's chosen, licensed medical professional prescribes.

The exception to this is a health maintenance organization (HMO), which maintains its own staff or network of medical professionals, who operate under the medical standards established by the HMO. Those medical standards can embody cost-benefit considerations. But in this case, the patient chooses to contract that power to the HMO in return for lower costs. A consistent patient power philosophy would allow the consumer to make this choice. But recognize that is a patient choice *not* to choose the patient power solution, but instead to give the decision of what health care to consume over to the third-party payer. This is why patient power advocates disfavor, but tolerate, HMOs. I have always viewed them as privatized, socialized medicine. They should be legal, but I would never choose one for me or my family, or advise anyone else to do so.

An American Health Care Vision

In August 2009, the *Wall Street Journal* published a paradigm-shattering commentary by Craig S. Karpel titled, "We Don't Spend Enough on Health Care." "Americans are being urged to worry about the nation spending 17% of gross domestic product each year on health care—a higher percentage than any other country," Karpel began. He noted that President Obama has repeatedly argued that the 17% of GDP America spends on health care is weighing down our economy and threatens future economic growth. However,

> No one thinks the 20% of our GDP that's attributable to manufacturing is weighing down the economy, because it's intuitively clear that one person's expenditures on widgets is another person's income. The $2.4 trillion Americans spend each year for health care doesn't go up in smoke. It's paid to other Americans.

Karpel continues: "The U.S. health-care economy should be viewed not as a burden but as an engine of growth." He cites the comprehensive economic modeling of Stanford University economists Robert Hall and Charles Jones, which concludes that "maximizing social welfare in the United States" would require "the development of institutions consistent with spending 30% or more of GDP on health by" 2050. Karpel concludes, "The administration's health care plan is biased towards bean counting rather than designed to maximize American physical and mental well-being. We need to ask ourselves whether there is truly anything more valuable to us than our loved ones and our own health and longevity."

The truth is that no one can really say that spending 17% of GDP on health care is too much, or too little. Any such judgment would be arbitrary central economic planning. The real answer depends on how Americans value the benefits of health care against the costs. That can only be determined in a competitive marketplace where consumers reveal their true preferences based on the decisions they make. That can work only if the consumers making the choices are really weighing the costs against the benefits. Once the decision over what health care to buy is united with market incentives to control costs in the patients themselves, then the people themselves can decide what percentage of GDP should be devoted to health care, through their collective decisions in the marketplace. That actually is the only rational way to decide. The people may effectively decide by their choices in the market that 17% is too much. Or over time, as the nation gets richer and richer, and technology makes desirable results more and more possible, they may decide they want to spend a lot more on health care, maybe even the 30% of GDP estimated by Hall and Jones.

The American people do seem to prefer, even crave, the best, most advanced health care in the world. The imagination is captured by a vision of a steady march of breakthrough miracle drugs slaying deadly diseases and defeating crippling pain. Of breakthrough individualized cures going straight to each body's particular source of life-threatening deterioration. Of the modern technological revolution in miniature going to work deep inside the body to fight for life, liberty, and the pursuit of happiness.

Patient power makes such a health care future possible.

CHAPTER 5

THE WELFARE EMPIRE

Liberate the Poor and Taxpayers

A fundamental misconception about America's welfare state misleads millions of voters to reflexively support an ever bigger and more generous government. William Voegeli fingers the attitude in his book, *Never Enough: America's Limitless Welfare State*: "no matter how large the welfare state, liberal politicians and writers have accused it of being shamefully small" and "contemptibly austere."[1] Barbara Ehrenreich expresses the attitude in her book *Nickel and Dimed*: "guilt doesn't go anywhere near far enough; the appropriate emotion is shame" regarding the stingy miserliness of America's welfare state.

But America's welfare state is not a principality. It is a vast empire bigger than the entire budgets of almost every other country in the world. We saw in the last chapter that just one program, Medicaid, cost the federal government $275 billion in 2010, which is slated to rise to $451 billion by 2018. Counting state Medicaid expenditures, this one program cost taxpayers $425 billion in 2010, soaring to $800 billion by 2018. Under Obamacare, 85 million Americans will soon be on Medicaid, growing to nearly 100 million by 2021.

But there are 184 additional, widely recognized, federal means-tested welfare programs, most jointly financed and administered with the states. In addition to Medicaid is the Children's Health Insurance Program (CHIP). Also included is the food stamp program, now officially called the Supplemental Nutrition Assistance Program (SNAP). Nearly 42 million Americans were receiving food stamps in 2010, up by a third just since November 2008. That is why President Obama's budget projects spending $75 billion on food stamps in 2011, double the $36 billion spent in 2008.

But that is not the only federal nutrition program for the needy. There is the Special Supplemental Nutrition Program for Women, Infants, and Children (WIC), which targets assistance to pregnant women and mothers with small children. There is the means-tested School Breakfast Program and School Lunch Program. There is the Summer Food Service Program for Children. There are the lower-income components of the Child and Adult Care Food Program, the Emergency Food Assistance Program, and the Commodity Supplemental Food Program (CSFP). Then there is the Nutrition Services Incentive Program for the elderly. All in all, literally cradle-to-grave service. By 2010, federal spending for food and nutrition assistance overall had climbed to roughly $100 billion ($99.3 billion to be exact).

Then there is federal housing assistance, totaling $77 billion in 2010. This includes expenditures for over 1 million public housing units owned by the government. It includes Section 8 rental assistance for nearly another 4 million private housing units. Then there is Rural Rental Assistance, Rural Housing Loans, and Rural Rental Housing Loans. Also included is Home Investment Partnerships (HOME), Community Development Block Grants (CDBG), Housing for Special Populations (Elderly and Disabled), Housing Opportunities for Persons with AIDS (HOPWA), Emergency Shelter Grants, the Supportive Housing program, the Single Room Occupancy program, the Shelter Plus Care program, and the Home Ownership and Opportunity for People Everywhere (HOPE) program, among others.

Besides medical care, food, and housing, the federal government also provides cash. The old New Deal–era Aid to Families with Dependent Children (AFDC) is now Temporary Assistance for Needy Families (TANF), which pays cash mostly to single mothers with children. There is the Earned Income Tax Credit (EITC), which sends low-income workers checks even though they usually owe no taxes to be credited against. The Child Tax Credit similarly provides cash to families with children. The Supplemental Security Income (SSI) provides cash for the low-income elderly, blind, or disabled persons. In 2010 such income security programs accounted for nearly another $200 billion in federal spending.

The federal government also provides means-tested assistance through multiple programs for child care, education, job training, and the Low Income Home Energy Assistance Program (LIHEAP), the Social Services Block Grant, the Community Services Block Grant, and the Legal Services Corporation, among other programs.

The best estimate of the cost of the 185 federal means-tested welfare programs for 2010 for the federal government alone is nearly $700 billion, up a third since 2008.[2] Counting the state spending, total welfare spending for 2010 reached nearly $900 billion, up nearly one-fourth since 2008.[3] Yet by 2008, Robert Rector and others report, total welfare spending already amounted to $16,800 per person in poverty,[4] and was four times as much as the Census Bureau estimated was necessary to bring all of the poor up to the poverty level and thereby eliminate all poverty in America.[5] That would be $50,400 per poor family of three. Indeed, Charles Murray wrote a whole book explaining that we already spend far more than enough to completely eliminate all poverty in America.[6]

The soaring welfare spending since 2008 is not a temporary increase reflecting the recession, since it is not projected to decline after the economy recovers. By 2013, total annual welfare spending will have grown still more, to nearly $1 trillion ($993 billion).[7] Over the ten-year period from 2009 to 2018, federal and state welfare spending will total $10.3 trillion.[8] This does not include Obamacare's massive expansion of Medicaid to nearly 100 million Americans, or the massive new entitlement providing subsidies for families making close to $100,000 per year and beyond. Together, this abusive entitlement spending will add trillions more.

Even in 2005, government spending on these means-tested welfare programs was 25% more than was spent on national defense, and that was at the height of the wars in the Middle East.[9] Government overall—federal, state, and local—spends more only on the big entitlements for retirees, Social Security and Medicare, and on education, primary, secondary, and postsecondary.[10] Total welfare spending may have even shot beyond education by now. Indeed, over the past two decades, total welfare spending has been growing faster than Social Security and Medicare, about twice as fast as education, and nearly three times as fast as national defense.[11]

By 2013, total government spending on welfare will be 50% more than for national defense under President Obama's budget policies.

Indeed, federal spending alone on welfare will be 10% higher than national defense spending by that year.

Of course, the big picture in entitlement programs includes Social Security and Medicare. Social Security spending for 2010 was $721.5 billion, and Medicare spending totaled $457 billion for the year, for a combined total of $1.179 trillion. Adding in federal welfare spending for the year leaves a combined total for entitlement spending of $1.879 trillion. The total federal budget for that year was $3.720 trillion. So entitlement/welfare state spending overall for that year was just over 50% of the entire budget. Not exactly stingy.

Indeed, the federal budget reports the total for "mandatory" human resource programs in 2010, minus federal employee retirement programs, which are not means-tested welfare programs, as $2.06 trillion, which would be 55% of the entire federal budget for the year. "Mandatory" is the budget's polite word for entitlements. Human resources covers precisely Social Security, Medicare, and all means-tested welfare, so it may be a better approximation of the total.

The War on Poverty famously began in 1965. From 1965 to 2008, the total spent only on means-tested welfare for the poor (not counting Social Security and Medicare) in 2008 dollars was nearly $16 trillion.[12] Rector and others report that it was more than all spending on all military conflicts from the American Revolution to today, which would be $6.39 trillion in 2008 dollars.[13] The total cost of World War II in 2008 dollars was $4.1 trillion, only about one-fourth as much as for the War on Poverty.[14] Since the War on Poverty began, total annual inflation-adjusted welfare spending has soared by 13 times, or 1,200%, while the total U.S. population has grown by only 50%.[15]

What have we gotten for all of that spending? Poverty fell sharply after the Great Depression, before the War on Poverty. The poverty rate fell from 32% in 1950 to 22.4% in 1959 to 12.1% in 1969, soon after the War on Poverty programs became effective. Progress against poverty as measured by the poverty rate then abruptly stopped.

The poverty rate bounced up and down around that 1969 level throughout the 1970s, before starting to rise again in the late 1970s. From 1978 to 1982, the poverty rate rose by almost a third, to 15.0%, reflecting the chaotic economy of the 1970s, as discussed in Chapter 6. It never fell below the

1969 level again, except briefly during the three-year period 1999 to 2001. In 2009, the U.S. poverty rate stood at 14.3%, about where it was right after the War on Poverty began, despite the expenditure of $16 trillion. In other words, we fought the War on Poverty, and poverty won.

But it's not all gloom and doom. Something has been working for the poor. Besides reporting the official poverty rate, the Census Bureau collects comprehensive data on the living conditions of the poor. Robert Rector, of the Heritage Foundation, regularly reviews that data and issues reports on the material condition of the poor in modern America. As Rector explains in his latest report in 2007,[16] the Census Bureau data shows that 43% of all poor households own their own home. The average home owned by the poor is a three-bedroom house with one and a half baths, a garage, and a porch or patio. The typical poor American has more living space than the *average* individual living in Paris, London, Vienna, Athens, and other cities throughout Europe. About half live in single-family homes. Only 6% of poor households are overcrowded with more than one person per room; *two-thirds have more than two rooms per person.*

The average consumption of protein, vitamins, and minerals is virtually the same for poor and middle-class children, Rector continues, and in most cases is well above recommended norms. Poor children actually consume more meat than do higher-income children and enjoy average protein intakes 100% above recommended levels. Overconsumption of calories is actually the biggest nutrition problem among the poor, as it is with the general U.S. population. Most poor children today are, in fact, "super nourished," as Rector puts it, based on the data. Today's poor children consequently grow up to be, on average, one inch taller and ten pounds heavier than the GIs who stormed the beaches of Normandy in World War II, as Rector further explains. Concerning hunger, 89% of the poor report their families have enough food to eat, while only 1.5% say they often do not have enough to eat.

Nearly three-quarters of poor households own a car; nearly a third own two or more cars. In addition, 80% of poor households have air-conditioning, while in 1970 only 36% of the entire U.S. population enjoyed air-conditioning. Moreover, 97% of poor households own a color TV, with over half owning two or more, 78% own a VCR or DVD player, 62% have cable or satellite TV, 89% own microwave ovens, more than half own a stereo, and more than a third own personal computers and automatic dishwashers. A third of poor households have both cellular and landline phones.

Rector adds that the typical poor family with children is supported by only 800 hours of work during a year, which amounts to 16 hours of work per week. If work in each family were raised to 2,000 hours per year, which is the equivalent of one adult working 40 hours per week throughout the year, nearly 75% of poor children would be lifted out of poverty.[17]

THE POVERTY OF WELFARE

Even though the poor in America don't live in material suffering, they nevertheless do suffer a real poverty. Not a poverty of material conditions, though there is some real material deprivation, but a poverty of social conditions, which does involve real misery. And the root cause of that poverty is the perverse, counterproductive incentives arising from the welfare system itself.

In 1984, Charles Murray's book *Losing Ground* shocked the nation by documenting how thoroughly we did indeed lose the War on Poverty. He showed that on a wide range of key social indicators, such as work, marriage, legitimacy, crime, and alcohol and drug abuse, among others, the condition of the bulk of the poor actually worsened in response to the massive increase in government welfare programs that started in the mid-1960s with the War on Poverty.

One key reason that poverty stopped declining after the War on Poverty started is that the poor and lower-income population stopped working, leading to all of the other deteriorating social conditions Murray cites. In 1960, nearly two-thirds of households in the lowest-income one-fifth of the population were headed by persons who worked.[18] But by 1991 this work effort had declined by about 50%, with only one-third of household heads in the bottom 20% in income working, and only 11% working full-time, year round.[19]

This was not a matter of the poor not being able to find work. As we discuss in Chapter 6, while the economy was chaotic during the 1970s, during the 1980s and 1990s America enjoyed a historic economic boom creating millions of jobs. The proof is in the pudding, or in how people actually voted with their feet. Millions of illegal aliens surged across the border to gain those jobs and participate in America's economic golden age, with the unemployment rate collapsing into insignificance by the end of the 1990s.

With the government offering such generous and wide-ranging benefits, from housing to medical care to food stamps to outright cash, and many others, to those with low incomes or who are not working at all, naturally many choose to reduce or eliminate their work effort and take the free benefits. Incentivewise, it is as if the government is generously paying people not to work and to have low incomes. To distinguish this from other perverse incentives of welfare, I call this the "whirlpool effect," as it sucks the poor and low-income down deeper into long-term poverty.

A seminal study by the federal government in the 1970s further confirms this argument. Under the experiment, the government provided special, even more generous packages of welfare benefits to groups of beneficiaries in Seattle and Denver. The welfare packages basically included everything more liberal policy makers could hope for, effectively providing a generous guaranteed income. Conducted from 1971 to 1978, the effort became known as the Seattle-Denver Income Maintenance Experiment, or "SIME/DIME."

The dramatic bottom-line result: for every $1 of extra welfare given to low-income persons, they reduced their labor and earnings by 80 cents.[20] No wonder the War on Poverty failed!

The Poverty Trap

Welfare benefits from the different benefit programs typically phase out at 150–200% of the poverty level, affecting about one-third of the workforce. This raises another work disincentive problem, labeled by Art Laffer and Steve Moore as the poverty trap.[21] As welfare is phased out as income rises, the loss of welfare benefits is economically the same as a tax on the rising earnings. Take the example of someone suffering in poverty who receives $12,000 a year in welfare benefits. Suppose she gets the opportunity for a new job earning $16,000 a year. But if she loses 50 cents in welfare benefits for every dollar earned, that is like a 50% tax effectively taking away $8,000 of the earnings from work. The payroll tax will take another 7.65% of the earnings, federal income taxes another 10% on the margin, and state income taxes roughly another 5% on the margin on average. That leaves an effective marginal tax rate of 72.65%, leaving little incentive for the poor to work.

Laffer and Moore write,

Needs tests, means tests, and income tests exclude people [from welfare] as their incomes progressively increase, ensuring that funds are not squandered on those who are less in need. While "needs" tests may be rationalized on both moral and budgetary grounds, when combined with payroll and income taxes, the phased reduction of welfare benefits has meant that spendable income actually rises very little as gross wages increase, and for some income thresholds, spendable income (total spending power) actually declines as wages increase.[22]

The reality of the poverty trap is actually worse than suggested above. In a pathbreaking paper in 1983, Laffer examined the total effect of all the needs tests and taxes affecting an inner-city family of four on welfare in Los Angeles.[23] His discovery:

What was clear from this analysis is that marginal tax rates for inner city inhabitants were prohibitively high—in some cases, the poorest people actually faced the highest marginal tax rates of all income groups. Over the entire range from no wages to wages of $1,300 per month, the family in my analysis faced marginal tax rates (net increases in spendable income) that ranged from a low of 53% (a poor family gained only $47 in spendable income when its gross monthly wages increased from $0 to $100) to a high of 314% (a poor family lost $214 in spendable income when its gross monthly wages increased from $1,000 to $1,100 a month).[24]

A 1996 Urban Institute study by Linda Ginnarelli and Eugene Steuerle on the same issue similarly found that the poor faced effective marginal tax rates of 70–101%.[25] The authors wrote, "A significant portion of the population faces tax rates of 100 percent or more for work at a full-time minimum wage job or for increasing their work effort beyond some minimal level. The net impact of this system, in our view, is pernicious."[26]

Laffer and Moore also note the blog of economics professor Jeff Frankel of Harvard University's Kennedy School of Government, recounting the concrete story of a single mother:

She had moved from a $25,000 a year job to a $35,000 a year job, and suddenly she couldn't make ends meet any more. . . . She really did come out behind by several hundred dollars a month. She lost free health insurance and instead had to pay $230 a month for her employer-provided health insurance. Her rent associated with her section 8 voucher went up by 30% of the income gain (which is the rule). She lost the ($280 a month) subsidized child care voucher she had for after school child care for her child. She lost around $1600 a year of the EITC. She paid payroll tax on the additional income. Finally, the new job was in Boston, and she lived in a suburb. So now she has $300 a month of additional gas and parking charges.[27]

The National Center for Children in Poverty similarly reported the financial incentives faced by Becky Evans, a single mother with two children living in Philadelphia:

Even with the help of government work supports, Becky can't cover her family's basic expenses until her earnings reach about $23,000. . . . She can almost make ends meet at about $19,000 in earnings, but by $20,000, her family is no longer eligible for food stamps and falls farther behind. If her earnings increase beyond $23,000, Becky will have a small cushion in her budget that could be used to cover an emergency. But if her income reaches $36,000, she will lose her child care subsidy. Subsequent earnings gains will be reduced as her children lose their health insurance, and Becky begins to pay premiums. Becky's earnings will have to increase to $40,000 before she breaks even again. The bottom line is that Becky's family is no better off financially if she earns $40,000 than if she earns $23,000.[28]

As indicated above, these work disincentives of the poverty trap spread throughout the bottom one-third of the workforce, below 200% of the poverty line, which makes it a big problem. But if we try to counter it by phasing out welfare benefits more slowly, reducing the effective marginal tax rate, that would spread the remaining work disincentives (the above whirlpool effect and the remaining poverty trap effective tax), and the dependency and spending burden of welfare, to higher and higher income levels, accounting for more and more of the population. Indeed, that would spread welfare dependency well into the middle class. The reforms discussed below will explain how to address this problem successfully.

The work disincentives of welfare spread their devastating effects throughout entire low-income and minority communities, like a tornado growing in force. As more and more people in a poor neighborhood languish with little or no work, the entire local culture begins to change. Daily work is no longer the expected social norm. Extended periods hanging around the neighborhood neither working nor going to school become more and more socially acceptable, reinforcing the counterproductive incentive effects.

Idleness is the devil's playground, so the ancient wisdom says. With productive activity not making any economic sense because of the work disincentives of the welfare plantation, ultimately counterproductive social activities proliferate. The resulting alcohol and drug abuse, recreational sex, illegitimacy, and family breakup that Murray notes become the new, expected social norms. Crime, a tax-free activity, becomes the natural outlet for the more enterprising, otherwise idle, young males, promoting a spreading culture of violence. The end result is the culture of poverty, a self-reinforcing, vicious downward spiral.

In the Middle Ages, the endless quest was the search for the Holy Grail. In modern America, the equivalent is the quest for "the root causes of poverty." One of the two root causes of poverty: nonwork. As the discussion above shows, this nonwork results from the counterproductive incentives of our vast welfare empire itself. Before this chapter is done, we will review reforms that will effectively eliminate those perverse incentives while maintaining a fully adequate safety net for the poor, hence eliminating real poverty. In other words, we will propose a reform "surge" that will reverse our fortunes and finally win the War on Poverty.

Incentives for Family Breakup and Illegitimacy

Prior to the War on Poverty, black families remained intact, and the overwhelming majority of black babies were born to two-parent families. But coinciding with the War on Poverty, the black illegitimacy rate soared from 28% in 1965, to 49% in 1975, to 65% in 1990, to about 70% in 1995, where it remains today.[29]

This effect has not been limited to blacks. Among whites, illegitimacy soared from 3% in 1965, to 11% in 1980, 21% in 1990, 25% in 1995, and 28% today.[30] Among white high school dropouts, the illegitimacy rate is 48%. Among Americans overall, the illegitimacy rate has soared from 7% when the War on Poverty began to 40% today.[31] Basically, families and legitimacy among the lower-income population have been obliterated since the start of the War on Poverty.

Out-of-wedlock births and single-parent families in turn have very negative effects on children in general. A wealth of data, research, and studies now show the following:[32]

- Children from single-parent homes on average have lower educational achievement, perform poorly on standardized tests, and even score lower IQs. They are also three times more likely to fail and repeat a year in grade school and are twice as likely to drop out of school altogether.
- Children from single-parent families are more likely to use drugs and to commit suicide.
- These children are also two to three times more likely to experience mental illness or other psychiatric disorders. Around 80% of children admitted to psychiatric hospitals come from single-parent homes. These children are also more likely to exhibit behavioral problems such as hyperactivity, antisocial behavior, and anxiety.
- White women raised in single-parent families are 165% more likely to bear children out of wedlock themselves, and 111%

more likely to have children as teenagers. They are also 92% more likely to get divorced. Similar effects are found for black women.

• Children raised by never-married mothers are 2.5 times more likely to be sexually active as teenagers. Boys from single-parent homes are twice as likely to father a child out of wedlock.

Illegitimacy is also a major cause of crime. Studies show that 75% of adolescent murderers, 70% of juvenile delinquents in state reform institutions, 60% of repeat rapists, and most gang members come from single-parent homes.[33] Young black men raised in single-parent families are twice as likely as black men from two-parent families to commit crimes, and three times as likely if they come from a neighborhood with many single-parent families.[34] A seminal study published in the *Journal of Research in Crime and Delinquencies* found that crime in a community was closely correlated with the percentage of single-parent families living there, rather than race or poverty.[35]

Such illegitimacy is the second key cause of poverty, in addition to nonwork. The poverty rate for female-headed households with children is 44.5%, compared to 7.8% for married couples with children. The poverty rate for married black Americans is only 11.4%, while the rate for black female-headed households is 53.9%. Moreover, it is primarily these single-parent families that remain poor and dependent on welfare for the long term. Indeed, single-parent families perpetuate poverty into the next generation. Children raised in single-parent families are seven times more likely to become welfare recipients as adults. The negative effects on children from single-parent families, and crime resulting from illegitimacy, also perpetuate poverty over the long term. As Rector again explains, "If poor women who give birth outside of marriage were married to the fathers of their children, two-thirds would immediately be lifted out of poverty. Roughly 80 percent of all long-term poverty occurs in single-parent homes."[36]

Family breakup and illegitimacy are again the natural result of the incentives created by our massive, overgrown welfare empire. Most welfare benefits are restricted to families with children. If you are a nonelderly adult in America without children, you are pretty much expected to support yourself. That is a sound principle. But it means that having a baby is the gateway to a generous package of government benefits.

Moreover, if the mother is married to a man who earns a significant income, then the benefits are lost. Indeed, if the mother is married to a man who is not working, but the government requires him to take available work before benefits are paid, then the benefits will be lost in any event, whether he refuses to work, or if he works and earns an income that eliminates benefits.

Once again, it is as if the government is paying women to have children out of wedlock. As Rector aptly puts it, "Welfare . . . converts the low-income working husband from a necessary breadwinner into a net financial handicap. It transformed marriage from a legal institution designed to protect and nurture children into an institution that financially penalizes nearly all low-income parents who enter into it."[37]

But the impact of welfare in causing illegitimacy is even more insidious than this. Basically, it makes illegitimacy economically feasible. Young women do not need to worry about who will support their children. If they have a baby out of wedlock, the government will support them. So they can go ahead and have children at a young age without marriage or developed income-producing skills of their own. Indeed, if they do so they get their own household and separate source of income, courtesy of the government, a very appealing package for a teenager.

Similarly, young men know they can exercise their sexual inclinations and father children without any financial or other responsibility. They know they need not support the children they produce. Moreover, with the above incentives for young women, welfare essentially provides these young men with willing female partners.

President Clinton recognized this problem in a national TV interview in 1993:

I once polled a hundred children in an alternative school in Atlanta, many of whom had been babies born out-of-wedlock. And I said if we didn't give any AFDC to people . . . after they had their first child, how many of you think it would reduce the number of out-of-wedlock births? Over 80% of the kids raised their hands.[38]

Apparently, low-income children understand the above analysis, even if many so-called liberals supposedly don't.

Indeed, even the "liberal lion," the late senator Ted Kennedy, recognized the problem. He said at the annual conference of the Michigan NAACP in Detroit in 1978:

> We go to a young girl, who's now 18 or 16 or even younger and this is what we say, "abandon all of your hopes, your schools will not teach you, you will not learn to read or write, you will never have a decent job, you will live in the neighborhoods of endless unemployment and poverty with drugs and violence," but then we say to this child, "wait, there is a way, one way, you can be somebody to someone, that will give you an apartment and furniture to fill it; we will give you a TV set, and telephone, we will give you clothing and cheap food and free medical care and some spending money besides, and in turn you only have to do one thing, that is go out there and have a baby."[39]

These effects were documented in the SIME/DIME experiments. As Robert Carleson, the senior welfare aide to Ronald Reagan both when the latter was governor of California and when he was president, reports,

> [T]he study found a higher rate of marital collapse for families with guaranteed income. The results showed that when families received guaranteed income at 90% of the poverty level, there was a 43% increase in black family dissolution and a 63% increase in white family dissolution. At 125% of the poverty level, the black family dissolution rate showed a 73% increase while for white families dissolution increased at a rate of 40%.[40]

These incentives for family breakup and illegitimacy reinforce the cultural trends discussed above. They further contribute to the rise of the poverty culture of drug and alcohol abuse, illegitimacy, crime, violence, and youth gangs, as young single males are more likely to engage in all of these activities. The proliferation of fatherless children from single-mother homes dominating poor neighbors dumps fuel on this social bonfire, as such children are more likely to engage in all of these counterproductive activities as well. And the rise of this culture of socially counterproductive activities just reinforces such activities, as everybody in the neighborhood is doing it, and such activities become the new social norm. Is this a picture of social dysfunction you recognize?[41]

So, besides costing the taxpayers a fortune, welfare has produced disastrous results among the low-income population, promoting the collapse of work and family, and perpetuating rather than ending poverty as a result. America is going into bankruptcy for this? There is a better way.

WELFARE REFORM BEGINS

The Origins of Welfare Reform

The process of welfare reform began in California under Governor Ronald Reagan, who was elected in 1966 and then reelected in 1970 on a platform including opposition to the then-exploding welfare system. Right after his reelection, Reagan appointed his deputy director of the California Department of Public Works, a former career city manager named Robert Carleson, to be his director of the California Department of Social Welfare.[42] Carleson developed the first serious effort to reform the War on Poverty welfare programs.

Over the previous ten years, the welfare rolls in California had almost quadrupled from 600,000 to over 2.2 million people, and the available funds were spread so thin that benefit payments for the truly needy were inadequate.[43] The first reform goal was to restrict welfare benefits to those who were actually poor, the "truly needy," as Carleson called them. Liberals had argued for phasing out welfare eligibility slowly as income of the recipient rose, to reduce the disincentives and effective tax of the poverty trap on increasing work and income. But this had little impact in reducing the downward draft of welfare on the poor, resulting from the work disincentives due to the government providing free income to those not working, or the whirlpool effect, as discussed above. Rather, it just drew more and more people above poverty into the perverse disincentives of welfare, because they could still qualify for some assistance at higher income levels as a result, which greatly increased costs for taxpayers. Reagan and Carleson reduced welfare rolls substantially first in California in the early 1970s, and then nationally in the early 1980s, by restricting welfare more tightly to those who were actually poor. At the same time, they actually increased benefits for the neediest.

Their second goal was "workfare," but this was more difficult to achieve. Reagan and Carleson wanted to require that if a welfare recipient could not find a private sector job, he or she would have to work in community service for a number of hours each week sufficient to "earn" their benefits at an implicit wage rate roughly equivalent to the minimum wage. They rightly reasoned that requiring work for welfare would greatly reduce both the nonwork and illegitimacy incentives of welfare, as recipients would now have to work in any event.

Reagan and Carleson made some headway with workfare innovations in California, but federal law prevented them from adopting the full program. After Reagan became president (I worked directly for Carleson in the White House Office of Policy Development at the time), they faced a roadblock in the Democrat-controlled House in getting the necessary changes in federal law to implement workfare nationwide. Finally, in 1987, Reagan won changes that would allow states to experiment with a broad range of work requirements and other welfare innovations, with a federally granted waiver of traditional program requirements.

Many conservatives did not expect this bill to be effective at first. But it helped to spawn a welfare revolution among the states, with the most comprehensive and successful reforms achieved by Governor Tommy Thompson in Wisconsin, with the assistance of his welfare-policy aide, Jason Turner, who later became the highly effective welfare commissioner for New York City under Mayor Guiliani. Thompson and Turner were basically able to finally implement the full workfare plan of Reagan and Carleson. The Thompson reformers were granted a waiver for the plan by President George H. W. Bush's Department of Health and Human Services, in probably the best domestic policy move of the entire administration of Bush 41.

The key to the Thompson reforms was a true work requirement for those on welfare, the first that had ever been fully implemented. Recipients who could not find private sector jobs were required to do community service work. If the recipient did not work the required hours, the AFDC and food stamp benefits for that recipient's family were reduced proportionately. If the recipient did not work at all, then no AFDC or food stamp benefits would be paid at all for the recipient's family.

Thompson and Turner added a further innovative component. To ensure incentives for the state's welfare bureaucracy to fully and faithfully implement the reforms, funding for each local welfare office was dependent on the office's success in getting recipients to work. Moreover, the Thompson reforms provided that offices that proved unable to get recipients to work would lose their own workload, to be contracted out to private entities. With these incentives, the Wisconsin welfare bureaucracy implemented the reforms with startling efficiency and enthusiasm.

The results of the Thompson reforms were truly dramatic. The AFDC caseload in Wisconsin declined a shocking 81%. In the state outside Milwaukee, the caseload declined 95%. Even in inner-city Milwaukee, welfare cases dropped 60%.

The Wisconsin reforms began to spread to other states across the country to varying degrees. Idaho and Wyoming achieved caseload reductions of 68%. Alabama, Mississippi, and New Mexico cut their caseloads in half. Nationwide, caseloads for the AFDC program dropped by one-fourth in the period from September 1995 to September 1997.

Welfare Reform Goes National

By 1996, welfare reform was ready to go national. House Speaker Newt Gingrich and Representative Clay Shaw (R-FL), chairman of the Welfare Subcommittee of the House Ways and Means Committee, led the effort to achieve the ultimate welfare reform goal of Reagan and Carleson: block grants back to the states.[44] President Clinton vetoed the reforms twice, but just before the 1996 election he signed the bill, which the Republican Congress had passed for a third time.

The legislation focused on the old Aid to Families with Dependent Children (AFDC) program, which was originally adopted in the 1930s as a central component of the New Deal. That program primarily paid cash to single mothers with children, embodying all of the perverse incentives of welfare. Federal funding for the program was based on a matching formula, with the federal government giving more to each state the more it spent on the program. Most states got a federal dollar for each dollar they spent, but some got as much as four federal dollars for every state dollar, depending on average incomes in the state. This created another whole level of counterproductive incentives, effectively paying the states to spend more. In response, they did, signing up more and more welfare recipients for the program in good economic times and bad, thereby bringing more federal funds to their states. Those who tried to reduce welfare spending in their states, like Governor Reagan in California, were fought with the argument that they would be losing federal funds for their state.

Under the reform legislation, the share of federal spending on this program was returned to each state in a "block grant" to be used in a new program designed by the state based on mandatory work for the able-bodied. The key is that the block grant is finite, not matching, so it does not vary with the amount the state spends. If the state spends more, it must pay for the extra costs itself. If the state spends less, it can keep the savings. This reverses the counterproductive incentives of the old system, with positive incentives to weigh costs against benefits.

To give the states broad flexibility in designing the new replacement program, the federal eligibility standards and benefit level requirements of the old AFDC program were repealed. That entailed, indeed, repealing the entitlement status of AFDC, as states could not be free to redesign their programs if their citizens were entitled to coverage and benefits as specified in federal standards. States were explicitly authorized to use program funding for child care so that parents could work, and for wage supplements for those who had moved into private employment. The one remaining condition of federal funding is that the new state programs were mandated to require work as a condition of receiving cash benefits. To reflect this new emphasis on work rather than extended dependency, the name of the program was changed to Temporary Assistance for Needy Families (TANF).

The reform was bitterly opposed by the liberal welfare establishment. Their view was well expressed by Senator Daniel Patrick Moynihan, of the Urban Institute, and others who predicted that the reforms would produce a "race to the bottom" among the states, and that within a year a million children would be subject to starvation.[45]

But quite to the contrary, the reform was shockingly successful, exceeding even the predictions of its most ardent supporters. The old AFDC rolls were reduced by two-thirds nationwide, from a high of 14.2 million in 1993, the year before the state waiver experiments began to have their effect, to 4.6 million in 2006.[46] The rolls were reduced even more in states that pushed work most aggressively: Wyoming (97%), Idaho (90%), Florida (89%), Louisiana (89%), Illinois (89%), Georgia (89%), North Carolina (87%), Oklahoma (85%), Wisconsin (84%), Texas (84%), Mississippi (84%).[47] By 2006, the percent of the population receiving TANF cash welfare was down to 0.1% in Wyoming, 0.2% in Idaho, 0.5% in Florida, 0.6% in Georgia, Louisiana, North Carolina, and Oklahoma, and 0.7% in Arkansas, Colorado, Illinois, Nevada, Texas, and Wisconsin.[48]

Ron Haskins of the Brookings Institution reports in his 2006 book evaluating the 1996 welfare reforms, *Work Over Welfare*, "the number of families receiving cash welfare is now the lowest . . . since 1969, and the percentage of children on welfare is lower than it has been since 1966."[49] Indeed, the percentage of American children on AFDC/TANF was reduced from 14.1% in 1994 to 4.7% in 2006.[50]

Moreover, in addition to those who left the AFDC/TANF rolls for work, or for marriage to a working husband, of those adult parents still receiving assistance from the program, over 22% were working by 2006, up from 6.6% in 1988.[51] That at least reduced their need for assistance.

As a result, total federal and state spending on TANF by 2006 was nearly 10% below the peak AFDC spending in 1995.[52] That reduction could and should have been a lot more, given the reduction in caseloads. But political compromises in the original legislation limited both federal and state spending reductions. Note, however, that total AFDC spending had increased by 67% in just eight years, from 1987 to 1995.[53] So total spending on the program was effectively reduced by close to half of what it would have been by 2006, eleven years later, under the old system at prior trends. Moreover, in real dollars, after adjusting for inflation, total TANF spending by 2006 was down 31% from AFDC spending in 1995, and down by more than half of what it would have been under the old system.[54]

Child care funding for low-income working parents has become a central component of the program, accounting for 19% of its expenditures.[55] That is further helping to maximize work and minimize dependency.

Requiring able-bodied recipients to work for their benefits eliminated the old welfare work disincentives, promoting work among recipients. But probably even more important were the reversed incentives for state administrators. With the state now paying all added costs, and gaining the savings, the administrative focus changed dramatically to getting recipients out to work.

As a result, Haskins reports, "from 1993 to 2000 the portion of single mothers who were employed grew from 58% to nearly 75%, an increase of almost 30%," and "employment among never married mothers, most of whom join the welfare ranks within a year or two of giving birth, grew from 44% to 66%," an increase of 50%.[56] Haskins adds, "Before 1996 never married mothers were the ones most likely to be school dropouts, to go on welfare, and to stay on welfare for a decade or more."[57]

Because of all this renewed work effort, the total income of these low-income families formerly on welfare increased by about 25% over this period. Haskins further reports,

> Between 1994 and 2000, child poverty fell every year and reached levels not seen since 1978. In addition, by 2000 the poverty rate of black children was the lowest it had ever been. The percentage of families in deep poverty, defined as half the poverty level . . . also declined until 2000, falling about 35% during the period.[58]

This decline in poverty "was widespread across demographic groups," and "the decline was caused by increased employment and earnings of female headed families."[59] Based on total income, poverty among these female-headed households declined by one-third, which meant that nearly 4.2 million single mothers and children climbed out of poverty. Haskins cites a study by the liberal Isabel Sawhill of the Urban Institute and Paul Jargowsky, concluding,

> So great was the decline in poverty that the number of neighborhoods with concentrated poverty fell precipitously, as did the

number of neighborhoods classified as underclass because of the concentration of poverty and the high frequency of problems such as school dropout, female headed families, welfare dependency, and labor force dropout by adult males.[60]

The Child and Youth Well-Being Index, published each year by Ken Land of Duke University, and based on twenty-eight key indicators of child well-being, increased by 30 percentage points from 1995 to 2005.[61] Haskins concludes:

> The pattern is clear: earnings up, welfare down. This is the very definition of reducing welfare dependency. Most low income mothers heading families appear to be financially better off because the mothers earn more money than they received from welfare. Taxpayers continue making a contribution to these families through the EITC and other work support programs, but the families earn a majority of their income. This explosion of employment and earnings constitutes an enormous achievement for the mothers themselves and for the nation's social policy.[62]

Consequently, the new reformed program is actually better for the poor, as it draws them into work and out of poverty. At the same time, it is better for taxpayers as well, saving huge sums particularly as compared to the spending if the regular annual increases had continued.

WINNING THE WAR ON POVERTY

There was only one big problem with the 1996 AFDC reforms. They reformed only one program, the old New Deal AFDC. The federal government operates another 184 means-tested welfare programs. The same wildly successful reforms to AFDC can and should be extended to every one of these federal programs as well. The suggestion that all these programs could be reformed, just as AFDC was in 1996, came to me through the files of Ron Haskins, who was the chief of staff for Shaw's Welfare Subcommittee.

This would effectively amount to sending welfare back to the states, but with continued major federal assistance in financing. As Reagan's welfare guru, Carleson, writes,

> Until President Lyndon Johnson sought to establish his Great Society, welfare in America was primarily a state, local, and private responsibility. Federal spending was modest. But following Washington's takeover of welfare during the 1960s War on Poverty, government welfare spending soared.[63]

With the states in charge, each state would have the flexibility to structure their welfare systems to suit the needs and circumstances of their particular state. The administrative savings alone from this flexibility in reorganizing the spending from these 185 programs would be quite substantial. State control would also allow experimentation among the states to try different reform ideas, with real-world results proving what works and what doesn't. Economic and political competition among the states would then lead them to adopt what has proved to work best.

The best estimate of the total current cost of these 185 means-tested welfare programs, federal and state, is the above-cited $10.3 trillion for the period 2009 to 2018. The states would enjoy control over this entire cauldron of money to finance an entirely new, redesigned welfare system for each state. The resulting savings would be on a par overall with the savings from the 1996 AFDC reforms, though with the major differences among these programs, the results will not be the same for each. I recommend below how the states should use their new powers to redesign the new welfare system. For the reasons I explain, I estimate that the ultimate savings would be at least half, or $5 trillion over the first full ten years, maybe more. This new system as recommended would eliminate poverty in America, finally winning the War on Poverty.

This would also achieve the ultimate dream of Reagan and Carleson in restoring the original federalism and state control over welfare. It follows the spirit of the new Tea Party movement across the country in restoring power to the states and gaining control over government spending, deficits, and debt. But in effectively eliminating poverty in

America, and finally winning the War on Poverty, it would also fulfill the ultimate dream of the Kennedy brothers, Lyndon Johnson, Hubert Humphrey, and the American liberal/left as a whole.

The biggest of the programs is Medicaid; in Chapter 4 we discussed block-granting that program back to the states. Besides TANF, the next biggest programs are food stamps and the collection of federal housing assistance programs.

Ideally, all of the 185 programs would be block-granted back to the states, not individually, but in one big pot, with the states free to use the money for assistance to the poor as they each deem best and most effective. Practically, this would involve a number of separate bills, coordinated to work together. One for Medicaid, big enough for its own bill, and others perhaps grouped in their own bills. But the federal funding for each would be provided through finite block grants, not with matching federal funding formulas giving more money to each state the more the state spends. To the extent the state spends more on its redesigned welfare system, the state would pay for it out of its own pocket (meaning the pockets of its taxpayers). To the extent the state spends less, it can keep the money for other uses.

Just what these other uses are would be the subject of some debate. Undoubtedly, the legislation would include some maintenance of effort (MOE) requirement on the states requiring them to maintain some level of state spending on assistance for the poor out of the state's own funds. The 1996 legislation included an MOE of 75% of previous state spending on AFDC. Given the enormous potential savings from the reforms, it should not be higher than that, and should probably be lower. The truth is that the more discretion the states are allowed, the more efficient and effective the ultimate results will be. As we will see in Chapter 8, it may be that flooding some low-income, crime-ridden communities with police protection would be the most effective antipoverty initiative of all.

The federal funding for these 185 programs should be apportioned among the states utilizing current federal funding formulas to the extent possible. That reflects political compromises already reached. The reform will be endangered only by reopening this most political of all battles. Federal requirements on the use of these federal funds by the states should be limited to just three. First, they must be used to assist poor and low-income families. Second, they must be used without discrimination, in accordance with federal civil rights laws. Third, the assistance must be provided in return for work, except in the case of the disabled, or retired seniors who should no longer be expected to work. As Carleson advises, "Assistance could only be provided in return for work from the able-bodied adults in the family, and the states would be free to carry this out."[64] He further explains, "Able-bodied people must work first in order to receive any welfare benefit; benefits will be earned before the money flows."[65]

What could the states do with all this new power and control over the funds? The fundamental concept in designing a new welfare system is to focus on the basic incentives. All the perverse, counterproductive incentives for nonwork, family breakup, and illegitimacy need to be eliminated, and replaced with positive, pro-growth incentives for work, savings, investment, entrepreneurship, and prosperity. Accompanying policies to break down any barriers to such opportunities would be mutually reinforcing; most of them are already in place thanks to good work coming mostly from the liberal/left over the years (though with critical support from Republicans and conservatives at times, such as with the 1964 Civil Rights Act, which would not have passed without Republican support).

The basic strategy is to rely on modern labor markets as much as possible to provide essential income support for the basic needs of the poor and lower-income families. That in turn would minimize the burden on taxpayers. With incentives to inspire the low-income population to work, that population would join in contributing to a booming economy.

Let me outline a new welfare system that would do that. But I need to emphasize that this new welfare system would be at the discretion of the states. It would not be required or even discussed in the federal legislation, which only needs to be structured so that states would have the power to adopt this system if they chose to do so. Remember as well that as Charles Murray and Robert Rector have shown, we already spend far more than enough on our welfare system across the nation to lift every American out of poverty. So there is tremendous scope for doing far more with far less. Indeed, Murray has argued that we could achieve enormous savings by just cashing out all current welfare programs and granting all of the poor enough cash to lift them out of poverty. But that free cash grant would produce its own perverse incentives and would be unfair to taxpayers. The system below effectively cashes out the current system, but only in return for work from the able-bodied.

The foundation of this new welfare system would be a guaranteed offer of work for the able-bodied. Those who reported to their local welfare office before 9 a.m. would be guaranteed a work assignment somewhere paying the minimum wage in cash for a day's work, eight hours. A private job assignment would be the top priority. But if that were not available for that day, the applicant would be assigned to some government-directed and financed activity, serving the community in some way, whether city, county, or state. The worker would be paid in cash at the end of the day. Those who needed more would come back the next day.

The government would provide free day care for those with small children who desired it. While the children were there, Medicaid-financed doctors would be available to examine and treat them if necessary.

For those who come back regularly, the welfare office would find them a private job assignment. Organizing local employers to offer such jobs would be a function for private charitable efforts, as well as the welfare administrators. In some prosperous local economies, employers could be ready and available to absorb everyone who shows up needing work. Organizing that could be a function of the chamber of commerce and other local business groups, as well as local church organizations. The more people and groups involved in this, the better for everyone. This smacks of real social solidarity.

Those who work a minimum number of hours each month would get a Medicaid voucher sufficient to purchase basic private health insurance. Those who work for a continued period establishing a regular work history would be eligible for new housing assistance focused on help in purchasing a home.

The federal minimum wage is now $7.25 an hour. These workers would receive the Earned Income Tax Credit (EITC) and the Child Tax Credit under current federal tax laws, or if those are included in the block grants back to the states, under the new system's welfare policies.

The EITC is now worth $3,000 for one child, $5,000 for two children, and $457 with no children. The Child Tax Credit is an additional $1,000 per child. These tax credits are refundable, which means the recipient gets these amounts regardless of tax liability. Then there is the value of the child care and the health insurance.

A single mother alone with two children would be guaranteed $21,500 in cash income under this system for full-time work, year round, plus child care and health insurance. That includes $14,500 in wages for the work, plus $5,000 from the EITC, and $2,000 from the Child Tax Credit. That is enough to take the family out of poverty. But note that every child comes with a father somewhere, and under this system fathers would no longer have an excuse to not help provide for their children. The family unit as a whole, therefore—father, mother, and two children—would be guaranteed cash income of $36,000, again plus child care and health insurance, but only in return for work of course.[66] That is quite adequate as a minimum safety net.

The state can choose to provide additional assistance for transportation if it deems that desirable. It can even provide additional assistance for education and training. But that should not be allowed to become an excuse for extended nonwork, which is a proven problem with such programs. Preferably, that education and training could occur at night, with child care if necessary. The state could choose as well to provide additional wage supplements to the extent it thinks that is necessary.

Consider how this system transforms all of the perverse incentives of the current welfare system into incentives for positive, productive actions. The incentives for family breakup and illegitimacy are eliminated entirely. No free benefits are handed out any longer for bearing a child out of wedlock. If the mother has a child without a husband, then the mother must go to work to support the child. Even the Child Tax Credit can and should be tied to work, as the EITC is, if it is included in the block grants back to the states, as it should be.

Moreover, there is nothing to be gained under this system by avoiding marriage or by couples splitting up. No benefits are provided to the mother for being unmarried. A government welfare check does not become a substitute for a working husband. If the father has to work to support himself anyway, and will be charged for child support, then he has no economic incentive to stay away from the family, either. So this system does not discourage marriage or encourage family breakup.

To the contrary, since living together will reduce living expenses that the couple will have to work to pay for in any event, the incentives are for family unification rather than family breakup. Couples staying together can also help each other by sharing the necessary work. Indeed, a single mother can avoid work altogether by marrying a working husband. So the system provides reinforcing economic incentives for marriage search. Alternatively, a single mother may return to live with her own parents to reduce living expenses and the need to work to pay for them. This is another form of family reunification, which also reduces the dependency burden on taxpayers.

The incentives for nonwork are reversed as well. There is nothing to be gained under this system by not working. No free benefits are passed out to those who choose not to work. So there is no whirlpool work disincentive. Rather, the incentive is to take whatever private sector job is available, since the able-bodied will have to work to support themselves in any event, and in the private sector the worker will gain skills, raises, promotions, and new opportunities over time. Instead of taxpayers paying the bottom 20% of income earners not to work, employers would be paying them to work.

Moreover, this system automatically shuts down the gaming that currently results when a welfare recipient takes an unreported job off the books and continues to draw benefits. That is because anyone who already has a job won't be free to even show up for the day jobs in the new system. (Unless their other job is at night, in which case, more power to them; we don't need to devote resources to counter such "excessive" work.) So the numbers showing up for the guaranteed day jobs would be sharply constrained, limited to those who have truly fallen on desperate times.

Moreover, even their need is likely to be short-term, as the incentive is for them to take available private sector jobs that do open up. People are not going to show up for these day jobs for years in a row, as many have done for free welfare.

In addition, for those who do show up, their public support will be minimized in any event, as the state agency finds them private employment that will provide the bulk of their support in place of the taxpayers.

That private employment will grow into or lead to permanent employment, bringing the worker out of public assistance with wage gains due to experience, learned skills, promotions, and the new opportunities that work will lead to over time.

The resulting incentives would reduce dependency, and the burden on taxpayers, in other ways, too. Under the current free welfare system, working at modest-income jobs makes a man economically harmful to his low-income family, and the free welfare becomes an economic substitute for husbands. It's not surprising, then, that young men in low-income communities lose interest in work. But under the new system, based on work, employment makes a man more desirable to the opposite sex, as he becomes a means for his lady to avoid otherwise necessary work. The incentive consequently reverses to promote work.

These incentive effects add up to a changing culture. Everybody in the neighborhood, except perhaps women supported by working men, is now getting up early every morning to go to work. That becomes reestablished as the social norm. Moreover, having babies without husbands, and family breakup, is now recognized by everyone as a costly practice not to be emulated. Having children only after marriage will be recognized as the smart practice. These new cultural realities will further encourage socially productive choices and actions.

This guaranteed offer of work will produce much better results than the old workfare model, where benefits calculated under some government formula are paid first, and then the bureaucrats are supposed to chase after the beneficiaries to make them work a sufficient number of hours to work off the benefit at the minimum wage. Once the benefits are already paid, the recipients have no incentive to work, and they come up with endless imaginative excuses as to why they cannot. Penalties to enforce the work requirement become socially difficult to enforce, and are too easily characterized as mean impositions on needy people.

With work first and payment later in return, this intractable situation is reversed. The beneficiaries have every incentive to work, and will be eager to do so, without penalty or enforced requirement. If they decide not to work, then that is their choice. The taxpayers lose nothing as a result. Of course, low-income parents are under the same legal obligation to provide for their children as everyone else. If they fail to do so, with a guaranteed offer of work always waiting for them, that is sanctionable neglect.

Nevertheless, the new system would still retain some work disincentives. These arise from the supplemental benefits in addition to the actual wages earned by working. The child care, the health insurance, even the wage supplements, which must be phased out at income levels above the minimum wage or else be provided to everyone, would still result in an effective poverty trap tax. Only a continuing effective Child Tax Credit that is provided to everyone in return for work, regardless of income, would not have this effect, because it would not be phased out at higher income levels.

This effective poverty trap tax will not prevent people from working under this system, because they must work to get benefits in any event. It will not prevent them from taking available private sector jobs, as long as the same benefits are available at the same income levels for the private sector jobs as for working at guaranteed public sector work, as they should be to avoid effectively discouraging private sector work. The only counterproductive effect of these disincentives would be to slow increased work effort and acquisition of increased productive skills over the income ranges at which the phaseouts apply, and hence slow the rate at which people grow out of receiving these additional benefits. That in turn would slow down some of the cost savings that might otherwise result from the reform.

Yet adding up the positive effects of all the reversed disincentives resulting from the reform indicates a dramatic potential for reduced costs and burdens on taxpayers. As discussed above, only a fraction of the ablebodied receiving benefits under the current system would show up for the guaranteed offer of work. The rest would get private sector jobs, or marry someone with a private sector job. Those who did show up for the guaranteed work would do so for only a short period of time, until they could find a private sector job, and meanwhile even they would be earning their own benefits through productive work, rather than burdening taxpayers. Reduced illegitimacy and family breakup will result in far less social need. The changing cultural environment will reinforce all of these positive effects. The new system would thus cost only a fraction of the current system, saving trillions of dollars over the years.

Even more savings would result from the administrative simplicity of the new system. There would be no need to maintain and investigate eligibility requirements. The incentives would take care of that adequately. If Warren Buffett or Bill Gates wanted to show up for a work assignment before 9 a.m., it would be no big deal. Trying to weed out higher-income people from showing up and working at an assigned day job is not worth the administrative costs. This would also save lower-income people in need of assistance a lot of hassle in dealing with requirements to demonstrate their need.

This new system would categorically end poverty in America. Everyone would have a place to go where they would be assured work in return for a sufficient income to keep them above the poverty line. There may be some who would still choose not to work even though they are capable of doing so. But they should be free to make that choice, as long they do not leave children suffering in neglect as a result. They would still always be backed up by the safety net, and they would have their compensating reasons for making that choice. They may have friends or relatives taking care of their needs, or they may have other arrangements. As long as this is their free choice, it should not be considered real poverty. It should be considered chosen leisure.

Of course, for the disabled who cannot work, or for retirees who should no longer be expected to work, a separate system would provide for their needs. Under the personal account reforms advanced in Chapter 3, every worker would have private disability insurance, or Social Security disability protection if that was their choice. Moreover, seniors would enjoy much higher retirement incomes due to the savings and investment in their personal accounts, minimizing poverty among that age-group. Generous programs should be provided for those who cannot work, or no longer should work, but who would otherwise remain poor. The cost of such programs would not remotely outweigh the valid social need.

Some on the right may complain that this suggested new system smacks too much of the make-work jobs of the 1930s. But they need to recognize that this system would replace a vast welfare state empire costing over $10 trillion over the next ten years, and would cost only a fraction of that, with much better results. In a modern, civilized society, the public is going to politically demand some social safety net for the poor that is more certain than private charity alone. These proposed reforms provide that at tremendous financial and social savings. There is no other politically feasible way to achieve those same savings.

Moreover, some on the left may complain that the poor will be deprived of dignity if they have to work to gain the basic necessities of life. Those with this view believe somehow that we owe everyone a living at taxpayer expense. The great majority of Americans will not share this perverse moral view. It is living at the expense of others, the taxpayers, when you are perfectly capable of providing for yourself, that is undignified.

For a real-world perspective on how the poor would see these proposed reforms, I recommend a fascinating little book, *Scratch Beginnings*, by Adam Shepard. The author recounts his experiences taking on the challenge at age twenty-four of his own social experiment, starting out on the lowest possible rung of the economic ladder to determine if he could rise out of poverty after a year of his best efforts.

He leaves his home in North Carolina with nothing but a tarp, a sleeping bag, an empty gym bag, the clothes on his back, and twenty-five dollars in his pocket. He takes a train to Charleston, South Carolina, a city where he has never been before and doesn't know anybody. His goal is to devote one year to climbing the job ladder to achieve a settled lifestyle. He forgoes using his college education or any family or professional contacts to help himself.

He arrives at nightfall, later than planned, and immediately starts looking for the nearest homeless shelter to spend the night. He finds a shelter run by Crisis Ministries that takes him in, and in the morning he begins working at odd jobs until he can find regular work a couple of weeks later with a moving company. He moonlights on weekends to add to his income, makes friends and contacts that help him find jobs and housing, and advances economically over time.

He receives his first raise in less than five months working for the moving company, to ten dollars an hour. In less than nine months, he earns a second raise to eleven dollars an hour. Moreover, when he moved out of the homeless shelter after three months, delayed by a month because he broke his foot while moving furniture, he moved into a room he rented in a large house in an upscale part of town. It was owned by a friend of a contact he developed working a second job on weekends. A little over a month later, he moved into a two-bedroom duplex with the cousin of one of his coworkers, a run-down place they devoted a weekend to making like new. His share of the $600 per month rent was $325 because he took the master bedroom. After just ten months of steady work, he was living in his own furnished apartment, with his own car, and $5,300 in savings.

His personal experience is illuminating, but so are the stories he tells about the attitudes of the other low-income people he meets on the way. What the book shows is that most real poor people in America would dearly love a safety net based on ensuring them of *work* whenever they need it.

These reforms work because, as Charles Murray and Robert Rector have shown, we are already spending far more than enough to eliminate poverty in America. Replacing the enormously counterproductive incentives of the current system with productive incentives that inspire the lower-income population to work and to establish and maintain intact families would result in enormous savings as compared to the current system, enabling us to categorically eliminate poverty in America, while avoiding national bankruptcy.

CHAPTER 6

THE END OF THE AMERICAN DREAM?

How the Government Caused the Financial Crisis

Since the 16th century, people have been coming to America from the world over. If we were to ask today the question "What is an American?" as American farmer Hector St. John de Crèvecoeur famously did in 1781, we would answer that an American is English . . . or French, or Italian, or African, or Irish, Spanish, German, Polish, Russian, or Greek. An American may also be Indian, Chinese, Japanese, Australian, Asian, or Arab, or Pakistani, or Afghan.

We would answer that an American is Christian, or he could be Jewish, or Buddhist, or Hindu, or Muslim. In fact, there are more Muslims in America than in Mecca or Tehran. The only difference is that in America, Muslims are free to worship as each of them chooses. An American is also free to believe in no religion. For that he will answer only to God, not to the government, nor to armed thugs claiming to speak for God.

Today America is a virtual Noah's Ark among nations, with people from every land, city, and town, every religion, every race, every creed, every nook and cranny around the world. Which leaves the question, why did they come?

And why do they still come? Over deserts, across rivers and oceans, sometimes in dangerous makeshift craft, losing their lives.

Well, it's not for the food stamps, or the public housing, or even Social Security and Medicare. America's world-leading prosperity dates all the way back to the early 18th century. The roots of that prosperity can be seen in the Declaration of Independence, which recognizes the God-given right of each man and woman to pursue happiness. And that is why they came. They came because America has always been the land of freedom and prosperity and opportunity. They came because of the American Dream, that in this nation every man and woman enjoys the freedom and opportunity to rise to achieve their dreams, regardless of family background, class, race, or religion.

Is that over now? Is America just another nation now, like Greece, as President Obama has suggested? In fact, just like Greece? Is the American Dream done? Is that what is meant by the "New Normal"? Or is that just a phrase to provide political cover for the realities of a new socialism, where everyone, as Churchill explained, shares equally in the curses of misery, rather than unequally in the blessings of capitalism?

In previous chapters, we discussed the contours of America's coming bankruptcy, and how to address the causes of that threat with sweeping fundamental reforms that reinforce rather than short-circuit the American Dream, liberating working people, the disadvantaged, and the poor to participate in and enjoy that dream more than ever before. But we can't truly replace entitlement and debt dependency with prosperity independence without restoring traditional robust American prosperity and economic growth. How to do that specifically is the subject of this chapter and the next.

FOUNDATIONS OF PROSPERITY

The foundations of prosperity, and of American prosperity in particular, are not hard to understand. They have been proved over and over throughout history, and around the world, not just in America. Prosperity requires the rule of law, with disputes settled in objective forums applying settled law. It requires secure property rights, so investors can know that their developed and accumulated capital will not be stolen from them. It requires freedom of contract, so that people will be free to exchange and trade what they produce. And that must apply not just between Americans, but between Americans and everyone in the world, to maximize prosperity.

Prosperity also requires minimum taxation, so that producers will not have the fruits of their endeavors taken from them. It requires not a complete absence of government regulation and oversight, but the minimum in regulatory barriers to production and in regulatory costs on production. It requires sound money tethered to real-world values, providing a stable medium of exchange and a stable medium for savings and investment.

We know how to re-create world-leading American prosperity. In fact, we did just that the last time the American economy fell into big trouble, in the 1970s. What we did then to rescue the American Dream is instructive for what we need to do now.

HOW WE FIXED IT LAST TIME

A big problem today is that no one under forty was even of sufficient age to have experienced the 1970s, and most of those over forty have so enjoyed the prosperity of most of the past thirty years that they have forgotten it.

The economics of the 1970s really begins in 1969. Inflation had climbed to 5.5% in that year, up from 1.6% in 1965. To counter that, the Fed slammed on the monetary brakes. That resulted in a recession beginning in December 1969, ending the 1960s economic boom, which stemmed from the sweeping Kennedy income tax rate cuts. The Fed returned to easy money to get the economy growing again, and the recession ended in eleven months.

But with the easy money to end the recession, by 1973 inflation was back to 6.2%, even higher than before. So the Fed reversed itself again to tighten money to counter the inflation. That produced the steepest and longest recession up to date of the post–World War II era, starting in November 1973 and lasting sixteen months. Somehow inflation also reached a new peak of 11% in 1974, followed by 9.1% in 1975. Under the reigning economic doctrine of the time, Keynesian economics, this inflation and recession at the same time should not have been possible. But just as with the physics that says the bumble bee should not be able to fly, still the bee does fly.

Keynesian economics arose in the 1930s in response to the Great Depression. The doctrine holds that economic growth is stimulated by increased government spending, deficits, and debt. That is supposed to increase demand, which is supposed to lead to increased production to satisfy that demand, restoring economic growth. It never worked in the 1930s, as the recession of 1929 extended into the decade-long Great Depression.[1] Under Keynesian economics, recession is caused by too little aggregate demand and inflation is caused by excessive aggregate demand. Since it is impossible to have both too much and too little demand at the same time, recession and inflation together is not supposed to be possible under this doctrine. Yet somehow America suffered 8.5% unemployment in 1975, up from 3.5% in 1969, to go with the 9.1% inflation.

The Fed returned to easy money to end the steep 1973–75 recession, and by 1979 inflation was back to a new peak of 11.3%. For 1980, inflation roared to 13.5%, even while the economy suffered still another recession, lasting six months. The prime interest rate reached 21.5% in 1980,[2] with home mortgage interest rates soon climbing as high as an absurd 14.7%.[3] Unemployment began an upward climb during the Jimmy Carter years that eventually peaked at over 10% in 1982.[4]

The poverty rate actually started increasing in 1978, eventually climbing by an astounding 33%, from 11.4% to 15.2%.[5] A fall in real median family income that began in 1978 snowballed to a decline of almost 10% by 1982.[6] Average real family income for the lowest-income 20% declined by 14.2%.[7] Indeed, during the Carter years (1977–80), real income declined for every quintile, from the lowest 20% to the highest 20%.[8] Real average income of U.S. households was, in fact, in a long-term decline, down rather than up from 1970 to 1980.[9] In addition, from 1968 to 1982, the Dow Jones Industrial Average lost 70% of its real value, reflecting the overall collapse of stocks.[10]

In the classic 1964 James Bond movie, *Goldfinger*, archvillain Auric Goldfinger plots a dirty bomb attack on America's gold reserves at Fort Knox that would leave the reserves poisoned by deadly radiation for over fifty years. Goldfinger, aided by a Red Chinese agent seeking economic chaos in the West, gloats to his prisoner, Bond, while the plot is under way that he conservatively estimates that the value of his own gold stock will soar tenfold as a result. The plot is foiled only because Bond is able to seduce Goldfinger's lover, Pussy Galore, into helping him, and Bond defuses the bomb with 007 seconds left on the timer.

Proving that truth is stranger than fiction, in the 1970s U.S. economic policies were able to achieve the results sought by both Goldfinger and his Red Chinese agent through their evil plot, as explained by Brian Domitrovic in his brilliant book, *Econoclasts*.[11] In 1964 the price of gold was fixed at $35 per ounce. By 1979 it had soared to $350 an ounce. In 1980 the price more than doubled even from those stratospheric heights, to $800.

Reagan explicitly scrapped Keynesian economics in favor of the new supply-side economics, which holds that economic growth results from the incentives for production. Reagan assigned to the Fed and monetary policy the sole goal of reducing inflation through tight money policies. To stimulate the economy, Reagan adopted supply-side policies to sharply increase incentives through lower tax rates and reduced regulatory burdens.

Reagan, in fact, campaigned on a recovery plan with four specific components, which he then implemented after he was elected:

1. Cuts in tax *rates* to restore incentives for economic growth, which was implemented first with a reduction in the top income tax rate of 70% down to 50%, and then a 25% across-the-board reduction in income tax rates for everyone. The 1986 tax reform then reduced tax rates further, leaving just two rates, 28% and 15%;

2. Spending reductions, including a $31 billion cut in spending in 1981, close to 5% of the federal budget then, or the equivalent of about $175 billion in spending cuts for the year today. In constant dollars, nondefense discretionary spending declined by 14.4% from 1981 to 1982, and by 16.8% from 1981 to 1983.[12] Moreover, in constant dollars, this nondefense discretionary spending never returned to its 1981 level for the rest of Reagan's two terms![13] By 1988, this spending was still down 14.4% from its 1981 level in constant dollars.[14] Even with the Reagan defense buildup, which won the Cold War without firing a shot, total federal spending declined from a high of 23.5% of GDP in 1983 to 21.3% in 1988 and 21.2% in 1989.[15] That's a real reduction in the size of government relative to the economy of 10%;

3. Anti-inflation monetary policy restraining money supply growth compared to demand, to maintain a stable value of the dollar;

4. Deregulation, which saved consumers an estimated $100 billion per year in lower prices. Reagan's first executive order, in fact, eliminated price controls on oil and natural gas. Production soared, and the price of oil declined by over 50%.

These policies came straight out of the foundations of prosperity discussed above. And they worked spectacularly. The Reagan recovery started, official records state, in November 1982 and lasted 92 months without a recession until July 1990, when the tax increases of the 1990 budget deal killed it.[16] This set a new record for the longest peacetime expansion ever, the previous high in peacetime being 58 months.[17]

During this seven-year recovery, the economy grew by almost one-third, the equivalent of adding the entire economy of West Germany, the third largest in the world at the time, to the U.S. economy.[18] In 1984 alone, real economic growth boomed by 6.8%, the highest in fifty years.[19] Nearly 20 million new jobs were created during the recovery, increasing U.S. civilian employment by almost 20%.[20] Unemployment fell to 5.3% by 1989.[21]

Real per capita disposable income increased by 18% from 1982 to 1989, meaning the American standard of living increased by almost 20%.[22] The Carter decline in income for the bottom 20% of income earners was reversed, with average real household income for this group rising by 12.2% from 1983 to 1989.[23] The poverty rate, which had started increasing during the Carter years, declined every year from 1984 to 1989, dropping by one-sixth from its peak.[24]

The shocking rise in inflation during the Carter years was also reversed. Astoundingly, inflation from 1980 was reduced by more than half by 1982, to 6.2%.[25] It was cut in half again for 1983, to 3.2%.[26] The contractionary, tight-money policies needed to kill this inflation inexorably created the steep recession of 1981 to 1982, which is why Reagan did not suffer politically catastrophic blame for that recession.

The prime rate was cut by two-thirds by 1987, to 8.2%, on its way down to 6.25% by 1992.[27] New home mortgage rates also declined steadily, reaching 9.2% by 1988, on their way down to 8% by 1992.[28] Note that opponents of the Reagan tax cuts had argued that the cuts would increase interest rates.

The stock market more than tripled in value from 1980 to 1990, a larger increase than in any previous decade.[29] Real personal assets rose by nearly $6 trillion, from $15.5 trillion in 1980 to $21.1 trillion in 1990, an increase of 36%.[30] Total real private net worth rose by $4.3 trillion from 1980 to 1989, totaling $17.1 trillion in constant dollars, an increase of one-third.[31]

In their 2008 book, *The End of Prosperity*, supply-side guru Art Laffer and *Wall Street Journal* chief financial writer Steve Moore point out that this Reagan recovery grew into a twenty-five-year boom, with just slight interruptions by shallow, short recessions in 1990 and 2001:

> We call this period, 1982–2007, the twenty-five year boom—the greatest period of wealth creation in the history of the planet. In 1980, the net worth—assets minus liabilities—of all U.S. households and business . . . was $25 trillion in today's dollars. By 2007, . . . net worth was just shy of $57 trillion. Adjusting for inflation, more wealth was created in America in the twenty-five year boom than in the previous two hundred years.[32]

They add, "The economy in real terms is almost twice as large today as it was in the late 1970s."[33]

Similarly, Steve Forbes wrote in *Forbes* magazine in 2008,

> Between the early 1980s and 2007 we lived in an economic Golden Age. Never before have so many people advanced so far economically in so short a period of time as they have during the last 25 years. Until the credit crisis, 70 million people a year [worldwide] were joining the middle class. The U.S. kicked off this long boom with the economic reforms of Ronald Reagan, particularly his enormous income tax cuts. We burst from the economic stagnation of the 1970s into a dynamic, innovative, high tech–oriented economy. Even in recent years the much maligned U.S. did well. Between year-end 2002 and year-end 2007 U.S. growth exceeded the entire size of China's economy.[34]

In other words, the *growth* in the U.S. economy from 2002 to 2007 was the equivalent of adding the entire economy of China to the U.S. economy.

Contributing to this extension of the Reagan recovery into the twenty-five-year boom were the tax cuts and other pro-growth policies adopted by the Gingrich-led congressional majorities in the 1990s, and the much-maligned Bush tax cuts adopted in 2001 and 2003. Congressional Republicans pushed through a capital gains tax rate cut of nearly 30% in 1997, from 28% down to 20%, expanded IRAs, and adopted other tax cuts on capital. Despite the 30% capital gains rate cut, actual capital gains revenues were $84 billion higher for 1997 to 2000 than had been projected before the rate cut.[35]

Gingrich's Republicans also cut spending, even though the Republicans later lost control of spending after Gingrich left. Total federal discretionary spending, as well as the subcategory of nondefense discretionary spending, declined from 1995 to 1996 in actual nominal dollars. In constant dollars, adjusted for inflation, the decline was 5.4%. By 2000, total federal discretionary spending was still about the same as it was in 1995 in constant dollars. As a percent of GDP, it was slashed by 17.5% in just four years, from 1995 to 1999. Total federal spending relative to GDP declined from 1994 to 2000 by an astounding 13.3%, a reduction in the federal government relative to the economy of nearly one-seventh in just five years. This was accomplished not just by reducing discretionary spending, but through fundamental structural reforms of some programs, such as the old AFDC program, and the phaseout of Depression-era farm subsidy programs through Freedom to Farm, the latter unfortunately later reversed.

Bush's 2001 tax cut included some nongrowth tax reductions, such as increasing the Child Tax Credit, but it also reduced the top marginal income tax rate from 39.6% to 35%, a reduction of only 11% he had to fight for tooth and nail. Bush's 2001 tax cuts also reduced the rate for the lowest-income workers by 33%, from 15% down to 10%. In 2003, Bush cut the capital gains tax rate by 25% and the income tax rate on corporate dividends by over half.

Though President Obama insists on calling these Bush tax cuts the "failed economic policies of the past," they quickly ended the 2001 recession, despite the contractionary economic impacts of the terrorist attack of September 11, 2001, and the economy continued to grow for another seventy-three months. After the rate cuts were all fully implemented in 2003, the economy created 7.8 million new jobs and the unemployment rate fell from over 6% to 4.4%.[36] Real economic growth over the next three years doubled from the average for the prior three years, to 3.5%.[37]

In response to the rate cuts, business investment spending, which had declined for nine straight quarters, reversed and increased 6.7% per quarter.[38] That is where the jobs came from. Manufacturing output soared to its highest level in twenty years.[39] The stock market revived, creating almost $7 trillion in new shareholder wealth.[40] From 2003 to 2007, the S&P 500 almost doubled. Capital gains tax revenues *had doubled* by 2005, *despite the 25% rate cut!*[41]

The deficit in the last budget adopted by Republican congressional majorities was $161 billion for fiscal 2007. The day the Democrat congressional majorities took control, January 3, 2007, the unemployment rate was 4.6%. George Bush's economic policies, again "the failed policies of the past" in Obama's rhetoric, had set a record of fifty-two straight months of job creation.

THE END OF PROSPERITY: THE FINANCIAL CRISIS

But these good times came crashing to an end in the financial crisis of 2008. What went wrong? And how can booming prosperity be restored?

The root causes of America's financial crisis, which ended the twenty-five-year Reagan boom, lie in departing from the policies that created the boom. As Laffer and Moore write,

So what explains our sudden turn toward pessimism? Why do we now forecast the End of Prosperity? The short answer is that we aren't just optimists, we are first and foremost realists. And we are now witnessing nearly all of the economic policy dials that were once turned toward growth being twisted back towards recession. . . . [O]ur politicians in both parties, but especially the liberal Democrats, are getting everything wrong—tax policy, regulatory policy, monetary policy, spending policy, trade policy. We call this the assault on growth. The political class seems to be almost intentionally steering the United States economy back into the abyss—and, to borrow a phrase from P. J. O'Rourke, the American electorate, alas, seems to be willing to hand them the keys and the bottle of whiskey to do it.[42]

In other words, by 2008 the two parties in Washington together had abandoned every one of the four planks of Reaganomics.

The first of these was abandonment of the Reagan plank involving sound, anti-inflationary monetary policy maintaining a stable value of the dollar. Federal Reserve Board Chairman Alan Greenspan, and other governors at the Fed, eventually departed from Reagan's injunction that monetary policy focus solely on maintaining stable prices, and started trying to stimulate the economy through old Keynesian policies of easy money. The central role of the resulting Fed policies in causing the financial crisis was most authoritatively explained by Stanford economics professor and monetary-policy guru John Taylor in his timely book, *Getting Off Track*.[43] Taylor begins,

> The classic explanation of financial crises, going back hundreds of years, is that they are caused by excesses—frequently monetary excesses—that lead to a boom and an inevitable bust. In the recent crisis we had a housing boom and bust, which in turn led to financial turmoil in the United States and other countries. I begin by showing that monetary excesses were the main cause of the boom and the resulting bust.[44]

Economics professor Lawrence H. White, now of George Mason University, elaborates:

> In the recession of 2001, the Federal Reserve System, under Chairman Alan Greenspan, began aggressively expanding the U.S. money supply. Year-over-year growth in the M-2 monetary aggregate rose briefly above 10 percent, and remained above 8 percent entering the second half of 2003. The expansion was accompanied by the Fed repeatedly lowering its target for the federal funds (inter-

bank short term) interest rate. The federal funds rate began 2001 at 6.25 percent and ended the year at 1.75 percent. It was reduced further in 2002 and 2003, in mid-2003 reaching a record low of 1 percent, where it stayed for a year. The *real* Fed funds rate was negative . . . for two and a half years. In purchasing power terms, during that period a borrower was not paying but rather gaining in proportion to what he borrowed. Economist Steve Hanke has summarized the result: "This set off the mother of all liquidity cycles and yet another massive demand bubble."[45]

From early 2001 until late 2006, as White further explains, "the Fed pushed the actual federal funds rate below the estimated rate that would have been consistent with targeting a 2 percent inflation."[46] That estimated rate is determined by what is known in economics as the Taylor Rule. Forbes adds, "In 2004, the Federal Reserve made a fateful miscalculation. It thought the U.S. economy was much weaker than it was and therefore pumped out excess liquidity and kept interest rates artificially low."[47]

White continues:

The demand bubble thus created went heavily into real estate. From mid-2003 to mid-2007, while the dollar volume of final sales of goods and services was growing at 5 percent to 7 percent, real estate loans at commercial banks were growing at 10–17 percent. Credit fueled demand pushed up the sale prices of existing houses and encouraged the construction of new housing on undeveloped land, in both cases absorbing the increased dollar volume of mortgages. Because real estate is an especially long-lived asset, its market value is especially boosted by low interest rates.[48]

Or as Taylor concluded, "[T]his extra-easy [Fed monetary] policy accelerated the housing boom and thereby ultimately led to the housing bust."[49]

The Housing Bubble

In other words, the Fed's persistent overexpansion of money and credit from 2001 well into 2006 generated overinvestment in housing markets across the country, as extreme low-interest policies and apparent abundant supply of capital led investors to believe that such housing investments were desirable. This ultimately stimulated the housing bubble, with wild housing overinvestments betting on continued rapid price increases in the housing sector.

The Fed's loose monetary policies during this period also generated sharp declines in the dollar. For example, the dollar was worth 1.15 euros near the start of 2002, but it declined by close to 50% to near 0.6 euros by the start of 2008.[50] The price of gold soared from $350 near the end of 2002 to almost $1,000 by the start of 2008.[51] Even inflation, defeated twenty-five years previously, started to come back, increasing from 1.55% at the end of 2001 to as high as 5.6% in July 2008.[52]

When the Fed finally realized it had to rein in its loose monetary policy, soaring housing prices slowed, flattened out, and then tipped into declines. The housing bubble burst, producing more rapid declines. The Case-Shiller Home Price Index shows that housing prices across the country declined an average of about 27% from their peak in July 2006 to the end of 2008.[53]

The steep decline in housing prices produced chaos throughout the financial industry in the United States, and ultimately the world, as widespread financial assets based on housing collapsed in value. This process is discussed further below.

Note that the monetary policies creating the housing bubble *misled* businesses and investors into making the overinvestments that inevitably were doomed to fail and produce the bust or recession. The process does not involve malfeasance, or greedy, immoral, or illegal behavior by businesses and investors. No doubt some improper activity by particular businesses or financial firms was involved. But that is not a cause of general economic recessions.

Negative real interest rates in particular effectively pay or subsidize investors and financial institutions to borrow and speculate. That is where the excessive leveraging by Wall Street firms that was exposed during the financial crisis and now seems so reckless in retrospect came from. Wall Street leaders and managers should have been wise enough to avoid that blunder, but government policies affirmatively misled them into making it.

The nasty political rhetoric blaming Wall Street for the crisis, and the simpleminded media reporting that fuels such propaganda, is just boob bait calculated to mislead the gullible into supporting the Obama political machine. As Taylor concludes, "In this book I have provided empirical evidence that government actions and interventions caused, prolonged, and worsened the financial crisis. They caused it by deviating from historical precedents and principles for setting interest rates that had worked well for twenty years."[54] Moreover, "They prolonged it by misdiagnosing the problems in the bank credit markets and thereby responding inappropriately, focusing on liquidity rather than risk. They made it worse by supporting certain financial institutions and their creditors but not others in an ad hoc way, without a clear and understandable framework."[55]

The primary culprit for this monetary policy disaster is the Republican Bush administration. The secretary of the Treasury, the President's Council of Economic Advisors, and the director of the Economic Policy Council are all supposed to monitor monetary policy and alert the president when it starts to run off course. Where were they while the Fed reduced interest rates so sharply for so long that the federal funds rate was negative for two and a half years, from 2002 to 2004? Where were they while the Fed maintained an excessively easy monetary policy from 2001 to 2006? Steve Forbes suggests that they actually favored these disastrous Fed policies:

> Why didn't the Treasury Department—behind the scenes—tell the Fed to strengthen the enfeebled greenback? Because the Bush Administration likes a weak dollar, feeling that it will improve our trade balance by artificially making our exports cheaper. Not since Jimmy Carter has the U.S. had such a weak dollar administration. This mania would never have reached the proportions it did had the Fed and Treasury had a strong-dollar policy.[56]

Those holding these economic posts are also responsible for helping the president determine whom to appoint to the Fed. The Bush Fed appointees consistently supported Greenspan's reckless policies during this period, and in some cases were even more aggressive than he was.

A central player in causing the entire financial crisis has, in fact, been the current Fed chairman, Ben Bernanke. Bush appointed Bernanke to the Federal Reserve Board of Governors in 2002, where he continued to serve until 2005. As economist Steve Hanke writes,

> There is plenty of blame to go around, but the main culprit is the Federal Reserve. In late 2002 Ben S. Bernanke, then a Fed governor and now the chairman, persuaded Alan Greenspan, then chairman, that the U.S. was in the grip of deflation. In consequence, the Fed pushed down on the monetary accelerator. By July 2003 the Fed funds rate had been squeezed down to 1%, where it stayed for a year. This artificially low interest rate set off the mother of all liquidity cycles.[57]

In the Bush administration, such failure was more than its own reward, as Bush appointed Bernanke as chairman of the President's Council of Economic Advisors in 2005, and then as chairman of the Federal Reserve Board when Greenspan retired in 2006. Bernanke was central to the entire financial crisis, and wreaked further havoc in these later posts.

But the Democrats cannot claim much credit in this chapter of the financial crisis, either. Not one of them spoke up during the Fed's runaway easy-money spree. Indeed, Democrats in Washington historically have supported exactly the easy-money Fed policies that produced the financial crisis. The last time they were completely in control of Washington for an extended period was the hopeless 1970s, when the Fed generated the worst sustained inflation since the Revolutionary War and helped to spawn a series of worsening recessions.

THE "AFFORDABLE HOUSING" FIASCO

But all of the above is only one part of the story of how the 2008 financial crisis was created. The second chapter of that story is "affordable housing" policies going back many years, spawned by liberals and progressives. These increasingly extreme and unbalanced policies began the housing bubble even before the Fed's miscalculations started in 2001. Moreover, because of these affordable housing policies, when the bubble burst and housing prices stopped their run-up and started to decline in 2006, the entire mortgage market, and ultimately the U.S. financial industry, was vulnerable to collapse.

Some of the institutions ultimately abused in the name of affordable housing go back to the New Deal. The Federal Housing Administration was created in 1934 to guarantee mortgages against default, which expanded their availability to more working families. Income and mortgage-size limitations focused the program's insurance on more lower-income borrowers over time, which made sense because private mortgage insurance became available for more average- and above-average-income earners and for bigger mortgages.

In 1938, Congress created the Federal National Mortgage Association, FNMA, which became known as Fannie Mae due to this acronym. Fannie Mae started by purchasing mortgages insured by the FHA, which expanded the capital available for mortgages. Over time it packaged these and other purchased mortgages into pools and sold shares in them in the open market, a process known as securitization. This made even more capital available for mortgages, and worked fine for many years.

In 1968, Fannie Mae was rechartered as a private, stockholder-owned corporation, removing its growing financial operations from the federal budget but still retaining federal ties. Fannie Mae continued to securitize a growing share of mortgages in the United States, without any requirement that they be insured, either publicly or privately. A separate government agency was also established that year named the Government National Mortgage Association (GNMA), which became known as Ginnie Mae. This agency securitized and insured mortgages issued to government employees and veterans.

In 1970, the government chartered a new private, stockholder-owned corporation named the Federal Home Loan Mortgage Corporation (FHLMC), which became known as Freddie Mac. This organization operated just like Fannie Mae, established to provide competition in the securitization market. Because of their continued federal ties, Fannie Mae and Freddie Mac became known as government-sponsored enterprises, or GSEs.

Affordable Housing "Innovations" Begin

All of these institutions worked fine for many years. But a seemingly minor turn down a road paved with good intentions took place in 1977, with adoption of the Community Reinvestment Act (CRA). The CRA required banks to lend throughout the entire geographic area in which they operate, from the rich suburbs to the poor inner-city ghettoes. The regulatory examination of each bank each year produces a CRA compliance score that rates the bank as to how well it has been doing in complying with the CRA. Congress also had enacted in 1975 the Home Mortgage Disclosure Act (HMDA), which required banks to publicly release detailed information regarding mortgage applications they receive.

Still, not much happened until housing activists, led in particular by the far-left Association for Community Organizations for Reform Now (ACORN), developed the strategy and tactics to leverage the CRA to maximum advantage. When a bank seeks regulatory approval to open a new branch or to merge with another bank, outside organizations can file challenges to the approval based on the CRA performance of the bank. ACORN started doing this in the late 1980s, settling its challenges for agreements by the banks to provide specified amounts of mortgages for nontraditional, lower-income, minority borrowers, as well as some extra cash for ACORN itself.

ACORN and its allies were greatly aided by provisions in the 1989 savings and loan bailout and in 1991 amendments to the HMDA requiring banks to report mortgage data by race, gender, and income. This data fueled public charges of racism against banks, further empowering the housing activists to win more bank payoffs.

This data was also used by the Federal Reserve Bank of Boston to produce a notorious study in 1992 purportedly showing that minorities were denied mortgages at higher rates than whites even after controlling for creditworthiness.[58] But the study was based on bad data, as University of Texas economics professor Stan Liebowitz explains:

> In fact, the study was based on such horribly mangled data that the study's authors apparently never bothered to examine them. . . .

The authors of the Boston Fed study, however, stuck to their guns even in the face of overwhelming evidence that the data used in their study was riddled with errors.[59]

Liebowitz led a review of the study that concluded, "[W]e were shocked at the poor quality of the data created by the Boston Fed. . . . When we attempted to conduct a statistical analysis removing the impact of these obvious data errors, we found that the evidence of discrimination vanished."[60]

The Boston Fed followed up the 1992 study with a manual for banks regarding how to expand mortgage lending to low- and moderate-income minority applicants. The publication began by reminding bankers of the potential compulsion behind its recommendations, with a helpful sidebar saying: "*Did You Know?* Failure to comply with the Equal Credit Opportunity Act . . . can subject a financial institution to civil liability for actual and punitive damages in individual and class actions." [61]

The manual then went on to advise "best practices" in serving low- and moderate-income and minority applicants. These included discounting bad credit history, no credit history, no savings, lack of steady employment, a high ratio of mortgage obligations to income, undocumented income, and inability to finance down payment and closing costs, leaving the purchaser with no substantial stake of his own money in the home.[62] Another "best practice" recommendation was to count unemployment benefits as income in qualifying for a mortgage.[63]

Liebowitz concludes, "What was the impact of this attack on lending standards? As you might guess, when government regulators bark, banks jump. Banks began to loosen lending standards. And loosen and loosen and loosen, to the cheers of the politicians, regulators, and GSEs." [64] Note this debasing of lending standards was an effect of government regulation, not a lack of regulation.

Clinton's Subprime Mortgage Revolution

ACORN and other housing activists began lobbying Fannie and Freddie to ease the mortgage underwriting standards for qualification for securitization. The organizations resisted, though they did agree to some relatively small-time "pilot projects." The housing activists then turned to congressional Democrats to assist in lobbying Fannie and Freddie. This bore bigger fruit, with Fannie and Freddie committing $13.5 billion to the purchase of low-income "affordable housing" loans in 1992 and 1993.[65]

The housing activists found even more powerful allies in the Clinton administration in 1993. Secretary of Housing and Urban Development (HUD) Henry Cisneros began regular monthly meetings with ACORN on "affordable housing" issues. Eventually, Cisneros allowed the extremist, far left ACORN "to redraft many of Fannie Mae and Freddie Mac's loan guidelines."[66] Moreover, Fannie and Freddie were increasingly populated at the highest ranks by Clinton administration appointees highly sympathetic to the cause of the housing activists. This included Fannie Mae's chairman and chief executive officer, James A. Johnson, an advisor to the 2008 Obama campaign.

But the big breakthrough came when President Clinton himself got on board. Stanley Kurtz explains:

> Finally, in June of 1995, President Clinton, Vice-President Gore, and Secretary Cisneros announced the administration's comprehensive new strategy for raising home-ownership in America to an all-time high. Representatives from ACORN were guests of honor at the ceremony. In his remarks, Clinton emphasized that: "Our home-ownership strategy will not cost the taxpayers one extra cent. It will not require legislation." Clinton meant that informal partnerships between Fannie and Freddie and groups like ACORN would make mortgages available to customers "who have historically been excluded from homeownership." In the end, of course, Clinton's plan cost taxpayers an almost unbelievable amount of money.[67]

Thus the subprime mortgage market was born.

A colorful example of mortgage lending practices in the new "affordable housing" market is provided by Kurtz, who quotes an April 1995 *Chicago Sun-Times* article as saying, "You've only got a couple of thousand bucks in the bank. Your job pays you dog food wages. Your credit history has been bent, stapled, and mutilated. You declared bankruptcy in 1989. Don't despair. You can still buy a house." [68] The article went on to refer prospective home buyers who fit the profile "to a group of far left 'community organizers' called ACORN." [69] At that very time, Barack Obama himself was shoveling money to ACORN to fund precisely these and other programs, from his posts as a director at Chicago's Woods Fund and as chairman of the board of the Chicago Annenberg Challenge, originally founded by Weather Underground leader Bill Ayers.[70]

HUD reinforced this subprime mortgage market through new regulations greatly strengthening CRA enforcement. As Peter Wallison explains in the *American Spectator*,

> In 1995, the regulators created new rules that sought to establish objective criteria for determining whether a bank was meeting CRA standards. Examiners no longer had the discretion they once had. For banks, simply proving that they were looking for qualified buyers wasn't enough. Banks now had to show that they had actually made a requisite number of loans to low and moderate income (LMI) borrowers. The new regulations also required the use of "innovative or flexible" lending practices to address credit needs of LMI borrowers and neighborhoods.[71]

In other words, President Clinton and his progressive, liberal/left allies were now effectively looting the banks by force of compulsion to promote their "affordable housing" policies.

Also in 1995, HUD established quotas requiring Fannie Mae and Freddie Mac to devote 40% of their funds in 1996, and 42% in 1997, to low- and moderate-income housing. Former Texas senator Phil Gramm notes in the *Wall Street Journal*,

> By the time the housing market collapsed, Fannie and Freddie faced three quotas. The first was for mortgages to individuals with below-average income, set at 56% of their overall mortgage holdings. The second targeted families with incomes at or below 60% of area median income, set at 27% of their holdings. The third targeted geographic areas deemed to be underserved, set at 35%.[72]

Both HUD and the Justice Department also began bringing lawsuits against mortgage lenders that turned down a higher percentage of minority applicants than white applicants.[73] Note again that all of this was the result of government regulation, not the lack of regulation.

The debasement of lending standards for the subprime market soon spread throughout the mortgage markets. As Wallison explains, "Once the standards were relaxed for low-income borrowers, it would seem impossible to deny these benefits to the prime market. Indeed, bank regulators, who were in charge of enforcing CRA standards, could hardly disapprove of similar loans made to better qualified borrowers."[74] By 1997 Fannie Mae was offering a 97% loan-to-value mortgage, and by 2001 it was offering 100% financing with no down payment at all.[75]

By 2006, subprime and similar "Alt-A" loans amounted to one-third of the U.S. mortgage market. In fact, Wallison further reports, by that point about half of all mortgage loans made in the United States could be classified as nonprime for one reason or another.[76]

Through their securitization practices, Fannie Mae and Freddie Mac then spread the unrecognized high risks of these mortgages throughout the financial world, selling shares in pools of them to other financial institutions and investors, in America and overseas. Because the capital markets believed, rightly as it has turned out, that the bonds issued by Fannie and Freddie to raise money for their mortgage financing were effectively government guaranteed, the two organizations were able to raise huge sums at low interest rates to pump into these mortgages and their securitization, exploding their pollution of U.S. and world financial markets to toxic levels. Fannie and Freddie alone eventually held a total of $1.6 trillion in subprime and Alt-A loans.[77]

The newly emerging subprime and Alt-A mortgage markets, and the explosion in mortgage financing led by Fannie and Freddie, meant an equivalent explosion in housing demand. That in turn began a housing bubble of rising home prices. That effect intersected with the Fed's over-expansion of money and credit from 2001 to 2006, producing a horrendous overinvestment in the U.S. housing sector.

The rising prices of this housing bubble, however, obscured and delayed the negative effects of the weakened and debased mortgage lending standards. Buyers took a chance on purchasing bigger houses than they could afford, figuring they could always refinance or sell out, probably at a profit, if they got into trouble. This alternative of selling out into a market of continually rising prices kept mortgage defaults at a minimum. This low default rate and the opportunity to sell any homes that were obtained through foreclosure at continually rising prices misled lenders into thinking that this mortgage business involved little risk. As Liebowitz writes, "Rating agencies could suggest that these loans were no more risky than the old antiquated loans and provide empirical support for that conclusion, given the still-low default rates at the time."[78]

Gramm adds, "This mentality permeated the market from the originator to the holder of securitized mortgages, from the rating agency to the financial regulator."[79]

The Failure of Regulation

The ratings agencies (Moody's, Standard & Poor's, Fitch) in particular let everyone down, because they were set up within a regulatory framework, protected from competition, to be the early-warning system of trouble down the line. Government regulations mandated that certain central financial institutions, such as insurance companies and money market funds, invest only in securities rated by these agencies as AAA, to protect the institutions from excessive risk. Other institutions, such as commercial banks and investment banks, in the United States and around the world, based what they thought was an acceptable distribution of risk in their portfolios on the ratings these agencies gave various securities.

But the entire regulatory system broke down when the rating agencies were seduced into going along with the fashionable liberal/left subprime mania and failed to see through the fog of the housing bubble (which was their job). They consistently rated shares in securitized pools of mortgages, even subprime and Alt-A mortgages, as AAA, causing the downfall of major financial institutions. But they were so caught up in the "affordable housing" mind-set, and so misled by the apparent safety of the housing market in the bubble environment, that in one famous comment an S&P spokesman responded to questions about whether their ratings were overoptimistic by saying, "The market can go with its gut; we have to go with the facts."[80] Those facts, they believed in the middle of the housing bubble, showed that the mortgage-backed securities were not particularly risky.

As Liebowitz wrote,

> In spite of their inaccurate ratings, the rating agencies, nevertheless, were making great profits from rating mortgage-backed securities, a quasi-sinecure created by the government that required many financial organizations (e.g. insurance companies and money market funds) to invest only in highly rated securities as certified by government approved rating agencies. . . . Given that government approved rating agencies were protected from free competition, it might be expected that these agencies would not want to create political waves by rocking the mortgage boat, endangering a potential loss of their protected profits.[81]

Liebowitz added, "Seemingly everyone went along. And most felt morally upright doing so since they were helping increase home ownership, especially among the poor and minorities."[82]

But not everyone was misled by the housing bubble. As far back as April 2001, the Bush administration warned that the size of GSEs Fannie Mae and Freddie Mac was "a potential problem" because "financial trouble of a large GSE could cause strong repercussions in financial markets, affecting Federally insured entities and economic activity." By September 2003, the administration was proposing "legislation to create a new Federal agency to regulate and supervise the financial activities of" Fannie Mae and Freddie Mac.

But Democrats almost uniformly opposed such regulation in the name of "affordable housing." Barney Frank, ranking Democrat on the House Financial Services Committee, said in October 2003, "these two entities—Fannie Mae and Freddie Mac—are not facing any kind of financial crisis. . . . The more people exaggerate these problems, the more pressure there is on these companies, the less we will see in terms of affordable housing."

At a House hearing on this issue in 2003, the Republicans sought to expand supervision and regulatory controls over Fannie Mae and Freddie Mac. Federal regulators testified that their reckless financial practices threatened the entire financial system. The Republicans called for a new regulatory authority to impose standard bank regulation on them.

But the Democrats excoriated the Republicans for criticizing what they saw as the highly successful practices of Fannie and Freddie in achieving their goals of affordable housing. Representative Frank led the counterattack, saying, "I believe there has been more alarm raised about potential unsafety and unsoundness than, in fact, exists" and "I think we see entities [Fannie Mae and Freddie Mac] that are fundamentally sound financially." The shameless Massachusetts Democrat added, "I want to roll the dice a little bit more in this situation towards subsidized housing. . . ." And that is what we did.

The ever-insightful Democrat Maxine Waters of California said,

> Mr. Chairman, we do not have a crisis at Freddie Mac, and in particular at Fannie Mae, under the outstanding leadership of Mr. Franklin Raines. Everything in the 1992 act has worked just fine. In fact, the GSEs have exceeded their policy goals. . . .

Franklin Raines was the former Clinton budget director who went on to serve as president of Fannie Mae. He expertly testified that the mortgage-related securities of Fannie and Freddie, which came to rock the entire financial world, were "riskless."

But the Democrats insisted that Republican concerns over safety and soundness were all just trumped up to frame the brilliant leadership of Mr. Raines, and just showed once again that Republicans don't care about the middle class and the poor. Indeed, the Democrats *attacked the regulators*, who had precisely provided the evidence that Fannie and Freddie were increasingly threatening the safety and soundness of the entire financial system.

In 2004, the Bush administration renewed its proposal to impose strengthened, standard banking regulation and supervision over Fannie and Freddie. But Barney Frank accused the president of creating an "artificial issue," saying "people tend to pay their mortgages. I don't think we are in any remote danger here."

By 2005, as American Enterprise Institute economist Kevin Hassett noted at Bloomberg.com, Alan Greenspan was warning that if Fannie and Freddie "continue to grow, continue to have the low capital they have, continue to engage in the dynamic hedging of their portfolios, which they need to do for interest risk aversion, they potentially create ever-growing potential systemic risk down the road. . . . We are placing the total financial system of the future at a substantial risk."

That same year, John McCain, supported by the Bush administration, was one of three cosponsors of legislation to impose such regulatory supervision and controls over Fannie and Freddie. But the Democrats shouted these proposals down as an assault on affordable housing for the middle class and the poor. Taylor writes,

> The government sponsored agencies Fannie Mae and Freddie Mac were encouraged to expand and buy mortgage-backed securities, including those formed with risky subprime mortgages. Although legislation, such as the Federal Housing Enterprise Regulatory Reform Act of 2005, was proposed to control those excesses, it was not passed into law. Thus the actions of those agencies should be added to the list of government interventions that were part of the problem.[83]

Hassett writes further regarding this bill,

> If the bill had become law, then the world today would be different. In 2005, 2006, and 2007, a blizzard of terrible mortgage paper fluttered out of the Fannie and Freddie clouds, burying many of our oldest and most venerable financial institutions. Without [Fannie's and Freddie's] checkbooks keeping the market liquid and buying up excess supply, the market would likely have not existed.

Yet Barack Obama joined with the Democrats to kill McCain's bill.

Government-backed Fannie and Freddie came to be plagued with outright corruption. Clinton had turned it into a feeding trough for Democrat cronies, led by Fannie chief Raines, who copped $90 million for himself in bonuses for his great work. Fannie and Freddie sought to protect their ongoing racket by hefty political contributions to key political angels. The second-highest recipient of such contributions was Senator Barack Obama of Illinois.

These disastrous "affordable housing" policies fall under the category of bad and excessive banking, finance, housing, and mortgage regulations. They effectively constitute the abandonment of a second plank of Reaganomics, the elimination of excessive, overly costly regulatory burdens. As a result, it wasn't just the Fed misleading investors, financial institutions, and the markets. It was regulators and their kept watchdogs the rating agencies as well. While the bad monetary policy that was so powerful in causing the financial crisis was primarily due to Republicans, as discussed above, this bad banking and mortgage regulation policy that was an equally huge factor was primarily caused by Democrats.

THE BUSH ADMINISTRATION BUNGLES THE CRISIS

As discussed above, housing prices peaked in July 2006, and the housing bubble burst as the Fed finally restrained its monetary policy. Without the bubble's continuing run-up in housing prices to mask the underlying problems, foreclosures started to rise soon thereafter.[84] Those who were granted mortgages and houses they couldn't afford under the new, debased affordable-housing lending standards could no longer just refinance or sell out if they got in trouble. Speculators who bought second or even third homes to turn over and make a quick buck could no longer sell at a profit, and were burdened instead with excessive mortgage service obligations they couldn't carry. So they just walked away from those homes.

The financial institutions foreclosing on those homes just forced housing prices down further when they tried to sell them to recoup their loans, contributing to more foreclosures in a downward spiral. The increased foreclosures affected not just the housing and mortgages that were foreclosed upon. They affected all housing, mortgages, and mortgage-backed securities that had been distributed throughout the U.S. financial system, and the world, through securitization. The increased foreclosures indicated increased risk for mortgages, reducing the value of all mortgage-related securities and instruments (including derivatives and credit default swaps). The declining housing prices meant that the value of the collateral backing up mortgages was lower, which reduced the value of all mortgage-related securities and instruments still further.

Those institutions with heavy concentrations of mortgages and mortgage-related securities were particularly vulnerable to these declines in value. Their capital reserve margins declined as a result, which led credit-rating agencies (finally waking up too late) to downgrade their credit ratings. Declining capital margins and downgraded credit ratings caused the stock prices of these institutions to decline.

The vulnerable companies tried to borrow to maintain liquidity and capital. But downgraded credit ratings and declining stock values made such borrowing more difficult, and costly.

Companies that became more highly leveraged in recent years, carrying lower capital margins to begin with, were especially vulnerable to this process. This, again, is one of the ways that the Fed's loose monetary policies misled financial institutions. Those Fed policies made leveraging with borrowed funds so cheap and easy that the increased leveraging seemed highly desirable.[85] The high credit ratings on mortgage-related securities further misled financial institutions into this greater leveraging.

Declining credit ratings and stock values led the markets to shun efforts by these institutions to raise more capital by issuing new bonds or stock. So the institutions turned to selling the mortgage-related securities to raise the capital. Moreover, because these firms were trying to raise capital quickly, they had to accept even lower prices to get rid of the securities faster. The resulting further declines in their market prices led others to try to dump their mortgage-related securities as well, quickly leading to panic selling, and crashing their market prices to virtually nothing. Adding to the problem was that no one really knew which mortgage-related securities might be plagued with the worst subprime mortgages backing them, or the most mortgages in default. So no one really wanted to buy any mortgage-related securities.

Mark-to-Market Death Spirals

But this is where further bad regulation kicked in to doom these institutions, including big Wall Street names. The Securities and Exchange Commission (SEC) had just adopted an obscure accounting regulation known as mark to market in 2006 (also known as fair value accounting). This regulation required the balance sheets of financial institutions to list assets at their current market prices every day, rather than their historical costs, or their expected values based on their probable future income streams. This meant that when panic selling by some troubled institutions to raise capital drove the value of mortgage-related securities to virtually zero, *all institutions had to change their books to reflect this minimal market value of the securities.* An institution could be receiving all of the payments due on its mortgage-backed securities just fine, with nothing in default. But overnight they had to list these securities as worthless nevertheless, because of the desperation, panic sales of others.

Consequently, balance sheets under mark-to-market accounting suddenly started to show insolvency, or near insolvency, for more and more institutions. All lending to these companies shut down, so they lost all liquidity (cash on hand) needed to keep company operations going. Stockholders, realizing that they would be wiped out if the companies went into bankruptcy, or got taken over by the government, started panic selling even when they knew the underlying business of the company was still viable.

This is how, even with more than 90% of mortgages still paying on time, major companies like Merrill Lynch, Bear Stearns, AIG, and Lehman Brothers found themselves suddenly bankrupt almost overnight. These companies may well all have survived under the accounting rules followed for decades until recently (known as historical cost accounting). But under the misguided new mark-to-market regulations, increasingly widespread panic threatened the entire economy.

Steve Forbes further explains the process:

[T]he crisis never would have become so unprecedentedly destructive but for a seemingly arcane accounting principle called mark-to-market, or fair value, accounting. The idea seems harmless: Financial institutions should adjust their balance sheets and their capital accounts when the market value of the financial assets they hold goes up or down. That works when you have very liquid securities, such as Treasurys or the common stock of IBM or GE. But when the credit crisis hit there was *no* market for subprime securities. Yet regulators and lawsuit fearful auditors pressed banks and other financial firms to relentlessly knock down the book value of this subprime paper, even in cases where these obligations were being serviced in the payment of principal and interest. Mark-to-market became *the* weapon of mass destruction.

When banks wrote down the value of these assets they had to get new capital. The need for new capital was a signal to ratings agencies that these outfits might be in need of a credit-rating reduction. This forced financial firms to increase capital for credit default swaps—which meant more calls for new capital. Result: Investment banks that still had positive cash flows found themselves in a death spiral. Of the $600-plus billion that financial institutions have written off, almost all of it has been *book* writedowns, not actual *cash* losses. . . . If this accounting asininity had been in effect during the banking trouble in the early 1990s, almost every major commercial bank in the U.S. would have collapsed. We would have had a second Great Depression.[86]

The Sarbanes-Oxley Act, passed after Enron and other financial scandals, threatened accountants with punitive lawsuits and even criminal prison terms for making accounting judgments that seemed mistaken in retrospect. So they were particularly aggressive in enforcing the mark-to-market accounting rules, which further helped to crash major investment firms, Wall Street, and the economy.

William Isaac, chairman of the FDIC in the 1980s under President Reagan, explained further:

During the 1980s, our underlying economic problems were far more serious than the economic problems we're facing this time around. . . . The country's 10 largest banks were loaded up with Third World debt that was valued in the markets at cents on the dollar. If we had marked those loans to market prices, virtually every one of them would have been insolvent.

Isaac continued:

This is contrary to everything we know about bank regulation. When there are temporary impairments of asset values, due to economic and marketplace events, regulators must give institutions an opportunity to survive the temporary impairment. Assets should not be marked to unrealistic fire sale prices. *Regulators must evaluate the assets on the basis of their true economic value (a discounted cash flow analysis).* If we had followed today's approach during the 1980s, we would have nationalized all of the major banks in the country and thousands of additional banks and thrifts would have failed. *I have little doubt that the country would have gone from a serious recession into a depression.* (emphasis added)

The Bush administration had the authority to relax this mark-to-market accounting through the SEC, and allow firms to value their mortgage-related securities under historical cost accounting, so if the underlying mortgages were still paying on time, and there was no reason to sell the security overnight, there was no reason to mark down the security's accounting value. But the Bush SEC never adopted this change.

Dredging Keynes up from the Dead

The Bush administration, however, did recognize by the end of 2007 that the economy was weakening. So they cut a deal with congressional Democrats for a $168 billion stimulus package based on tax rebates, basically cash grants refunding a portion of taxes.

This was yet another departure from Reaganomics, which was based on cuts in tax *rates*. It is tax rate cuts that stimulate the economy, because they allow taxpayers to keep a higher percentage of what they produce, expanding the incentive to produce. A tax rebate check, by contrast, does nothing to change incentives. Whatever the taxpayer produces after receiving the check is subject to the same incentives as before.

The rationale behind the tax rebates is that they give taxpayers more money to spend, and that increased spending will stimulate the economy. But that is an old Keynesian rationale, which failed so miserably in the 1970s and before, and which Reagan left for dead in favor of the new supply-side economics—rate cuts and incentives—which worked so spectacularly. The old Keynesian theory does not work because borrowing $168 billion from the economy to give taxpayers $168 billion to spend adds nothing to the economy on net, and does nothing to expand incentives.

And of course, the Bush–congressional Democrat stimulus package did not work. The economy seemed to ignore it completely, and just worsen instead. Then-senator Obama fully supported this failed stimulus at the time, and called for still more.

Some Republicans defended Bush's embrace of this policy by arguing that the Democrats would not have agreed to another round of supply-side tax rate cuts, and that the president needed to show the country that he could work together with the Democrat congressional majorities. But this was more foolishness. In embracing a policy that would not and did not work just so they could get agreement from the Democrats, it was Bush and the Republicans who were held responsible for the failed results, leading to disastrous defeats in the fall.

What Bush should have done instead is propose a plan in December 2007 based on Reaganite supply-side economics, which would have worked. One of the top problems in our economy is the outdated high federal corporate tax rate of 35%, as discussed further in Chapter 7, which also applies to corporate capital gains. Bush should have proposed slashing that rate to 20%, with the corporate capital gains rate reduced to 15% like the individual rate. He also should have proposed making the Bush tax cuts of 2001 and 2003 permanent. Along with the repeal of mark-to-market accounting, and other factors, this would have stimulated an end to the financial crisis.

The Democrats would then have faced a severe dilemma. If they refused to go along with this reprise of Reaganomics, they then could have been held politically responsible for the downturn if it continued, or worsened, as it did. If enough of them did not want to take that risk, however, and they went along with this program, the worst of the financial crisis would have been avoided, and the economy would have recovered after a year at most.

This was the critical point where the Bush administration completely lost its way, broke the governing consensus behind Reaganomics and free market economics, and let us fall all the way back to the confused, outdated Keynesianism of the 1970s. Despite the early 2008 Keynesian stimulus package, the economy continued to worsen over the summer and into the fall.

Paulson's Panic

Not much in economic history can match the utter confusion and long cascading disaster of Secretary of the Treasury Henry Paulson's $700 billion bailout proposal in mid-September 2008. By then the earlier stimulus plan developed by his brilliant Keynesians was such an ineffective failure that no one even remembered it anymore. So Paulson and Bush, backed by Bernanke—ever ready with bad advice—went before the nation to argue that they needed Congress to pass a bill providing $700 billion to bail out the banks, *or else the nation was going to fall into another Great Depression!*

This message, repeated constantly until Paulson's proposal was passed, panicked the entire U.S. economy, and then the world economy. That $700 billion was just under one-fourth of the entire federal budget at the time. If that enormous sum was needed to save us from a banking collapse and another Great Depression, how much trouble were we in? The answer: much more than we were before Paulson came up with his brilliant idea. In the following weeks, even though Paulson's plan passed, the stock market tanked thousands of additional points. We now know the economy also went into free fall, collapsing backward by 6.8% in the fourth quarter of 2008, one of the worst performances on record. Paulson's words may have done at least as much to destroy asset values worldwide as the bombing of the Axis powers by the Allies in World War II.

Moreover, Paulson proclaimed his urgent insight just a few weeks before a hotly contested national election. McCain and his running mate, Sarah Palin, were surging ahead of Obama and Biden in mid-September before Paulson spoke up. They and the rest of the Republican Party had no hope after Paulson's panicky message was delivered to the nation. How could Republicans hope to win anything after their own president, brilliant Treasury secretary from Wall Street in tow, went before the nation to say that the result of eight years of his administration was a nation on the brink of collapse into a Great Depression, one that could be prevented only by the taxpayers coughing up $700 billion to bail out the banks? McCain, Palin, and the rest of the Republicans were lucky to do as well as they did with this Great Depression monkey on their back. Paulson's Panic consequently achieved what the old Soviet polit-buro tried and tried to accomplish for decades but never could—a leftist takeover of the United States.

It was even worse than that. Not only did Paulson's panicked blunder turn over the country to the most liberal/left government in the history of America; it established the precedent for unlimited, runaway govern-ment spending. For if the taxpayers could be gouged for *$700 billion* to bail out the banks, how could anything be denied for the poor, the sick, the lame, the halt, the young, the old, the homeless, and the increasingly wretched refuse of our teeming shores produced by Paulson's panicked economy? All that would soon be energetically sought by the leftists and liberals that Paulson's foolishness put in charge of our government. We are lucky they have gouged us for only a couple of trillion dollars so far.

Yet by the end of the year, Paulson had still only spent half the $700 billion. He said he needed the money to buy the bad mortgage-related assets on bank balance sheets to get banks lending again. But after he got his way, he changed course and didn't use the money for that, instead trying to use the funds to rebuild bank capital in return for preferred stock and other interests in the banks, a partial bank nationalization. He wasted a substantial part of the money in forcing some of the big-gest banks to take this capital infusion even though they didn't need it and didn't want it. He didn't want the market to downgrade those banks that did need and receive federal assistance, and thought they would fare better if even the healthy big boys were taking federal assistance as well.

The Great Panic that Paulson spawned was not necessary. What Paulson should have done was rely on the enormous financial safety nets that already existed in the FDIC, the Fed, and the Treasury. Instead of announcing the coming of another Great Depression, Paulson should have quietly asked Congress for an open line of credit to the FDIC for whatever it needed to assure depositors would be paid. Along with the extension of deposit insurance coverage to all bank deposits and money market funds, which was adopted in the bailout package, done quietly, this would have reassured markets and the nation, rather than panicked them. Eliminating mark-to-market accounting would have done more to rescue the banks than all of Paulson's bailout spending, and at no cost to taxpayers.

The Fed also already had the authority it needed to buy securitized shares in pools of mortgages and other loans, to revive the securitization process that had become the foundation of so much lending in the modern economy. Indeed, the Fed has now already pursued this policy.

Banks and other institutions that were in or near insolvency but appeared to have a reasonable chance of climbing out of it could have been given temporary regulatory waivers to allow that to happen, as the regulators had done in previous financial crises. For banks that appeared hopelessly insolvent, the FDIC already had plenty of existing authority to take them over, and either merge them with other healthy, willing banks or ax the shareholders who had let the bank collapse, replace them with the bondholders, and reopen them far healthier, without the burden of debt to the bondholders. The FDIC has long shown it can do that for several banks at a time in a weekend. Paulson did not favor this, apparently because he was too focused on making sure all the bondholders got paid, having become too familiar with them during his long tenure at Goldman Sachs.

Did Deregulation Cause the Crisis?

During the 2008 presidential campaign, Barack Obama alleged over and over again that the financial crisis was due to the right-wing philosophy of deregulation, "a philosophy that views even the most commonsense regulations as unwise and unnecessary." The charge was echoed by fellow Democrats such as House Speaker Nancy Pelosi, who notified us that the financial crisis was all due to the Bush administration's "right wing ideology of anything goes, no supervision, no oversight, no regulation."

But they were never too clear about exactly what deregulation they were talking about. An early foil was the 1999 repeal of the hopelessly outdated, sixty-five-year-old Glass-Steagall Act, a repeal pushed through

Congress by then–Senate Banking Committee chairman Phil Gramm. In late September, Obama was blasting Gramm as "the architect in the United States Senate of the deregulatory steps that helped cause this mess." Glass-Steagall mandated separation of commercial banking, based on deposits, from investment banking, based on issuing and trading securities such as stocks and bonds. The financial community had long ago eaten gaping loopholes into this Swiss cheese chunk of regulation, attempting to compete with the universal banks of Europe, which had never suffered such confused regulatory barriers.

Such long-overdue deregulation played no role in the financial crisis. Bill Clinton, who signed the legislation, and the Treasury secretary who advised him to do so, later Obama advisor Robert Rubin, have both said as much. The securitization of mortgages, so troubled in the financial crisis, is part of the core securities business of investment banks, and even with Glass-Steagall they could buy or even make mortgages if they wanted. Glass-Steagall repeal, in fact, passed the Senate 90–8, with the votes of Obama supporters Joe Biden, Chuck Schumer, John Kerry, John Edwards, Chris Dodd, and Tom Daschle.

Indeed, exactly contrary to Obama's wild claims, *the repeal of Glass-Steagall was a major factor that helped to counter the financial crisis.* The repeal allowed Bank of America to buy out Merrill Lynch, JPMorgan Chase to buy out Bear Stearns, and Barclays Bank to work on buying up the remains of Lehman Brothers. It allowed investment banks Goldman Sachs and Morgan Stanley to take refuge as diversified bank holding companies. If investment banks Bear Stearns and Lehman Brothers had diversified more into commercial banking, taking commercial deposits, that might have provided them with the superior capital cushions needed to survive. As John Carney put it, "[T]he first line of defense of the financial system has been combining our investment banks with strong depository banks. If we hadn't repealed Glass-Steagall we'd be in much worse shape."

Note that the least regulated of our financial institutions, hedge funds, fared the best in the financial crisis. Derivatives and credit default swaps not based in the broken mortgage market also did not have any trouble. Note also that government regulation is estimated to cost America over $1 trillion per year, about $8,000 in lost output for every U.S. household, almost as costly as the entire individual income tax.

Under the 1999 repeal of Glass-Steagall, banks were not allowed to engage in the risks of investment banking using government-insured deposit funds. Rather, a holding company was allowed to own both a commercial bank, taking deposits, and an investment bank; the two remained separate corporations linked only by common ownership by a third corporation, the holding company. This is a sound regulatory framework that enables the U.S. financial community to remain competitive in the global marketplace with other major financial centers that all operate under the same or looser regulatory constraints.

The full truth was once again recognized by Liebowitz, who wrote in the *New York Post* that the argument that the financial crisis was due to deregulation has it *"exactly* backward." The problem arose *"because* of regulation—regulation driven by liberals and progressives, not free market 'deregulators.' Pushed hard by politicians and community activists, the regulators systematically and *deliberately* altered financially sound lending practices."[87]

Liebowitz is talking here about the CRA and the plethora of associated regulations forcing the debasement of traditional lending standards upon banks, as discussed above. Liebowitz writes further,

> What you will not find, if you read the housing literature from 1990 until 2006 [which reflected the liberal, progressive view], is any fear that perhaps these weaker lending standards that *every government agency* involved with housing tried to advance, that congress tried to advance, that the presidency tried to advance, that the GSEs tried to advance—and with which the penitent banks initially went along and eventually enthusiastically supported— might lead to high defaults, particularly if housing prices should stop rising.[88] (emphasis in original)

The banks were penitent because they soon discovered that if they didn't go along with the new hip housing credit standards debasement, they would be prosecuted by HUD or even by the Justice Department under the new, irresponsible regulatory regime. The mark-to-market accounting regulations represented further regulatory failure contributing to the crisis.

The real cause of America's financial crisis, therefore, was that during the Bush years the president and Democrats and Republicans in Congress departed from every one of the four planks of the Reagan economic program discussed at the outset of this chapter. Bush's Fed created an enormous bubble in housing prices through absurdly loose monetary policies from 2001 to 2006 that overexpanded the money supply and even left the federal funds rate negative in real terms for years. When that bubble burst, as was inevitable, the resulting sharp decline in housing prices brought down wide swaths of America's financial system, which had become heavily invested in mortgages and mortgage-related securities.

The housing bubble began even earlier with the regulatory creation of the subprime mortgage market and the debasement of traditional mortgage lending standards led by liberals and Democrats during the Clinton administration in pursuit of supposedly progressive "affordable housing" policies. This effect, caused by regulation, intersected with the later Fed monetary policies to grow the housing bubble to levels that eventually threatened our entire economy.

Bush and the Democrats and Republicans in Congress also lost control of federal spending during these years, contrary to Reagan's budget-cut policies and reduction of federal spending as a percent of GDP. While Reagan reduced federal spending by about 10% as a percent of GDP, and the Gingrich-led Republican congressional majorities in the 1990s reduced it by another 13%, President Bush and his Congresses had increased it back by nearly 14% by 2008.

Then, when the crisis became apparent at the end of 2007, Bush and congressional Democrats reacted to it not with Reaganite supply-side tax rate cuts, but with old-fashioned, outdated Keynesian economics in the form of tax rebates, or cash grants, which sought to stimulate the economy by increasing spending, rather than through powerful incentives for productive activities like saving, investing, starting and expanding businesses, job creation, entrepreneurship, and work. This reflected the lack of understanding of economic policy by Treasury Secretary Paulson, who had demanded control of administration economic policy as the price of taking the Treasury job from his lofty perch as the head of Goldman Sachs. Paulson's maladministration of economic policy during the rest of 2008 may be referred to as Paulson's Panic, culminating in his

$700 billion bailout plan, which finally panicked the rest of the economy over the edge into deep recession.

The deregulation distraction was never a matter of economics, but of political propaganda. It was advanced to serve the political goals of blaming Wall Street for the financial crisis, and to deflect blame from the real causes in misguided government policies.

OBAMANOMICS

What was most striking about President Obama's economic policies from the very beginning is that they were so thoroughly and carefully structured to follow exactly the opposite of every one of the planks of Reaganomics.[89] Instead of the Reagan budget cuts of 1981, Obama led enactment in his first year of a stimulus bill adding nearly $1 trillion to government spending, probably the largest increase in government spending in world history. That was followed by a $400 billion omnibus spending bill, a $275 billion housing bailout proposal, another $350 billion in TARP bailout spending, and another $250 billion set aside for further bank bailouts. Reagan cut welfare spending back to focus on the truly needy. Obama increased federal welfare spending by one-third in his first two years alone. By 2010, federal spending overall had been increased by 25% in just two years. That does not even count the addition or expansion of three new entitlement programs in Obamacare, at a cost of further trillions.

Instead of Reagan's sharp cuts in income tax rates, President Obama's policies involved comprehensively increasing the top tax rates for every major federal tax. That included a nearly 20% increase in the top two income tax rates, counting the phaseout of deductions and exemptions. The top capital gains tax rate was scheduled to soar by nearly 60%, counting the application of Obamacare's new 3.8% tax on investment income. The tax rate on dividends was scheduled to nearly triple, from 15% to 43.4%, counting the new Obamacare tax as well. The Obamacare legislation also increased the Medicare HI payroll tax rate by 62% for higher-income earners, meaning the nation's employers and investors. The estate tax, more popularly known as the death tax, which had been phased out completely by 2010 under the Bush tax cuts, was scheduled to return from the grave with a 55% top rate.

Reagan pursued tight, anti-inflation, strong-dollar monetary policies, which caused a rising dollar in the 1980s. President Obama's Fed has pursued wildly easy monetary policies, keeping interest rates at record lows near zero for record periods. That has caused gold to soar to all-time records—with its price per ounce higher than the S&P 500 index for the first time ever—and the dollar to decline, buoyed occasionally only by even greater weakness in some other currencies, such as the euro. Reagan assigned to the Fed the sole task of maintaining a stable currency without major inflation. But Obama's Fed took major, if not primary, responsibility for stimulating economic recovery through easy monetary policy, which was a return to the Keynesian monetary policies of the 1970s. Indeed, by the end of 2010, the Fed was announcing a new policy of restoring inflation to stimulate the economy and reduce unemployment.

President Reagan's deregulation saved the economy and consumers ultimately at least $100 billion a year. Included in that was his immediate deregulation of oil prices, and unleashing of the private sector, as Reagan put it, to solve Carter's energy crisis through increased production. President Obama, in sharp contrast, first promoted the multitrillion-dollar cap-and-trade tax, and now, administratively, even more onerous EPA regulation of carbon dioxide emissions under the Clean Air Act. If that EPA regulation, which lacks adequate scientific grounding,[90] is not stopped, it will deprive the nation of the low-cost, reliable energy supplies essential to a modern booming economy.

But President Obama's regulatory policies are shutting down energy production even more directly. Besides the unnecessary and legally unjustifiable Gulf of Mexico oil drilling moratorium, the Obama administration has also shut down oil shale production in the American West, already approved and permitted drilling off the coast of Alaska, and even some onshore production. Despite much rhetoric about favoring nuclear energy production, permits for new projects are not coming fast enough to allow America to keep pace with other major economic competitors around the world in nuclear power, particularly China.

Moreover, sweeping, costly new regulatory burdens under the financial reform legislation will constrain the essential credit needed for job creation and recovery, including access to consumer credit. Yet contrary to President Obama's rhetoric, the legislation includes nothing to address the root causes of the financial crisis.

But this is all just part of a sweeping reregulation firestorm from the Obama administration that is sharply increasing costs and shutting down business expansion and creation, and the resulting jobs, in manufacturing, mining, oil and gas refineries, chemical plants, communications, utilities, railroads, airlines, diesel transportation, natural gas production and use, coal production and use, lithium battery production, agriculture, and food labeling and marketing.[91] Additional problems and costs arise out of antitrust and Occupational Safety and Health Administration reregulation.

Prior to this latest recession, since World War II recessions in the United States have lasted an average of ten months. The longest recession previously was sixteen months, officially scored by the National Bureau of Economic Research (NBER) as starting in December 2007. As discussed above, it was treated from the beginning not with Reagan's supply-side economics, but with the Bush-Obama reprise of Keynesian economics. That started with the February 2008 so-called stimulus package negotiated between Bush and the Democrat Congress, followed by the Obama stimulus one year later, but five times larger and enacted on the promise that it would keep unemployment below 8%.

Yet by September 2010, *thirty-three months* after the recession began, *the economy was still losing jobs overall!* Another 41,000 jobs were lost that month; roughly 350,000 jobs had been lost from May to then. Moreover, in a regular annual benchmark revision to calibrate unemployment rates for updated data, the Bureau of Labor Statistics (BLS) reported a further 366,000 jobs lost for March. In August 2010, the unemployment rate was still rising, climbing to 9.6%.

African-Americans were suffering a depression, with unemployment persisting at 16.1%, stuck in that neighborhood for a year or more. Hispanics had been suffering long-term double-digit unemployment as well, at 12.4% in September. Obamanomics was hitting teenagers the most, with unemployment stuck at 26% for the long term.

The total number of Americans unemployed stood at almost 15 million, with close to half of those classified as long-term unemployed, job-

less for more than six months, and close to a third unemployed for over
a year, the highest since the Great Depression. In addition, the number
employed part-time for economic reasons rose to 9.5 million in September. The BLS reported, "These individuals were working part time because their hours had been cut back or because they were unable to find
a full time job."

Another 2.4 million were defined as marginally attached to the labor
force, an amount stuck at that total for a year. The BLS explains that these
individuals "wanted and were available for work, and had looked for a job
in the prior 12 months," but were not counted among the unemployed because they had not looked for work in the prior four weeks. These included
1.1 million discouraged workers, up 352,000 over the prior year, who were
not currently searching for work and therefore were not counted as unemployed, because they believed no jobs were available for them.

The total army of the unemployed and underemployed consequently
stood at over 26 million Americans. The BLS reported the U6 unemployment rate, which includes the unemployed, those marginally attached to
the labor force (discouraged), and those working part-time for economic
reasons, at 17.1%. That was the highest point since the recession began,
and probably since the Great Depression.

But the job and unemployment numbers in the headlines don't give a
complete picture of the economic troubles America has suffered. In the
Wall Street Journal on August 10, 2010, American Enterprise Institute vice
president Henry Olsen examined the revelations provided by the civilian-
employment population ratio. As Olsen explained, while the unemployment rate measures the percentage of working-age Americans who are
actively seeking jobs but do not have one, "the civilian-employment population ratio measures the percentage of working age Americans who
have a job, whether they are seeking one or not." The trend of this ratio
reflects the full extent of the missing discouraged workers who have
been left hopeless, the full jobs gap that has to be made up, and how far
we are falling behind in terms of jobs that need to be created.

Olsen reported,

Looking at this ratio, America is suffering its largest drop since
World War II. When the economy was at its Bush-era height, in

2007, a little over 63% of adult Americans had jobs. Friday's [July jobs] report shows that only about 58.4% [now] do, a decline of nearly 5 percentage points. While the unemployment rate remains steady at 9.5%, the employment-population ratio continues to fall each month. In April it was 58.8%, in May 58.7%, and in June 58.5%.

Also by September 2010, thirty-three months after the recession began, the U.S. Census Bureau reported an all-time record for the number of Americans in poverty, 44 million, the highest for the fifty-one years that the Census Bureau has been tracking poverty, up 4 million over the prior year, for a poverty rate of 14.3%. Consistent with that, the number of Americans receiving food stamps also hit an all-time record. Within a few years, under Obamacare, a record 97 million Americans will be on Medicaid. September 2010 also saw a new record of 100,000 foreclosures.

On September 20, 2010, the NBER finally decided that the recession had technically ended more than a year earlier, in June 2009. That was still a record eighteen months. But that just means that some economic growth has resumed, and the economy has stopped falling in terms of overall output. Even with this, the above sorry economic record almost three years after the recession began shows how badly President Obama's Keynesian economic policies have failed America.

Historically, the worse the recession, the stronger the recovery. Real economic growth in the first four quarters of Reagan's recovery from the deep 1981–82 recession was a whopping 7.7%. Even the recovery under President Gerald Ford from the deep 1973–74 recession sported real economic growth of 6.2%. A similar boom was generated after the 1960–61 recession by the Kennedy tax rate cuts, even though that recession was not so severe.

But under President Obama's policies, economic growth already fell into another downward spiral in the first year of recovery, with real growth falling from 5% in the fourth quarter of 2009, to 3.7% in the first quarter of this year, to near 2% in the second and third quarters. Indeed, in September 2010, more than a year after the recovery supposedly got under way, GDP was still well below its last previous peak in the fourth quarter of 2007. By contrast, in the Reagan recovery, the economy soared past its previous peak in six months.

As economist John Lott summarizes, "For the last couple of years, President Obama keeps claiming that the recession was the worst economy since the Great Depression. But this is not correct. This is the worst *'recovery'* since the Great Depression." Given the background of postwar recessions, which lasted on average ten months, with the longest previously at sixteen months, and given that the steep recession technically ended in June 2009, the American economy by Election Day 2010 should have been enjoying its second year of a booming recovery, with steadily declining unemployment.

With President Obama's actual recovery the weakest in modern times, potentially even sliding downward into a double-dip recession, the Fed announced in October and November 2010 an ominous new turn in policy. It would ease monetary policy further to the point of re-creating inflation if necessary to spawn a more vigorous recovery and bring down unemployment. In response, gold soared, further beyond the S&P 500. Other commodities, including, most menacingly, oil, followed suit. In turn the dollar began a worrying decline, which meant that everything Americans bought from overseas cost more, portending a declining standard of living.

Federal Reserve Chairman Ben Bernanke is quite certain that he can maintain complete control over inflation. But that is delusional. We are on course to revive inflation expectations, which will require still more, extended recession to quell. If foreign countries decide to embrace a new currency for their foreign trade and their reserve currency because the dollar has become too unreliable, they will dump their dollar reserves at an accelerating rate. This will accelerate the decline in America's standard of living and the revival of uncontrollable inflation.

President Obama's economic policies are not taking America forward to a new vision of prosperity, despite all the self-glorifying, overheated rhetoric. His Rip van Winkle school of economics, studiously ignoring everything that has happened since 1980—indeed, playacting as if none of it ever happened—is only taking us backward to the policies of the 1970s, or even the 1930s. What President Obama is treating us to is effectively a historical reenactment of the 1970s, if not the 1930s, so those of us paying close attention can all see firsthand just how those economic tragedies happened.

Indeed, if President Obama's policy of across-the-board increases in the top rates for every major federal tax is pursued before full recovery, the probability of a double-dip recession will soar to 100%. That is because those higher rates will sharply slash incentives for production and leave American producers, businesses, and employers uncompetitive in the global economy. In that case, instead of the tax increases raising revenue to help close the deficit, the recession will cause the deficit to soar past $2 trillion.

With the top 1% of income earners already paying more in federal income taxes than the bottom 95% of income earners combined, there was never any serious prospect that trying to raise taxes on "the rich" was going to raise much more in revenue in any event. The more likely result would be a capital strike, as those with capital withdraw from the real economy into tax safe havens, and even outright capital flight, as capital flees the country altogether. We can expect, in fact, that just as President Obama is so studiously following the opposite of President Reagan's economic policies in every detail, the result will be the opposite as well, as Art Laffer has argued. What would be the implications of that?

The extension of the Bush tax cuts for two years allowed the long-overdue recovery from the recession to flower, as discussed in Chapter 2. But the results of the Fed's monetary policies may collide with that recovery to produce rising inflation and interest rates this year and next. When the Fed pulls back on its expansionary monetary policies to counter the inflation, the contractionary results may well show up in 2013, when President Obama's scheduled comprehensive tax rate increases for every major federal tax on the nation's employers and investors would go into effect. The combined impact of those two forces, exacerbated by Obama's regulatory tsunami, would produce one whopping recession, just the opposite of Reagan's economic boom that took off in 1983.

CHAPTER 7

THE PROSPERITY OF FREEDOM

Let's Get America Booming Again

The foundation for averting the coming bankruptcy of America is to restore booming economic growth. Only such growth can produce the surging tax revenues to begin to close long-term deficits and sufficiently reduce government spending for essential assistance to those in need. Booming growth will also by itself reduce the national debt as a percent of GDP, because GDP will grow steadily larger over time relative to the debt. If budget surpluses result from the surging revenues and reductions in spending over time, debt as a percentage of GDP will decline that much faster.

We know how to create another twenty-five-year, generation-long economic boom. We did it the last time America got into trouble, in the 1970s, by following timeless principles of economics. Similar to the four planks of Reaganomics discussed in the previous chapter, the planks of this Let's Get America Booming Again economic program are:

- reductions in tax rates to maximize incentives for economic growth;
- reductions in government spending to balance the budget, reducing debt burdens to manageable levels as a percent of GDP;
- sound monetary policies to maintain a stable value of the dollar, without inflation or deflation;
- reductions in regulatory barriers and costs on the economy and production.

The specific policies in each of these areas to restore a new American economic boom are discussed below.

TAXATION: PRINCIPLES, FACTS, AND POLICIES

Marginal Tax Rates

The key to understanding the impact of taxes on the economy is to focus on tax rates, particularly marginal tax rates, which is the tax rate that applies to the last dollar earned. The tax rate determines how much the producer is allowed to keep out of what he or she produces. For example, at a 25% tax rate, the producer keeps three-fourths of his production. If that rate is increased to 50%, the producer keeps only half of what he produces, reducing his reward for production and output by one-third. Incentives are consequently slashed for productive activity, such as savings, investment, work, business expansion, business creation, job creation, and entrepreneurship. The result is fewer jobs, lower wages, and slower economic growth, or even economic downturn.

In contrast, if the tax rate is reduced from 50% to 25%, what producers are allowed to keep from their production increases from one-half to three-fourths, increasing the reward for production and output by one-half. That sharply increases incentives for all of the above productive activities, resulting in more of them, and more jobs, higher wages, and faster economic growth.

Moreover, these incentives do not just expand or contract the economy by the amount of any tax cut or tax increase. For example, a tax cut of $100 billion involving reduced tax rates does not just affect the economy by $100 billion. The lower tax rates affect every dollar and every economic decision throughout the economy. That is because every economic decision is based on the new lower tax rates. Indeed, the new lower tax rates affect every dollar, or unit of currency, and every economic decision throughout the whole world regarding whether to invest in America, start or expand businesses here, create jobs here, even work here, because all these decisions will be based on the new lower tax rates. Tax rate increases have just the opposite effect on every dollar and economic decision throughout the economy and the world.

In addition, marginal tax rates do not just affect the incentives of those to which the rates currently apply. They also affect those to which the rates may apply in the future. For example, consider a small business owner. If he invests more capital in the business to expand production, or hires more workers to increase output, that may result in higher net taxable income. It is the tax rate at that higher income level, not at his current income level, that will determine whether he undertakes the capital investment, or hires more workers.

These incentive effects explain the basis of Hauser's Law discussed in Chapter 2. Over the past sixty years, with top federal income tax rates as high as 92% and as low as 28%, the resulting revenues still persisted at 18–19% of GDP. That is because the higher rates deflated incomes and production so much at the highest income levels, while the lower rates inspired so much more income and production at those income levels, that the end result was basically the same income levels as a percent of GDP. This is why the higher income tax rates make no sense regardless of your political philosophy (unless your philosophy holds that it is good for America to be a poorer nation).

Flat Rate Versus Progressive Rates

A so-called "progressive" tax rate structure applies progressively higher rates to higher incomes. Those higher rates impose all the counterproductive incentives of higher marginal tax rates. The "progressive" tax rate structure effectively imposes a penalty for producing and earning more. Consequently, it naturally results in less productive activity, reducing economic growth and GDP.

Despite these negative economic effects, the progressive tax rate structure is advanced in the name of fairness, on the grounds that it is supposed to be fair for "the rich" to pay more. But it is the flat rate tax structure that is the most fair, not the progressive rates. Under a flat tax rate, if Taxpayer A earns 10 times what Taxpayer B does, then Taxpayer A pays 10 times what Taxpayer B does. But under the progressive tax rate structure, if Taxpayer A earns 10 times what Taxpayer B does, then Taxpayer A pays more than 10 times what Taxpayer B does. That is an unfair penalty on production, which is also economically counterproductive.

For example, consider a pure flat rate tax of 20% applied to all. Taxpayer A makes $500,000 a year; Taxpayer B makes $50,000. Under the 20% tax rate, Taxpayer A would pay $100,000 in taxes; taxpayer B would pay $10,000 in taxes. Consequently, Taxpayer A makes 10 times what Taxpayer B does, and pays 10 times what Taxpayer B does.

Now consider a pure "progressive" income tax that applies a 20% rate to the first $100,000, 25% to the next $100,000, 30% to the next $100,000, 35% to the next $100,000, and 40% to all income above that. Taxpayer B who makes $50,000 a year would still pay $10,000 under that tax. But Taxpayer A, who makes 10 times as much at $500,000 per year, would pay $150,000, which is 15 times as much as Taxpayer B. This penalty on higher incomes is both economically counterproductive and unfair. A flat rate tax with loopholes closed so that a taxpayer who makes 10 times as much pays 10 times as much, but not more, would provide incentives to maximize economic growth, and would be the most fair.

Multiple Taxation of Capital

These incentive effects are compounded in our tax system through the multiple taxation of capital. Capital income is taxed not once, but in fact several times in federal and state tax codes. For example, consider a saver who invests a dollar in a corporate enterprise. Any dollar that corporation earns is taxed at the corporate income tax rate, totaling roughly 40% in America on average now, counting federal and state corporate income taxes. If the remainder of that dollar is paid to the investor in dividends, then it is taxed again through the individual income tax at the dividends tax rate. With President Obama increasing the dividends tax rate from 15% to 43.4%, applying that 43.4% tax rate to the 60 cents remaining after paying the corporate income tax leaves just 34 cents for the investor out of the original dollar earned.

A third layer of taxation of capital income is represented by the capital gains tax. Consider an asset such as a share of stock. When the price of that asset increases, that is reflecting an increase in the expected value of the future income stream to that asset. That future income will be taxed by both the corporate income tax and the individual income tax when earned. If that asset is sold now, taxing the increased value by the capital gains tax is effectively taxing that future income stream a third time.

The death tax (the popular name for the estate tax) is still another, fourth layer of taxation of capital income. If the investor in our example above saves the 34 cents remaining on that dollar of corporate earnings after paying the corporate and individual income tax, and leaves it to his children at death, applying the death tax to it would take roughly half of what is left, leaving his children just 17 cents out of the original dollar earned.

Our tax system further burdens capital income through depreciation rather than immediate expensing. Except for capital investment in plant and equipment, all other business expenses are deducted in the year they are incurred, because the income tax is supposed to be on net income after expenses. But deductions for the expenses of acquiring capital equipment must be spread out over many years under arbitrary depreciation schedules. Capital equipment is what makes American workers the most productive, and hence the most highly paid with the highest standard of living, in the world. With such capital equipment, for example, workers can use mechanized, computerized, modern crane shovels, rather than their bare hands, for digging and building. Or they can use modern computers rather than just computing in their heads. The effective result of extended, arbitrary depreciation schedules instead of immediate deductions or expensing is higher taxes on investment in capital equipment, which means less of such capital equipment, slowing growth in jobs, productivity, and wages.

Kennedy Got It

While President Obama and his administration fail to understand any of this, President John F. Kennedy did. Kennedy proposed legislation to reduce income tax rates across the board by nearly 30%. Kennedy explained,

> It is a paradoxical truth that tax rates are too high today, and tax revenues are too low and the soundest way to raise the revenues in the long run is to cut the tax rates. . . . [A]n economy constrained

by high tax rates will never produce enough revenue to balance the budget, just as it will never create enough jobs or enough profits."[1]

Kennedy added,

Our true choice is not between tax reduction, on the one hand, and the avoidance of large federal deficits on the other. . . . It is between two kinds of deficits—a chronic deficit of inertia, as the unwanted result of inadequate revenues and a restricted economy—or a temporary deficit of transition, resulting from a tax cut designed to boost the economy, produce revenues, and achieve a future budget surplus.[2]

Kennedy explained further that the best way to promote economic growth "is to reduce the burden on private income and the deterrents to private initiative which are imposed by our present tax system—and this administration is pledged to an across-the-board reduction in personal and corporate income tax rates."[3]

Kennedy's proposed tax rate cuts were adopted in 1964, cutting the top tax rate from 91% to 70%, as well as reducing the lower rates. The next year, economic growth soared by 50%, and *income tax revenues increased by 41%!*[4] By 1966, unemployment had fallen to its lowest peacetime level in almost forty years. *U.S. News & World Report* exclaimed, "The unusual budget spectacle of sharply rising revenues following the biggest tax cut in history is beginning to astonish even those who pushed hardest for tax cuts in the first place."[5] Arthur Okun, the administration's chief economic advisor, estimated that the tax cuts expanded the economy in just two years by 10% above where it would have been.[6]

President Obama's Tax Welfare

President Obama claims that he has cut taxes to revive the economy, too, for 95% of workers in fact. But those "tax cuts" all involved tax *credits* rather than reductions in tax *rates*. The centerpiece is a $400 per year "Making Work Pay" tax credit, $7.69 per week, that is scheduled to expire soon.

Such tax credits do not work to stimulate economic growth, because they do not change the fundamental incentives that govern the economy. A $400 tax credit involves the government either explicitly or effectively sending you a check for $400. But after that, you and everyone else still face the same tax rates and same economic incentives as before.

Tax cuts do not expand the economy by "putting more money in people's pockets," thereby leading to increased spending. Increased welfare benefits would put more money in people's pockets as well. But this is an outdated Keynesian rationale from the 1930s, which, again, does not work, for two reasons. First, the government has to borrow or tax the money from someone else in the economy to give you the tax credit or increased welfare check. So, if it takes $400 out of the economy to give you $400 through the tax credit or increased welfare, it has not added anything to the economy on net. Second, again, there is no change in fundamental incentives.

Note also that Obama's tax credits are refundable, which means if you do not have enough income tax liability for the credit to offset, the government will send you a check for the difference. The tax credit in this case is entirely indistinguishable from welfare, which is never going to be the foundation for a booming economy. Obama's own budget documents show that 35% of his supposed income tax cuts go to people who do not pay income taxes, and therefore those are not tax cuts at all, but welfare checks. This is why Obama's own budget accounts for this portion of his supposed tax cuts as outlays rather than revenue reductions. You can't *cut* income taxes for people who do not pay income taxes.

The Rich and Their "Fair Share"

Even before President Obama was elected, official Internal Revenue Service data showed that in 2007 the top 1% of income earners paid 40.4% of all federal income taxes, almost twice their share of adjusted gross income.[7] The top 5% paid 60.6% of all federal income taxes, while earning 37.7% of adjusted gross income.[8] The top 10% paid 71.2% of all income taxes, while earning 48% of adjusted gross income.[9]

By contrast, the bottom 95% of income earners paid 39.4% of all federal income taxes.[10] That means the top 1% of income earners paid more federal income taxes than the bottom 95%!

Again, this was *before* the comprehensive tax rate increases for every major federal tax, a central part of President Obama's economic plan, and which he justified by saying they were necessary to ensure that the rich paid their fair share of taxes. But the data above raises the question, just what would be their "fair share"?

IRS data also shows that those on whom President Obama wants to increase taxes, earning more than $200,000 a year, constitute just 3% of taxpayers. Yet that 3% pays more in income taxes than the bottom 97% combined.[11]

Given these facts, increasing taxes on the top 1%, or the top 3%, in the name of "fairness" would effectively enshrine in the tax code the morality of pirates, or of Willie Sutton, who explained that he robbed banks because "that's where the money is." Because of the gross imbalance in the tax code that already exists, attempting to raise taxes further on this small sliver of the population is not going to generate any significant additional revenues, and more likely will lose revenue overall, especially if a recession results.

The Middle Class, the Working Poor, and Reagan's Republicans

The facts also demonstrate the falsehood of the charge made by Obama and the Democrats that Republicans cut taxes for the rich but haven't "given a break to folks who make less." The share of federal income taxes paid by the top 1% was 17.6% in 1981, when President Reagan brought his supply-side economics to Washington.[12] After a quarter century of rate cuts, that share had more than doubled by 2007, as indicated above. That is because with the lower tax rates, incomes boomed along with the economy, and high-income taxpayers had the incentives to pull their money out of tax shelters and invest it in the real economy, fueling the boom while increasing their reported income.

But in 2007, again before President Obama was even elected, the bottom 40% of income earners as a group paid no federal income taxes.[13] Instead they received net payments from the income tax system equal to 3.8% of all federal income taxes.[14] In other words, they paid negative

3.8% of federal income taxes. The middle 20% of income earners, the actual middle class, paid 4.7% of all federal income taxes.[15]

This is the result of the Republican supply-side economics that began with Reagan and Jack Kemp in the 1970s and 1980s, continued through Newt Gingrich and his Contract with America, and further played out with the Bush tax cuts of 2001 and 2003. Reagan and his Republicans abolished federal income taxes on the poor and what liberals call the working class. Moreover, they almost abolished federal income taxes on the actual middle class (the middle 20%).

The origins of the Earned Income Tax Credit (EITC), which has done so much to reduce income tax liabilities for lower-income people, can be found in Ronald Reagan's famous testimony before the Senate Finance Committee in 1972, where he proposed exempting the working poor from all Social Security and income taxes as an alternative to welfare. It was that testimony that led Congress to adopt the credit in 1975. As president, Reagan cut federal income tax rates across the board for all taxpayers by 25%. He also indexed the tax brackets for all taxpayers to prevent inflation from pushing workers into higher tax brackets.

In the Tax Reform Act of 1986, President Reagan reduced the federal income tax rate for "folks who make less" all the way down to 15%. That act also doubled the personal exemption, shielding more income from taxation for everybody, but a higher percentage of the income of lower-income workers.

Gingrich's Contract with America adopted a child tax credit of $500 per child that reduced the tax liabilities of lower-income people by a higher percentage than for higher income people. President Bush doubled that credit to $1,000 per child and made it refundable, so that low-income people who do not even pay $1,000 in federal income taxes could still get the full credit. Bush also adopted a new lower tax bracket for the lowest-income workers, 10%, reducing their federal income tax rate by 33%. Again, he cut the top rate for the highest-income workers by just 11.6%, from 39.6% to 35%.

These tax changes are the reason that by 2007, the bottom 40% of income earners paid no income taxes. Many conservatives do not think it was a good idea to exempt so many from paying any income taxes at all. Nevertheless, the charge that the Republicans cut taxes only for the rich is factually groundless. Under Reagan Republican tax policies, the share of income taxes paid by "the rich" has soared to arguably excessive, even abusive, levels, while income taxes were abolished for the poor and working class, and almost abolished for the middle class.

Instead of bemoaning this, it would probably be wiser for conservatives and Republicans to take credit for it. Indeed, the politically wisest course would probably be to support tax reform that finishes zeroing out any income tax liability for the middle class (again the middle 20% of income earners) as well as lower-income earners, which would not result in much additional revenue loss. The last two Democrat presidents won by running on a tax cut for the middle class, which would then no longer be possible. While conservatives fear the politics of a majority of voters paying no income taxes, conservative candidates could then run arguing that the tax-exempt should vote for them to protect their exemption from tax-voracious big-government liberals, just as liberals run while arguing that seniors should vote for them to protect their Social Security benefits from budget-cutting conservatives. A politically untouchable exemption from the income tax for the bottom 60% of income earners would mean a sharp limitation on the revenues that could be raised for big-government spending. Moreover, even the tax-exempt would oppose raising taxes on top income earners if they feared losing their jobs and a horrible economy as a result.

In any event, I do not think it would be viable for conservatives to run for office arguing that taxes must go up on the bottom 60% of income earners because "everybody needs to pay something," all the more while arguing for tax rate cuts for top income earners and corporations to provide full incentives for economic growth. That is why even flat-tax advocates have always included in their reforms exemptions for the lower-income earners that do not pay taxes under the current system.

Taxes and Economic Freedom

Instead of judging taxes by the morality of tax piracy, the only reasonable way to judge taxes is by their impact on economic growth and prosperity, and on economic freedom. Higher taxes mean less personal freedom, because that reduces personal control over your income, and the government rather than you decides how it is spent or saved. Lower taxes mean more personal freedom, because that increases personal control over your own income, and leaves you with more of your own income to choose to save, spend, or invest as you desire.

Therefore, taxes as a percentage of GDP should be taken as a reverse indicator of economic freedom. Higher taxes as a percentage of GDP mean less economic freedom; lower taxes as a percentage of GDP mean more freedom.

Maximizing Economic Growth—the 15% Solution

Based on the above discussion, an income tax code maximizing economic growth would keep rates as low as feasible, and tax capital income only once, just as labor income is. That would mean eliminating the multiple taxation of capital and all discriminatory taxation of capital income. It would also mean a flat rate rather than progressive income tax.

I offer below proposed tax reforms along these lines designed to help stimulate another twenty-five-year, generation-long economic boom and generate enough revenue to achieve a long-term balanced budget, given the spending policies discussed below and the other reforms proposed in this book. The reforms are designed based on a dynamic rather than static analysis, which means all the positive economic growth effects are considered in estimating the resulting revenues.[16]

INDIVIDUAL INCOME TAXES

The flat income tax proposals of others over the years, such as Robert Hall and Alvin Rabushka, Art Laffer, Steve Forbes, Dick Armey, and Steve Moore, generally indicate that a single flat income tax rate of 17–19% would generate the same revenue as the current income tax system, on a static basis, meaning without considering the positive economic effects of the reforms. These proposals have mostly included generous personal exemptions essentially leaving tax-exempt the low-and moderate-income workers who pay little or no tax under the current tax system.

A single flat rate income tax of 15% would quite possibly generate the same revenues as the current income tax, considering dynamic economic growth effects. This is with a generous personal exemption of $10,000 that would leave low- and moderate-income families untaxed. Apart from deductions for expenses incurred in generating income, so that the tax remains a levy on net rather than gross income, all other deductions, credits, and loopholes should be eliminated (except for the Consumer Choice Tax Credit, discussed in Chapter 4). That would leave a simple flat tax that could be filed on a postcard, saving millions of hours and billions of dollars on tax record keeping and preparation

The deductions eliminated should especially include those for state taxes, such as for income, sales, and property taxes. Such deductions only encourage higher state and local taxes and spending. Similarly, it would be desirable to eliminate the deduction for interest on newly issued state and local government bonds (leaving the deduction for bonds already purchased intact), for that only encourages more state and local government debt.

The deduction for home mortgage interest is a big revenue loser and inefficiently distorts more investment into housing and away from other productive opportunities. But compromises can be made for political reasons. That is true for the deduction for charitable contributions as well. Note that reducing all tax rates to 15% sharply reduces the revenue lost from all deductions, since the deductions would be taken against a lower rate. For example, a $1,000 deduction taken against a 35% tax rate reduces tax liability by $350. But a deduction taken against a 15% rate loses only $150 in revenue. The key implication of this is that keeping a deduction with the lower single rate doesn't cost as much in terms of lost revenue.

Note as well that the tax reform does not need to be revenue neutral. It can be a net tax cut. Indeed, trying to strictly adhere to a requirement of revenue neutrality would probably leave the whole reform effort politically infeasible. That is because strict revenue neutrality inevitably means that some people will pay more under the reform while others pay less, a perfect formula for political gridlock. No reform is going to leave everyone paying exactly the same as under the current system. A net tax cut would allow for everyone to pay a little less, making sweeping reform politically feasible.

Another way to dampen special interest opposition to the elimination of tax loopholes and deductions is to make the new flat tax system optional, as proposed by Steve Moore of the *Wall Street Journal*. Taxpayers can be allowed a choice of whether to file under the new, simple flat tax system, or under the old system, with all its loopholes and deductions. Those to whom some loophole or deduction of the current system was most important could then still file under that system.

The current tax code also loses huge chunks of revenue due to the exclusion of employer-provided health insurance from taxable income. As discussed in Chapter 4, that should be transformed into the Consumer Choice Tax Credit, empowering all workers with the same tax advantages as enjoyed by those with employer-provided insurance. While that credit is not ideal from the perspective of tax policy, from the perspective of health policy, and given the current policy framework of Obamacare, it is probably necessary as a political matter.

But virtually all other credits in the income tax code should be eliminated as the worst form of economic distortion, special interest vote buying, and abuse. An exception can be made for the R & D tax credit, which can be justified as compensating for the general social benefits of advancing technology, which are not fully captured by the inventors, innovators, and producers of that technology.

The EITC and the Child Tax Credit should be block-granted back to the states with the other welfare programs discussed in Chapter 5. The EITC has proved to be very effective as welfare policy, but subject to lots of fraud and abuse as tax policy. The states can each decide how best to provide their own wage supplements to carry out the policy of the EITC, which can involve direct cash grants rather than tax credits. The Child Tax Credit does have a desirable social goal in promoting families and a stable domestic population, to avert the economically and socially destabilizing population declines that threaten other countries due to collapsing fertility rates, particularly Russia, Japan, and some Western European countries. But in the United States each state can decide what child supplements to provide and how. The $10,000 personal exemption of the proposed flat tax also largely serves the function of the Child Tax Credit.

Note that the single flat-rate tax eliminates any marriage penalty in the tax code entirely. It also eliminates any possibility that inflation will force working people into higher tax brackets.

CORPORATE INCOME TAXES

The federal corporate income tax rate in the United States is 35%. Counting state corporate income tax rates as well pushes the average corporate U.S. tax rate close to 40%, virtually the highest in the industrialized world. That is because other countries have learned the lessons of Reaganomics, even as President Obama wants to pretend it never happened. As a result, in the last ten years, the average corporate tax rate for the European Union has been reduced from 38% to 24%. Germany enjoys a 15% national corporate rate, as does Brazil; Canada's 18% rate is scheduled to fall to 15% in 2012. Even China, still run by the Communist Party, enjoys a 25% corporate tax rate.

How are America's companies supposed to compete in the global marketplace with this corporate tax rate disability? How can America's companies provide good jobs at high wages to American workers, when the companies are not internationally competitive due to crippling tax burdens?

America's international competitiveness would be restored with a 15% corporate tax rate, matching the individual income tax rate. State corporate income taxes would then leave America's rate close to 20% on average, unless the states wisely follow the recommendation in Chapter 8 to eliminate state income taxes. The federal corporate income tax currently accounts for only 7% of federal revenues, so sharply reducing the rate is not going to decimate federal finances. But closing the extensive corporate tax loopholes in the reform in return for the lower rates, and considering the revenue feedback from the positive dynamic effects of the reform, the overall result could well be little or no revenue loss on net, if not actual net revenue increases from the corporate income tax as the economy booms.

CAPITAL GAINS TAXES

Based on our discussion at the outset of this chapter, the capital gains tax should be zeroed out, for both individuals and corporations, since it basically taxes an additional time the present discounted value of income that would be taxed when it is earned. It is one of the additional, multiple layers of taxation on capital income. Such multiple taxation discourages capital investment, reducing GDP, economic growth, jobs, and even wages, which are strongly affected by the amount of capital available to each worker. It particularly discourages the venture capital essential to the start-up of significant new companies, as that initial capital investment is banking on an eventual sharp run-up in the capital value of the company. These are the reasons why fourteen out of thirty OECD countries, plus China, Taiwan, Hong Kong, Singapore, and others, already enjoy zero capital gains taxes.

The current income tax code taxes individual capital gains at 15%, reflecting the 2003 Bush tax cuts, with corporate capital gains still taxed at 35% at the federal level. While ideally these rates should be zeroed out, there are some advantages to taxing capital gains at 15% for both individuals and corporations. In particular, the 15% capital gains rate would be a revenue bonanza, especially in an economic boom, without too much of a negative economic effect. Moreover, as previously indicated, over the past forty years, every time the capital gains tax has been cut, revenues have increased, and the 15% rate would involve a major cut in corporate capital gains. Given America's financial difficulties, the country needs revenue that can be obtained without significant economic harm.

Moreover, taxing all apparent income at the same 15% rate has political appeal, even if it effectively involves taxing the same income twice at that 15% rate. Many policy makers are not intellectually capable of understanding the concept of present discounted value of the future income stream, or at least they are good at pretending they don't, and they would be mollified by the across-the-board 15% rate.

Dividends Tax

Based on the principle of taxing capital income only once, either the corporate income tax should be completely abolished or corporate dividends should be made tax-free. A 15% corporate tax rate would mean a zero tax for corporate dividends.

But again, the dividends tax rate under current law is 15%, reflecting the 2003 Bush tax cuts. In an economic boom, continuing that rate also would provide bountiful, much-needed revenues without an excessive adverse economic effect. And the uniform applicability of the 15% rate would appeal to those who can't understand the concept of double taxation, or see its unfairness.

EXPENSING

Based on the discussion at the outset of this chapter, all investment in plant and equipment should be deductible in the year the expense is incurred, just as with all other business expenses. Depreciation would then be abolished for all such investment. This would provide maximum incentives for investment in tools and technology for production, ensuring that American workers will enjoy the most modern and productive equipment and plant facilities in the world.

As a result, American workers would continue to be the most productive in the world. Wages in the marketplace are determined by productivity, so this provision would maximize wages and wage gains for working people.

PAYROLL TAXES

As discussed in Chapters 3 and 4, workers should be allowed the freedom to choose to save and invest eventually all of their payroll taxes in a personal savings, investment, and insurance account that would take over responsibility for financing all the benefits currently financed by the payroll tax. That would allow the payroll tax to be eventually phased out entirely. This would free labor income from double taxation and lower the cost of labor for employers, which would mean more jobs and higher wages.

DEATH TAXES

To maximize economic growth, the death tax, or estate tax, should be abolished as well. As we have seen, that is just another layer of taxation on lifetime savings that was already taxed several times when it was earned. The rich don't pay the death tax, because they have the money to employ accountants to get around it. Only more middle-class, small-business persons pay this tax when they try to leave the family business to their children. Several economic studies show that abolishing this tax would enable greater and more efficiently allocated capital investment, maximizing overall economic growth and quite possibly resulting in more overall revenue rather than less.

ALTERNATIVE MINIMUM TAX

The Alternative Minimum Tax (AMT) was adopted at the end of the Johnson administration based on the supposed scandal of some of the richest few hundred taxpayers avoiding any income tax at all through the thorough exploitation of legal tax loopholes and tax shelters (including in particular the tax exemption for interest on state and local government bonds). But the income thresholds for this tax were never indexed for inflation, so now the tax threatens to apply to more middle-class taxpayers, particularly in higher-tax states (primarily because the deduction for state and local taxes is one of the qualifying factors for the AMT). So Congress now routinely extends an exemption from the AMT to avoid this middle-class tax increase.

Congress should just abolish the AMT charade entirely. It is just yet another layer of taxation, and with the flat tax reform recommended above, the tax loopholes and shelters that can shield even the richest from any income taxes would be directly abolished.

HOW TO BALANCE THE BUDGET

The fundamental strategy to balancing the budget is to start with the tax code that would maximize long-term economic growth, and then to shoehorn spending into the revenues produced by that tax code. That would produce the highest wages and the most jobs for working people.

This would require both short-term spending reductions and long-term fundamental reforms of major spending programs. Since I do not believe in human suffering, I am not an advocate of pain and sacrifice through budget cuts, except for commercial special interests living off the public who should not be, and others taking advantage of the taxpayers through sweetheart deals. Consequently, while the spending cuts I propose sharply reduce federal spending, they are carefully structured so that no one in need is left without essential assistance. Following that principle will make the spending cut proposals more politically feasible and even popular. To be sure, various special interests who benefit from that spending, and doctrinaire liberals who believe government spending no matter what is good, would vigorously oppose these cuts.

But given the deep financial dangers facing America, including outright bankruptcy, those unworthy sentiments can be defeated. That is a good thing, because another principle of mine is that it's a waste of time to advocate political kamikaze missions.

I do believe, however, in challenges that will require elected political leaders to learn the appealing populist virtues of complex proposals, and how they would benefit working people, the middle class, and the poor, and then articulately explain those proposals to the general public. Too much of the political conflict we see in Washington is not actually due to a fundamental clash of values, but to a failure of political leaders to dig into and understand the key issues, to communicate them articulately, and to try to understand what the apparent opposing side is actually saying.

The traditional Washington-establishment approach to balancing the budget is to negotiate an agreement on a package of spending cuts and tax increases. This is what President Obama's Deficit Commission did in proposing to raise taxes by nearly $1 trillion over ten years, though the commission deserves credit for proposing tax reforms that recognize the fundamental importance of reducing tax rates, and for many sweeping proposed spending reductions. But the tax increase/spending cut approach never works, and has no prayer of ever working.

That is because the tax increases are permanently adopted into law. But the spending cuts are never fully adopted, or if they are they are soon swept away in the next liberal budget. Then the tax increases don't raise the revenue projected, and budgeted to be spent, due to the negative incentive effects of the increased taxes. So the deficit reappears and worsens until voters can be fooled by the whole charade again. This is exactly what has happened several times at federal and state levels.

The federal experience goes back to 1982, when congressional Democrats promised President Reagan $3 in spending cuts for every $1 in tax increases. Reagan went to his grave still waiting for those spending cuts.

Then there was the 1990 budget deal, where President George H. W. Bush agreed to violate his famous 1988 campaign pledge, "Read my lips, no new taxes," for a supposed balanced budget. But the deficit increased from $221 billion in 1990, to $269 billion in 1991, to $290 billion in 1992, when voters booted him out for violating the tax pledge that got him elected.

In 1993, President Clinton tried for a balanced budget, with a Democrat Congress voting through a tax increase as part of the deal. By 1995, the new Republican Congress, elected to replace the tax-increasing Democrat Congress, was greeted with a Clinton budget projecting $200 billion deficits indefinitely into the future.

House Speaker Newt Gingrich led Congress to undertake a different approach, the one tried-and-true way to balance the budget. It is a simple two-step process. One: cut tax rates to improve incentives for savings, investment, job creation, business creation, business expansion, entrepreneurship, and economic growth, to get the economy booming. You can't balance the budget by constantly chasing lower than expected revenues. With the economy booming, revenue surges consistently. Step two: cut spending growth, and let revenues surge past it.

As discussed in Chapter 6, the new Republican Congress cut the capital gains tax rate by 40% and reduced other tax burdens on capital investment, leading to a resurgent economy. Then they sharply restrained federal spending. Indeed, in six years, from 1994 to 2000, they cut total federal spending relative to GDP by one-seventh, more even than Reagan did, though he was constrained by the need to raise defense spending, which won the Cold War without firing a shot, in Margaret Thatcher's famous phrase.

As a result, $200 billion annual federal deficits, which had prevailed for over fifteen years, were transformed into surpluses by 1998, peaking at $236 billion by 2000.

This is the approach we should adopt now to balance the federal budget again. The above tax reforms constitute the first step: reducing tax rates and adopting other reforms to maximize long-term economic growth. The central strategy for the shorter-term spending reductions is to return spending for all federal budget line items, except Social Security, Medicare, and Medicaid, and debt interest, back to the levels in the fiscal 2007 budget. That was just four years ago, and America survived just fine with those spending levels. Apart from the three major excluded entitlement programs, which would be slated for fundamental, long-term structural reforms, as discussed in previous chapters, there is no other federal program or spending category, including national defense, that could not perform perfectly well at 2007 spending levels (except debt interest). Based on the president's own budget documents, this would save $527 billion in annual spending to start, growing over time since the long-term baseline would be lower. Even if Congress just returned discretionary spending back to 2007 levels, that would reduce spending by $374 billion in the first year, and $1.56 trillion over ten years.[17]

In the process, we should ensure that all unspent stimulus spending is repealed. The failure of that Keynesian spending strategy has now been demonstrated so many times, in theory as well as in practice, that university economics departments should stop teaching it. Failing that, I would favor legal recognition of a cause of action by failed small businesses and unemployed workers against said university economics departments for malpractice.

A second central theme to balancing the budget is a full-scale assault on all corporate bailouts and corporate welfare throughout the entire budget. This would include, of course, terminating TARP and all other bailouts, and returning the money to the federal Treasury rather than recommitting the money to any further bailouts. Fannie Mae and Freddie Mac, those twin engines of the financial crisis that have already sucked up $150 billion in taxpayer bailouts and counting, should be phased out over the years, replaced by private financial institutions securitizing mortgages in competitive markets.

Former assistant Treasury secretary Emil Henry Jr. explained how to do that in the *Wall Street Journal* in November 2010.[18] Fannie and Freddie raise funds to buy and securitize new mortgages by issuing debt to the public in the form of bonds, which the market assumes are backed by the federal government, providing the two mortgage giants with an overwhelming interest rate advantage that has driven out almost all private competition. Under current law, the secretary of the Treasury has the power to phase down the issuance of new debt by these two GSEs. Henry recommends phasing down that newly issued debt to zero over an eight-year period, which would allow private securitization firms to flourish and ultimately replace Fannie and Freddie entirely. Fannie and Freddie could then be liquidated after this period. This would not only end all further taxpayer bailouts of these GSEs, but also terminate an indiscriminate government housing subsidy provided broadly throughout the market. Under the thorough welfare reforms advanced in Chapter 5, each state could then decide how to use the extensive current low-income housing subsidy funds for the worthy goal of helping responsible low- and moderate-income families attain home ownership.

This budget-balancing theme would also mean terminating or phasing out the traditional corporate bailouts and welfare well ensconced in the general budget. That would include such stale programs as the Overseas Private Investment Corporation and the Export-Import Bank, which raid taxpayer funds to support job creation overseas.

Another outdated form of corporate welfare is the agriculture subsidies left over from the New Deal era seventy-five years ago. There is no reason why farming and agriculture cannot operate without taxpayer subsidies just like any other business. Most crops, in fact, do. The Gingrich-led Republicans in the 1990s adopted Freedom to Farm, which provided for phasing out farm subsidies in return for removing government controls over what farmers could grow. This was a long-overdue reform, but Congress backed off it in 2002 after Gingrich left office. That needs to be brought back, with ten-year budget savings of $290 billion.[19]

But there is a whole new family of corporate welfare bailouts in President Obama's "green" energy subsidies for wind, solar, and other alternative fuels, now amounting to tens of billions of dollars per year, and slated to explode further. The fallacy of these subsidies is illustrated by the proposed Shepherds Flat wind farm project in Oregon, sponsored by General Electric Company and Caithness Energy, LLC. Counting federal and state subsidies, taxpayers are to cover 65% of the costs of the project, involving 338 GE wind turbines, while the corporate developers are to put up only 11% of the costs themselves.[20] Yet the project is still expected to charge its power consumers above-market rates, as compared to traditional energy sources.

Another example is the proposed world's largest solar-thermal power plant, to be built on seven thousand acres of federally owned land near Blythe, in the Southern California desert. The federal government would finance nearly a third of the $3 billion investment for the first half of the project, expected to provide only three hundred permanent operating jobs when fully completed.[21] Yet the project would still result in higher energy costs for power users, including businesses and consumers in Southern California.

Overall, the U.S. Energy Information Agency reports that taxpayer subsidies for wind and solar projects average nearly 100 times those for oil and natural gas, nearly 50 times those for coal, and even 15 times those for nuclear production.[22] A globally cited Spanish study found that such supposed "green jobs" subsidies in Spain ended up costing $774,000 per job.[23] In Denmark, the subsidy per green energy job created was $90,000 to $140,000 per year, 250% as high as the average pay per worker in Danish manufacturing.[24] In Germany, the government subsidy per green job was as high as $240,000 per year.[25]

In return for these huge costs per job created, the resulting energy costs far more for power users, which includes job-creating businesses, especially manufacturers, as well as consumers.[26] That is why these green jobs subsidies have been shown to destroy many more jobs than they create. The Spanish study shows 2.2 jobs destroyed for each green job created in that country. An Italian study showed even worse net results for the green jobs subsidies in that country.

The economy would go broke with taxpayers so heavily subsidizing entirely new energy industries, which in turn produce higher cost energy for the economy to run on. Market competition, prices, and supply and demand must decide whether and when alternative "green" energy is the wave of the future, not taxpayer subsidies. President Obama's green energy subsidies need to go the way of President Carter's ill-fated Synthetic Fuels Corporation; that would save $170 billion over ten years.[27]

President Obama's Debt Commission came up with further good deficit spending cuts. One was to reduce the federal workforce by 10%. President Clinton recognized as a former governor that just the number of public employees was a powerful force in the growth of spending, and he helped gain control of federal spending by sharply restraining the number of federal civilian employees. President Reagan maintained a federal hiring freeze for most of his two terms as well.

Obama's Debt Commission also proposed freezing federal pay for three years, which is quite justifiable given studies showing an explosion in federal pay in recent years, well beyond comparable private sector compensation standards. From 2005 to 2010, the number of federal workers making over $150,000 per year surged more than tenfold, from 7,420 to 82,034; the number making over 170,000 soared by 21 times from

1,322 to 27,845; and the number making over 180,000 rocketed by 21 times as well, from 805 to 16,912.[28] In 2009, average pay and benefits for federal civilian employees climbed to more than double that of private sector workers, $61,051 to $123,049.[29] Since 2000, federal compensation in real terms after adjusting for inflation grew by 37%, compared to 9% for private sector workers.[30]

The Debt Commission also proposed merging the Small Business Administration with the Department of Commerce. But given all the other reforms in this book, the remaining functions of the departments of Agriculture, HUD, Labor, and Commerce could all be merged into a new Department of Economic Growth, with the mission of promoting pro-growth economic policies. Given its remaining functions, the Department of Energy could be split into the departments of Interior and Defense. And the remaining functions of the Department of Education could be block-granted back to the states, since education is primarily a state and local function.

Some other spending cuts are just long overdue, as further recognized by the Debt Commission. With modern satellite television and radio, not to mention cable TV, we cannot justify borrowing money from the Chinese to finance National Public Radio and public television. They need to finance their own way in the private sector. The same goes for Amtrak. Also overdue are repealing the top-dollar wage requirements for federal projects required by Davis-Bacon, freezing all further urban mass-transit projects for now, privatizing air-traffic control, and terminating AmeriCorps and the Small Business Administration, for a ten year savings altogether of $205 billion.[31] The costly defined benefit Civil Service Retirement System for federal employees should be replaced by a defined contribution plan with specific contributions to worker investment accounts, as proposed for state and local workers in Chapter 8. The federal government also owns millions of acres of surplus federal properties that do not involve public parks or environmentally sensitive lands, which should be sold into private ownership for productive uses, which would add to the economy and provide additional federal revenues. To the extent necessary to balance the budget in the short term, well within the ten-year budget window, all nondefense discretionary spending should be frozen until that is achieved.

Repealing Obamacare and replacing it with the patient power alternatives would save over $3 trillion in spending over the first ten years of full Obamacare implementation, and more than double that in the second ten years, as indicated by the analysis in Chapter 4. The other entitlement reforms discussed in this book would more than balance the budget over the long run, sharply reducing federal spending well below the postwar average of 20% of GDP. That would include block-granting the remaining 184 federal means-tested welfare programs back to the states, as discussed in Chapter 5, saving trillions over the first ten years. It would also include expanding the personal accounts, as discussed in Chapter 3, to eventually finance all the benefits now financed by the payroll tax, ultimately reducing federal spending by 10% of GDP, itself the largest cut in government spending in world history.

Finally, with a balanced budget and booming economic growth, the national debt as a percentage of GDP would plummet. That means the relative debt burden would plummet as well, slashing debt interest spending as a percentage of GDP. Based on CBO's projections, that could ultimately reduce federal spending by another 10% of GDP.

The net result of it all would eventually be to cut the federal behemoth at least in half from where it would otherwise be, maybe more. But remember, with all of the above reforms, worthy federal functions would not go unserved. Most of them would be served instead far better through the private capital and insurance markets (retirement and health care), the private labor markets (welfare), and the states.

MONETARY POLICY AND A STABLE DOLLAR

Milton Friedman won his Nobel Prize for his work and insights on monetary policy.[32] And one of his primary insights was that an economy may get a short-term sugar high from an increase in the money supply brought on by an expansionary easy-money policy, but ultimately such a policy does not increase economic growth. Easy monetary policy, increasing money in excess of the demand for money, ends up simply increasing prices in inflation, with no positive effect on real economic

growth. Moreover, Friedman taught that the price of bringing down inflation would always be temporarily higher unemployment.

Another key Friedman insight was that the Fed's monetary policies
operate with long lag times, a year or even two after a policy action,
whether easing monetary policy to expand the economy or tightening
policy to counter inflation and slow a runaway economy. So if the Fed is
trying to ease to counter recession, by the time it recognizes the recession is ending and it cuts back on stimulative policy, it is too late. The
stimulative policy would really be having its effect one to two years later,
by which time the economy would be in a recovery boom, and the result
would just be to contribute directly to inflation. If the Fed then tightens
to stop inflation, by the time it recognizes that inflation is declining and
it relaxes monetary policy, it is too late. The restrictive, contractionary
policy would still be affecting the economy a year or two later, when unemployment has risen as the price of fighting inflation, and the contractionary policy would then just be contributing to higher unemployment
and recession. That is how the 1970s got into four ever-worsening cycles
of recession and inflation from 1969 to 1982.

These are the central reasons why Reagan was so right to end the
Fed's game of trying to manage the economy through recessions and
inflation by easing or tightening monetary policy. Trying to counter
recession with easy money would just end up in inflation that would
cause higher unemployment and end up in further recession down the
road. The idea that the Fed could expand the real economy through easy
money was another Keynesian notion based on the fallacy that economic
growth is caused by increasing demand, through printing up more dollars in monetary policy, or increasing government spending, deficits,
and debt in fiscal policy. But what actually promotes economic growth
is enhanced incentives for increased production, through lower tax rates
on that production, or reduced regulatory cost burdens on production,
which is what the more modern supply-side economics teaches, rooted
in the work of Robert Mundell and Art Laffer.[33]

But while Milton Friedman's critique of Fed policy intellectually
demolished Keynesian monetary policy prescriptions, Friedman's own
prescription for Fed policy had flaws of its own. Friedman argued that
the Fed should just provide for stable, consistent growth in the money

supply, through preferably a fixed rate of targeted growth meant to match long-term growth in the economy. That was sensible because the supply of money needs to keep up with the demand for money to avoid deflation and recession.

But the supply of money in the economy at any one time turned out not to be easy to determine. Do you just count actual cash, or do you consider as well checking accounts, or savings accounts, or money market funds, or other liquid investments?

Another problem that became more obvious over time is that the demand for money is not stable, so a stable rule for the money supply would create its own problems. Reduced money demand, reflected for example through decreased velocity, or circulation, of money, needs to be matched by reduced supply, or else inflation will result. Increased money demand reflected through increased velocity of money, as may be caused by a real economic boom, needs to be matched by increased supply, or else the boom will be squelched.

While attention to the money supply remains important for all the reasons Friedman explained, the supply-siders advanced a more practical prescription. They argued that the Fed's monetary policy should be guided by prices in real markets, particularly the most policy-sensitive commodity prices, such as oil, silver, copper, and other precious metals, but especially gold, the most policy-sensitive commodity of all, given its ancient tradition as a store of value and money in itself.

This prescription came to be known as the price rule. When such prices started to rise in markets, that signaled the threat of inflation was rising, and the Fed should tighten monetary policy and the money supply. When such sensitive prices started to fall, that signaled the threat of recession or even deflation, and the Fed should ease monetary policy. Following such monetary policies would avoid inflation and deflation, and cyclical bubbles and recessions, and maintain a stable value of the dollar.

That promotes economic growth because investors know that the value of their investments will be maintained without depreciation due to inflation or a declining value of the dollar, and cyclical recessions that might crash their investments will be minimized. This is the policy the Fed should follow to promote economic growth, and ultimately another economic boom.

But President Obama and Fed Chairman Ben Bernanke have adopted their Rip van Winkle economics, doggedly forgetting all the learning and experience provided in recent decades by the Friedman monetarists and the supply-siders, whose approach is exactly what ended the Great Inflation of the 1970s and stopped the cycles of boom and bust that had been pushing the American economy toward collapse during that era. They have insisted on returning to the Keynesian fallacies of the 1970s as if Milton Friedman, the monetarists, the supply-siders, Ronald Reagan, Jack Kemp, and the twenty-five year economic boom—without significant inflation or recession—never happened. And if the rest of us prove unable to stop them before they proceed all the way to bringing back the disastrous policy results of the 1970s, both Obama and Bernanke will have betrayed the responsibility of their offices, and the American people, through gross public policy malpractice.

REDUCING REGULATORY BARRIERS AND COSTS

Energizing America

The most important and urgent deregulatory policy for creating another economic boom is to unleash the private sector to enable it to produce a plentiful supply of low-cost energy. That would provide a lower cost foundation for the entire economy, effectively equivalent to another major tax cut.

America enjoys the resources to be the world's top oil producer, the world's top natural gas producer, the world's top coal producer, and the world's top producer of nuclear energy. The problem is that our own government has stood perversely in the way, preventing America from using its own resources to produce a reliable supply of low-cost energy. Historically, nations have gone to war to ensure their access to essential energy supplies, most notably the Japanese in World War II. By foreclosing America from its own energy supplies, the federal government has effectively committed an act of war against the American people.

Just think of the direct benefits alone to the American economy of holding within its own confines the world's top oil , coal, natural gas, and nuclear power industries. That would involve millions of high paying jobs in those industries alone. And it would involve trillions in revenues to federal, state, and local governments.

But the reliable low-cost energy supplies they produce would create millions and millions of new jobs throughout the entire economy, and ultimately trillions over the years in new revenues due to the booming overall economy that low-cost energy would support. Such energy is critical to manufacturing in particular, which requires extensive amounts of it.

To achieve this, federal and state governments must remove onerous restrictions on offshore and onshore oil drilling. They must remove the excessive regulatory burdens that have prevented the construction of new oil refineries and nuclear power plants for decades. They must allow the development of the boundless new supplies of natural gas that recent discoveries and technological breakthroughs have made possible. They must allow the construction of new power plants, including modern, clean coal plants.

This can and should be done while maintaining all essential environmental standards and requirements. Despite the 2010 BP oil spill in the Gulf of Mexico, modern drilling maintains a strong safety and environmental record, with less oil spilled than in importing oil through tankers, or, indeed, from natural seepage from the environment. Modern energy production technology can afford to bear all necessary costs of maintaining sound environmental standards.

None of this is to say that we as a society must forget about alternative energy such as wind and solar power. Any unnecessary restrictions on their production should be removed as well. But we cannot restore traditional American economic growth and prosperity, and avert the coming bankruptcy of America, while putting our nation's energy industry on welfare to produce high-cost energy that will only kill rather than create jobs, growth, and prosperity.

Correcting the Financial Crisis Mistakes

Despite the passage of President Obama's financial regulatory reform bill, none of the misregulation that contributed to the financial crisis, as explained in Chapter 6, has been corrected. Providing the foundation for another economic boom requires removing that misregulation.

Instead of ending, as advertised, the "too big to fail" doctrine, the financial regulatory reform bill actually institutionalized it. "Too big to fail" refers to the policy of providing federal bailouts to some financial institutions when they get into economic trouble, because of the fear of what their collapse will do to the economy. That practice just makes it more likely that big institutions will fail, because their owners and management take bigger risks, and the markets are willing to finance those risks, because of the expectation that the institutions will be bailed out. President Obama's legislation institutionalized this practice by providing the federal government with the permanent power and the permanent funding to take over and bail out whatever institution the administration thinks is necessary.

This policy is based on the same fallacy as the TARP bailouts adopted in the fall of 2009. As long as the fundamentals of economic prosperity discussed at the beginning of Chapter 6 are maintained—the rule of law, property rights, freedom of contract, low marginal tax rates, the minimum regulatory barriers and costs necessary, sound money, and a stable dollar—the failure of no institution, or even group of institutions, can bring down the entire economy. Financial institutions that fail will quickly be replaced by others to perform the essential functions of lending and finance.

Wall Street veterans who felt their own heads were too close to the chopping block in 2008 will deride this. The titans of Wall Street will never understand how they can go down without bringing the whole economy down. In fact, every ten years or so some of those major players get themselves into serious trouble, and come to Washington selling that same snake oil, that the fate of the world depends on their survival as rich fat cats, even if they temporarily have to pose in welfare-queen drag to survive. In 2008, then–Treasury secretary Hank Paulson, formerly of

Goldman Sachs, was too close to that patrician titan culture himself, and that is why he was so easily and disastrously panicked.

This periodic I'm-too-big-to-fail raid on the taxpayers can and should be stopped by reforming the bankruptcy code to provide for rapid bankruptcy—the unwinding and dissolution of failed financial institutions—preferably in thirty days or less. What money and value is still there in the institution can be rapidly used to pay off creditors and claimants. Parts or even all of the institution still functional can be sold off if possible. But whatever losses have been incurred are gone and can't be brought back. They can be spread only by a bailout to the innocent victim taxpayers, rather than borne by those who took the risks for the potential rewards they usually get in return—the institution's owners, management, and creditors.

Yes, in the case of widespread failures there would be some short-term economic fallout throughout the economy as the panic worked itself through. But just as the average recession since World War II has ended in less than a year, so would any such downturn be over in a year or less, and prosperity quickly restored. For the general public, that is, not for the failed fat cats of the institution. In contrast, haphazard bailouts of the kind we saw in 2008 only prolong and deepen the crisis. Long historical experience with the business cycle confirms this.

But once this policy of rapid bankruptcy replaces too-big-to-fail, the periodic panics will be far more rare. That is because all market players will know they are on their own and must take precautions to protect themselves from any possible contingency by reducing risks and increasing reserve cushions. What is needed is a couple of good, quick, big Wall Street bankruptcies to prove this policy out. I can't wait. The monetary policies described in the last section will further avoid the government creating artificial bubbles with their inevitable busts.

Note that even though, as explained in Chapter 6, the 2008 financial crisis failures were actually caused by bad government policies misleading major Wall Street players into bankruptcy, not their own malfeasance or even misfeasance, rapid bankruptcy and liquidation for such failures is still the right policy. It is the job of these Wall Street fat cats not to be misled into bankruptcy. If they are, there should be no get-out-of-jail-free bailout card letting them skip directly to GO again. If they want to play the Wall Street fat cat game, they must suffer the market consequences if they stumble, whatever the causes. A policy of private gain but socialized losses just robs the taxpayers and spreads further harm throughout the economy. The monetary policies discussed in the last section would help to avoid the government misleading market players in the future (but they can't guarantee the government still won't find a way to do it, as with the subprime mortgage fiasco).

Another deregulatory change that needs to be made is to repeal the Community Reinvestment Act, which Clinton began to use to browbeat bankers into making what turned out to be bad subprime mortgage loans. Especially without too-big-to-fail, bankers need to be free to restrict their lending to demonstrably creditworthy borrowers. If society decides that some assistance to help lower-income families acquire homes is desirable, that assistance can and should be provided through safety net programs, not by looting the banks.

Of course, this also means that lending discrimination lawsuits against banks must be limited to cases involving actual discrimination, not refusals to fund bad credit risks, which as we saw in the financial crisis, just gets everyone in trouble.

Another necessary, corrective regulatory change is to repeal the mark-to-market requirements, for the reasons discussed in Chapter 6. Forcing all financial institutions to write down their assets because some of them tipping into failure have to engage in panic sales just spreads the panic and failure unnecessarily. Traditional accounting based on the expected payment streams from the assets would be quite sufficient.

With Fannie Mae and Freddie Mac phased out, correction of all the causes of the financial crisis would be complete.

ANOTHER GENERATIONAL ECONOMIC BOOM

With no marginal tax rate over 15%, producers will be able to keep 85% of what they produce. The result will be an unprecedented boom in production, and in the activities that lead to higher production—saving, investment, work, starting businesses, expanding businesses, entrepreneurship, and job creation.

Businesses will get an immediate deduction for investing in new plant and equipment. This ensures that American workers will enjoy the latest, most advanced capital equipment to work and produce, which will make them the most productive workers in the world by far. That will mean higher wages and rapidly increasing living standards.

Businesses, investors, and savers can be confident in a sound, strong dollar without inflation. These policies will attract investment to America from the world over, creating still more jobs and higher wages in America. That will bid up the dollar to new highs, securing its role as the world's reserve currency. That strong dollar will buy more goods and services from abroad, making Americans richer. The only drawback is that domestic investment strategies based on a cheap dollar will not be viable. But there will be more than enough other opportunities. Also, under these policies, gold will no longer be a good investment option. But its price will be stable over the long run.

A balanced budget with this monetary policy will keep interest rates moderate and stable over the long run. That will further promote growth. With Social Security and Medicare shifted to personal accounts, welfare shifted to the states, all forms of corporate welfare abolished, outdated agencies and bureaucracies terminated, and unnecessary spending of all kinds slashed, federal spending will eventually stabilize at half or even less than half of what it would be otherwise.

The unfunded liabilities of Social Security and Medicare will be gone. Instead the programs will be fully funded with savings and investment. With no more federal deficits, there will be no more additions to federal debt. With the economy booming, federal debt as a percent of GDP will decline consistently. Instead of bailouts, debt guarantees, and too-big-to-fail, we will have accelerated bankruptcy for financial institutions that get into trouble. This will further avoid government liabilities for such bailouts. Financial institutions will take care to avoid excessive risk, overleveraging, and other economic vulnerabilities, because they will know that if they make a mistake, they will be gone. This all adds up to America's debt problem being solved.

Instead of heavy payroll taxes discouraging work, every American worker will be contributing to the nation's productive savings and capital investment through their own personal accounts. Over time, this will add trillions to the nation's capital stock, adding still more to booming economic growth. That money will be funding the latest new technologies made possible by rapidly advancing science, making America's workers all the more productive and booming the economy even further. Replacing the payroll tax with personal account savings and investment will also maximize the labor force, contributing still more to growth. Workers will also each be choosing their own retirement age, with powerful incentives to delay retirement as long as possible to accumulate still more funds in their personal accounts, leading to still more prosperous retirement years. Those that can will consequently likely choose to retire later and later. This will further maximize the productive workforce. Instead of taxpayers bearing the burden of paying the lowest-income 20% of the population not to work, those who can will be working instead of staying dependent on welfare, further maximizing the productive workforce and contributing to economic growth.

Moreover, the nation's states and cities will no longer be dragging America down into bankruptcy with still more runaway debt, taxes, spending, and unfunded liabilities. Instead states will be further contributing to growth and positive incentives by phasing out their own income taxes, achieved by controlling their own runaway spending. The unfunded liabilities of state and local pensions will also be gone, replaced with savings and investment, further contributing to booming economic growth. The new focus on law enforcement in our nation's cities will add further zones of booming economic growth, contributing still further to our national prosperity. We will explore these new avenues to prosperity in the next chapter.

America will enjoy a powerful, world-leading energy industry in oil, natural gas, coal, and nuclear power. If science can make alternative energy like solar power or wind power viable and cost competitive, without putting the industry on welfare, America will be number one in that, too. This will mean an abundant low-cost supply of energy with which to fuel booming economic growth.

Patient power incentives will be controlling health costs, as a result of the choices of each patient and their families, further reducing the cost burdens on production. That also will be another effective tax cut. America will also enjoy a booming health care industry, liberated from the bureaucratic socialism of Obamacare. People will continue to come from the four corners of the world to get their lifesaving health care in America.

This all will maximize economic freedom as well as prosperity. With low tax rates, people will enjoy the maximum freedom to control the fruits of their own labor, to decide what their own money will be spent on, how much they will save and invest, and where they will invest it, how much to contribute to charity, and where. With sharply reduced government spending and debt, free men and women acting in the private sector and the free market will determine where more of our nation's resources go, maximizing efficiency, which will further maximize growth.

This all adds up to more than a Reagan-like boom—a new economic Golden Age. The 21st century will be another American century.

CHAPTER 8

FAILED STATES

Renewing Prosperity for Your State

The politicians who have run the city of Detroit for the last sixty years have uniformly campaigned as champions of the poor and working people. But what they have uniformly done is sacrifice the interests of the poor and working people to the liberal/left special interests that form the backbone of their dominant political machine. Economists talk about the phenomenon of "market failure," but what we have in Detroit today is a case of "political failure."

By 1950, the population of Detroit had multiplied to 1,800,000 people, and the city enjoyed the highest median income of all major cities in America.[1] Over the ensuing decades, in which the city's politics was a competition solely among the most extreme left wing of the Democratic Party, we saw working people, the middle class, businesses small and large, and capital investment increasingly flee the city and its high taxes, oppressive regulations, and poor services. Today the city is a shrunken shell of its former self, with less than 40% of its former population at 714,000 people.[2] Moreover, its median household income now ranks sixty-sixth among major American cities.[3]

The city government itself is the second-largest employer in Detroit, right behind the city's public school system. In fact, of the city's twenty-five biggest employers, the state, county, and city governments account for 40% of all jobs.[4] The city employs one worker for every 50 city residents remaining, compared to Indianapolis, which employs one worker for every 223 residents.[5]

This municipal socialism is not working. In late 2010, unemployment in Detroit was stuck at 13.4%, which was 40% higher than the national average at the time. This reflected not a cyclical problem, but a long-term depression in Detroit. One-third of Detroit residents live in poverty.

Less than one-fourth of the public school students in Detroit graduate on time from high school, the lowest graduation rate in the country.[6] Yet spending per pupil in Detroit public schools is higher than in wealthy Marin County, California, where the high school graduation rate is 97%.[7] Indeed, for their performance, Detroit public school teachers enjoy the highest pay in the country among major metropolitan areas, at $47.28 per hour.[8] Yet citing supposed budget reductions, the Detroit public schools actually asked parents to provide toilet paper for the schools.[9] A Bill and Melinda Gates Foundation study cited the Detroit public school district, the eleventh largest in America, as the worst major-city education bureaucracy in the entire country.[10]

With Detroit's dramatic loss in population over the decades, half the housing stock in the city is now vacant. Recent city government deliberations have considered just demolishing all this vacant housing. What this means is that over half a century of uniform governance by liberal/left politicians has led to the city now literally starting to disappear beneath their feet.

The political and economic repression has more recently started to spread across the whole state of Michigan. Michigan's downturn began well before the financial crisis, with the state losing 336,000 jobs from 2000 to 2006.[11] Michigan's unemployment had been as low as 3.3% under then-governor John Engler, but by late 2010 it was stuck at 12.4%, the second highest in the nation.

Under liberal governor Jennifer Granholm, Michigan scored among the national leaders in unemployment for several years. Yet refusing to learn from experience, she persisted with tax-increasing policies. In 2007 she led enactment of a $1.4 billion tax increase, jacking up the state income tax rate, and the Michigan business tax rate by 22%.[12] In 2009, with double-digit unemployment in the state, she proposed another $700 million tax increase.[13] The Michigan legislature, distinguishing the state from Jonestown, Guyana, refused the deadly Kool-Aid and declined her request. In 2010 she was back proposing another $550 million tax increase.[14] With double-digit unemployment in her state for several years, she advocated junking the state's flat tax for a graduated tax rate structure that would punish, with higher and higher tax rates, those that produce more.[15] That would of course only chase still more investment, businesses, and jobs out of the state.

The tax increases didn't balance the budget. Instead tax revenues ran nearly $1 billion below projections, and the deficit reappeared at nearly $3 billion.[16] The state ran up costs providing bailouts to specific politically favored businesses. The Michigan Economic Development Corporation doled out $3.3 billion in tax credits for these crony capitalist favorites, with the state adding another $1.6 billion in bailouts for specific investments that supposedly created jobs. This represents just the opposite of sound tax policy, which involves eliminating special interest breaks and subsidies in return for lower rates. But the businesses favored with this taxpayer loot often returned the favor with contributions and other support for the Granholm political machine.

Part of the taxpayer loot was used for a national TV ad campaign featuring actor Jeff Daniels, star of the Hollywood movie *Dumb and Dumber*, touting the Michigan Economic Development Corporation and its corporate welfare handouts.[17] Meanwhile, a study by economist Michael Hicks of Ball State University found that every $1 million of the "economic development" tax credits was tied to a "strongly statistically significant" correlation with the loss of 95 jobs in the county of the business receiving the handout. By 2010, over 750,000 private jobs had fled the state over the prior decade, about 20% of private nonfarm payroll employment.[18] Michigan employed 637,000 state and local government workers, with less than 500,000 manufacturing jobs left in the state.[19]

But unlike in the city of Detroit, there is political life in the Wolverine State yet. In the 2010 elections, not only did the governor's office change party control, but control over the Michigan House of Representatives almost exactly reversed from 65 Democrats and 42 Republicans to 63 Republicans and 47 Democrats. Republican majority control over the Michigan Senate soared to over 2 to 1.

This is how democracy is supposed to work. When the party in power fails the people, the people throw it out. This is not meant to be a politically partisan point. One of the worst recent governors in the country on tax, budget, and economic policy was Republican governor Jodi Rell of Connecticut.[20] One of the best was Democrat governor

Joe Manchin of West Virginia.[21] It is all about the policies they adopt, not the party.

But democracy is not functioning this way in Detroit, and in other cities headed down the same road. On its current course, eventually there will just be one resident left in Detroit. He will be a lifelong liberal/left Democrat, lifelong city government employee, and lifelong member of AFSCME. He will elect himself mayor of the late great city of Detroit, raise taxes again one last time, and then leave the city a ghost town, as he moves out because he can't afford the taxes, either.

STATE AND LOCAL GOVERNMENT BANKRUPTCY

Detroit is a microcosm of failed city government. But the phenomenon is not limited to Detroit. It is just at a more advanced stage of the same process occurring in Cleveland, Pittsburgh, Baltimore, Washington, D.C., Buffalo, Newark, Oakland, and elsewhere, with New York, Philadelphia, St. Louis, and even Los Angeles and Chicago headed down the same road. These and other American cities are increasingly haunted by the growing specter of political, economic, and ultimately financial bankruptcy.

The same political malfunction at the root of these problems is now threatening the fiscal solvency of entire major states, from California to Illinois to New York, as well as Michigan and New Jersey, though a revival of political competition in the last two offers the hope of a long-term change. But these same problems exist in varying degrees among state and local governments across the entire country, threatening to speed up the timer even further on America's ticking bankruptcy bomb.

By the third quarter of 2010, state and local debts had accumulated to $3.062 trillion,[22] more than doubling since 2000. Municipal securities alone totaled $2.388 trillion.[23] This is all on top of the federal national debt.

In just 2008, the last year for which the Census Bureau publishes combined data, state and local governments ran a deficit of $178.4 billion.[24] At the beginning of 2011, states faced another $124 billion in combined deficits, as estimated by the federal Government Accountability Office.[25]

But this is a long-term structural problem. By 2060, GAO projects, state and local government deficits will themselves total 5% of GDP, which would be $750 billion this year.[26]

In part today's soaring state deficits are due to the recession, which caused the steepest drop in state revenues in fifty years.[27] In the first quarter of 2010, total state tax revenues were down over 8% from the year before.[28] But as Laffer and others explain, "The major driver of the state fiscal meltdown is that states partied hard during the bull market expansion of the 1990s and then again during several years of the past decade."[29] As they elaborate,

> When times were good, states added new programs for fully funded pre-kindergarten, expanding Medicaid to those with incomes often double the poverty level, building space launch programs, providing laptops to every public school student, while building convention centers, sports stadiums, and casinos. Nothing was unaffordable.[30]

State lawmakers seemed to think the good times would last forever.

As a result, real state and local spending, after adjusting for inflation, grew an average of 41.5% among the states from 1997 to 2007.[31] The Reason Foundation in California reports that nationally, state general fund spending on average grew at twice the rate of growth of population plus inflation.[32] If states had just restricted their spending to grow no faster than the rate of population growth plus inflation in each state, they would be enjoying budget surpluses now instead of budget deficits.[33] Michael Flynn and Adam Summers explain in the Reason Foundation report, "If legislators had chosen to be responsible, they could have maintained all current state services, increased spending to compensate for inflation and population growth, and still enacted a $500 billion tax cut."[34]

Instead, twenty-nine states raised taxes in 2009, amounting overall to close to $24 billion in higher tax burdens.[35] California raised its top income tax rate to 10.55% and added another half-percentage point to the sales tax rate, which is now over 10% in some localities with the local sales tax add-on. As a result, California is now the only state in the nation with double-digit income as well as sales tax rates. Oregon and

Hawaii vied to outdo California in tax piracy, with the top income tax rate in Oregon rocketing to 11% on incomes over $250,000, and the top income tax rate in the Aloha State matching it at 11%, but on incomes over $200,000. On his way out the door, New Jersey governor Jon Corzine raised the state's top tax rate to 10.75%, just two years after the previous income tax hike. Illinois, now uniformly ruled by Democrats, started 2011 by raising its state income tax rate by 67% and its corporate income tax rate by 50%. New York State raised income taxes again as well, with the top rate now virtually 9%. With New York City's add-on local tax, the top individual tax rate there is now 12.35% and the top business tax rate is 15.95%, easily the highest in the country. As state and local income tax rates, these are on top of federal income tax rates, leaving New York City's total combined corporate tax rate of 50.95% the highest in the developed world. None of these states promised that these would be the last tax hikes, and if political leadership is not changed, they won't stop until the tax burden is the same as Cuba's.

One reason states raised these taxes was to pay for uncontrolled state and local hiring of still more public employees and runaway salaries and benefits. In 2008, the first year of the recession, state and local governments continued hiring, adding an additional 338,000 employees, even while the private sector began losing jobs, cutting back employment by 289,000.[36] By the end of 2009, 8 million private sector jobs had been lost, but state and local employment was still up 2%, or close to 400,000 jobs.[37] It was not until 2010, the third year after the recession began, that state and local governments began to cut back hiring.

Moreover, state and local government workers are paid on average 45% more than private sector workers,[38] with an average hourly wage of $26.25, and $13.56 in hourly costs for benefits, for total hourly costs of $39.81, or $80,000 per year on average.[39] As a result, in 2008, total employment costs for state and local workers climbed to $1.1 trillion, which was half of total state and local government spending.[40] For 2009, in the teeth of the recession, pay and benefits for state and local workers rose by another 6%, twice the rate of inflation.[41] Virtually all state and local workers also enjoy sumptuous health plans. For public school teachers in Milwaukee, for example, the cost of family health coverage is $26,844, for which the teachers pay nothing.[42] That is why Governor

Scott Walker has fought so hard there for fundamental structural reform of the system.

Besides this extravagant compensation, state and local workers also enjoy lavish retirement benefits. Typically, state and local pension plans provide for retirement as early as fifty-five after thirty years of service, with monthly benefits equal to 60% or more of their last salaries. Public safety workers, such as police and firefighters, can retire even earlier, usually by age fifty after twenty years of service, with benefits equal to 50% of peak pay. This adds up on average to annual benefits of $27,600 (on top of Social Security), more than twice average private sector pensions of $13,100.[43]

Josh Barro and E. J. McMahon provide some examples of how extreme even ordinary public pension benefits can get. In a *New York Post* exposé they offer the example of a teacher in Albany County, New York, retiring at fifty-nine after a thirty-seven-year career. His final salary of $89,000 qualifies him for an annual pension benefit starting at $62,745 plus annual cost-of-living adjustments.[44] The present value of that pension is $1.25 million.[45] Or take the example of a Yonkers, New York, teacher who, after earning a master's degree and completing some additional coursework, qualifies for a public school salary of $110,000 after thirty-seven years of employment.[46] That teacher is eligible to retire at fifty-nine with an annual pension of $78,255, plus cost-of-living adjustments, worth a present value of more than $1.5 million.[47] In fact, more than 3,700 retired New York State employees now receive lifetime pensions of over $100,000 per year.[48] Oh, and that pension is completely exempt from state and local income taxes, while private pensions are subject to tax on income over $20,000 a year.

Annual pension costs for New York City have multiplied by 10 times in the last ten years,[49] and now consume 20% of city tax collections, expected to rise still further in coming years.[50] McMahon writes, "For the amount of added money they're now pouring into pension funds each year, compared with a decade ago, New Yorkers could nearly double what they spend on police and fire protection—or rebuild their aging transit system without borrowing a penny."[51] Barro and McMahon report that over the next five years, payments by state and local governments in New York into their pension systems will triple.[52] For school districts, those payments are expected to quadruple over that time, requiring an 18% increase in property taxes just for those pension costs alone.[53]

State and local governments officially admit cumulatively $1 trillion in unfunded liabilities for their public employee pension systems.[54] But an eye-opening 2009 study by Robert Novy-Marx and Joshua Rauh indicates that if state and local pension liabilities are evaluated the same as private sector corporate pension plans, the liability is more realistically $3.8 trillion.[55] This is in addition to the debt liabilities noted above. In Illinois, less than half the pension promises for state and local workers are funded.[56] The unfunded liabilities in Colorado total $3,624 per resident.[57] In Kansas, it is nearly $3,000 per resident.[58]

Lush public employee retirement health plans, a benefit rarely seen in the private sector, add further, enormous unfunded liabilities, estimated by Chris Edwards and Jagadeesh Gokhale at an additional $1.4 trillion.[59] Retired state and local employees in New York can keep their former employer-provided health insurance for little or nothing paid themselves, worth $14,000 per year. Once these retired workers qualify for Medicare, the taxpayers in New York pay for their Part B premiums and for generous Medigap coverage.[60]

President Obama's February 2009 trillion-dollar stimulus package provided over $200 billion in increased funding to aid the states. But that actually only worsened state budget problems. As indicated in Chapter 2, with that money states spent nearly half a trillion more in the last two years than they collected in taxes, and the stimulus windfall still didn't prevent them from raising taxes, which President Obama suggested it would when his stimulus was whooped through the Congress. The stimulus funding was only a temporary measure that was supposed to revive the economy, not a permanent increase in the burden on federal taxpayers. That money was like a narcotic for state politicians, temporarily relieving them of the need to address the dramatic budget problems they had created. But as Art Laffer, Steve Moore, and Jonathan Williams ask in the 2010 *Rich States, Poor States*, "What happens when the money runs out?"[61]

What will happen is that most states will then face a budget hole that has only grown deeper while state budget policy makers were sedated by the stimulus. Indeed, the terms of the stimulus itself deepened those holes with "maintenance of effort" requirements that prevented states that received the federal aid from reducing spending. As Laffer and company write,

> Let it be known that the 2009 federal stimulus bill arguably turned out to be the greatest power grab by the federal government and usurpation of states' rights in decades. It allowed Congress to dictate to state lawmakers what programs in their own budgets they could and could not cut and by how much.[62]

A study by Washington State's Evergreen Freedom Foundation illustrates the dramatic impact of this problem on state budgets, explaining, "because state lawmakers accepted $820 million in education stimulus dollars, only 9 percent of the state's $6.8 billion K–12 budget is eligible for reductions in fiscal year 2011."[63] The study found, in fact, that stimulus restrictions prevented state lawmakers from adopting reductions in 75–90% of the budget![64] As the authors of *Rich States, Poor States* point out, "This has left well over half of state budgets untouchable this year and next in terms of making the necessary cuts to balance their budgets."[65] All the worse, the stimulus effectively required that states receiving the money maintain state spending in major program areas at levels equal to the peak of the prior spending sprees, which was when the economy was booming.

State lawmakers found themselves politically locked in to runaway spending. For example, in South Carolina, to spend the hundreds of millions in increased funding for the state's Head Start education and child care programs, the state had to sign up thousands of new families. Then-governor Mark Sanford explained, "There is no way politically we're going to be able to push people out of the program in two years when the federal money runs out."[66]

Most troubling are the financial fiascos in the worst "failed states," a term that up until now has been applied to Third World countries with disintegrating governments, such as Somalia. California may be in the worst shape of all. Its state budget soared from $75 billion in 2003 to $99 billion in 2007, a 31% increase in just four years.[67] At the same time, the state's tax burden is narrowly focused on the highest-income earners, with the top 1% paying 48%, nearly half, of all state income taxes.[68] That meant when the financial crisis hit, the state's revenues nosedived along with the incomes of the highest flyers. Despite double-digit income and sales tax rates, both virtually the highest in the nation, the state ended up with a $40 billion deficit, and had to issue $3.2 billion in IOUs to pay some of its outstanding bills.[69] Those double-digit tax rates are the major reason the state also suffers double-digit unemployment at 12.4%, tied for second highest in the nation. That is only further contributing to persistent deficits. At the beginning of 2011, California faced another $28 billion budget deficit.

In addition, over the past decade, California public employee pension obligations have soared by 2,000%,[70] leaving nearly $55 billion in unfunded liabilities.[71] The state now spends more on its public employee pensions than on its university system.[72] This is all why Jamie Dimon, chairman of JPMorgan Chase, told reporters last year that California poses a greater risk of default than Greece.[73] Indeed, in 2009, the Fitch credit-ratings agency downgraded California's credit rating all the way to junk status at BBB, the same rating as Puerto Rico at the time.[74]

Meanwhile, in New York State, per capita state and local spending is nearly 20% higher than in California.[75] As a result, the Empire State suffered a $6 billion deficit even before the financial crisis, and the deficit seems to reappear year after year in spite of, or perhaps because of, the yearly tax increases. The top 1% of income earners in New York already pay 41% of state income taxes, and recent tax increases on "the rich" in the state have generated only about half the revenue projected (and spent in the budget).[76] Moreover, public employee pension liabilities, compensation, and employment are wildly out of control in the state. Its unfunded pension liabilities alone are now probably over $100 billion.

The state passed a $1.7 billion tax increase in April 2008. In December 2008 it added a $1.5 billion payroll tax on New York City workers to fund mass transit, on top of the world-leading city tax rates discussed above. In 2009, the state adopted another $5 billion tax increase, making its income tax rates among the highest in America. In 2010, the state adopted still another cigarette tax, bringing the total tax in New York City to $5.85 per pack. Yet going into 2011, the recurring annual state budget deficit persisted.[77]

New Jersey suffered a higher top state income tax rate than either

California or New York, at 10.75%. The top 1% of income earners pay 46%, or almost half, of all state income taxes as well.[78] Yet the state also bears the third-highest property taxes in America.[79] The state raised the top income tax rate by 41% in 2004 to try to close its deficit.[80] But after that didn't work, Governor Corzine increased taxes two more times before he was booted out of office in 2009, leaving newly elected governor Chris Christie the highest deficit yet.

On top of these deficits are an unfunded state worker pension liability of $46 billion, plus another $16 billion for health benefits for retired state workers.[81] The New Jersey government has failed to make its contribution to the state pension fund in 13 of the last 17 years, raising unfunded liabilities even faster in the process.[82]

The Garden State's finances were in such bad shape that Christie had to slash the state budget by 26%, including a billion in cuts to education increases that resulted in the layoff of thousands of teachers statewide. Yet Christie still faced another budget deficit of $10 billion for 2011.[83]

Illinois has been spending twice as much each year as it collects in taxes.[84] The state fell six months behind in paying its bills, with a stack of $5 billion in outstanding bills waiting to be paid.[85] Some Illinois legislators were evicted from their offices because the state didn't pay their rent.[86] State troopers have been turned away from gas stations because the station would not take their state credit card.[87] "The state of Illinois is known as a deadbeat state," Illinois comptroller Dan Hynes told CBS's 60 Minutes in December 2010.[88]

A last fine example of fiscal foolishness offering instructive lessons is provided by Maryland. In 2007, Maryland imposed a special tax bracket for millionaires that was 30% above the income tax rate paid by most workers in the state. The combined state and local tax rate for millionaires climbed as high as 9.3%. Instead of the projected $107 million in higher revenues from the tax increase, tax returns filed by millionaires declined by one-third, resulting in a net *loss* of $257 million in income tax revenues.[89] The wealthiest county in the state, Montgomery County, by itself lost $4.6 billion in taxable income in one year alone.[90]

As Art Laffer once explained, the problem with Robin Hood and his merry men robbing the rich in Sherwood Forest is that, pretty soon, the rich stop riding through that forest.

STATE AND LOCAL PROSPERITY

Just as at the national level, rescuing state and local governments from bankruptcy will first require reigniting long-term state and local economic growth. Only booming growth will provide the revenues to pull state and local governments back from the beckoning financial abyss. Only such vital growth can promote financial independence among working people and the poor while minimizing the burdens of government assistance. Only a booming economy can restore the American Dream.

Just as state and local governments have their own roles and responsibilities in our system of federalism, their formula for contributing to strong economic growth is somewhat different as well. Tax rates, regulatory costs, and government spending burdens are still critical factors, but state and local governments have no role in monetary policy and the currency. Instead they are primarily responsible for critical state and local government services that make the economy, as well as everyday life, functional. The most critical of these for vibrant long-term growth are law enforcement, education, and essential infrastructure such as roads, highways, and bridges.

Here is what state and local governments must do to avert bankruptcy and help restore a long-term economic boom in their states and cities.

Taxation Liberation

Nine states survive perfectly well with no state income tax at all. These include large states such as Texas and Florida, medium-size states such as Tennessee and Washington, and smaller-population states such as New Hampshire, Nevada, South Dakota, Wyoming, and Alaska.

Income taxes are the most economically destructive of all taxes. That is because income levies tax directly the reward for work, savings, investment, and entrepreneurship. As discussed in Chapter 6, with the reward reduced, the incentive for pursuing these economically productive activities is reduced. The result is less work, less saving, less investment, fewer new businesses, less business growth, less job creation, lower wages and income, and lower overall economic growth. Higher marginal tax rates reduce these incentives still more. A marginal tax rate of zero, as with no income tax, maximizes these incentives, at least as far the burden of income taxes is concerned.

High income taxes also cause wealthy and high-income individuals to leave the state for more favorable tax climates, particularly the states with no income taxes. Those who have accumulated substantial wealth see the returns to that wealth eaten up by high income tax rates just because they live in a certain state. It is so easy for these high net worth families and individuals to buy a home in a more favorable state and live there enough to claim that state as their taxing jurisdiction. The original state then loses all the tax revenue from these fleeing taxpayers.

Experience and economic studies bear this out. The latest work was produced by Laffer, Moore, and Williams and published in the 2010 edition of *Rich States, Poor States*. Economic growth, as measured by gross state product, raced ahead from 1998 to 2008 in the nine states without income taxes almost 50% faster than in the nine states with the highest top personal income tax rates. Job growth, as measured by nonfarm payroll employment, rocketed ahead more than twice as fast in the nine income-taxless states as compared to the nine states with the top income tax rates. Yet total state tax receipts in the first nine states still grew 30% *faster* than in the latter nine.[91]

The authors then went on to look at the economic performance of the eleven states that have adopted a state income tax in the last fifty years. In each case, they compared the performance of the state in the five years before the state adopted an income tax with performance following adoption of the income tax. All eleven states grew more slowly than the rest of the country after adoption of the income tax. Michigan adopted a state income tax in 1967. By 2008, its gross state product as a percent of total U.S. GDP had fallen by 47%. Ohio adopted its state income tax in 1971. By 2008, its gross state product had fallen by 38% as a percent of total U.S. GDP. For Illinois, which adopted an income tax in 1969, the decline by 2008 was 31%. For Pennsylvania, which adopted its state income tax in 1971, the decline by 2008 was 31% as well.[92]

Moreover, after Michigan adopted its income tax, its personal income per capita fell from 129.97% of the U.S. average to 88.8% by 2009, a decline of 41 percentage points. Indiana personal income per capita declined from 113.84% of the U.S. average to 85.79% by 2008, a decline of 28 percentage points. Ohio declined from 114.57% of the national average to 89.33% by 2008, a decline of 25 percentage points. These states consequently all declined after adoption of a state income tax, from personal income per capita well above the national average to well below the national average by 2008. But per capita income declined substantially compared to the U.S. average after adoption of income taxes in all eleven states. As the authors state, "Personal income per capita is the closest measure to be found that represents the state's standard of living; gross state product is the truest measure of a state's output."[93] The results show that in each state that has adopted a state income tax in the last fifty years, "the state's economy has become a smaller portion of the overall U.S. economy, and the state's citizens have had their standard of living dramatically reduced."[94]

Yet in nine of the eleven states, after adoption of the state income tax, total state and local tax revenues as a percentage of all state and local revenues in the U.S. declined as well, in some cases sharply. Michigan's share of taxes, for example, declined by 34%. In West Virginia, the decline was 33%, in Indiana, 28%, in Pennsylvania, 23%, in Illinois, 21%. Thus the only thing the people in these states got for having a state income tax was a lower standard of living.

The authors further contrast the economic performance of Tennessee, with no state income tax, with the performance of neighboring Missouri, which is considering a reform to replace its income tax with a 5.11% sales and use tax applying to purchases of services as well as goods. From 1998 to 2008, Tennessee's gross state product grew 27% faster than Missouri's, and Tennessee's lead in GSP will only continue to widen in future years. Over the same period, jobs grew 29% faster in Tennessee. Yet over that period, total state revenues generated by Tennessee's faster-growing economy grew 39% faster than Missouri's.[95]

If Missouri's economic growth just caught up to the average of the states with no income tax, which are growing 50% faster, Missouri would enjoy $100 billion in increased state GSP and income over the next ten years.[96] From 1998 to 2008, the average job growth among the no-income-tax states was 349% (more than four times) faster than in Missouri. The growth in GSP per capita, or standard of living, was 80% faster. If GSP per capita over 1998 to 2008 had grown in Missouri at the same average rate as for the no-income-tax states, income for each Missouri resident would be more than $12,000 higher on average.[97]

Texas, with no state income tax, can also be contrasted with California, with nearly the highest state income tax rates in the nation. While the top personal income tax rate in California is now 10.55%, even the average income earner pays a marginal income tax rate on the next dollar earned of 9.30%. The Texas personal income tax rate, by contrast, is 0%. The top California income tax rate of 10.55% also applies to capital gains and to corporate dividends. But Texas has not just no income tax, but also no capital gains tax and no tax on corporate dividends. Moreover, even the sales tax rate is higher in California at 8.25% than in Texas at 6.25%. Not surprisingly, with all these higher taxes California government spending per capita is almost 50% higher than Texas government spending.

Even with all of California's advantages as a land of beguiling climate, movie stars, beautiful Pacific beaches, unsurpassed natural ports, and the economically pathbreaking Silicon Valley, since 1998 the rate of real economic growth in Texas has been almost 20% higher than in California.[98] Since the end of the tech boom and the post-9/11 recession, the rate of real economic growth in Texas has been astoundingly almost 50% higher than in California.[99]

From 1998 to 2007, real personal income in Texas grew 21% faster than in California.[100] Since 2002, the gap has widened, with real personal income growing 46% faster in Texas.[101] Moreover, since the end of the tech boom and the post-9/11 recession, jobs in Texas have grown more than twice as fast as in California.[102]

Starting with the Gold Rush of 1849, California has been the destination of choice for Americans, with migrants coming originally in wagon trains over thousands of miles, then by railroad, by plane, and finally by car over interstate highways. But no more. From 2000 to 2007, a net 1.2 million U.S. residents left California.[103] Texas, by contrast, enjoyed net interstate migration during that time of over one-half million, the third highest behind Florida and Arizona.[104] Over the decade 1998–2007, a net 1,438,480 Americans fled California.

As Laffer, Moore, and Williams write in the 2009 edition of *Rich States, Poor States*,

Our competition between California and Texas demonstrates how economic theory actually works in the real world. Pro-growth tax and economic and regulatory policy leads to rising employment, income, home values, population and tax revenues, while high levels of taxes and spending have the opposite effect.

They add,

When comparing California with Texas, U-Haul says it all. To rent a 26 foot truck one-way from San Francisco to Austin, the charge is $3,236, and yet the one-way charge for that same truck from Austin to San Francisco is just $399. Clearly what is happening is that far more people want to move from San Francisco to Austin than vice versa, so U-Haul has to pay its own employees to drive the empty trucks back from Texas. The great thing about this example is that it's a market price set in the real world—you don't need to rely on a fancy economic model to see our point.[105]

The phenomenon of Americans voting with their feet to flee high taxes is not limited to California. It is happening all over America, and has been for quite some time. From 1990 to 1999, nearly 2.9 million Americans moved from the forty-one states with income taxes into the nine states without income taxes.[106] In 2004 alone, the nine states with no income tax gained an additional 323,579 residents from the forty-one states with income taxes.[107]

Americans for Tax Reform's Center for Fiscal Accountability regularly reports IRS data regarding interstate migration of taxpayers. Their latest report shows that in 2007 the nine states with no income tax gained 235,000 residents from the other forty-one states.[108] These residents took with them $11.8 billion of net adjusted gross income.[109] The center further reports that in 2007, the ten states with the highest tax burden,

California, Connecticut, Hawaii, Idaho, Maine, Maryland, New Jersey, New York, Rhode Island, and Wisconsin, together lost 441,000 residents, taking with them $12.8 billion in income.[110]

Moreover, the center reports that from 1997 through 2007, the ten states with the highest tax burden lost over 3 million residents.[111] Those residents took with them during that period a staggering $82 billion in income.[112] Yet the nine states with no income tax enjoyed during that same period a net in-migration of over 2.6 million residents from the other forty-one states, bringing with them almost $100 billion in additional income.[113]

In addition, from 1997 to 2007, a net 2.3 million Americans moved to the ten states with the lowest tax burden: Alabama, Alaska, Florida, Louisiana, Nevada, New Hampshire, South Dakota, Tennessee, Texas, and Wyoming.[114] These new residents produced $88.7 billion in income in their new states during that period.[115]

The study by Laffer, Moore, and Williams in the 2010 edition of *Rich States, Poor States* found that from 1999 to 2008, population in the nine states with no income taxes grew 152% faster than in the nine states with the highest income tax rates.[116] The population of Texas swelled by 20.6%, including a net 736,000 Americans who moved to Texas from other states.[117] In contrast, New York's population grew by only 3.8%, including a net 1.7 million New Yorkers who fled the state over this period, analogous to East Germans fleeing to the West after the fall of the Berlin Wall.[118] Another net 1.4 million Americans fled California during this ten-year period. The total of Americans leaving Illinois was a net 637,979; the total for Michigan was 445,493; the total for New Jersey was 418,928.

By contrast, the population of Florida, with no state income tax, soared by 19% over this period, including 1.3 million Americans who moved into the state from across the country.[119] This is not just a matter of Americans moving to the Sun Belt. The population of New Hampshire, free of state income taxes, grew by nearly 10%. Income-tax-free Washington State grew by nearly 14%, including a net 200,000 Americans who moved into the state from elsewhere.

Moreover, all eleven states that adopted state income taxes in the last fifty years suffered declines in their population as a percent of the total U.S. population. For Pennsylvania, the decline was 30%; for Ohio, 28%;

West Virginia, 38%; Michigan, 24%; Illinois 23%.[120] As Laffer and his colleagues remind us, "There's an old saying that high taxes don't redistribute wealth, they redistribute people."[121]

Further studies and experience demonstrate that the incentive effects of higher income taxes harm the economy. From 1957 to 1997, growth in real personal income was more than twice as high in states that did not raise their income taxes significantly as compared to states with the biggest increases in income taxes, as the Heartland Institute reports.[122] A study by the Joint Economic Committee (JEC) of Congress found that from 1990 to 1993, the ten states that raised income taxes the most experienced a net gain of only 3,000 jobs, an increase in the unemployment rate of 2.2 percentage points, and a real decline of $484 in personal family income. But the ten states that cut income taxes the most over that period experienced a net gain of 975,000 jobs, an increase in the unemployment rate of only 0.3 percentage points (due to the recession in the time frame), and a real increase of $148 in personal family income.[123]

An earlier JEC study comparing tax policies in the fastest-growing states with those in the slowest-growing states in the 1970s found quite similar results. It concluded that state income growth is inversely related to the total level of state and local tax burdens, changes in the level of state and local tax burdens, the degree to which the state relied on income taxes, and the progressivity of the state's income tax rates. The study reported,

> The evidence is strong that tax and expenditure policies of state and local governments are important in explaining variations in economic growth between states, far more important than other factors frequently cited such as climate, energy costs, the impact of federal fiscal policies, etc. It is clear that high rates of taxation lower the rate of economic growth, and that states that lower their tax burdens are rewarded with an enhancement in their economic growth. Income taxes levied on individuals and corporations are particularly detrimental to growth, more so than consumption based taxes or user charges that do not reduce incentives to work or form capital. Progressive taxation not only lowers the rate of economic growth compared with proportional or regressive tax-

ation, but in the process hurts the very persons that progressive taxes are designed to help: the poor.

The authors of *Rich States, Poor States*, 2009 edition, also compared the ten states with the lowest marginal corporate income tax rates with the ten states with the highest rates over the period 1997 to 2007. Economic growth during this period was 37% higher in the low-tax-rate states as compared to the high-tax-rate states.[124] Personal income grew 41.5% faster.[125] Population grew 136% faster, or substantially more than twice as much.[126] Jobs grew by 120% more, also substantially more than twice as much.[127] The authors conclude that "states which penalize corporate profits have slower growth in income and population."[128]

A 1979 study by Robert Genetski and Young Chin performed a cross-sectional analysis on all fifty states plus the District of Columbia, relating changes in relative economic growth to changes in relative tax rates from 1969 to 1976. With a three-year lag, a strong negative relationship was found between above-average tax increases and economic growth. The authors concluded:

> [M]uch of the slower than average economic growth experienced in many of the Northeastern states, such as New York, Connecticut, Rhode Island, Vermont, New Jersey, and Massachusetts, appears to be related to the sharp increases in relative tax burdens in those states. In contrast, New Hampshire's relative tax burden was lowered during this period, and its economic growth was above the national average. Similarly, the above average economic growth experienced in many Western and Southern states during this period is associated with decreases in relative tax burdens.[129]

A 1979 study by Robert Newman analyzed employment growth in the South relative to the rest of the nation in sixteen manufacturing industries and six other major industries.[130] He found that changes in relative corporate tax rates, as well as unionization and right-to-work laws, were the major factors causing the shift of industry toward the South.

Many other studies have found similar results.[131] What these studies and the real-world experience portend are dramatic and fundamental economic, social, and political changes for America. The South from Texas to Florida is rising as the new industrial base, and economic powerhouse, of the nation. The Northeast is in long-term decline, falling behind the rest of the country. The poorest state in the union is no longer Mississippi or West Virginia. It is upstate New York. Liberal northeastern media outlets can shelter their populations from competing, alternative points of view. They cannot shelter their populations from reality. These fundamental economic realities will translate into fundamental political realities and regional changes in national political leadership more and more over time.

The Midwest from Wisconsin, Iowa, and Missouri east to Pennsylvania and even New Jersey is still showing signs of intellectual, political, and economic life, fighting for the future, with the exception perhaps of Illinois. But northeastern intellectual elites are locked in a brain freeze circa the 1930s. If that freeze does not thaw, the rest of America, and even economically emerging nations abroad, will pass them by.

A TAXPAYER BILL OF RIGHTS

The conclusion from the above analysis is that to maximize economic growth, jobs, and prosperity, the forty-one states with state income taxes should phase theirs out as well. The feasibility of such sharp cuts in state tax rates is further demonstrated by real-world experience.

In 1978, Delaware found itself in the ridiculous trap of suffering the highest marginal state income tax rate in the nation at the time, at the absurd rate of 19.8%. Again, this was on top of federal income tax rates. Then-governor Pete DuPont consulted with Art Laffer to devise a plan that resulted in a dramatic reduction in the tax rate down to 6.95%, phased in over eight years. Yet from 1979 to 1999, annual individual income tax revenue in the state soared fourfold, from $200 million to $800 million.[132]

Similar results were achieved in the early 1990s in New Jersey under then-governor Christine Todd Whitman. On the advice of Steve Forbes and Larry Kudlow, she implemented a plan cutting state income tax rates by 30%. Proposing that plan just two months before the 1993 elections also rescued her campaign from otherwise sure defeat, which should indicate to future state candidates the political feasibility and appeal of such sweeping reforms.[133]

The key to understanding how such reform can work is to recognize the fundamental fallacy in sitting down with pie charts of state revenues and spending at any point in time, and asking, "Okay, without the income taxes that generate x percent of state revenues, where do we cut x percent of state spending?" Establishment insiders know, and keep to themselves, the essential truth that real-world budgets can't be intelligently analyzed on that static, point-in-time basis. What you have to understand is this—*all those budget numbers are continuously changing!* Not just year to year, but even month to month. To understand the true, feasible policy options, you have to analyze the budget on a dynamic basis, meaning you have to look ahead and see where the budget numbers are going to be in future years. That will reveal how you can phase in dramatic tax rate cuts.

When Whitman cut New Jersey income tax rates by 30%, she didn't cut state spending by 30%. Nor did DuPont cut Delaware state spending by two-thirds when he slashed the top income tax rate from 19.8% to 6.95%. In fact, total state spending in each case continued to grow throughout the entire phase-in period of those dramatic tax rate cuts. But if you just slow the growth of spending, you can use the savings to finance tax rate cuts. With the revenue feedbacks from the resulting more rapid economic growth, you can finance still more rate cuts. Note how the data discussed above showed that state revenues grew more rapidly in states without income taxes than in states with income taxes. This is how Governors DuPont and Whitman accomplished their reforms.

The key tool to achieve the phaseout of state income taxes in every state is known as the Taxpayer Bill of Rights, or TABOR. Colorado voters adopted a TABOR in 1992, which limits growth in state taxes and spending to the rate of growth of population plus inflation. The state government is required to rebate annual tax revenue increases in excess of this limit back to the taxpayers. As a result, Colorado rebated $139 million in 1997, $563 million in 1998, $679 million in 1999, and $941 million in 2000, for a total of $2.3 billion over that period.[134] From 1997 to 2007, a cumulative total of $6.7 billion was rebated to taxpayers, while the state income tax rate was cut from 5% to 4.63%.[135]

Jobs in Colorado grew twice as fast in the ten years after TABOR was adopted as in the ten years before. Per capita personal income also grew twice as fast in the ten years after TABOR. In the fourteen years before TABOR, per capita income growth in Colorado was below the national average.[136] In the fourteen years after TABOR, per capita income growth was almost 20% higher than the national average.[137]

A similar limit was adopted in California in 1979 by the Gann Amendment. As a result, California's average annual rate of spending growth in real terms after inflation fell from 9% in the 1970s to 2% in the 1980s.[138] State spending per capita fell from 7th in the nation in 1979 to 16th in 1990.[139] With the Gann Amendment limiting spending, and Proposition 13 limiting taxes, the California economy soared, increasing gross state product by 132% from 1979 to 1988, 30% faster than the hot national economy at the time.[140]

These are very reasonable limits on state spending. Spending rising at the rate of population growth and inflation means the same amount of spending can be maintained per person in real terms over time. That prevents government spending from growing faster than the economy and becoming a bigger relative burden over time.

As noted above, however, in recent years state and local spending have grown at twice the rate of growth of population plus inflation. If a state just holds spending growth to the TABOR limit, however, and devotes the savings each year to reducing income tax rates, then enough savings would be generated along with new revenues from the resulting economic growth to phase out the state's income tax completely in less than ten years. That would apply to the state individual income tax, the state's corporate income tax, and the state's capital gains tax, the latter two usually not raising a lot of money. All three can and should be phased out through this means. This was shown for the state of Virginia in a study I completed in 2010 for the Virginia Institute for Public Policy.[141] But the same study could be done for each state. The job could be completed through this means in less than ten years in every state.

With the burden of state income taxes lifted, economic growth in the state would soar, new jobs would be created, and wages and incomes would rise, as we have seen above. Revenues from the remaining taxes would rise more rapidly as well, along with the booming economy. After state income taxes are phased out, the TABOR spending limit should remain to ensure that state spending doesn't get out of hand again in the future.

SUPERMAJORITY REQUIREMENTS

Another desirable protection for taxpayers besides the TABOR spending limit is for each state to adopt a supermajority requirement for raising taxes. By legislative rule, statute, or constitutional amendment, this would require a supermajority of at least 60%, and preferably two-thirds, in each house of the legislature before a tax increase could be adopted. This supermajority requirement is justified by the principle that there should be a broad consensus among taxpayers before a higher proportion of their incomes is taken from them by force of law rather than by their individual consent. That would prevent a logrolling, special interest, pork-savoring coalition from easily joining together to burden taxpayers and undermine prosperity contrary to the broader public interest.

Balancing the Budget

A TABOR spending limit would keep state taxes and spending under control over the long run. But further spending reforms are necessary to keep that spending limit feasible, and to solve the shorter-term budget crisis.

The key to restoring budget balance in the shorter term is to reduce all budget line items back to the levels of 2007. This would implement a budget reset that would match spending to revenues still suffering from the effects of the recession and the housing crisis. The states were doing just fine with the spending in 2007, just a few years ago, and America can survive with that level of spending restored once again. This is similar to the budget strategies followed by Governor Bob McDonnell in Virginia, and Governor Chris Christie in New Jersey. But more fundamental budget strategies are needed to maintain the TABOR spending limits over the longer run.

PENSION LIBERATION

Long-term state and local budget solvency requires fundamental pension reform to eliminate unfunded liabilities and intractable taxpayer burdens. Under the traditional defined benefit (DB) pension model, workers are promised a specific benefit amount for each month in retirement. The employer pays retirement contributions into a common investment pool for all covered workers. The workers may be required to make some contribution as well. The employer then invests the funds in the common pool,[142] which is used to pay the promised benefits in retirement.

Under the defined contribution (DC) model, the employer simply contributes a specified percentage of the worker's salary to an individual investment account for the worker. The worker may be required to make a contribution as well. The worker then directs investment of the funds over the years, within certain limits. The worker's retirement benefit then equals what the accumulated funds can finance by that time.

The standard notion of a pension plan used to be the defined benefit model. But over the past thirty years, the world has been racing away from this old DB model to the new DC model. Today, the great majority of private employers have switched to DC plans for their workers, with just 16% of private sector workers still in the older DB plans.[143] But among full-time state and local workers, 90% are still in the old-fashioned DB plans.[144]

As indicated above, the typical state and local government public employee pension plan provides for retirement at age 55 or later with 30 years of service. The retiree then typically gets a monthly benefit for life equal to 2% of final salary times the number of years of service. So the worker at 55 can get 60% of final salary for life. But the worker does not have to stop working altogether to get those payments. He can get another job elsewhere and still get the pension payments. The plans often also include survivors, disability, and retirement health benefits.

The standard myth is that DB plans are better for the workers than DC plans. But the DB plans are typically structured to serve the union's interest in longer-term workers who stick with the union for most or all of their careers. As a result, the plans generally involve a lot of redistribution away from the shorter-term workers and toward the longer-term ones. But in our modern, mobile workforce, the great majority of workers that ever work for a state or local government are shorter-term workers, staying with the government employer for less than 15–20 years. As will be shown below, these workers would be better off with the DC plans. Indeed, even longer-term workers can do better with their own DC plans. Moreover, the DC plans are clearly much better for the taxpayers.

The first state to adopt major reforms replacing an older defined benefit plan with a comprehensive defined contribution plan was Michigan. Then-governor John Engler proposed the reform in November 1996, and it was quickly enacted by the legislature. This was the best policy action undertaken by the state government in Michigan in the last fifteen years.

The reform provided that all new state employees hired after March 31, 1997, will be in the new DC plan. Under that plan, the state contributes a minimum of 4% of the worker's salary to an individual investment account for each worker. The employer matches voluntary employee contributions up to an additional 3% of salary, making a total possible contribution of 10%. The worker can contribute up to an additional 10% of salary without employer match at the worker's choice.

Current employees at the time were allowed to choose to switch to the new DC plan only during an open enrollment period in the first four months of 1998. If they did make the switch, their share of past contributions to the old DB plan were transferred to the DC plan. In addition, for workers who were vested in the DB plan, an amount equal to the present value of their accumulated retirement benefits was transferred to their DC account as well.

Investment options are structured for workers to make investing easy for them. First, they can choose from three core investment funds with set percentages of asset allocations in different investment areas, reflecting a range of risk and return variations. State Street Global Advisors, the third-party administrator for the plan and one of the largest pension investment firms in the world, maintains these three funds, choosing the particular investments and holding to the preset asset allocation requirements.

Second, the worker can choose from among twelve preselected mutual funds considered the best in their primary investment areas, whether stocks, bonds, or other private investments. Finally, the worker can choose a self-directed option that includes the choice of hundreds of mutual funds determined to be sound and suitable for retirement investment.

Workers who leave state employment under the DC plan can leave their assets in the same structured investment system, or roll them over into an IRA or a retirement plan maintained by their next employer. Workers who switch to the DC plan receive the same retiree health benefits as under the old DB plan. For new workers in the DC plan, the state pays 3% of the cost of the health benefits for each year of service, up to a maximum of 90%. The retiree pays the rest. These benefits vest after ten years of service. Retirees can choose any alternative private health plan and direct the state premium contribution toward payment of that plan. This includes private Health Savings Account plans.

The state's reform plan provides for no change in the benefits of current retirees. Moreover, there will be no change in benefits for employees who choose to stay in the old DB plan, either.

The state Department of Management and Budget estimated that Michigan would save almost $100 million in the first year alone because of the new DC plan, primarily because of reduced administrative costs. Yet 45% of state employees and 65% of public school employees who effectively received no benefits under the old plan because they left state employment too early are now able to benefit under the new system after state employment of only two years, with fully vested benefits after only four years.

The many advantages to taxpayers of such a DC pension plan include:

No investment risk. The most obvious advantage for taxpayers of a defined contribution plan is that it eliminates investment risk for them. With the government managing a common pool of investment funds under a defined benefit plan, the taxpayers bear the complete risk of poor investment performance. If such poor performance leaves the pool unable to pay the promised defined benefits, then the taxpayers will have to make up the difference. A GAO report indicates that state and local pension funds lost 27.6% of their value in 2008 due to the financial crisis.[145]

Under the defined contribution plan, however, the taxpayers simply make a specific contribution to the accounts of the workers each month. The government is then not liable for the investment performance of the funds. Workers' benefits equal whatever the accumulated funds can finance. Taxpayers consequently are not subject to any risk of investment performance.

No political risk. DC plans eliminate another set of risks for taxpayers that are usually overlooked—political risks. With the government specifying benefits far in the future, as under defined benefit plans, there is always a strong danger of political giveaways by shortsighted politicians. These politicians can promise higher retirement benefits, while leaving future officials and taxpayers to pay for them. Indeed, one of the major reasons for the unfunded liabilities faced by public pension plans throughout the nation is the extent to which, flush with investment returns during the stock market boom years, politicians greatly sweetened the benefits retirees would enjoy. Under a DC plan, where the government does not specify future benefits but only makes regular investment contributions, this risk is eliminated.

Moreover, a large government investment pool, as under a defined benefit plan, is always subject to the danger of political interference that could raise costs. Political favoritism may influence investment policy, prohibiting some investments and forcing the fund into others. By taking the focus off simply maximizing investment returns, such political favoritism reduces investment returns and increases the cost of funding the specified defined benefits.

Politicians may seek to raid the large, tempting investment pool in other ways as well. They may seek to withdraw funds for other uses, claiming an excess of funds that may be temporary or chimerical. Or they may fail to pay the full required contributions into the pool, using the money for other purposes instead. These actions again raise costs for taxpayers in the long run.

Government management of the funds also creates the risk of mishandling of the funds by bureaucrats who lack the incentives, competitive pressures, and expertise of private investment managers. Attempts to insulate the funds from bureaucratic control by contracting out to private investment managers will not eliminate political risks because the government bureaucrats still decide who to hire and fire and can put restrictions in the governing contracts.

Finally, a large government investment pool creates the risk for taxpayers of greater government control of the private economy. Through such a pool, the government may end up owning large shares of private companies. The government will also hold a large share of investment capital that it could use to impose effective mandates on the private sector, dictating conditions to companies for investment or lending from the pool. Even where there has been a good record of avoiding such abuse in the past, the danger is always present.

None of these risks arising from a large government investment pool exists, in a DC plan, where the government does not maintain such a pool.

No unfunded liability. DC plans also eliminate all unfunded liabilities in public pensions. Under a DB plan, any shortfall in the common investment pool that leaves the pool short of funds to pay future promised benefits, creating an unfunded liability, must be covered by the taxpayers, regardless of the cause of the shortfall. In the defined contribution plan, where the government does not maintain a common investment pool but only pays a specified amount to each worker's individual account each month, and benefits equal what those accounts can finance, there is no possibility of an unfunded liability that taxpayers would have to cover.

Greater control over costs. Costs under a DB plan, where the government has pledged to provide a certain benefit regardless of cost, can vary greatly, depending on a wide range of factors outside the government's control. Retirees can live longer, greatly increasing costs. More workers may stay with the government employer long-term, increasing costs. Interest rates or the stock market may decline, requiring increased contributions to make up the difference.

With a DC plan, by contrast, the government is responsible only for a specified contribution each month. This is completely under the government's control, depending only on what the government agrees to pay. This means in turn greater certainty and predictability in budgeting. There is no possibility that taxpayers will be surprised with a large, unexpected cost that will require increased taxes.

Reduced costs. A defined contribution plan can also significantly reduce pension costs. Defined benefit plans have large administrative costs for the government employer. The government must maintain and pay for the management of the large common pool of assets. It must pay for an actuarial firm to conduct audits and compile annual reports. Moreover, federal law imposes many regulatory requirements on such plans, regarding distribution of benefits, eligibility, investment policies, etc. Complying with and reporting on these requirements significantly adds to costs.

With a DC plan, by contrast, administrative costs are negligible. The government simply pays an amount into each employee's own account as part of payroll processing. The worker takes over administration of the account after that.

A defined contribution plan can save the government huge amounts on funding costs as well, depending on the regular contribution specified in the plan. The Michigan DC plan costs the state 4–7% per worker for retirement benefits, depending on the degree to which each worker contributes to the plan. This is probably less than the payroll costs of any other state's defined benefit plan, which typically run into the double digits as a percent of payroll. Yet the resulting retirement benefits are plenty adequate.

Improved employee recruitment. Finally, because of the advantages to employees noted above, DC plans can help employers attract better employees. Highly talented workers may not be willing to commit to state or local government employment long term. But they may be willing to work for a state or local government for a few years. The DC plan would make it easier to recruit such workers because it is fully portable, and the workers can take the saved contributions with them when they leave. Moreover, these and other workers would favor the freedom of choice, personal control, and possibly higher benefits that they could get through DC plans. These are the reasons why college professors across the country are typically covered by a TIAA-CREF defined contribution retirement plan.

The many advantages to workers of a defined contribution pension plan include:

Portability and immediate vesting. The most obvious advantage of DC plans for workers is portability. Since the contributions are paid directly into individual accounts for each worker, it is easy simply to allow workers to take their accumulated funds with them when they change jobs. As a result, workers get to keep the full past contributions made on their behalf and their full accrued benefits.

Moreover, in a pure DC plan, the employer's contributions to the individual account become the full property of the worker immediately upon payment, and the contributions begin earning full market investment returns from that moment on, growing geometrically over the years. The returns earned by the invested contributions also become the full property of the worker from the moment they are earned. As a result, the worker enjoys immediate vesting of all retirement funds, which again workers can take with them when they leave for other jobs and opportunities. The Michigan plan included a slight delay in vesting of two years for 50% of contributions and four years for 100%. But this is not an inherent or necessarily desirable feature of DC plans.

In a defined benefit plan, by contrast, the contributions for each worker are kept by the government in a common pool where each worker's share is not separately identified. The worker's rights to benefits from that pool typically vest only after long periods, of ten years or so. Even then, the formula defining their benefits generally disadvantages the worker until at least fifteen to twenty years of service.

These portability and immediate vesting features of defined contribution plans strongly benefit the majority of those who are ever state and local government workers, who are not going to stay with one employer for their entire careers, or even for fifteen to twenty years. The old-fashioned defined benefit plans tie workers to their current employers and make it costly to take advantage of new opportunities from other potential employers. Indeed, these old plans were intentionally designed to have that effect, which is highly detrimental to workers.

Personal control. In the DC plan, the retirement funds for each worker are under the control of the worker in their own individual accounts. Workers can consequently adopt the investment strategies and benefit plans that best suit their own individual needs and preferences. As a result, even longer-term workers could end up with higher benefits than under a traditional defined benefit plan.

Moreover, under the DC plan, workers don't have to worry about politicians mishandling the funds, accumulating unfunded liabilities, or running out of money to pay their benefits, or the political winds turning against them. In other words, they don't suffer the political risks involved with politicians handling huge amounts of reserve funds, or the vagaries of political fortune.

Fairer benefits. Under a traditional defined benefit plan, the benefits are skewed to favor the longer-term and oldest workers over others, in at least three ways. First, the vesting requirements eliminate benefits for those working less than ten years or so, with the funds then devoted to the longest-term workers. Second, the benefits are a percentage of final salary, which tends to be much higher for those who have worked for the employer the longest, or for older workers.

Third, granting the same percentage of final salary for each year worked (2% or so) does not grant the full benefit of the contributions for younger workers, especially for those who leave for other employment after a few years. For example, take a worker who enters government employment at twenty-two, works for fifteen years, and then leaves for a private sector job. Under a traditional defined benefit plan, he will qualify for benefits when he reaches retirement. But he will only receive the same 2% or so of final salary for each year worked as other workers under the benefit formula. Yet the contributions paid for him during employment continued to earn investment returns for many years after he left employment. The worker, however, receives no benefit from these additional investment returns.

Indeed, contrast the younger worker above with an older worker who enters government employment at age fifty and continues to work there for fifteen years, retiring at age sixty-five. The contributions for this worker earned investment returns for far fewer years than those for the younger worker, and compounded for far fewer years. Yet this older worker will get the same 2% or so of final salary for each year worked as the younger worker. And that will be the same percentage of the usually much higher salary for older workers. The younger workers are consequently denied the full benefit of their contributions, which are redistributed to others. Instead, the older workers are actually favored over them.

Higher benefits. The great majority of workers would get higher benefits through the defined contribution plan. As discussed above, the entire system is skewed to favor the longer-term workers. But the great majority of all workers who ever work for a single government employer are shorter term. In Michigan, 45% of state employees and 65% of public school employees effectively received no benefits under the old defined benefit plan because they left state employment in ten years or less. In California, 70% of state and local workers stay with one government employer for less than ten years. In fact, the Michigan DC plan discussed above can pay higher benefits than a typical defined benefit plan to younger workers who stay with their government employer for less than 15–20 years, depending on exactly how early shorter-term workers are allowed to retire under the DB plan.

To demonstrate this, consider the example of a worker who enters government employment out of school at age twenty-two, earning $35,000 in his first year. He receives a 2% real increase in salary each year, and contributes 3% of salary to the DC plan to maximize the employer match, for a total contribution to the DC account of 10% of salary each year. His invested funds earn the same standard, long-term, real return of 5% discussed in Chapter 3. He works for the government employer for fifteen years, and then departs public employment for better opportunities in private business at age thirty-seven.

By the age of thirty-seven, his government salary had reached $47,105 a year. With a defined benefit of 2% of final salary times the number of years of employment, he would be entitled to an annual benefit of 2% of $47,105 times 15, equaling $14,131 a year after he reaches the retirement age. But by age fifty-nine under the defined contribution plan, his DC account would have accumulated $290,288, which would be enough to pay him $14,514 out of the continuing investment returns alone every year for the rest of his life, enabling him to leave the entire accumulated account fund of nearly $300,000 to his family.

Now suppose the worker instead worked for twenty years for the public employer, and then left to work in private business at age forty-two. By then his government salary would have reached $52,008. The typical DB plan would pay him at retirement 2% of $52,008 times 20, or $20,803 a year in later retirement. But by age sixty-two under the DC plan this worker would have accumulated $412,879, which would be enough to pay him $20,643 every year out of the continuing investment returns for the rest of the worker's life, enabling him to leave the entire $400,000-plus dollars to his family.

This would be achieved under the design of the Michigan plan while gaining the tremendous savings for taxpayers that plan would provide. More generous DC plans with employers paying a higher percentage of salary into the account would enable a higher proportion of workers to actually do better in the DC plan as compared to the DB plan. For many state and local DB plans, major savings could still be achieved even while paying somewhat more into the replacement DC plan than in Michigan. But with the specter of bankruptcy haunting so many state and local governments, and the burdens on taxpayers and the economy, the Michigan plan should be recognized as plenty generous enough.

Freedom of choice. More broadly and fundamentally, the DC plan expands the freedom of choice of workers. Workers can choose their own investments, investment strategies, and investment managers, within limits. They can also choose their own benefit structures and vary their benefits over time, perhaps leaving more in the accounts to accumulate further earnings. Current workers at the time of the reform can also choose whether they want to be in the DC plan or stay in the DB plan.

The survivors, disability, and retiree health benefits of the DB pension plans could be provided in exactly the same way as add-ons to the DC plans. Or they could be provided through private life, disability, and health insurance in the DC plans. But there is no good reason why state and local taxpayers should have to pay for health benefits for former employees who have gone on to work in the private sector. Moreover, Medicare is plenty generous enough for former workers past age sixty-five, so state and local taxpayers should likewise not have to be burdened with further health benefits for former workers of this age.

Such reform of state and local public employee pensions is perfectly analogous to the Social Security reforms based on personal accounts discussed in Chapter 3. Public and private DC pension plans would be perfect complements to those Social Security personal accounts, increasing the possibility that middle-income Americans can accumulate close to a million dollars or more over their working years. In regard to the broader national bankruptcy issue, if we are going to solve that problem, all unfunded future retirement benefit promises need to be replaced with fully funded systems backed by real savings and investment.

Critics of DC pension plan reforms will argue that state and local governments with DB plans can better handle investment risk than workers in DC plans. But workers can fully handle the investment risk posed by DC plans, for two main reasons. First, retirement investments are very long-term. The worker is investing not only for his entire career, but, indeed, for his entire life, as the remaining retirement fund will continue to be invested to support benefits throughout retirement. With such a long-term investment horizon, perhaps sixty years or more, workers can weather many ups and downs in investment performance, with the average return on a diversified portfolio very likely over the long run to close in on the average long-term market return.

Second, workers can easily invest in simple, widely available, highly diversified pools of stocks, bonds, and other investments, through mutual funds and other vehicles. Such diversified pools will track the general long-run market investment returns. Indeed, with a sufficiently broad-based investment pool, the worker would basically own a piece of the economy as a whole. If the entire economy collapses, state and local governments will not be able to support DB plan promises, either.

Workers, indeed, may be able to handle this investment risk better than state and local governments. For they can do so without all of the political risks discussed above. Moreover, what is not sufficiently appreciated is that defined benefits are subject to depreciation through inflation risk. DC plans, by contrast, inherently maintain at least some inflation protection as the worker's investment returns would rise along with inflation over the long run, reestablishing standard, real, above-inflation market rates of return. DC plans, with their full portability and immediate vesting, are also better equipped to weather layoffs or job cutbacks, which can sharply reduce a worker's DB plan benefits.

Critics may also argue that most workers are too unsophisticated about investing to handle the responsibility of directing their own retirement investments. But as with the retirement investment plans discussed in Chapter 3, under the Michigan plan workers must choose only from among a range of carefully selected, broadly diversified, professionally managed funds. Even unsophisticated farmworkers in the South American nation of Chile have been able to handle that responsibility well.

Union-affiliated actuaries always try to drown proposals to change from DB plans to DC plans under a blizzard of technical arguments that the transition would be costly because the government will have to pay the workers leaving the DB plan their share of accumulated funds to take to the new plan. But if the DB plan is fully funded, then it will have the money to pay the departing workers that has been saved in its common trust fund. If the DB plan is not fully funded, then it needs to be in any event, and the government will have to bear that cost anyway. Moreover, experience shows that those who leave DB plans to take a defined contribution option are primarily the shorter-term and younger workers with little in accumulated funds in the DB plan.

State and local governments should at a minimum adopt DC reforms for all new public employees, and provide an option for all current workers to switch, along the lines of the Michigan plan. Moreover, they should encourage that transfer for current employees by cutting back on overly generous current DB plan benefits. Police officers and firefighters probably should enjoy the opportunity to retire at fifty-five. But there is no reason to burden taxpayers with paying for retirement for other state and local workers before the normal Social Security retirement age.

State and local governments should be aggressive in demanding such concessions from public employee unions. Unlike private companies, state and local governments are not required by federal law to recognize and negotiate with unions. As discussed in Chapter 10, public employee unions are not subject to the market, political, and legal checks that keep private sector unions within reasonable bounds. State and local governments should refuse to renew or extend public employee union contracts unless the above reasonable changes are made to public employee pensions. The American tradition of prohibiting strikes by public employees should also be uniformly recognized and enforced across the country. State and local governments also need not and should not collect dues for public employee unions. All such dues should be voluntarily paid by the workers to the extent they desire to do so. Ultimately, if necessary, the state bankruptcy option discussed at the end of this chapter could be used to reform excessive public employee pensions, and to implement the other employment policies discussed below.

OTHER EMPLOYMENT POLICIES

With compensation for public employees accounting for at least half of state and local spending, great strides can be achieved by recalibrating employment policies. Particularly in the jurisdictions that are in the most financial trouble and have hired the most new workers in recent years, a four-year hiring freeze would be justifiable, workable, and highly beneficial in averting state and local bankruptcy. Given how much public employee pay has raced ahead of private compensation, a pay freeze for state and local workers for four years would be highly justifiable as well, generating tremendous savings from current spending trends.

PRIVATIZATION

Another good strategy for reducing state and local spending is privatization of public services. This involves providing a formerly government service through the competitive private market instead. This can be done through any of several means, including contracting out the service through competitive bid to a private company, franchising a private company to provide a service to a particular geographic area, with consumers paying the company directly for the service, or simple "load shedding," which means the government just withdraws from providing the service and leaves it to the competitive private market.

As a general matter, the competition and incentives of the private market will lead the private firm to produce higher-quality service at lower costs than a public bureaucracy not subject either to market competition or incentives. For this reason, privatization is now a well-established practice among state and local governments and has demonstrated success in achieving budget savings while improving services.[146] As explained in the Heartland Institute's *The Patriot's Toolbox*, a helpful policy guide for federal, state, and local governments from the Tea Party perspective, "Thousands of national, state, and local government agencies in the United States have successfully privatized scores of services. Researchers have documented the successful privatization of airports, electric and telecommunications utilities, prisons, schools, transportation, and many other services."[147]

Indeed, *The Patriot's Toolbox* goes on to list thirty categories of public services that can and often should be privatized, including, besides the above, bridge and road maintenance, day-care facilities, golf courses, parking lots, rubbish collection, school construction, cafeteria services, driver's education classes, stadium and convention center management, street cleaning, snow removal, swimming pools, and toll roads.[148] Former Indianapolis mayor Stephen Goldsmith, a national trailblazer in privatization policies, advocates a "Yellow Pages" test for determining what services should be privatized, arguing that if a service can be found in the Yellow Pages, the state or local government should buy it from the private vendor, rather than produce it. Indeed, five cities famously known as "contract cities" contract out virtually all of their services, outside of public safety services such as the police and law enforcement.[149] But *The Patriot's Toolbox* and other authorities advocate a careful, case-by-case business evaluation of the costs and benefits of each privatization option.[150]

The International City/County Management Association (ICMA) reports that local governments contract out 17% of services to for-profit businesses, 16% to other government entities that can provide the service more efficiently at lower cost, 5% to nonprofit organizations, and 2% through franchising, volunteers, and other means.[151] The Reason Foundation, a national leader in researching and advancing privatization policies, reports cost savings through these means for state and local taxpayers of 20–50%, based on reviews of more than one hundred studies.[152]

The Patriot's Toolbox also advocates that state and local governments develop an inventory of all the real property assets they own, and evaluate which of these they could sell off while still maintaining essential services. They note that assets that have been fruitfully sold off by governments to private operators include water supply and distribution systems, electric and gas utilities, more than one hundred airports, and other basic infrastructure, in countries around the globe.[153] Increasingly, governments worldwide are turning to private developers to build the basic infrastructure in the first place, and then operate it under government contract.

OTHER COST-SAVING REFORMS

Another opportunity for major state and local budget savings is "economic development" programs and corporate welfare. Booming economic growth results from maintaining a general economic climate of low marginal tax rates and low regulatory costs. There is nothing that economic development programs and offices can meaningfully add to that. Rather, targeted giveaways and corporate welfare to particular companies and projects will only detract from general economic growth, since only the market can determine the most efficient and productive enterprises to prosper. Targeted handouts and corporate welfare will go instead to corporate cronies with the most political influence, adding up to a subtraction from the economy and a waste of taxpayer dollars. All these economic development programs and offices and all state and local corporate welfare should be zeroed out, adding up to considerable savings for the budget and taxpayers.

In addition, the health reforms to replace Obamacare discussed in Chapter 4 would add up to considerable savings in state Medicaid programs. States could maximize those savings by emphasizing opportunities for Health Savings Accounts for Medicaid beneficiaries, and even for the health plans for their own state and local employees. They could follow other successful state Medicaid reforms adopted around the country, such as those adopted by Jeb Bush when he was governor of Florida. The full scope of these proven reforms are monitored by the Center for Health Transformation in Washington, D.C.

The welfare reforms discussed in Chapter 5 would also provide broad savings for state and local governments, through the substantial administrative savings resulting from the welfare block grants, and much more so through the new incentives from providing welfare assistance for the able-bodied only through work. Altogether, these reforms would provide for sweeping reductions in state and local spending, sufficient to balance state and local budgets and avert state and local bankruptcy.

Serving the People

LAW ENFORCEMENT

Let's try a thought experiment. Suppose you could go anywhere in New York City any time day or night in complete physical safety, with no fear of crime or violence. What would be the economic implications of that?

All those abandoned, run-down residential properties in formerly dangerous neighborhoods would suddenly offer great economic opportunity. You could grab one at what would be a suddenly increasing but still-meager market value, and fix it up. You and others could go there any time of day or night to work on it, with no fear. You could install top-quality fixtures without worrying about theft or vandalism. You could then rent it out, or even live there yourself.

Anyone could then open a store in the neighborhood to serve the residents any time day or night, without fear of crime or vandalism. The growing population in the suddenly rejuvenating neighborhood would increasingly provide new business opportunities to service. Outsiders could invest money in the neighborhood, without fear that it would be trashed or stolen. Moreover, customers could come to the store from all over the city, without fear of crime.

What is true on a small, individual scale would be true on a larger scale. The low-cost land and property in the currently run-down, crime-ridden, drug-infested ghettoes would suddenly be the top investment and business opportunity in the city. Residential developers could buy up low-cost properties and restore modern housing to serve the flowering neighborhood. Commercial developers could establish more extensive retail and office enterprises on still relatively low-cost property in the neighborhood, and then construct new shopping malls, knowing people could come from all over the city to work, shop, and buy. New and better restaurants of all types would open to serve the new consumer and residential traffic. The now safe, newly prospering neighborhood would need more of everything, from grocery stores to auto mechanics to dentists to consumer banks.

These burgeoning new enterprises would mean new jobs, especially for the nearby residents looking for work. With the new welfare system described in Chapter 5, every able-bodied adult, and quite a few teenagers, would be looking for work. As employment in the neighborhood soared, there would be renewed and growing demand for all types of goods and services. That would mean still more business opportunity.

Youngsters in school would see this blossoming opportunity all around them, and would know there was a real future awaiting them if they would just finish school. Young women would be looking for young men who could support a family, as they would no longer have the option of marrying the government for their support. For young men, becoming a productive, working member of society would now be a top means of attracting young women.

Now imagine that the same new regime of physical safety and freedom from the threat of crime and violence was established in Detroit. Imagine you could go anywhere in Detroit day or night without fear of crime or violence. Imagine the same for Los Angeles, Chicago, St. Louis, Cleveland, Philadelphia, Newark, Camden, Baltimore, Atlanta, Buffalo. Imagine what that would mean for America. In the new climate of pro-growth investment incentives discussed in Chapter 7.

Maybe there was a reason that law enforcement and physical safety for person and property was the original purpose of government. Maybe we have reached a point in our civilization where mining the wisdom of the past can tell us as much as exploring the Zen of the future.

The lesson from this thought experiment is that local government must focus first and foremost on their original job—law enforcement and physical safety for person and property. This would do far more to help African-Americans, Hispanics, the poor, and other minorities than ever more and counterproductive income redistribution, which is really just institutionalized violence against property and productivity, which is why it is counterproductive. The new welfare system described in Chapter 5 satisfies the valid concern underlying income redistribution policy, securing the vulnerable from the suffering of deprivation and want. There is no helpful role for local governments to add to that (though they would have the vital, local role in the new welfare system). But with their own, local resources, local governments instead need to do their original job, providing physical security from crime and violence, instead of trying to add to counterproductive redistribution.

This would involve a massive transfer of local government resources into the police and law enforcement, to achieve the ultimate goal of providing physical security and freedom from crime and violence everywhere in the city, any time of day or night. That might involve networks of locals digitally hooked up to law enforcement and the police, like a continuous, online digital neighborhood watch. With cell phones, laptops, and other new technologies providing mobile Internet potentially continuously online, new vistas in law enforcement may be opening up that local governments need to learn how to exploit. But it should also involve a massive increase in police, detective, and other law enforcement personnel.

The new environment might produce quite a social jolt at first. But as the new peace, security, and prosperity is established, a deterrence effect would become predominant, just as the way to achieve peace is to be militarily strong enough to win any war (peace through strength). Everyone would recognize that, more than ever, crime does not pay, and that legal retribution is swift and powerful. The community at large would shift from increasingly foreclosed criminal endeavors to the newly emerging economic opportunities.

This renewed focus on law enforcement and physical security is the foundation for restoring economic growth, opportunity, and prosperity to America's inner cities.

EDUCATION AND SCHOOL CHOICE

Our current educational system today functions to serve the bureaucracy, rather than the people and specifically their children. And why not? You have to finance the system through your taxes, whether you like the job they are doing or not. Neither you nor any parent can influence a public school's finances in the way a customer of any private enterprise can affect it by taking their business elsewhere.

That is why our educational system is failing the people, and the children. Less than 30% of eighth graders scored proficient or above in the 2003 National Assessment of Educational Progress reading test.[154] In Chicago, it was only 15%, in Cleveland and Washington, D.C., 10%. Nationwide, the high school graduation rate is 74%, meaning that one-fourth of students drop out before graduating.[155] Moreover, on international tests of student achievement, American students score worse the longer they are in school.[156]

Yet federal, state, and local governments spend more on education than on national defense. Maybe one reason we get such poor performance in return is that 40% of school funds is spent on the bureaucracy rather than in the classroom.[157]

Public education exists to serve the children, not the bureaucracy, and not the teachers' unions. In other words, the money is for the children, not the school. That is why the public money for each child should follow the child to the school the family chooses, ideally whether public, charter, or private.

This would shift power from the public school bureaucracy to parents, students, and the family, which is why the bureaucracy opposes it so strongly. If parents and students have the power to determine where the funding goes, schools, teachers, administrators, and the bureaucracy would have to be maximally responsive to their concerns and preferences. No longer would complaining parents and students be treated as weird interlopers in the expert process of education. Instead we would have power to the people.

Each school would be in a fierce competition for funds, and would have to strive to satisfy parents and students to win that competition. The *incentives* facing school administrators and teachers would be transformed. This would spur each school to more carefully monitor its performance, move expeditiously to correct problems, and devote imagination and energy to timely innovation. As a result, the public schools themselves would change and improve sharply. It wouldn't be just the students whose parents choose to send them to a better-performing private school who would get a better education. The overall results would be much more like the performance the public gets with every other good and service in a competitive market.

In this new environment, the combined choices of parents, students, and families would automatically work school reform. Funding would automatically and immediately flow to the schools that best satisfied parents and students with the best teaching methods, materials, and subject matter. Schools that failed to change and serve would automatically lose funding. If they persisted in failing, they would ultimately lose their students to other, better-performing schools, and so would have to close.

This system would also promote decentralized experimentation and innovation, allowing more scope and opportunity for the demonstration of the virtue of new ideas and innovations. Experienced teachers with better ideas for instruction could more easily start their own schools to demonstrate the superiority and appeal of their innovations. The system would also allow for decentralized flexibility, with different schools striving to maximize the cultivation and flourishing of different talents and abilities, whether in math, science, music, the arts, or other disciplines. Parents and students could then each pick the school that best served their particular needs and preferences.

Pathbreaking, eye-opening research by Caroline Hoxby confirms that competition causes public schools to change and improve their performance, with better student achievement across the board as a result.[158] These improvements are further confirmed by other studies.

Charter schools are one way to introduce school choice. Charter schools are public schools that are allowed decentralized management to try to best serve their communities and students, sometimes with private sponsors and operators. Some student choice is allowed among charter schools within certain districts or geographic areas. But the choice and resulting competition is too limited, because private competitors are excluded and the number of charter schools is generally strictly limited.

A better option is to allow each student a school voucher for his or her share of public funds, which would then go to the public, private, or charter school the student and his family chooses. The same result could be achieved through a refundable tuition tax credit of equivalent amount. An additional desirable reform would be to allow citizens and businesses tuition tax credits for contributions toward private, supplemental vouchers for low-income and minority students.

There has been a scandalous failure of urban media watchdogs to protect the interests of low-income and minority students in school choice, and favor instead the special interest, public school teachers' unions, too often condemning these students to a lifetime of economic failure in the global economy without an adequate education. The transparent logic explained above demonstrates why school choice would serve the public far better than the current bureaucratic swamp in education.

Another school choice reform is known as "the parent trigger." Under that policy, a majority of parents with students attending a public school can sign a petition directing one of four or five fundamental, transformational changes at the school. One is to provide for the school to be transformed into a charter school, with the petition even directing a new private sector charter school operator for the school. A second option is known as "turnaround," which involves replacing the school principal, and granting the new principal broader powers to change school practices, procedures, teaching methods, and subject matter content.

A third option is known as "transformation," and involves specifying broader changes beyond replacing the principal, including replacing teachers, and directly specifying changes in all other operations of the school. Another option available when all else fails and the parents are convinced the school is hopeless is to require closure of the school, with the students reassigned to other public schools nearby.

The parent trigger idea was originally developed and advanced by left-leaning, "progressive" political institutions in California, where it was first enacted into law. But more recently it has earned broad support across the political spectrum. As enacted in California, parent trigger rights were limited to failing schools based on specified state criteria. But there is no reason why the same rights cannot be allowed to parents at every public school. The original parent trigger concept can also be broadened to allow parents to specify that all students at the school be allowed school vouchers or tuition tax credits to attend any public, charter, or private school of their choice. This would allow parents and students to break out of the limited choices of local public schools, which may be widely unsatisfactory.

Another liberating idea would produce a revolution at the college level. States could establish testing programs for earning professional licenses or certificates attesting to mastery of occupational knowledge. Once an applicant passed the test, he or she would be granted the license or certificate. This could apply to stockbrokers, accountants, insurance agents, real estate agents, even lawyers, or any other required license, except the more sensitive medical licenses where the public health is directly involved.

This would block the power of colleges to exact an exorbitant fee, and impose numerous other requirements for a broader college degree which are not necessary for a professional license or certification. This would be most important for younger students from minority and low-income families who cannot afford hefty tuition and the loss of so many earning years to gain an unnecessary college degree.

Prometheus Unbound

Of all state and local regulatory barriers, the most crippling for the economy is when states join into regional pacts to impose cap-and-trade burdens or so-called renewable energy standards on producers within their states. As explained in Chapter 7, cap-and-trade burdens would raise the cost of energy in the state for consumers and business. The extra costs would not only unnecessarily burden consumers; they would also slay jobs and slash economic growth, wages, and incomes.

"Renewable energy standards" require utilities to produce, and therefore both residential and business consumers to buy, certain quantities of so-called renewable energy, produced by wind, solar, and other alternative energy technologies. These energy sources today are far more costly than traditional energy, resulting again in higher energy costs for residential and business consumers in the state. Since these alternative energy sources cannot survive economically without massive public subsidies, that only adds further to the unnecessary burdensome costs.

If grassroots activists cannot convince current state and local policy makers to remove all such requirements as soon as possible, then political challengers should contest incumbents on these grounds, promising to unleash energy producers and state and local economies from these tragically unnecessary, arbitrary burdens.

WHEN BANKRUPTCY IS THE RIGHT ANSWER

The U.S. Constitution grants the federal government the power to enact a bankruptcy code for the entire nation. The current U.S. bankruptcy code already provides for municipal and other local governments to declare bankruptcy, terminating their debts and allowing them to start over with a clean slate. But there is no provision for states to declare bankruptcy.

Federal legislation should be enacted to add a new chapter to federal bankruptcy law, providing for states to file for bankruptcy when all else fails and they prove unable to get their financial affairs in order otherwise. This would be far preferable to federal bailouts for spendthrift states, which would only accelerate the coming bankruptcy of America.

States are sovereign institutions, and the new state bankruptcy code can be structured to respect that. It should provide that states could not be forced into bankruptcy by creditors. Bankruptcy filings would be solely at the discretion of each state. Moreover, federal bankruptcy judges would not have the power to order a state to do anything. That would violate state sovereignty and democratic control by the voters. The federal law would specifically provide that no judicial bankruptcy decree for any state could provide for a tax increase. That would take us all the way back to taxation without representation, which we fought a war to overturn.

States that wanted to exercise this new bankruptcy option would file a plan of reorganization with a federal bankruptcy court. The plan of reorganization would specify how the state's debt obligations would be readjusted and then paid off, including possible reductions or cancellations of outstanding debts as in any bankruptcy. The only requirement on the plan of reorganization, besides no tax increases, is that all creditors within the same class of priority would have to be treated equally within the usual established rules for all other bankruptcies.

The highest level of priority would be for bondholders, so that a state could file for bankruptcy without nullifying outstanding bonds, which would preserve its ability to borrow in the future when necessary and desirable. This would also help to avoid disruption in state bond markets. Note that municipal bond markets have continued to function over many years even with the possibility of municipal bankruptcy under federal law. The second level of priority would be for vendors and contractors to the state, granting those who have provided goods and services some protection even in bankruptcy to be paid, or at least be paid equally and proportionally with others. The third level of priority would be for union contracts. This would empower states to rewrite onerous pension obligations for state employees, or to freeze salaries and pay contrary to any outstanding contractual obligations.

The federal judge would have the power solely to accept or reject the state's plan of reorganization. If the judge accepted the plan, it would have the force of law, reordering the state's debts as provided. If the judge rejected the plan, he would have to issue an opinion explaining why. The state could then try again.

The federal law should provide that a state's bankruptcy could be triggered by a filing initiated by the state's governor; by the state legislature by passing the plan of reorganization, which would automatically send it to the court for approval; or by the people adopting the plan of reorganization by referendum, automatically sending it to the court as well.

For states that have become politically dysfunctional, as California may be, this would be the best solution, far better than spreading the responsibility for the debt of spendthrift states to other taxpayers across the country.

CHAPTER 9

THE EQUALITY OF FREEDOM

Equality of Rules Versus Equality of Results

The year was 2081, and everybody was finally equal. They weren't only equal before God and the law. They were equal every which way. Nobody was smarter than anybody else. Nobody was better looking than anybody else. Nobody was stronger or quicker than anybody else. All this equality was due to the 211th, 212th and 213th Amendments to the Constitution, and to the unceasing vigilance of agents of the United States Handicapper General.

So began Kurt Vonnegut's 1961 short story "Harrison Bergeron."[1] In that brave new world, the government forced each individual to wear "handicaps" to offset any advantage they had, so that everyone could be truly and fully equal. Beautiful people had to wear ugly masks to hide their good looks. The strong had to wear compensating weights to slow them down. Graceful dancers were burdened with bags of birdshot. Those with above average-intelligence had to wear government transmitters in their ears that would emit sharp noises every twenty seconds, shattering their thoughts "to keep them . . . from taking unfair advantage of their brains."[2]

But Harrison Bergeron was a special problem, because he was so way above average in everything. Vonnegut explained, "Nobody had ever borne heavier handicaps. . . . Instead of a little ear radio for a mental handicap, he wore a tremendous pair of earphones, and spectacles with thick wavy lenses."[3] Seven feet tall, "Scrap metal was hung all over him" to offset his strength, to the point that "Harrison looked like a walking junkyard."[4]

The youthful Harrison did not accept these burdens easily, so he had been jailed. But with his myriad advantages and talents, he had broken out. An announcement on TV explained the threat, "He is a genius and an athlete . . . and should be regarded as extremely dangerous."[5]

Harrison broke into a TV studio, which was broadcasting the performance of a troupe of dancing ballerinas. On national television, he illegally cast off each one of his handicaps. Then he did the same for one of the ballerinas, and then the orchestra, which he commanded to play. To shockingly beautiful chords, Harrison and the ballerina began to dance. Vonnegut explained the beauty of their dance:

> Not only were the laws of the land abandoned, but the laws of gravity and the laws of motion as well. . . . The studio ceiling was thirty feet high, but each leap brought the dancers nearer to it. It became their obvious intention to kiss the ceiling. They kissed it. And then, neutralizing gravity with love and pure will, they remained suspended in air inches below the ceiling, and they kissed each other for a long, long time.[6]

At that moment, in barged the Handicapper General, Diana Moon Glampers, with a double-barreled shotgun, and she shot the two lawbreakers dead to the floor.

We have spent most of this book explaining a new vision of a modernized, comprehensive, 21st century social safety net that would end deprivation and want. This is justified to prevent human suffering. In civilized societies, there is broad consent to such policies, which simply recognize the moral obligation of each to help their fellow man.

But once such policies are established, going beyond that to take from some by force of law what they have produced and consequently earned, to give to others merely for the purpose of making incomes and wealth more equal, is not justifiable. Vonnegut's story helps to explain why.

First, to achieve true and comprehensive equality would involve gross violations of personal liberty, as the talented and capable must be prevented from using their abilities and advantages to get ahead of others, or to make any feel inferior in any way. The more productive must be prevented from using their abilities to produce more than others, or at least any extra production must be seized from them to be redistributed to others (which is effectively the same as prohibiting the production in the first place). This is why in all those societies that have tried to enforce the more extreme vision of mandatory equality, totalitarian governments have emerged, trying to enforce that vision on all. A thoroughgoing government structure must develop to impose and enforce social control on the most productive, or on any potential outbreak of "excess" productivity.

Moreover, as Vonnegut's story illustrates, inequalities of wealth and income are not the only important differences in society. If equality is truly a moral obligation, then inequalities of beauty, intelligence, strength, grace, talent, etc., logically all should be leveled as well. That would require some rather heavy-handed government control and intervention.

Besides gross restrictions on liberty, we can see as well that this vision of equality is not actually fair. It is not fair to the beautiful to force them to wear ugly masks. It is not fair to the strong to punish them by holding them down with excess weights. It is not fair to the graceful and athletic to deprive them of their talents. In the same way, it is not fair to the productive to deprive them of what they have produced, merely to make them equal to others who have produced less. As Vonnegut's story shows, putting social limits on the success that people are allowed to achieve with their own talents and abilities makes for an ugly society, harshly restrictive on its best lights, who have the most to actually give to the benefit of all.

Finally, this vision of equality as a social goal, with equal incomes and wealth for all, is severely counterproductive economically, and so makes for a poor society as well. Pursuing such a vision would require very high marginal tax rates on anyone with above-average production, income, and wealth, which rates, experience as well as theory shows us, lead to less production. As we saw in our discussion of tax policy in Chapter 7, the less the productive are allowed to keep of what they produce, the less they will produce.

Indeed, if income and wealth is going to be equalized, why would anyone save or invest? Savings just adds to wealth, and wealth is anti-social under a social justice regime of equal wealth for all. Indeed, the only rational strategy for everyone under such a regime is to consume all income and not save anything. For anyone who saves more than others will see that savings expropriated, and anyone who saves less than others will be rewarded with a grant from the government to make their savings equal to all others.

With no savings, there can be no investment. But under the social justice of equal income and wealth for all, investment would similarly make no sense in any event. Investment is made only to earn returns, which means more income. Anyone who invests more than others would have an above-average income, which excess would be expropriated to maintain equality. But if you invest less than others on average, and suffer a below-average income, you would be rewarded with a grant from the government to ensure you enjoyed the same average income as everyone else. So, again, the only rational strategy for everyone would be to avoid all investment.

But the only difference between the prosperity of modern industrial society and the subsistence living of cavemen is savings and investment. All the tools and equipment that enable us to produce more than what was enjoyed during caveman days come from investment, made possible by savings. The caveman had the brute force of manual labor just as much as modern man, if not more so because they were more practiced at it. Indeed, even the caveman's club involved savings and investment. If Robert Reich and Paul Krugman were around at the time, they would have seen to it that the clubs of all the cavemen that bothered to make one were confiscated so that they were not unequally advantaged over the cavemen who focused only on hunting cavewomen to pull by their hair into their caves. So no one would have even bothered to make clubs, and there would be no human civilization to speak of. This is the natural, inevitable result of the social justice vision of equal income and wealth for all.

Actually, even this gives too much credit to that vision. For the same analysis applies to the concept of work itself. Under a social justice regime of equal income and wealth for all, there would be no reason for anyone even to work. If you worked more than others, and earned more income as a result, the above-average results of all that work would be expropriated. If you didn't work at all, then you would receive a grant from whatever government might possibly be functioning so that you still consumed the same average amount of goods and services as every-one else.

So under a social justice regime of equal income and wealth for all, the only rational strategy for everyone would be, literally, "Party till you drop." Maybe this is why the Bible tells us that envy is one of the seven deadly sins. Observe the similar logical results under a strict regime of "From each according to his ability, to each according to his needs." With above-average ability taxed at a marginal tax rate of 100%, any such ability will be very hard to find. With all needs heavily subsidized, expect a cornucopia of such need.

A thought experiment will further bolster these commonsense observations, and perhaps help younger students to see the point more clearly. Credit for this experiment belongs to Jay Richards and his book *Money, Greed, and God.*[7] Consider a college class where the professor announces that to demonstrate his commitment to social justice and equality, henceforth every student will get the same grade as the average grade achieved by the entire class. Above-average students would immediately recognize this as unfair, for they would get no reward and recognition for their hard work, talent, and abilities. Thoughtful average students would recognize this as unfair as well, for why should below-average students who did not devote the same hard work and ability get the same grade as they? Even honest below-average students would recognize this as unfair as well, for they would know that they did not deserve the grade earned by others.

But there would be an even more revealing secondary effect. The above-average students would stop working so hard and studying, for they would get no gain from doing so. They are going to just get the same average grade as everyone else in any event. So their grades would decline. *As a result, the average grade for the class would decline as well, hurting everyone.* Indeed, the same effect would result for every student. For each student would know that his own individual effort would not affect the average grade for the entire class significantly. *So the average students would stop studying as well!* And even the below-average students would recognize there is no point to whatever effort they were providing. So their studying would also decline, to nothing.

This means not only that the class grade would plummet precipitously. It means also that there would be no studying, and no one would learn anything. So the whole point of the class would be defeated.

This is exactly what happens to the economies of societies where the social justice vision of equal results for all is most assiduously followed. See, for example, North Korea or Cuba. Or compare North Korea with South Korea, or the old East Germany with the old West Germany. Or China of the 1960s and 1970s with the Japan of the time. Or China of the 1960s and 1970s with the China of today.

Such economic results lead to further restrictions on personal liberty. The more productive would naturally want to leave any regime of forced equalization of incomes and wealth, for they would just be plundered by the rest of society, and would be prevented from achieving their full potential. So the regime would have to maintain tight restrictions on emigration and international travel to avoid losing the society's most productive citizens. But this wouldn't just be a problem among the most productive. Most would not want to live in an economically stagnant, poor society. The great majority would want to flee as well to lands of greater opportunity and prosperity. So the regime would have to restrict everyone from leaving, imposing on the liberty of all. This is where the Berlin Wall comes from.

Some may protest, oh no, this is not what we mean. We are not so naive as to think that a policy of equal incomes and wealth for all is remotely workable. It would be an advance of civilization and science equivalent to Newton's discovery of gravity and Einstein's discovery of the theory of relativity for everyone to come together and agree, fully and finally, that equal incomes and wealth for all is not a desirable social goal. For throughout academia, journalism, the media, and the more liberal wing of our politics, the reigning assumption is that this is precisely the proper social goal.

Moreover, just as the absolute goal of equal incomes and wealth for all produces these unacceptable end results, any policy that goes beyond safety nets ending deprivation and want, to taxing and redistributing to achieve *more* equal incomes and wealth, takes us *toward* these unacceptable end results to the extent we pursue the equalization policy. To the extent we go down that path, we get less savings, investment, work, and prosperity, as well as less freedom, and ultimately less real fairness.

EQUALITY UNDER THE LAW

But the Declaration of Independence itself says, "All men are created equal." And equal justice and liberty for all is, indeed, a fundamental American ideal. But what is involved in these expressions is a different concept of equality than the social justice concept of equal incomes and wealth for all.

The original liberal, and traditionally American, concept of equality is "equality under the law." That means the same, equal rules apply to all, not the same equal results. Baseball is a fair game because the same rules apply to all players. That is equality under the law. But the game never ends with the same results, in a tied (equal) score for both teams. That would be social justice equality, or equality of results. Similarly, no two players ever end the season with exactly the same performance statistics across the board. That is not unfair inequality.

While a false notion of equality undermines the freedom and prosperity of all, including working people, a proper understanding of equality advances freedom and prosperity for all. Equality of rules equally protects the property of all, which encourages savings, investment, and work, because all are assured of the same protection for the fruits of their work and productive activities. Equality of rules ensures that all enjoy the same freedom of contract, empowering them to maximize value and production, and to plan investment knowing they can rely on their agreed contractual rights. Equality of rules provides a framework in which all are equally free to pursue their individual vision of happiness to the maximum.

Within this framework of equal rules for all, the outcome of the market in terms of income and wealth is fair, for two fundamental reasons. The first is that people basically earn in the market the value of what they produce. Economists say more formally that wages equal the marginal productivity of labor. That encompasses both the concept of the market value of the output of each worker, and the number of workers that can do the same thing. The more workers that can produce the same output, the less that output is worth in the market. If the worker's output is unique, that output will be worth more, to the extent that people value it, because only he can produce it.

Alex Rodriguez and LeBron James each make a lot more money than any teacher, or any doctor. In a broad social sense, what teachers do and what doctors do is worth a lot more than what athletes Rodriguez and James do. Not everyone can do what teachers do, and fewer still can do what doctors do. But only Alex Rodriguez and LeBron James can do what they do. What they do pleases millions every night of the long season that each plays, whether those millions experience it in person at the stadium, on the radio, on television, or in the paper reading about it in the morning. Each fan is willing to pay a little in return for the athletes' unique performance. Since the A-Rods and the LeBrons are the only ones who can provide that performance, what they get adds up to a large amount for each. What they get is not unfair. They earn it, through talent, hard work, and performance.

More generally, as the productivity of more average workers grows, they earn more. As their productivity and skills advance with experience, they earn more. This is why 97% of workers earn more than the minimum wage. The law compelling employers to pay is not the reason workers earn what they do. The productivity of workers in competitive markets is what determines their earnings. This is why labor earns roughly 70% of the total output of the American economy year after year, and capital earns only about 30%. Capital, too, earns the value of what it contributes to production. The return to capital equals the marginal productivity of capital. Political rhetoric is cheap. But reams of economic studies document these patterns in detail in the real world.

This is why it is even wrong to speak of the "distribution" of income and wealth. Income and wealth are not distributed. Income and wealth are produced, and in a fair society they come into the world attached to the rightful owner that produced them. As the late Harvard philosophy professor Robert Nozick wrote, "Whoever makes something, having bought or contracted for all other held resources used in the process . . . is entitled to it. The situation is *not* one of something's getting made, and there being an open question of who is to get it. Things come into the world already attached to people having entitlements over them." Indeed, if income and wealth are not born attached to the owner that produced them, they tend not to be born at all, which is what the discussion of tax policy in Chapter 7 showed.

Moreover, what is produced is not taken from anyone else. It is created by the worker. So the income and wealth that such production earns does not come at the expense of anyone else. The economy is not a fixed pie with slices being handed out. Each worker expands the pie, creating his own slices.

Another implication of this is that the notion of "the race of life" is not an accurate picture of the economic marketplace. The economics of income and wealth is not a matter of a fixed prize waiting to be awarded to the winner of a race. Each worker produces his own prize, without stopping any other worker from producing yet another prize for himself. So there is no need to be fixated on whether everyone starts out "at the same starting line." A worker starting out with more advantages may produce more. But that doesn't stop anyone else from producing. To the contrary, more productive workers to work and trade with will only expand opportunities for others to be more productive.

As a result, the question of whether natural endowments of talent, intelligence, or other productive characteristics are deserved is actually irrelevant. If natural endowments make a worker more productive, that does not harm anyone else. More production from worker X does not mean that worker Y must produce less. To the contrary, it means new opportunities for worker Y.

The second reason that the outcome of the market in terms of incomes and wealth is fair was developed by my former professor Nozick in his landmark book *Anarchy, State, and Utopia*.[8] In the market, incomes and wealth are obtained through the sum of innumerable voluntary exchanges. Those exchanges each involve the exercise by the individuals to the exchange of their economic liberty. "Capitalist acts between consenting adults," in Nozick's phrase.[9] Indeed, the individuals enter into the exchange because they both believe they benefit from it. Except when they are mistaken in that belief, the exchanges consequently produce mutual benefit, and thereby increase happiness and social welfare. In economic terms, the exchanges increase value and hence total production (or GDP). This process of individuals freely trading among themselves at their own choice is inherently fair, so the outcome of the process is fair. The incomes and wealth that result from this process of voluntary exchange are inherently fair. The social principle that results from this process is, as Nozick states, "From each as they choose, to each as they are chosen."[10]

Nozick elaborates on this principle through his celebrated hypothetical of the case of former basketball star Wilt Chamberlain:

> Now suppose that Wilt Chamberlain is greatly in demand by basketball teams, being a great gate attraction. . . . He signs the following sort of contract with a team: In each home game, twenty-five cents from the price of each ticket of admission goes to him. . . . The season starts and people cheerfully attend his team's games; they buy their tickets, each time dropping a separate twenty-five cents of their admission price into a special box with Chamberlain's name on it. They are excited about seeing him play; it is worth the total admission price to them. Let us suppose that in one season one million persons attend his home games, and Wilt Chamberlain winds up with $250,000, a much larger sum than the average income and much larger than anyone else has.[11]

What would be unfair about that resulting "inequality"? Nozick rightly asks. Each person attending the games freely paid the ticket price by their own choice for an experience they enjoyed, or at least believed they would enjoy. There is no sound moral basis for objecting to this process or to Chamberlain's resulting outsized personal income.

This argument makes most clear how the policy of mandatory, forced equality of incomes and wealth inherently must involve restrictions on personal liberty. Nozick explains:

> [N]o end-state principle or distributional patterned principle of justice [like equal incomes and wealth for all] can be continuously realized without continuous interference with people's lives. Any favored pattern [of distribution] would be transformed into one

unfavored by the principle, by people choosing to act in various ways; for example, by people exchanging goods and services with other people, or giving things to other people, things the transferrers are entitled to under the favored distribution pattern. To maintain a pattern one must either continually interfere to stop people from transferring resources as they wish to, or continually (or periodically) interfere to take from some person resources that others for some reason choose to transfer to them.[12]

These are two different explanations for why the pattern of income and wealth resulting from the market is fair: because the pattern represents what each has produced, and because the pattern results from an inherently fair process of voluntary exchange. But they are mutually reinforcing factors. The reason people usually choose to enter into voluntary exchanges with others is that they think what the other has produced is worth the price to be paid.[13] That shows that the exchange transactions are generally made for rational, not arbitrary reasons.

Moreover, the same policy arises from either explanation. People should be free to enjoy the incomes and wealth that arise from market transactions. It is no business of the government, or third-party interlopers, to redistribute such income and wealth merely for the purpose of making them more equal. This is the policy that maximizes total production, income, and wealth within the constraint of providing comprehensive safety nets to eliminate poverty, deprivation, and want, because it allows producers to otherwise keep what they produce, maintaining the incentives to produce. What the discussion earlier in this book showed is that if those safety nets are structured intelligently, to maximize the role of modern capital and labor markets in bearing the burden, with market incentives to maximize productive behavior, then the cost of that burden will be minimized. The cost of that burden will then be feasible, not seriously counterproductive, allowing for the maximum, just prosperity of all.

The great alternative to Nozick was previously developed by his Harvard philosophy colleague John Rawls, in his celebrated volume *A Theory of Justice*.[14] Rawls argued for a different distribution of income and wealth than that produced by the market. But he was too smart to advocate the principle of absolute equality of income and wealth, recognizing the validity of the above arguments regarding the impracticality of that principle.

Rawls derived a different principle through moral reasoning. His explanatory device was the concept of "a veil of ignorance."[15] Rawls posited a presocial "original position," in which all of society gathers together behind a veil of ignorance to decide what the proper principle of distributive justice should be to govern society. Behind the veil of ignorance, no one knows what their position in society will be under the governing principle of distributive justice. They don't know what their talents, abilities, desires, character, motivation, or family background will be. In this situation, with all considerations of vested or personal interest removed, Rawls determined the principle of distributive justice he believed most would choose.

Rawls believed the principle they would choose is equality of income and wealth, except that inequalities would be allowed only to the extent that the practical economic effect of such inequalities was to make the poorest and least advantaged members of society better off. In other words, inequality would be allowed when the resulting incentives from allowing the productive to keep a larger share of what they produce would result in higher production and economic growth that increased the incomes of the poor. But the imposition of equality would stop short of going so far that the resulting loss of production and growth actually left the poor even poorer, as in the analysis above, where total equality of incomes and wealth was shown to lead to the elimination of savings, investment, and work. Rawls called this the difference principle.

Rawls, however, provided no definitive logical proof that this difference principle is what the people behind the veil of ignorance would choose. To the extent that this principle would result in more redistributive taxation to make incomes and wealth more equal than would result from the principle of a comprehensive safety net to end poverty, deprivation, and want, and no more, as advocated in this book, then it would not maximize total production, income, and wealth within the constraint of the moral obligation to care for the poor. The principle would go beyond the taxation necessary to finance a comprehensive but well-structured safety net, to require additional redistributive taxation for equality just up to the point beyond which the counterproductive effects would be so harsh, through the counterproductive incentives as discussed above, that it actually resulted in less income and wealth for the poorest themselves. Such a principle would seem to allow for sufficient loss of production, income, and wealth that everyone else other than the lower-income citizens would be worse off, or at least most of the others would be worse off.

For this reason, I do not believe that, even under a veil of ignorance, most people would choose this principle. I do not believe that most people would choose equality resulting in lost production, income, and wealth as long as the poorest were not made worse off. I believe that most people would see as fair the pattern of income and wealth arising from the market, either because that pattern reflects the contribution to production of each participant, or because it results from an inherently fair process of voluntary exchanges, as long as there was a comprehensive social safety net as described in this book that eliminates poverty, deprivation, and human suffering. With such a safety net in place, most people would not want to go beyond that and suffer the loss of production, income, and wealth that would result from more redistributive taxation merely to achieve more equality. Human suffering would be eliminated under this principle, but no economic prosperity would be sacrificed to achieve more equality beyond that. Contra Rawls, this is what most people would choose.

But there is a little more to the full story. Redistributive taxation is not the only way to achieve greater equality of incomes and wealth. Greater equality can arise because the ability to produce becomes more equal. That can be achieved through more and better education, for example. Or greater equality can arise because more people choose to trade and transfer to achieve that result, such as through charity.

Greater equality achieved through these means does not have any of the counterproductive effects of greater equality achieved through redistributive taxation. It does not restrict anyone's liberty, it is not unfair to the producers (by effectively stealing their production), and it doesn't create counterproductive incentives reducing production, incomes, and wealth.

Another example along these lines is the personal savings, investment, and insurance accounts as an alternative to Social Security and Medicare. As discussed in Chapter 3, with all working people contributing to such accounts, ownership of wealth across the entire society would become far more equal, because the bottom half of income earners who save little or nothing today would accumulate huge savings and investment amounts in such accounts over their lives. This greater equality would be achieved not through redistribution of existing wealth, but through the creation of new wealth far more equally owned. With the investment income from this newly created wealth, income would be more equal as well. This greater equality is again achieved with none of the gross counterproductive effects of income and wealth redistribution.

Undoubtedly there are other means of achieving greater income and wealth equality in this way. Whenever that can be accomplished, everybody wins. The resulting greater equality does provide a measure of social peace and solidarity, while reducing social envy. The personal accounts make all workers capitalists as well, contributing to the end of perceived conflict between labor and capital. With all workers owning a share of the nation's business and industry, public and political support will increase for free market policies that will advance the growth and prosperity of that business and industry, and in consequence the general economy overall. The happiness of those who are almost religiously committed to the social goal of greater equality is increased, which effectively is another social gain.

More energy and attention devoted to building up equality of income and wealth in these ways, rather than tearing down the honest production, income, and wealth of others, would greatly benefit our nation.

More Equality Than You Know

For nearly twenty years now, major media institutions have been reporting growing inequality in America. But does what they are reporting reflect actual "inequality," or does it just reflect changing demographics in our society? Often the numbers they are reporting for changes over decades can't logically be compared because the composition of the numbers themselves has changed so much. Because this issue, and the media institutions themselves, are so ideologically contentious, much of what has been reported has been misleading at best, and deceptive at worst.

All of this has been best sorted out by Alan Reynolds in his brilliant book *Income and Wealth*.[16] Reynolds digs deep into the underlying data to show that what has been reported as rising inequality involves primarily changing demographics that reflects changing patterns of work and productive output, and even misunderstood changes in the meaning and composition of the numbers being reported themselves.

CHANGING DEMOGRAPHICS

As Reynolds reports, the top fifth of households in terms of income includes nearly six times as many full-time workers as the bottom fifth.[17] That is because the top fifth is heavily composed of two-earner couples with older children or other relatives that work. The bottom fifth, by contrast, is heavily composed of aged or young singles who are either retired or still in school. Of course, a household composed of one single person cannot have multiple workers in any event. Some in the bottom fifth are disabled and can't work; others are temporarily too sick to work or to work regularly. Some who do work are in the bottom fifth because their work is in the underground economy, or in crime, and so is not reported. Some in the bottom fifth don't work regularly because they suffer from alcoholism or drug addiction.

The result of all of these factors is that in 2004, 56.4% of households in the bottom fifth featured no work by anyone for the entire year, not even part-time work, leaving the average number of workers per household in the bottom fifth rounded down to zero by the Census Bureau.[18] By contrast, the average number of earners in the top fifth of households was 2.0.[19] The total number of full-time, year-round workers in the entire bottom fifth of households in 2004 was less than 3 million, compared to 16.4 million of such workers in the top fifth of households.[20] Differences in work are reflected throughout the income scale, as the average number of workers in the second-lowest fifth and in the middle fifth of households in terms of income was 1.0, in the second-highest fifth, 2.0.[21]

Those who don't work, for whatever reason, don't themselves expect to make as much income as those who do. That difference in income does not reflect unfair economic "inequality." It reflects differences in production, as the discussion above indicated.

In our generous society, the bottom fifth does receive a lot of transfer income from government programs, such as Social Security retirement and disability payments, all the federal, state, and local welfare programs discussed in Chapter 5, education assistance, etc. This transfer income enables many in the bottom fifth not to work even though they otherwise could and would do so. In the case of those retired or in school full-time, this is not undesirable. In the case of those on welfare, it is undesirable and socially and economically counterproductive, as discussed in Chapter 5.

As Reynolds reports, most income received by the bottom fifth of households is from such transfer payments, nearly 80% in 2001, for example.[22] For the top fifth, by contrast, such transfer payments represented less than 2% of household income.[23] But the measures of income usually reported as showing rising inequality do not even include such transfer payments in their definition of income. That grossly exaggerates actual income inequality. Family gifts that finance the living expenses of a college student who otherwise appears in the statistics as a low-income household are also not counted, again exaggerating income inequality.[24]

In addition, over time, income from work naturally increases with rising wages. Transfer payments are not linked to rising wages, however. So the income "gap" between households in the top fifth, with multiple workers, and households among the bottom fifth relying mostly on transfer payments is naturally going to grow over time, all the more so if the transfer payment income is not even counted. This will be especially true during economic boom times, when jobs, wages, and household and family incomes are rising even faster. Those households relying more heavily on income from work will prosper faster during such times, leaving those relying primarily on transfer payments falling further behind. This was reflected during the twenty-five-year Reagan economic boom, which was wrongly castigated by ideological media opponents as increasing economic "inequality," when what was actually happening was more prosperity for our society, involving more production from those working.

Another important difference in incomes can be found due to age and experience of workers. As Reynolds notes, median income of families where the head of household is 45 to 54 is close to three times as large as the median income of families where the head of household is younger than 25.[25] That reflects the raises and promotions that workers naturally earn over time. This, again, is not an unfair economic "inequality," most would agree. It reflects again increased ability to produce as workers gain experience and skills over time. The aging of the huge numbers of baby boomers in recent decades naturally exacerbated this social "inequality" as they grew into their peak earning years. Nothing remotely "unfair" about that.

Another important factor in income differences is education. Reynolds indicates the median income of households where the head holds a doctorate degree is about two and a half times as large on average as the median income of households where the head holds only a high school degree, and five times as large on average as for households where the head holds less than a ninth-grade education.[26] This, again, is not an unfair economic "inequality," most would agree. It reflects increased ability to produce as workers gain in education and human capital.

The explosion in women working over the last forty years naturally exacerbated these income differences. The rise of working women sharply increased the number of two-earner couples, resulting in more social "inequality" as compared to households with only one earner, or no earners. But this increasing "inequality" does not reflect the unfairness of Reaganomics, or our "oppressive" capitalist system. It reflects the increased production coming from two-earner households.

This increasing "inequality" was exacerbated by the increasing proportion of college-educated workers in recent decades, and the tendency of couples to match up with spouses of equivalent educational backgrounds. Households with two college-educated spouses working are going to earn a lot more than households with only one worker of lesser education, with an even wider difference with households with no worker. But these differences reflect, again, not unfair economic inequality, but rather differences in productive output.

At the other end of the spectrum, increasing numbers of single households are also increasing "inequality." Young people delaying marriage toward and past thirty are increasing those single households. So is the aging of the population, creating more single widows and widowers, an effect that will grow as the baby boom retires. But married couples earn on average three times the incomes of single people, as Reynolds reports, in part because single households cannot have two earners, and because younger people and widows tend to earn lower incomes.[27] Comparing household incomes across the decades would consequently appear to show increasing income inequality, again during the Reaganomics years. But this is not a valid comparison because it would not be comparing apples to apples given the changing household composition. The changing income pattern is not reflecting economic effects, but the effect of the demographic change of more lower-income single households instead of higher-income married households.

Another demographic change in recent decades is increasing numbers of single mothers with children, with the mother often lacking a high school diploma. Such households tend to suffer the lowest incomes and the highest poverty rates in the country. That would again appear to increase income inequality. But it would again be the effect of changing social demographics, rather than an economic effect, discrediting simple comparisons of changing household incomes over the years.

Increasing immigration in recent decades of lower-income, lesser-skilled workers with little education would also appear to increase income inequality. As Reynolds notes, "Countries that import millions of poor people are bound to end up with more poor people than otherwise."[28] But that again would not be an economic effect, but the effect of an immigration policy of allowing entry of more workers with little in productive skills.

STATISTICAL ILLUSION

Other fundamental errors arise from a failure to distinguish between more Americans getting richer, and only the rich getting richer. For example, major media outlets have decried a declining percentage of Americans in some fixed, moderate-income range, after adjusting for inflation, such as between $35,000 and $50,000 per year, which they take as indicating a shrinking or vanishing middle class.[29] But during periods of sustained economic growth, such as during the Reagan economic boom, growing incomes would naturally take a higher percentage of Americans past any fixed, moderate-income range. Reynolds notes that the data published in the very *Washington Post* feature raising such an alarm refuted the significance of the claim. It showed, in fact, that the percentage of households with real incomes higher than $50,000 increased from

24.9% in 1967 to 44.1% in 2003, while the percentage with real incomes lower than $35,000 fell from 52.8% in 1967 to 40.9%.[30] This represents the middle class getting richer, with incomes growing beyond the fixed income range, rather than a shrinking middle class. Reynolds cites *Wall Street Journal* senior economics writer Steve Moore, who demonstrated the soaring prosperity of middle America during this period: "in 1967 only one in 25 families earned an income of $100,000 or more in real terms, whereas now [in 2004], one in six do. The percentage of families that have an income of more than $75,000 a year has tripled from 9% to 27%."[31] An exasperated Reynolds rightly laments the statistical confusion reflected by major media institutions and even researchers who should know better:

> Such complaints—deploring the rapidly rising percentage of families earning more than $50,000–$100,000 per year—are persistent yet inexplicable. A larger percentage of Americans earning more income is apparently being confused with a quite different concept of "inequality"—namely, the same number or percentage of people earning more money. . . . Yet there is no sense in which a larger percentage of workers earning higher incomes can possibly have a harmful effect on other people with "less-skilled" jobs.[32]

If class warriors cannot get this simple point, they will never understand more complex statistical errors, which Reynolds has been an intellectual leader in exposing. Any top income group, whether you are measuring the top 1%, 5%, 10%, or 20%, by definition has no income ceiling like the lower-income groups. For example, the middle 20% will always be between some $X thousand per year and some $Y thousand. But the top 20% will include all incomes above the 80th percentile, up to the highest-earning individual billionaires in the country. The implication of that is that any average or mean of incomes in the top 20% will always be much higher than the median of incomes in the top 20%, which is defined as the income level with half of those in this fifth above and half below. The median will consequently always provide a much more accurate reflection of the typical income earner in any top income group than any average or mean. Discussions focusing on the change

in "average" incomes of the top 1%, or top 20%, or top anything in between are therefore always misleading. Reynolds provides this example:
"Mean income for the top 10 percent is about two-thirds larger than
median income, showing how mean averages *greatly exaggerate* the level
of typical incomes of top income groups."[33]

This becomes especially misleading when comparing the top income
group to any lower-income group, or to changes in their relative income
shares over time, when those income shares are measured by average incomes rather than median incomes. That is because in any lower income
group, with both an upper and lower bound to the incomes included, the
average or mean income will always be much closer to the median. So
in focusing on averages within each income group, the realities of lower-
income groups will be compared to a misconception of the top income
group.

Reynolds illustrates this by examining Federal Reserve data regarding incomes of different subgroups of American workers. In that data,
the average or mean income of the top 10% of households seems to increase much more from 1989 to 2004 than the average or mean income of
the next-highest 10%, or of any lower-income group. That would imply
growing inequality, with the rich getting richer faster than any other
group is improving. But when the more accurate median income is considered, the income of the top 10% grew at virtually the same rate from
1989 to 2004 as the bottom 20%, and as the second-lowest 20%.[34] That
indicates widespread and relatively even progress among all income
groups over the period.

A similar statistical problem arises from income changes affecting
the bottom limit, or threshold, of any top income group. The statistical illusion here is that rapidly rising incomes among households with
incomes below the top income group can appear to increase the incomes
of the top group. For example, as the incomes of those in the second
10% of income earners grow into what was formerly the top 10%, the
bottom limit, or threshold, defining the top 10% must increase, because
only 10% of income earners can fit into the top 10%. As the threshold
increases, the average of incomes above the higher threshold will inevitably be higher. That will appear to be an increase in incomes of the top
10%. But it is an effect of the increase in incomes of those below the

threshold. Any increase in incomes of the original top 10% would be in addition to this effect.

Reynolds illustrates the problem with this specific example. The top fifth of household incomes began at $68,352 in 1980 (in 2004 dollars). By 2004, the incomes of so many in the second 20% had increased above the former $68,352 threshold that the top 20% of income earners now started at $88,029. As Reynolds explains, "If you calculate a mean average of all the income above $88,029 in 2004, you are bound to come up with a larger figure than if you averaged all the incomes above $68,352 (as we did in 1980). The average in 2004 *excluded* incomes between $68,352 and $88,029—incomes that were included in the average in 1980."[35]

In this case, the average of the top 10% is being *"pushed up* from below by rising numbers of people moving up—leaving what used to be considered a 'middle class' income and 'joining the ranks of the rich.' "[36] Or as Reynolds more famously said previously, "so many people have been getting rich there isn't room for them all in the top fifth."[37] The essential point, to paraphrase Reynolds, is that this statistical effect does not mean the rich are getting richer; it means more people are getting rich, which is a reflection of rising general prosperity, rather than rising incomes at the top.

Confusion arising from this statistical illusion led to media reports insisting that the great majority of income growth, if not all, over substantial periods, such as 1970 to 2000, had occurred only among the top income group. These reports claimed that as a result, incomes of the bottom 80% had not increased at all over that period, or even had fallen. Reynolds cites New York Times writers David Cay Johnston and Paul Krugman as making such claims.[38] But as Reynolds notes, Census Bureau data showed not only real income gains among every income group over the period, but accelerating gains, with real incomes among the lower-income groups increasing even faster in the later years.[39] CBO data also showed real income gains for every income group over the period.[40]

APPLES AND ORANGES

Other studies and media reports raise alarms about supposed soaring incomes over recent decades concentrated among the top 1%. These statistics arise from trends of reported incomes on tax returns over these decades, going all the way back into the 1960s in some cases.

The fundamental blunder in all of these studies and reports is that the 1986 tax reform radically changed what is reported on income tax returns, so income before is not comparable to income after. As Reynolds notes, the Statistics of Income Division of the IRS itself tried to warn about this, saying, "Data for years 1987 and after *are not comparable* to pre-1987 data because of major changes in the definition of 'adjusted gross income' (AGI)."[41] But the studies and media reports of the class warriors began doing precisely that.

The most important change is that the much lower individual income tax rates after tax reform, from a top rate of 70% when Reagan entered office to 28%, caused billions in business income to switch from corporate tax returns to individual tax returns as subchapter S corporations, partnerships, limited liability partnerships, and proprietorships. These billions in business income naturally appeared primarily among the top 1% of income earners, causing the income to such upper earners to appear to soar during the 1980s, from before the 1986 tax reform to after it, exactly the period when the results of Reaganomics were coming in. Studies and media reports consequently sounded the alarm that Reaganomics was causing massive increases in inequality and the incomes of the richest to soar compared to everyone else. But this was all based on a misunderstanding of the data. All that had changed was the way in which the income of the highest-income earners was reported on different tax returns, as the IRS had tried to warn.

Moreover, more income from companies started since 1986 has also been reported on individual returns than would have been the case before the tax reform. That and the growth of the other businesses now reporting as individuals has made the top income shares measured by tax return data continue to appear to rise more rapidly since then. By 1997, more than half of all U.S. corporations were subchapter S corporations reporting their income on individual income tax returns, primarily among the top 1%.[42] By 2001, subchapter S corporations accounted for almost one-fourth of all before-tax corporate profits.[43] Starting in 1996, banks were allowed to report their incomes as subchapter S corporations.[44] By 2003, over 2,000 banks were doing so, with the largest at $9 billion.[45]

In addition, money-losing businesses with negative incomes that now began reporting on individual tax returns were counted after 1986 among the bottom income earners as a result, which would further exaggerate supposed inequality. As Reynolds reports, "What looks like a very low income 'household' in the tax return data can include many normally profitable businesses having a tough year."[46] Indeed, subtracting these business losses from the bottom income shares makes entire population subgroups seem to be earning less than they really are.

Another important change is that until the 1986 tax reform, interest income on the trillions in municipal bonds was not required to be reported on individual tax returns. Afterward, all that income concentrated among the wealthiest income earners was counted in the top income shares, again appearing to show rapidly rising inequality as a result of "Reaganomics," when it was really just a result of tax reform, changing how income is reported on tax returns.[47]

Moreover, most income from executive stock options is now reported as W-2 wage income, while before tax reform it was reported as capital gains when exercised.[48] So studies of wage, salary, and labor income count this large source of income concentrated among the top income earners in the later years, but not in the earlier years, showing a large increase in inequality and in the incomes of the top earners over the years. Yet that would be solely due to counting income in the later years that they did not count in the earlier years.

At the same time, after tax reform, investment income of the more middle-income workers was increasingly not counted because a rising share of that income was held in IRAs or 401(k)s, and so not reported on income tax returns. Indeed, the contributions to these accounts were even sometimes subtracted from taxable income, further reducing reported incomes among middle-income workers. Reynolds notes that with $10 trillion in these accounts by 2002, at just a 7% return that would amount to $700 billion in investment income that year alone mostly for more middle-income earners not reported on income tax returns, and therefore not counted by income distribution studies based on tax return data.[49]

Reynolds adds that the stock market boom in the 1990s caused IRA and 401(k) plans to triple during that decade, from about $2 trillion to nearly $6 trillion.[50] Yet while the great majority of that $4 trillion in capital gains went to the bottom 99% or even 90% of income earners, none of it was reported on income tax returns, and therefore none of it showed up in income distribution studies based on income tax return data. Yet the great majority of the capital gains of the rich from the stock market boom were outside such accounts and thus *were* reported on income tax returns. Reynolds says, "The top 1% also experienced big capital gains, but nearly all of those gains were taxable and therefore uniquely visible on tax return data."[51]

Studies trying to determine changes in income distribution from tax returns were consequently whipsawed by the explosion of these tax-preferred retirement accounts. Before the explosion, which started in the early 1980s, the investment income of the more middle-income earners was all counted on tax returns. By 2000, almost none of it was, even while investment income for these more middle-income earners was exploding. That would be reflected in a sharply increasing share of income going to top income earners in income distribution studies based on tax returns, misleading everybody. As Reynolds explains,

> Before these tax-favored savings plans became commonplace, virtually every dollar of investment income from the savings of middle-income taxpayers *was* reported as taxable income and therefore counted as income in studies that use those older tax returns to estimate income distribution. Today, by contrast, most investment returns from the savings of middle income taxpayers are rarely or never taxed. This makes it singularly inappropriate to use tax data to compare income shares *before* and *after* the explosion of tax deferred accounts.[52]

Tax reform's sharply falling tax rates themselves would cause the upper-income earners most punished by the former high tax rates to report more income after tax reform. The lower rates would cause more income to rise and be reported out of tax shelters, and to be taken in taxable and reportable cash rather than in tax-exempt benefits. The capital gains tax rate cuts in 1997 and 2003 caused a surge in reportable capital gains realizations outside tax-protected retirement accounts. The sharp cut in the tax rate on dividends in 2003 caused a similar surge in dividends paid and reported. All of these effects caused further sharp distortions in comparing the trends in incomes for top income earners compared to others, in the years before the tax changes relative to the years after.

Tax return data is unsuited for measuring income distribution for other reasons as well. Transfer payments are not reported as income on tax returns, so all of this income for lower-income households is missed. Moreover, many low-income families do not even file income tax returns. Such tax returns consequently cannot give an accurate picture of income inequality or concentration.

Reynolds notes finally that more accurate CBO data on income distribution trends shows that after the 1986 tax reform "the top 1 percent's share of pretax household income fell with the stock market crash of October, 1987 and surged with the stock market boom in 1996–2000, but otherwise showed no significant and sustained upward trend."[53] The media institutions that trumpeted the grossly misleading studies and reports of soaring tax returns based on confused tax return data over decades badly misled their audiences, and failed to do their job of reporting what is happening in the real world.

WAGE STAGNATION

Related to these misconceptions over income distribution is "the Wage Stagnation thesis."[54] This is the allegation that there has been little or no improvement, or even a decline, in the living standards or wages or compensation of all but the top income earners since 1970 or 1973.

As Reynolds notes, this allegation is usually based on a misreading of Bureau of Labor Statistics data regarding the "average earnings of production and nonsupervisory workers."[55] This is not to be taken as a measure of the wages of "blue collar workers," as "nonsupervisory workers" includes "physicians, lawyers, accountants, nurses, social workers, research aides, teachers, drafters, photographers, beauticians and musicians."[56]

Moreover, the average earnings reported have been heavily diluted over the years by the rise of millions of part-time jobs in retail and services. Those jobs greatly benefit the spouses, mothers, students, seniors, and others who would not want to take on full-time employment but are glad to be able to earn some extra family income. But over the last forty years, as more and more have taken such part-time jobs, averaging in their earnings with the earnings from full-time work brings down the average earnings sharply from what is earned by full-time work. That means comparing such average earnings from forty years ago to average earnings today is again comparing apples to oranges—average earnings from full-time work then to average earnings from much more part-time work today. As Reynolds says, "Because millions more 'payroll employees' work fewer hours per week than was true in the past, any comparison of what happened to average *weekly* wages over time is dishonest."[57]

At the same time, this earnings series also excludes the self-employed. That leaves out millions earning good and long-rising incomes in productive, skilled professional and entrepreneurial occupations.

Another distortion in the argument is starting the measure from the year 1973. Reported real incomes for that year were unusually high because price controls kept roaring inflation down for a time.[58] Earnings growth from that anomalous year would naturally be slower because of that. Why pick that year if we are trying to have an honest discussion of the issue?

Reynolds notes as well that by 2001 the Census Bureau was reporting that the poor enjoyed as much or more of the indicia of a comfortable, modern standard of living as the middle class thirty years before.[59] The poor enjoyed as many or more cars, trucks, clothes dryers, and refrigerators in 2001 as the middle class in 1971. They enjoyed twice the proportion of air conditioners and color TVs, and much more of the modern advances of microwaves, DVDs, VCRs, personal computers, and cell phones as the middle class thirty years before. That indicates a broad advance of prosperity.

The broadest and most accurate measure of living standards is real per capita consumption. That measure soared by 74% from 1980 to 2004, an unprecedented gain in that short a period.[60] If we measured it just during the twenty-five-year Reagan boom, it would be even higher. From 1973 to 2004, about thirty years, such real per capita consumption in America nearly doubled.[61] Over seventy-five years, 1929 to 2004, real per capita consumption by American workers increased by five times, and even faster since 1961 than before.[62] The fastest growth periods were 1983 to 1990, and 1992 to 2004, during the Reagan boom.

But even this measure has its shortcomings. The official inflation measures used to adjust it overstate inflation. Correcting for that would probably add a percentage point to the growth, which would double the gains after twenty years. Using the more modern chain-weighted index for personal consumption expenditures, or PCE deflator, developed by the Commerce Department's Bureau of Economic Affairs, would raise the gain from 1977 to 2005 by nearly 50%.[63]

Moreover, most measures of wage, earnings, or income growth do not include employee benefits, which have become a much larger share of worker compensation over the last forty years, especially health insurance and retirement benefits. Real per capita consumption may cover consumption of health care adequately, but probably not employer contributions to retirement accounts, and maybe not other employee benefits.

Moreover, throughout the entire economy, whenever an improvement in quality or capability of anything is not reflected commensurately in the price of the product or service, the improvement is almost always undercounted or not counted at all in economic statistics. All these statistics are compiled primarily on the basis of market prices. But the market price of a good or service does not typically rise commensurately with an improvement in quality or capability. More typically, such improvements are accompanied by a decline in price. Statisticians can try to make adjustments for those effects. But without market prices to define the improvement, their efforts are guesswork that never keeps up with the true utilitarian value of the improvements over time.

Even more difficult is accounting for the value of new inventions and products. Measurement of their contribution to GDP or other statistics begins with their market prices. Typically, the price of a new product or invention declines during the years after introduction, due to improvements in manufacturing and economies of scale, even while their quality and capability typically soars. How to account in the statistics for GDP, income, and wealth for the resulting improvement in living standards and quality of life from these technological advances? There is no good answer, which means as a result that they are never close to truly accounted for.

Probably the best example is the recent history of computers. A desktop computer today retailing for $999 has far more computing power than the mainframes of thirty years ago, which cost many times more. Moreover, that desktop today plugs into a worldwide Internet with millions of Web sites, which did not even exist thirty years ago. Our statistics as to growth in GDP, income, and wealth do not remotely begin to account for the resulting value created in our lives. Indeed, today we have laptops that mean we can take this resulting value with us wherever we go. Does the retail price of those laptops at Best Buy reflect their contribution to GDP, or value in our lives?

Another good example is cell phones, which could only be imagined in the 1960s as Agent Maxwell Smart talking into his shoe. Today, for a couple of hundred dollars or so, we not only can take with us a portable phone smaller than our hand anywhere we go, but that phone is itself is a portable computer that can give us portable Internet access everywhere we go, along with e-mail and text messaging capability, and even perhaps video. Does that couple of hundred dollars retail price, along with the monthly service fee, even remotely account for the value contributed to our lives, or real GDP?

The same effect is present in the improving quality and capability of homes and their appliances, cars, televisions, and every other consumer good or business tool. As W. Michael Cox and Richard Alm note, "Dozens of automotive innovations improve performance, safety, and comfort: anti-lock brakes, air bags . . . turbochargers, cruise control, automated air conditioning and heating, sun roofs, adjustable steering wheels, and windshield wiper delays. Today's cars are loaded with 'power.' They're more likely to have power steering, windows, seats, door locks, and rearview mirrors. They're also more likely to have radial tires and tinted glass."[64] Moreover, today's steel-belted radial tires "last more than 10 times longer than the old four-ply cotton lined tires."[65] Cox and Alm add, "today's models offer more powerful engines and travel 60 percent farther on a gallon of gas. A quarter century ago, cars needed maintenance twice a year. Now they routinely travel up to 100,000 miles between tune ups."[66] Moreover, "The cars that zoom down today's highways possess more computing power than the Apollo 11 landing module that first put astronauts on the moon."[67] Yet the typical car today costs less in terms of hours worked than the typical clunker from 1970.[68] That improvement is not remotely fully reflected in the statistics of GDP and income growth.

Cox and Alm offer a list of the new and greatly improved products and services since 1970.[69] Among those not already mentioned, they include camcorders, which allow the creation of personal home movies; CDs and CD players; videocassette recorders, which allow studio movies to be watched at home; fax machines, overnight delivery, fiber optic cables, laser printers, handheld calculators, e-mail, ATMs; Doppler radar, which greatly improves weather forecasting; satellite TV, satellite radio, big-screen TVs, small-screen TVs, high-definition TVs, 3-D TVs, home theaters, video games, digital photography, nonaspirin painkillers, food processors, aspartame, radial keratectomy, CT scans, bypass surgery, ultrasound, in vitro fertilization, organ transplants, soft contact lenses, LASIK eye surgery, gene therapy, and hair restoration. Yet again, our statistics on growth of GDP, income, and wealth do not even remotely account for the resulting value and improvements in our lives. Look around you and you will recognize far more the vast improvements in everyday life for working people that results from sustained economic growth.

There is nothing on this planet comparable to the prosperity that America has provided to working people.

CHAPTER 10

NEW LABOR: PROSPERITY UNIONS

Power to the People for Working Families

Eddie York, thirty-nine, was married with three children, ages seven, seventeen, and eighteen.[1] The family lived in Lenore, West Virginia, where Eddie worked for a small business, Deskins Contracting, owned by his brother-in-law, Russell Deskins. York was experienced in operating heavy equipment for the company, such as cranes, steam shovels, and backhoes.

Deskins was hired by the Apogee Coal Company for a short-term cleanup project at its Ruffner mining operation, one of the largest strip mines in the state. York's role in that project was to operate a backhoe to dredge sediment ponds that catch the runoff from the open coal pits.

On July 22, 1993, York joined a coworker, Marion Hensley, at the remote, rural work site, accessible by a single dirt road. He began work operating his backhoe, scooping mud out of one of the ponds. The United Mine Workers (UMW) was running a strike at the Ruffner coal facility, but York and Hensley were not coal miners, so the strike did not apply to them. Picketers nevertheless had assembled that day about three miles down the access road, trying to limit entry to the mining operations.

The UMW had tried to unionize Deskins two years earlier. But the small company with a handful of employees felt it could not absorb any increased costs, so the company declined. But in the process, four union members beat up Russell.

One of the UMW picketers down the road was Jerry Lowe, age forty-three, son of a former president of UMW Local 5958, and himself a career UMW coal miner. The stocky, five-foot six-inch, three-hundred-pound Lowe brought with him that day a Colt Trooper .357 Magnum, and a case of beer.

At the end of the workday, the coal company sent two security pickup trucks with six professional guards out to the Deskins work site to escort York and Hensley out. As the trucks passed the picket line on the way in, they were pelted with rocks and metal balls fired from slingshots. Among the picketers, then, was the current UMW Local 5958 president, Earnest Woods, armed with a .380 automatic pistol.

A caravan started back out from the pond with one security pickup truck in front, Hensley and York in their pickups following behind, and the second security truck bringing up the rear. They were again pelted by rocks and metal balls as they approached the picket line. But this time gunshots rang out as well. One hit the rear security truck. "Another tore through the back window of Eddie York's truck and entered his skull," *Reader's Digest* reported.[2] The truck went off the road into a ditch.

The bullet taken from York's dead body was fired from a Colt Trooper .357 Magnum. At York's burial three days later, a neighbor told reporters, "He was trying to feed his family. No lump of coal is worth getting killed for." Two years later, York's youngest son, Eddie, then nine, was quoted as saying, "Why did it have to be our daddy when there are so many mean people in the world?"[3]

The UMW alleged that the company security guards killed York, to whip up antiunion sentiment. But the guards had a perfect alibi. They were unarmed. Reed Larson, president of the National Right to Work Committee, reports that then "UMW President Richard Trumka all but danced on York's casket, saying, 'If you strike a match and put your finger in, common sense tells you you're going to burn your finger.'"[4] Trumka today is president of the entire AFL-CIO.

On November 2, 1993, a federal grand jury indicted eight members of Local 5958, including Lowe and the local president, Woods. Seven testified against Lowe as the killer, and so were sentenced to just 120 days in jail each. Lowe was sentenced to eleven years.

The sentence was so light because Lowe was only charged with illegal use of a firearm to damage a vehicle in interstate commerce, and illegal use of a firearm to incapacitate a driver in interstate commerce.[5] Union violence is often not aggressively prosecuted because local authorities are often politically dominated by the union, as with the UMW in West Virginia. And federal authorities are hampered by the 1973 U.S. Supreme Court decision in *U.S. v. Enmons*. The Court held in that case that federal antiextortion laws do not apply to union violence, even murder, as long as the violence is undertaken in pursuit of "legitimate" union objectives, such as wage increases or improvements in other conditions of employment.

So union violence often runs wild. In *Enmons*, three defendant members of the International Brotherhood of Electrical Workers (IBEW) were set free after shooting up utility company transformers with high-powered rifles and blowing up a transformer substation. Since the union was on strike at the time, the courts found these actions to be in pursuit of legitimate union objectives.

In another incident, Eldon Fowler was a twenty-six-year-old ordained minister moonlighting as a security guard at the Jarl Extrusion plant in Elizabethton, Tennessee.[6] One night after the United Steelworkers called a strike at the plant, union pickets suddenly moved away from the site Fowler was guarding. Fowler was then murdered by buckshot fired from a passing car; he left behind a young widow.

In 1986, a Teamsters "contract negotiating tactic" involved setting a series of fires at the Dupont Plaza Hotel, a popular vacation spot in San Juan, Puerto Rico.[7] Unfortunately, one of the fires burned out of control, killing nearly one hundred and injuring scores more.

The New York *Daily News* labor dispute in the late 1980s concerned proposed work rules changes that would eliminate jobs that were no longer necessary due to advances in technology and delivery methods, most of which were no-show jobs.[8] The union argued that it had bargained for those positions and was entitled to the money. But the *Daily News* was facing stiff competition from *Newsday* on Long Island and could no longer carry such unproductive costs.

On the first day of the strike, delivery trucks were pelted with stones and bricks. By the second day, over fifty delivery trucks had been burned.[9] Subsequently, the strikers began stealing *Daily News* papers from newsstands, and threatening newsstand operators with violence if they continued to carry the paper. Advertisers were similarly threatened. But the FBI declined to investigate union coordination of the violence, citing the *Enmons* decision.[10]

In March 1987, the IBEW struck a consumer-owned utility near Anchorage, Alaska, demanding that the utility deny jobs to nonunion workers.[11] On the second day of the strike, a high-powered rifle bullet was fired into a transformer, shutting off power to one thousand homes in the cold Alaskan winter. Strikers blocked and threatened repairmen trying to restore power, slashing tires on repair trucks. Further violence spread the outages to four entire communities served by the utility. Pickets threatened to rape and murder the wife of one nonstriking employee. One union militant was quoted in the local paper as threatening the utility's board of directors: "You settle it (the strike) or we'll bring this town down."[12]

It is the *Enmons* free pass for union violence that has enabled organized crime to gain influence over some unions, such as the Service Employees International Union (SEIU), the International Brotherhood of Teamsters, the Laborers' International Union of North America, and the Associated Building Trades Council, according to a presidential Commission on Organized Crime.[13] The mob uses violence to muscle in on the unions, placing its own syndicate members into local, district, and even national union offices. The crime commission concluded that the *Enmons* decision created a "loophole that allows organized crime figures to obtain . . . personal gains through the extortion of employees."[14] The commission explained how the mob bosses gain further by using the loophole to commit "violent acts against a non-union business competitor," and then claim they were done in pursuit of "a legitimate, nonprosecutable labor objective such as a union organizing effort, when the actual purpose was to eliminate unwanted business competition for the syndicate."[15]

This is just a sample of a long history of union violence. Of course, the stories of the victims of this violence are sad. But there should be a deep sense of sadness over the perpetrators, too. These union activists see themselves as just fighting for what every mainstream American wants—traditional middle-class American prosperity for themselves, their families, and their brothers and sisters in the union. What is sad is that they think this is what they have to do to get it.

The fundamental problem is a medieval concept of how to gain wealth—taking it from those that have it, by force or threat of force if necessary. When this was the predominant means of gaining wealth, during the aptly named Dark Ages, the constant threat of armed raiders riding in and plundering what the productive built and accumulated imposed a large risk, or effective tax, on investment and productive activity. That generally prevented investment and economic growth from getting off the ground, for centuries. Unions based on this medieval economics generate an analogous effect today, squelching industries that could and would provide good jobs with good wages for working people. The bottom line is that all union activity in America put together, including all the violence, physical intimidation, and even strikes, has not increased the share of national income going to labor. Throughout the postwar era, at least sixty years, labor's share of national income has been stable at about 71%.[16] Medieval economics doesn't work. Again, that's why we call it the Dark Ages.

PROSPERITY UNIONS

Our modern society has developed far better avenues to wealth and prosperity—producing, innovating, applying the advances of modern science, and riding the wave of resulting economic growth that can provide rapidly multiplying bounty for all. What is needed is a modern labor movement consistent with this modern road to wealth and prosperity. That would involve a New Labor, composed of modern, 21st century Prosperity Unions.

Prosperity Unions would not see relations with employers as tussles over sagging sand castles in fixed sandboxes. They would not seek to gain for their workers by imposing nonproductive, counterproductive practices such as featherbedding, which are just another effective tax on investment and production, slowing rather than advancing economic growth and prosperity for working people overall. They would not seek to impose work rules that detract from productivity and maximum efficiency.

The touchstone of a Prosperity Union would be to approach employers with the overarching question: "What can we do to be more productive so you can pay us more?" Such unions would still contract with employers to stop and reverse abuses, below-market pay, and dangerous or poor working conditions. But instead of counterproductive work rules, they would seek to maximize cooperation in creating the most efficient and productive working operations possible. Instead of featherbedding, they would seek more investment in their business that would expand opportunities and jobs for their members. And in return, they would rightly expect and gain wages commensurate with their newfound productivity, which would quite possibly be far higher than they ever believed possible.

Rather than resist such unions, employers would welcome them, even seek them out, as these Prosperity Unions would be productive partners in advancing a newly common cause of business success for workers, capital, and management. As a result, the labor movement, which is currently dying out except in government bureaucracies still based on medieval economics, would turn around and flourish. Labor unions would flower once again to become central components of modern, 21st-century prosperity.

Besides opening a whole new world of worker-employer relations, these Prosperity Unions would work for public policies that promote and maximize economic growth for all, like those advanced in this book. Their special focus would be to seek policies ensuring that working people participate in such general economic growth, and fully share in the resulting fruits, rightfully commensurate with their contributions to productivity and output. Prosperity Unions would help to spread the word among grassroots working people regarding the exciting opportunities to be opened through these and other reforms. And they would take the message to federal, state, and local elected officials that what working people need and want is precisely reforms to maximize economic growth, and the full participation of working people in the fruits of it.

There is no reason why unions have to be run by pseudo-Marxist philosophers, like former SEIU president Andy Stern, or by brownshirt thugs with third-hand Marxist notions, like AFL-CIO president Richard Trumka. The association of the far left with the labor movement arose out of the social traumas of the origins of the Industrial Revolution 150 years ago. It is long past time for society to get over those ancient battles.

Today's vestigial romanticism over those long-ago fights is just not cool anymore. That serves today only to hold back working people and society overall from the full modern prosperity we should all enjoy. We can only march together into the maximally productive, maximally prosperous future that has long been waiting for us, with labor and capital as the complements they must be, rather than antagonists.

American unions should be run by real, practical, blue-collar working people advancing the genuine interests of working Americans in traditional world-leading American prosperity and living standards, not some throwback notion of a global socialist movement, or outdated, late 19th century–style social revolution. Blue-collar reformists should arise to contend for control of their unions on these grounds. They should start genuine, new Prosperity Unions of their own. In this lies the worthy revival of the labor movement. There is a whole new world of opportunity here for younger people committed to new thinking in union leadership.

ECONOMIC GROWTH VERSUS REDISTRIBUTION

A central truth providing the intellectual foundation for Prosperity Unions is that economic growth provides vastly greater benefits for working people and the poor than redistribution does. It is economic growth that is the key to prosperity and the good life for the middle class, working people, and the poor.

If total real compensation, wages and benefits, grows at just 1% a year, after twenty years the real incomes of working people would be only 22% greater. After forty years, a generation, real incomes would be 50% more. But with sustained real compensation growth of 2%, after just twenty years the real incomes and living standards of working people would be nearly 50% greater, and after forty years they would be 120% greater, more than doubled. At sustained 3% growth in wages and benefits, after twenty years the living standards of working people will have almost doubled, and after forty years they will have more than tripled.

The U.S. economy sustained a real rate of economic growth of 3.3% from 1945 to 1973, and achieved the same 3.3% sustained real growth from 1982 to 2007.[17] (Note that this 3.3% growth rate for the entire economy includes population growth. Real wages and benefits discussed above is a per worker concept). It was only during the stagflation decade of 1973 to 1982, reflecting the deeply misguided reigning intellectual leadership of the time, that real growth fell to only half long-term trends.[18] If we could revive and sustain that same 3.3% real growth for twenty years, our total economic production (GDP) would double in that time. After thirty years, our economic output would grow by 2⅔. After forty years, our prosperity bounty would grow by 3⅔. This is a quite realistic prospect if the nation adopts the growth-maximizing policies advocated in this book. As Brian Domitrovic explained in *Econoclasts*, "The unique ability of the United States to maintain a historic rate of economic growth over the long term is what has rendered this nation the world's lone 'hyperpower.'"[19]

If we are truly following growth-maximizing policies, we could conceivably do even better than we have in the past. At sustained real growth of 4% per year, our economic production would more than double after twenty years. After thirty years, GDP would more than triple. After forty years, total U.S. economic output would nearly quadruple. America would by then have leapfrogged another generation ahead of the rest of the world. Achieving and sustaining such growth should be the central focus of national economic policy over the next decade, for it would solve every problem that plagues and threatens us today.

Such booming economic growth is the foundation for averting the coming bankruptcy of America. I am not saying that we can grow our way out of the current financial swamp. Saving America from bankruptcy requires all of the policies advocated in this book. That includes changing all of our nation's retirement programs to operate on a fully funded, fully invested basis. That includes transformed incentives to gain control over health costs. That includes transforming the welfare empire so that the poor and the near poor, the lowest 20% of our population in income, are working and contributing to our economic growth and prosperity to the extent possible. That includes terminating corporate welfare and making other spending reductions through the above reforms and more that would altogether virtually cut our federal albatross in half, and sharply reduce state and local spending as well. But without a foundation of booming economic growth, ultimate success for our nation is not possible.

Such economic growth will produce surging revenues that would make balancing the budget so much more feasible. Surging GDP will reduce the national debt as a percent of GDP relatively quickly, particularly with balanced budgets not adding any further to the debt. With everyone's retirement funds invested in the markets, a booming economy will make retirement all the more prosperous.

A booming economy, with the patient power incentives to control costs discussed in Chapter 4, will solve the problems of health care. The booming economy will mean higher GDP in the denominator, and the cost control incentives will mean lower health costs than otherwise in the numerator. The calamitous projections of health costs eating up our entire GDP will consequently never come to pass. But the booming economy will provide the resources to enable rapidly advancing modern science to solve tragic health problems that seem intractable today, meaning longer and healthier, more comfortable lives. People may still choose to spend more of their growing incomes on health care for themselves and their loved ones. That would probably be a wise decision.

Sustained, rapid economic growth is also the ultimate solution to poverty, as discussed further in Chapter 11. With sustained robust economic growth, maintaining the most powerful military in the world, and thereby ensuring our nation's security and national defense, will require a smaller and smaller percentage of GDP over time. That security itself will promote capital investment and economic growth in America. The booming economy will produce new technological marvels that will make our defenses all the more advanced. With the economy rapidly advancing, there will be more than enough funds for education. There will also be more than enough funds to clean up and maintain a healthy environment.

It was sustained, world-leading economic growth that produced the America of today, as Domitrovic has indicated. Real per capita consumption in the United States nearly doubled from 1973 to 2004, or about thirty years.[20] American living standards measured in this way grew by more than fivefold from 1935 to 2004, about seventy years.[21] As noted by Stephen Moore and Julian L. Simon in their underappreciated work, *It's*

Getting Better All the Time: 100 Greatest Trends of the Last 100 Years, real per capita GDP grew by nearly sevenfold from 1900 to 2000.[22]

And that data is also seriously understated because the official inflation measures used to adjust it overstate inflation. Moreover, those results were achieved with Americans staying in school much longer, and retiring earlier, so working much less over their lives.[23] Indeed, the average workweek declined by 50% from 1900 to 1950, and has stabilized at that level since.[24]

Moore and Simon also report that more financial wealth was created in the United States from 1950 to 2000 than in all the rest of the world in all the centuries before 1950.[25] Real financial wealth in the United States doubled from 1950 to 1970, and tripled from 1970 to 2000.[26] When we add housing equity to such real wealth, real assets in America soared from $6 trillion in 1950 to $40 trillion in 2000.[27]

And, no, this wealth is not all concentrated among a few plutocrats at the top. More than half of all Americans own stock today (52%), three times as many as belong to unions (14%).[28] Close to 70% own their own home. Median household wealth climbed to $71,600 in 1998, up 2.5 times since 1965, roughly thirty years.[29] And with the reforms discussed in this book, as average working Americans all migrate into retirement and health savings accounts, ultimately displacing even Social Security and Medicare, all Americans will participate in and enjoy such wealth creation even more. Ultimately, average-income couples could commonly retire as millionaires, especially considering all the sources of their wealth accumulation, including all their retirement accounts, health savings accounts, and housing ownership.

In addition, that typical home that most Americans own today is of far superior quality, bigger, less crowded, and stocked with a cornucopia of modern conveniences after decades of sustained economic growth.[30] The average new house by 2000 was 50% bigger than even in the 1960s, with two to three times as many rooms per person as in 1900.[31] Moore and Simon add,

> It is hard for us to imagine, for example, that in 1900 less than one
> in five homes had running water, flush toilets, a vacuum cleaner,
> or gas or electric heat. As of 1950 fewer than 20 percent of homes

had air conditioning, a dishwasher, or a microwave oven. Today between 80 and 100 percent of American homes have all of these modern conveniences.[32]

Indeed, in 1900 only 2% of homes enjoyed electricity.[33] As Cox and Alm note further in their insightful *Myths of Rich and Poor*, "Homes aren't just larger. They're also much more likely to be equipped with central air conditioning, decks and patios, swimming pools, hot tubs, ceiling fans, and built in kitchen appliances. Fewer than half of the homes built in 1970 had two or more bathrooms; by 1997, 9 out of 10 did."[34]

Such economic growth has produced dramatic improvements in personal health. Throughout most of human history, a typical life span was 25 to 30 years, as Moore and Simon report.[35] But "from the mid-18th century to today, life spans in the advanced countries jumped from less than 30 years to about 75 years."[36] Average life expectancy in the United States has grown by more than 50% since 1900.[37] Infant mortality declined from 1 in 10 back then to 1 in 150 today.[38] Children under fifteen are at least ten times less likely to die, as 1 in 4 did during the 19th century, with their death rate reduced by 95%.[39] The maternal death rate from pregnancy and childbirth was also one hundred times greater back then than today.[40]

Moore and Simon report, "Just three infectious diseases—tuberculosis, pneumonia, and diarrhea—accounted for almost half of all deaths in 1900."[41] Today we have virtually eliminated or drastically reduced these and other scourges of infectious disease that have killed or crippled billions throughout human history, such as typhoid fever, cholera, typhus, plague, smallpox, diphtheria, polio, influenza, bronchitis, whooping cough, malaria, and others.[42] Besides the advances in the development and application of modern health sciences, this has resulted from the drastic reduction in filthy and unsanitary living conditions, which economic growth has made possible as well.[43] In the present day great progress is being made against heart disease and cancer.

The dramatically declining cost of food, resulting from economic growth and soaring productivity in agriculture, has greatly contributed to the well-being of working people, the middle class, and the poor in America. As Moore and Simon report, "Americans devoted almost 50 percent of their incomes to putting food on the table in the early 1900s compared with 10 percent in the late 1900s."[44] While most of human history has involved a struggle against starvation, today in America the battle is against obesity, even more so among the poor. Moore and Simon quote Robert Rector of the Heritage Foundation: "The average consumption of protein, minerals, and vitamins is virtually the same for poor and middle income children, and in most cases is well above recommended norms for all children. Most poor children today are in fact overnourished."[45] That cited data comes from the U.S. Census Bureau. As a result, poor children in America today "grow up to be about 1 inch taller and 10 pounds heavier than the GIs who stormed the beaches of Normandy in World War II."[46]

That has resulted from a U.S. agricultural sector that required 75% of all American workers in 1800, 40% in 1900, and just 2.5% today, to "grow more than enough food for the entire nation and then enough to make the United States the world's breadbasket."[47] Indeed, today, "The United States feeds three times as many people with one-third as many total farmers on one-third less farmland than in 1900," in the process producing "almost 25 percent of the world's food."[48]

Moreover, it is economic growth that has provided the resources enabling us to dramatically reduce pollution and improve the environment without trashing our standard of living. Moore and Simon write that at the beginning of the last century,

Industrial cities typically were enveloped in clouds of black soot and smoke. At this stage of the industrial revolution, factories belched poisons into the air—and this was proudly regarded as a sign of prosperity and progress. Streets were smelly and garbage-filled before the era of modern sewage systems and plumbing.[49]

Redistribution, taking from those that have produced and accumulated wealth to give to working people and the middle class, to achieve more equal results for society overall, could never remotely produce the dramatic gains for working people and the middle class that economic growth has produced, and can in the future, if only we would let it rip. In fact, for the reasons explained in Chapters 7 and 9, such redistribution would actually slash economic growth, and even reverse it, as we have seen in extreme socialist and communist countries around the world. Indeed, such redistribution is just a sophisticated modern version of the medieval mind-set for obtaining wealth, and still holds the potential for producing another Dark Ages.

These are all the reasons why sustained, rapid economic growth must be the top priority of public policy. That is the most effective means by far—indeed, the only means for advancing the quality of life for working people, the middle class, and the poor. Extrapolate into the future and think what further wonders economic growth will produce for the common man and woman in the coming decades. That is why we must keep it going. When President Kennedy told us that a rising tide lifts all boats, he was only scratching the surface.

A LEGAL FRAMEWORK FOR PROSPERITY UNIONS

Current U.S. labor law as it has evolved over the 20th century is actually pretty well suited to the rise of new Prosperity Unions. New unions are started by workers signing cards calling for a union certification election. Once the signatures reach a required threshold, the National Labor Relations Board holds a secret ballot election. Workers can also decertify and remove a union through the same process.

Once a union is started, employers are required to bargain in good faith with it. But the government does not force employers to agree to union demands. Consequently, if union demands become excessive, and threaten the company's economic survival, the company can refuse to agree to them.

Labor law protects the union's right to strike. But there is a market check on that right. The company can hire replacements for striking workers. If the employer is offering below-market wages, however, it will not be able to attract sufficient replacement workers with adequate skills to stay in operation. The strike will then be maximally effective in forcing the company to agree to higher wages. But if the employer is offering market wages, and the union is demanding above-market wages that would leave the company uncompetitive, the employer will be able to hire sufficient replacements to keep operating. Moreover, employers are not obligated to fire those replacements and restore the former union employees to their former jobs once the strike is over. The strikers are only legally entitled to be rehired as openings become available. Unions are consequently constrained by the law and the market to keep their demands reasonable.

Moreover, unions are subject to democratic governance by the workers. They periodically elect their union officials in elections overseen by the NLRB. If union demands are excessive, and workers are losing job opportunities and work as a result, they can vote to replace the incumbents with new leadership, though physical intimidation and violence can add to the practical advantages of incumbency to leave this possible check less effective than it should be.

This legal framework generally makes private sector unions workable. They remain subject to market checks and balances, and some measure of democratic control by workers. But even under this framework, unions at times have exacted excessive demands, intimidating weaker-minded employers into giving in. That has left the companies uncompetitive in the marketplace, resulting in the decline of some major American industries that formerly provided good jobs and wages to working people. And as we have seen, under the current legal framework, unions have too often veered off into violence.

Reforms should focus first on ensuring that union elections are fair and open, and free of physical intimidation, to improve worker democratic control. But so-called card-check reforms would do just the opposite. They would deprive workers of the secret ballot in union certification elections, allowing unions to be certified upon a majority signing cards for the union. This would leave workers subject to physical intimidation and even violence by roving bands of union thugs demanding that workers sign the cards. Consequently, card-check reforms are not in the interests of workers and should be rejected.

As we have seen, reforms are also needed to stop union violence. There must be no special exemption in federal law for union violence. Federal antiextortion laws should be amended to close the *Enmons* loophole. Union officials who would oppose that self-identify themselves as immediate targets who should be displaced from office. Federal, state, and local laws must be applied to punish all forms of violence, including union violence. Such violence has not and cannot advance the cause of working people.

Another fundamental, continuing problem is the use of union dues for political purposes. The Supreme Court recognized a right of workers to refuse to pay the portion of their dues used for political purposes, and to get a refund for any that are, in the landmark case of *Beck v. Communications Workers of America*.[50] But unions have gotten away with just laughing off that requirement and refusing to comply with it. As the Supreme Court has recognized, dues used for political purposes have nothing to do with collective bargaining, which is what workers are required to pay dues for. Requiring them to pay dues for political causes they do not support violates their basic free speech and democratic rights. Therefore the *Beck* decision should be vigorously enforced. But if genuine, blue-collar working people arise to take control of their unions, transforming them into Prosperity Unions, they could themselves eliminate the union political payoffs and other union waste, and slash their own union dues. This would effectively be another tax cut for working people.

The ultimate protection for the freedom of workers, and check on abusive union power, is right-to-work laws. Those laws presently exist in twenty-two states, under federal authorization providing for states to adopt such laws at their option in the Taft-Hartley Act. Right to work protects the freedom of each worker to choose not to join a union, even if there is a union representing other employees of his company. That makes payment of union dues voluntary as well.

Right-to-work laws put unions on an equal footing with all other private sector American institutions, which are voluntary. Union membership should be at the free choice of each worker. No American should be forced to join a union as a condition of working at any particular company. Even the U.S. military is now an all-volunteer force. Unions must be based on voluntary membership as well.

With such right-to-work laws, unions would have to strive to provide good service and benefits to working people to attract members and dues. They couldn't just sign a contract with an employer forcing all of the company's workers into the union. Right to work would give the ultimate power to each worker, rather than to the union. Unions would have to serve the workers sufficiently to attract the approval of each one.

The argument against right-to-work laws is that workers who choose not to join and pay dues where a union is negotiating pay and working conditions at a company are free riders, receiving the benefits of the union's service without paying for it. But a worker is not a free rider if he doesn't want the service the union provides, for whatever reason, which could include use of dues to support politicians and causes the worker doesn't support. The independent worker is not asking or requiring the union to negotiate for him.

In contrast, forced unionism without right to work leads to counterproductive abuses of power, such as union corruption and waste, the pursuit of increasingly extremist politics with the hard-earned money of working people, and physical intimidation and even violence against the workers themselves. Here as elsewhere, power corrupts. Voluntary association is what makes institutions serve the people. We need to apply that to unions as well, to ensure that they actually serve the workers rather than their own institutional interests. The way to do that is for all fifty states to adopt right-to-work laws.

With these protections for workers, private sector Prosperity Unions would be ideal American institutions. But there would still be a fundamental problem with unions for public sector workers, whether for local, state, or federal government. Ultimately, in the private sector if a union pushes too far, the company will be driven out of business. Consequently, there is a market limit to how much a union and its members can plunder the public. Not so with a union for government workers. Federal, state, or even local governments cannot be driven out of business. They gain their revenue forcibly through taxes. As a result, there is no market limit to how much such unions can pirate from the public.

Indeed, public sector unions choose their own employers, by voting for the governing policy makers for each political entity. This creates an inherent conflict of interest, as a politician can be negotiating for pay and benefits for his own political supporters at public expense. It can lead to oppressive political corruption, where there is no political limit as well as no market limit to the plunder of the public by government worker unions.

That fundamental, unworkable problem with public employee unions used to be commonly understood, which is why even an ultimate liberal like Franklin Roosevelt would not recognize such unions. And that is why strikes by government workers have been commonly prohibited in American history as well. These workers are providing essential public services, and government unions should not be allowed to deprive the public of such services. But today this common understanding of the past has been lost in too many jurisdictions. As a result, we find exactly the oppression of the public discussed above in some local or even state jurisdictions.

POWER TO THE PEOPLE

The reforms advocated throughout this book open a whole new world to blue-collar working people and the middle class. Power is consistently shifted to them from federal, state, and local governments and other centralized institutions. In reform after reform, they become the central locus of decision making and power, and the entire economy is reoriented to serving them. The 1960s mantra of "Power to the People" would be achieved at last.

With a flat tax personal exemption of $10,000 per person, and a 15% tax rate after that, blue-collar working families would pay little or no federal income taxes. Nor would there be any state or local income taxes for them to pay under the reforms advocated in Chapter 8. Any income tax burden on the middle class, defined as the middle 20%, would be minor as well.

Moreover, instead of payroll taxes, which for most blue-collar working people and middle-class families is the largest tax today, they would be paying into their own personal savings, investment, and insurance accounts for their Social Security and Medicare benefits. The payroll tax would consequently be transformed from the highest tax on working people today to an engine of personal family wealth and prosperity. Workers with employer pensions would be accumulating additional savings and investment there as well. Health Savings Accounts would accumulate still more. As I have demonstrated, over a lifetime at just standard market investment returns, blue-collar and middle-class families would regularly approach a million dollars or more through these means, all the more so if the value of home equity is counted as well.

Remaining funds could all be left to their children and families at death, at the worker's choice. What a foundation that would be for the future prosperity of their children. Those funds could finance college and professional school educations. They could provide the start-up funds for new small businesses or professional practices. They could provide for the down payment for homes for the families of the grown-up children. They would provide a hilltop launching pad for a lifetime of savings and investment for these second-generation families as well.

As a consequence, with every worker accumulating his or her personal ownership stake in the nation's business and industry, the nation's savings and wealth would be far more equally owned. This would be achieved not by counterproductively redistributing existing wealth, but by the vast creation of new wealth. This would further promote capital and labor working together collaboratively as complements, with so much of the capital owned by labor.

With hundreds of millions of working Americans all over the nation contributing to such accounts, the result would be a tidal wave of new savings and investment that would carry the whole nation to a new level of economic growth and prosperity. Such increased savings and investment would create millions of new jobs, and finance the new technology and equipment to leapfrog the productivity of working people in America to new world-leading heights. That increased productivity would in turn finance rapidly increasing wages for working people.

Working people with personal accounts would also be free to each choose their own retirement age, rather than have the government choose their retirement age for them, as discussed in Chapter 3.

Working people and the middle class would be the power centers of the Patient Power health care system as well. With workers enjoying the same tax benefits for purchasing insurance as employers, workers would be free to choose among the full scope of insurance alternatives in the competitive marketplace. Moreover, they would be free to choose any health insurer across the entire country, not just those in their state. When they reach retirement, all of Medicare would be Medicare Advantage, and they would be free to choose any insurer across the entire country for their health insurance as well.

These insurers will be competing to serve the worker and patient who chooses them, not an employer who has a stronger interest in saving on health costs than in the worker's long-term health. Insurers who try to intrude too much on a patient's choice of health care will suffer an enormous competitive disadvantage. In any event, in this Patient Power world, no insurer will have the power to weigh health costs against benefits and tell the patient his or her health or even life is not worth the costs. Nor will an insurer have any power to cut off a paying insured customer because he or she becomes sick.

Among the worker's or retiree's choices for health coverage would be Health Savings Accounts, which would maximize patient power and control over his or her own health care. The patient would pay for any noncatastrophic health care he chose directly out of his own Health Savings Account funds, with no insurer role at all. The worker could use those funds for dental care, eyeglasses, contact lenses, hearing aids, prescription or over-the-counter drugs, birth control, or any other medical device.

Working and middle-class families would, most important of all, enjoy a health care system geared to maximizing the application of the latest science and medical breakthroughs to the health needs of the sickest and most vulnerable. The booming economy would join with the incentives of this health care system to accelerate the development of new wonder drugs, treatments, and miracle cures. This is what should be expected from the best, most advanced health care system in the world.

With school choice, working people and the middle class would find themselves in the same position of control in regard to the education of their children. Schools would all have to compete to attract each student, which would force them to compete to serve the interests and needs of the student and his or her parents. No longer would parents have to stand aside while education bureaucrats dictate hapless education experiments that leave their children behind, or deploy distasteful learning materials and subject matter that propagandize the children contrary to the values taught at home. The money would follow the choice of each student and his or her parents, so it would be their preferences that would be dominant and would be served.

Working people would also be in control of their new Prosperity Unions, which would be forced to cater to and serve them. These unions would be working every day to maximize the wage growth and job opportunities for their workers in maximally beneficial cooperation with their company and employer, rather than in counterproductive conflict. The union would not be forcing them into counterproductive strikes, threatening them with violence, or stealing their money through corruption. Nor would it be wasting their money on politics in favor of extremist, far-left causes the worker may not support.

With monetary policy tethered to a focus on stable prices, blue-collar and middle-class families would also not be plagued by the runaway costs of inflation, eating away at the value of their savings. With control over state and local spending, their property taxes would be kept down as well. With urban cores enjoying a new dawn of awareness that physical safety and law enforcement is job one, their communities, neighborhoods, and families would enjoy a new freedom from crime, and from the fear of crime.

Most important of all, instead of suffering the threat of the coming bankruptcy of America, working people and the middle class would enjoy a thriving, booming economy, providing abundant jobs and growing wages year after year. The American Dream would be open to them and their children more than ever. Rather than failing state and local governments undermining them, those governments would be following policies contributing to and reinforcing their prosperity and opportunity.

Indeed, with all of the reforms in this book, and booming economic growth, within a generation, average blue-collar working families in America could be earning over $100,000 a year, and retiring as millionaires. That should be the lodestar of American public policy.

All of the above adds up to the greatest breakthrough in the personal prosperity of working people in world history, a true workers' paradise.

CHAPTER 11

THE NEW CIVIL RIGHTS

Economic Empowerment

The civil rights struggles of the 20th century primarily focused on achieving equality under the law for African-Americans and other minorities. One can only shudder to realize that such basic equality, proclaimed as a fundamental principle of our Declaration of Independence, still had not been achieved at this late date in our history.

As a matter of law, however, such basic legal equality has now been mostly won. But that legal equality has not opened the door to the American Dream for too many African-Americans, Hispanics, and other minorities. In terms of income, wealth accumulation, education, health care, and other social indicators, the American Dream, or maximum possible personal prosperity, is still too remote for too many in minority communities. Something more is needed to achieve that. What is needed is economic empowerment.

For African-Americans, Hispanics, and others to achieve true economic justice and prosperity, the civil rights struggle must now expand beyond the battle for legal equality and address the nation's economic policies. Those policies must include economic empowerment for the poor and minorities.

The source of wealth and prosperity in America, and, indeed, the world over, is the open marketplace of the free economy. The interests of the poor and minorities will not be advanced by economic policies that hamper the operation of the market, stymie its productive engines, and short-circuit economic growth. Such divisive and counterproductive policies would only ultimately leave everyone poorer, including, or maybe especially, the most vulnerable among us.

Rather, what is needed are policies of economic empowerment and liberation that will throw open the doors to the productive market to the currently excluded. These are the policies of the New Civil Rights. These are the policies that have been advocated in this book.

ECONOMIC OPPORTUNITY AND GROWTH

The top priority of the New Civil Rights is sustained, robust, rapid economic growth. Without such growth, there is no hope for African-Americans, Hispanics, and other minorities to fully attain middle-class American living standards as a group. Only with such sustained growth can we open new vistas of prosperity to African-Americans, Hispanics, and the poor.

Though, as we saw in Chapter 5, progress against poverty has stalled since the explosion of welfare under the War on Poverty, it was economic growth that reduced U.S. poverty from roughly 50% in 1900, and 30% in 1950, to 12.1% in 1969. Among blacks, poverty was reduced in the 20th century from 3 in 4 to 1 in 4 through economic growth.[1] Child poverty of 40% in the early 1950s was also reduced by half.[2] It was economic growth that made the elimination of child labor possible as well. Moreover, as Steve Moore and Julian Simon note, "A family living at the U.S. poverty level today has an income that is about three times higher than the average per capita income for the world."[3] This is another result of robust American economic growth.

We saw in Chapter 5 how the living standards of the poor in America today are equivalent to the living standards of the middle class forty years ago, if not the middle class in Europe today. With sustained vigorous economic growth, forty years from now the lowest-income Americans will live better than the American middle class of today.

If real compensation growth for the poor can be sustained at just 2% a year, after just twenty years their real incomes will increase by 50%, and after forty years their incomes will more than double. If pro-growth economic policies could raise that real compensation growth to 3% a year, after just twenty years their real incomes would double, and after forty years it would triple. That is the most effective antipoverty program possible.

We discussed in Chapters 6 and 7 the policies necessary to restore booming economic growth in America. Because such sustained economic growth is essential to African-Americans, Hispanics, and other minorities, such policies are essential to the New Civil Rights as well. In contrast, policies that would undermine or short-circuit such growth, such as ideological redistribution to achieve equality of results as discussed in Chapter 8, are contrary to the New Civil Rights. Under the policies of the New Civil Rights, therefore, African-Americans, Hispanics, the poor, and other minorities would enjoy a booming economy full of opportunity and advancement.

WINNING THE WAR ON POVERTY

We discussed in Chapter 5 policies to ensure that the poor participate in such booming growth through a guaranteed offer of work. Such policies would categorically end real poverty in America. Through such policies, the poor can end their poverty at any time just by showing up for work, where the wages and other continuing assistance received only for work would raise them up at least to the poverty level.

This system would replace current federal and state means-tested welfare programs numbering in the hundreds and estimated to cost taxpayers $10.3 trillion over the next ten years. Most crucial is to recognize the effect of the incentives of this new system. It would reverse the plague of nonwork among those in the bottom 20% of income earners who are not disabled from working, which has arisen from the self-defeating War on Poverty. Since the able-bodied can only gain assistance by working, they will have every incentive to take whatever private sector job is available, where they can gain raises, promotions, connections, and real-world skills that will lead to higher and higher incomes over time. Indeed, the whole system would be geared to placing the poor in such private sector jobs.

Moreover, new incentives from this system would not just apply to the poor. The state bureaucrats administering the system would have transformed incentives as well. To the extent they place the poor in private sector jobs, they reap the savings for their state budgets and their taxpayers. To the extent they fail to do so, their state budgets and taxpayers must bear the full burden of supporting the poor. The astounding success of the 1996 welfare reforms indicates that such incentives are powerfully effective.

New incentives would apply as well to end the plague of family breakup and illegitimacy that is also fundamentally at the root of poverty. No additional money is available in this system for bearing a child out of wedlock. To the contrary, for every child that is born, someone will have to work to support the child: either the father, the mother, or both. As a result, gone are all incentives for illegitimacy.

Moreover, the incentives in this system are all in favor of marriage to working, productive men. Only that would reduce the burden of working that the mother must otherwise bear herself, or at least through her family, or friends willing to support her otherwise. Men always able to rescue their mates from poverty by working would become attractive marriage partners, rather than a burden penalizing the family. This in turn would be another factor promoting work. The result would be to promote rather than discourage marriage, ending the tragic, dramatically counterproductive incentives for family breakup of the current welfare system.

Under this system, moreover, the poor can no longer be tyrannized by welfare bureaucrats examining their personal lives to determine their eligibility. They can no longer be penalized by asset tests for saving some money to help them out of poverty, whether by paying for school or starting a business or profession. They need only to show up for work, no questions asked.

There would still be some disincentives to work resulting from the phaseout, as income rises, of supplemental benefits outside of wages for work. This effective poverty trap tax is unavoidable to the extent any such benefits, such as child care or health care subsidies, are provided that have to be phased out as income rises (or else be provided to everyone). But under the policies advocated in this book, there would be no federal or state income taxes on the poor or near poor, no payroll taxes, and no property taxes if they did not own real estate. So the poverty tax trap would be minimized.

As a result, poverty would be categorically ended in America. The poor and working people would enjoy a social safety net that guarantees available work and that no one need be in poverty, with incentives promoting work and family rather than disintegrating them. Moreover, those unable to work to support themselves because of disability or age, with no other means of support such as disability insurance or benefits, would be cared for through other, continuing programs.[4] As a consequence, the War on Poverty would finally be won.

EDUCATION LIBERATION

The current public school system is failing America's minority children. Across the nation, almost 60% of low-income fourth graders cannot read at a basic level, based on the government's own standardized tests. In Chicago schools, almost 90% of low-income and minority students fall below their grade level on standardized tests. The performance in other big cities is mostly the same. Indeed, big-city schools assign as much as one-fourth of African-American boys to classes for the handicapped.

Nationally, half of African-American and Hispanic students won't even finish high school, or graduate on time.[5] Among African-American males who drop out of high school, 72% suffer unemployment in their twenties, and 60% have served some time in jail by their midthirties.[6] That is why there are more African-American men in prison today than in college.[7] Those who do graduate from urban schools with high grade point averages often drop out of college because they cannot do the work.

In Detroit's public schools, which serve a predominantly minority and low-income student population, only one-fourth or less graduate from high school on time.[8] For inner-city school districts in New York and Baltimore, only about one-third graduate on time.[9] In Cleveland, Los Angeles, Miami, Dallas, and Denver, less than half do.[10]

Of course, our public schools are not only failing poor and minority children. But the failures are far worse for children of color, many of whom are trapped in dysfunctional inner-city schools that are not educating them. As a result, the system is stealing their future and condemning them to a life of poverty through no failure of their own.

Adding insult to injury, many in the education bureaucracy say the problem is minority students and their families themselves. They say public schools perform poorly in the inner cities because the students there come from disadvantaged and single-parent homes. These students, they say, just cannot be expected to perform as well as students from the affluent white suburbs.

Apart from the fact that public schools are not succeeding so well in the white affluent suburbs, this argument overlooks the performance of inner-city Catholic schools dealing as well with kids from poor, single-parent, inner-city families. Famed sociologist James Coleman found that poor children in Catholic schools scored higher on tests in science, math, reading, and vocabulary than those in public schools. He also found the Catholic schools to be more integrated and to have higher graduation rates. Indeed, studies have found that Catholic schools increase high school graduation rates of inner-city children by over 40%.

A 1999 Heritage Foundation study of African-American children in Washington, D.C., found that Catholic school students outperformed public school students in math by a wide margin. The average eighth grade African-American Catholic school student scored higher than 72% of the public school eighth graders.

Private non-Catholic schools have produced dramatic results as well. KIPP (Knowledge Is Power Program) Academy in the South Bronx is 45% black and 55% Hispanic. It is housed in the same building and draws from the same neighborhood area as the lowest-performing public school in the district. After just two years, students at KIPP scored in the 64th percentile in reading and the 79th percentile in math. After three years, the scores rose to the 78th percentile in reading and 82nd percentile in math.

Moreover, we have several examples across the country where strong local leaders have dramatically improved the performance of public schools in low-income areas. Nancy Ichinaga, as principal of Bennett-Kew Elementary School in Inglewood, California, raised that school's reading performance from the 3rd percentile in the state to the 50th percentile in four years. Hellen DeBerry took over Earhart Elementary in Chicago in 1991. By 1998, the school's sixth graders were scoring in the 78th percentile in reading and the 85th percentile in math. At a charter school in Detroit, University Preparatory Academy High School, 95%

of students graduate on time, and 100% of graduates attend college or a postsecondary school program.[11] Cornerstone Schools operates charter schools and faith-centered private schools in Detroit with a high school graduation rate of over 90%.[12]

The problem in the public schools is not a lack of money, either. As noted in Chapter 8, education spending has soared over the past forty years, with more now spent on education than national defense.[13] Detroit, with its heavily minority and low-income student population, spends more per pupil on its public schools than wealthy Marin County, California, which has a 97% high school graduation rate.[14] That same comparison holds true across the entire country. Metropolitan Detroit public schools were paying the highest teacher salaries of all major metropolitan areas in the country in 2008, at $47.28 an hour.[15]

But under the New Civil Rights, African-Americans, Hispanics, the poor, and other minorities will enjoy school choice, as discussed in Chapter 8. That means they will be free to choose to leave failing inner-city schools, and choose the schools, public or private, that will best educate their children, in accordance with the needs and preferences of each parent and student. If the child has a special talent, whether math, science, or music, the family can choose a school that will best cultivate that talent. If the public school offends their values, they can choose another school that will not.

Moreover, minority families and the poor will benefit from the resulting competition among schools, as each school, public or private, will realize that they must serve the students and their families to attract their attendance, and funding. This is the best possible spur to get failing inner-city schools to transform. The end result of that competition will be vastly superior schools as compared to what they suffer today, providing real hope, opportunity, and future for their children.

Minority parents know this is true. That is why they have proved so ready to exercise school choice when the opportunity has arisen. When Congress enacted the Scholarship Opportunity Program for the District of Columbia in January 2004, over 6,000 students applied for just 1,800 slots. Despite the growing demand for such school choice among D.C.'s minority communities, one of the early acts of the 2009 Pelosi-Reid Democrat Congress was to terminate the program.

Even before this battle, Wall Street financier Ted Forstmann and the late Walmart heir and philanthropist John Walton teamed up to offer a thousand scholarships to low-income students in Washington, D.C., enabling the students to attend the school of their choice. After just a few months, with no media coverage and no advertising, they were swamped with almost eight thousand applications.

This enormous demonstrated desire for education liberation prompted Forstmann and Walton to increase their effort dramatically. In June 1998 they founded the Children's Scholarship Fund (CSF). Donating $100 million of their own money and raising $70 million more, they funded forty thousand scholarships for low-income children. Joining in support of this effort were former Atlanta mayor Andrew Young, Southern Christian Leadership Conference president Martin Luther King III, YWCA Center for Racial Justice founder Dorothy Height, Colin Powell, former Clinton White House chief of staff Erskine Bowles, baseball slugger Sammy Sosa, and former Senate majority leader Tom Daschle.

While Forstmann and Walton originally planned to offer these scholarships in forty cities in three states, they ultimately offered the scholarships to every family in America with an annual income of less than $22,000 that was willing to apply $1,000 of its own money each year to the chosen school's tuition.

Within sixth months of first publicly announcing this offer, CSF received 1.25 million applications. The applications came from 22,000 cities and towns in all fifty states, including 26% of all eligible families in Chicago, 29% in New York, 33% in Washington, D.C., and 44% in Baltimore.

But Forstmann and Walton were not the first to chart this trail. In 1991, the late J. Patrick Rooney, formerly the chairman of the Golden Rule Insurance Company, founded the first privately funded voucher program, the Education CHOICE Charitable Trust. That fund offered 750 scholarships of $800 for low-income students in Indianapolis. Within three days, he received two thousand applications.

In 1996, Virginia Gilder, chairman of the Empire Foundation for Policy Research in Albany, New York, led the establishment of a program offering Brighter Choice Scholarships. The scholarships were offered to all students at the perennially worst-performing school in the city—Giffen Memorial Elementary School. The scholarships would pay 90% of tuition up to $400 for any student at the school to attend the private school of their choice. Within six months, almost one-fourth of the student body at the school, 105 out of 458 students, had used the scholarship program to leave Giffen for a private school.

Probably even more would have left, except that a funny thing happened. In response to the new competition, *Giffen improved!* The principal and 20% of the teachers were replaced and the entire curriculum was revamped.

Eventually, close to seventy privately financed voucher programs sprouted up across the country. A national organization, CEO America, led by Fritz Steiger, provides funding and expertise to help these programs get started.

Many African-American leaders and writers recognize the importance of school choice for their community. Andrew Young told the NAACP in 1999, "If you are in an . . . underachieving school, then you have a right to seek a voucher to go to a school where you can be guaranteed some level of achievement." Alveda King, niece of slain civil rights leader Martin Luther King Jr., told the press in 1997, "I believe that if Martin Luther King and [his brother] A. D. King were here they would say 'do what is best for the children.' It [school vouchers] may sound radical, but so were they. Is it moral to tax families, compel their children's attendance at schools, and then deny choice between teaching methods, religious and secular education, and other matters?"

Former Baltimore mayor Kurt Schmoke told the press in 1996, "If parents of students have the right to choose so many other basics in their lives—such as where they live, where they go to church, where they work—then they also ought to have the right to choose where their children go to school." Now retired Wisconsin state representative Polly Williams, who led enactment of a school choice program in Milwaukee, states, "Choice is the best thing to come around for my people since I've been born. It allows poor people to have those choices that all those other people who are fearing it already have."

Finally, liberal *Washington Post* columnist William Raspberry wrote in 1998, "If I find myself slowly morphing into a supporter of charter schools and vouchers, it isn't because I harbor any illusion that there is something magical about these alternatives. It is because I am increasingly doubtful that the public schools can do (or at any rate will do) what is necessary to educate poor minority children."

Supposedly "liberal" opinion, however, has sided with the teachers' unions against the interests of minorities and the poor in school choice freedom. Those unions are against school choice transparently because they favor the rigid public school monopoly that protects them from competition. That gives them maximum power to feather their own nests, as well as to pursue their ideological frolics at the expense of the children they are supposed to serve and the taxpayers. What is "liberal" about that?

Is what passes for liberalism today so intellectually fossilized that they cannot see what is going on here? Or are they shamefully just more interested in serving the liberal political machine, of which the teachers' unions are a central component, than the children of minorities and the poor? Either way, it is time for today's "liberalism" to change or die on this issue. Minorities and the poor need to seize control of their own future, and the futures of their children. If supposed liberalism won't change on this critical issue, then minorities and the poor need to have the courage and independence to drop out of the so-called liberal political coalition and transfer their allegiance to new leaders.

But under the New Civil Rights, poor and minority families would benefit from another highly effective tool to control and transform their schools as well. They would enjoy the power of the parent trigger, as also discussed in Chapter 8.[16] For schools with a consistent, demonstrated record of failure, if 50% of the parents with children in the school sign a petition supporting the change, they can direct specific reform of the school, as they choose. They can direct that the school be transformed into a charter school with much greater freedom to determine its own subject matter, teaching materials, instruction methods, and school personnel. They can even specify a particular charter operator with an established record of success in nearby neighborhoods.

Or they can choose a school turnaround or transformation option that would allow for replacing the principal and other administrators, and some or all of the teachers, with new instruction methods, teaching materials, and subject matter. Or they can choose a school choice option that would allow the parents to each choose to opt for a voucher that would pay for some or all of the costs of any other school of their choice, public or private. They could even choose to close the school if they are convinced it is hopeless, providing for reassignment to other public schools.

This parent trigger concept originated in the inner city, first developed by the Los Angeles Parents Union, and promoted by its spin-off Parent Revolution, a self-described progressive community activist group. It would again empower parents with control over their schools and the education of their children. The mere threat of the parent trigger options would generate a new attitude and responsiveness by school administrators and teachers to parents and their concerns. As Parent Revolution deputy director Gabe Rose told *School Reform News*, "This is the first time parents have ever had this sort of power."[17]

Within a year of enactment of the parent trigger in California, more than 60% of parents with children in McKinley Elementary School in the minority Compton neighborhood in south-central Los Angeles petitioned to demand the school be converted into a charter school. Los Angeles mayor Antonio Villaraigosa and former state senator Gloria Romero, who sponsored the state's parent trigger legislation, supported the petition signers. As Compton parent organizer Shirley Ford said, "The Parent Trigger finally gives parents the opportunity to make real decisions about their children's education."[18]

McKinley Elementary is in the bottom 10% of schools in the entire state, with the latest scores for African-American students continuing to decline. A state audit of the Compton Unified School District in 2010 found that administrators and teachers often demonstrated a lack of civility and respect for parents, concluding, "We remain deeply concerned about the commitment to student achievement across the district, and have grave reservations at this time about the capacity of the District to make significant gains for students."[19] That will change now, or schools throughout Compton will be triggered.

These education liberation policies are central components of the New Civil Rights.

PATIENT POWER FOR THE POOR

The problems of America's health care system are most acute for minorities and the poor. They have no alternative but to take what the system gives them, whether employers or the government. They do not have the resources to pay for better coverage or care on their own. Those on Medicaid are directly under government control. Increasingly, they do not even have the choice of doctors, for they must accept whatever doctors are willing to work for the measly compensation Medicaid offers them. We know that this has resulted in reduced quality of care and health. Moreover, minorities and the poor are also prone to more illness at an earlier age. They suffer lower life expectancies as a result. So health care choice, control, and quality are an even more urgent issue for them.

But the New Civil Rights would liberate minorities and the poor from this trap of poorer care and health, through patient power. Instead of miserable Medicaid, which is just a sophisticated, politically acceptable means of denying them health care, minorities and the poor would enjoy the same health coverage and care as the middle class, because with Medicaid vouchers they would enjoy the same health insurance as the middle class. With that standard—market insurance paying market rates to doctors, hospitals, and other health providers—minorities and the poor would enjoy far greater access to health care.

Minorities and the poor would be free to choose to maximize their choice and control over their own health care through Health Savings Accounts. These HSAs would work best for the poor. They would have funds in the accounts to pay for routine checkups, tests, and all forms of preventive care. The account funds would be available to pay for dental care, eyeglasses or contact lenses, hearing aids, birth control, and other items that standard insurance may not pay for. With HSAs, minorities and the poor would be able to pay for alternative medicine they may choose that insurers may not finance, and that they would otherwise probably not have the funds to pay for, unlike higher-income workers. Minorities and the poor would also benefit the most if they kept themselves healthy and minimized health costs through aggressive shopping among health providers, resulting in more money remaining for them in the HSA.

Finally, under the New Civil Rights, minorities and the poor would be backed up by a true health care safety net ensuring access to essential health coverage and care, while maintaining their freedom of choice and control.

A SOCIAL SECURITY DECLARATION OF INDEPENDENCE

Workers in the top half of income earners earn substantial capital income through 401(k)s, IRAs, stock options, etc., in addition to their higher income from work. But those among the lower half of income earners are missing out, as they do not have the funds to make significant capital market investments. As a result, they are just falling further and further behind. Not only do the higher-income earners make more in wages, but they also enjoy a second source of income in the capital markets, in which the lower-income workers cannot even afford to participate.

Because the African-American population receives lower incomes on average, major wealth differences exist along racial lines as well. The typical white household has ten times the net worth of the typical black household, which amounts to only $7,500.[20] Indeed, over half of black households suffer with no net financial assets at all.[21] This wealth gap is reflected in inheritances as well. African-Americans on average only inherit one-tenth as much as whites.

This wealth gap results in a substantial difference in home ownership as well. A Federal Reserve study shows that while about 70% of white working-age families own their own home, only 42% of similar-age African-American families do. Those without significant saved wealth lack the necessary funds for a down payment. Less saved wealth in the African-American community means that blacks do not have the same assistance from parents or their family members in obtaining down payment funds as whites do. A study by Kerwin Kofi Charles of the University of Michigan and Erik Hurst of the University of Chicago found that while 27% of white home buyers received financial assistance from family members, only 8% of African-Americans did.

The major investment for low-income workers and minorities is Social Security. The Social Security benefit formula is skewed to favor lower-income workers with higher returns. Yet even with the extra benefits, these workers are still promised low, below-market returns. Single workers and two-earner couples who each earn the equivalent of today's minimum wage throughout their careers are still promised a real return by Social Security of only about 2%.

Perversely, the program promises an even worse deal for African-Americans. Because of their lower life expectancies, they tend to live fewer years in retirement to collect benefits, resulting in even lower returns. A black male born today has a life expectancy of 68.2 years.[22] But the Social Security retirement age for that worker in the future will be 67 years. That means on average a black male would receive Social Security retirement benefits for about a year.

The Heritage Foundation took this into account in a groundbreaking study calculating promised Social Security returns for African-Americans.[23] The study found that the promised Social Security return for a low-income single black male worker today would be a negative 0.66%. This means that the worker does not receive a return on what he pays into Social Security, but effectively pays money for the privilege of paying into the program. For an average-income single black male, the promised return is negative 1.5%. A two-earner, low-income, black couple with two kids would only receive a return of 1%. For the same couple with average income, the return would be zero percent. A 1996 study by the RAND Corporation similarly found that effective rates of return under Social Security for African-Americans were a full percentage point lower than the returns for whites, primarily due to their lower life expectancies.[24]

The difference between these redistribution Social Security returns and long-term standard returns on savings and investment—with the long-term real return on stocks of 7% or more, and on bonds of 3.5% to 4%—adds up to a true fortune over a lifetime. This fortune is effectively being robbed from lower-income workers through Social Security. Going back to the study we examined in Chapter 3, take an example of a low-income two-earner couple each earning the equivalent of today's minimum wage each year throughout their career. Suppose again that they could save and invest in personal accounts over their entire careers what they and their employers would otherwise pay in taxes into Social Security. The study again accounted for private life and disability insurance benefits to replace Social Security survivors and disability benefits and for administrative costs.

Earning a net real return of 5% on their investments over their career, this lifetime low-income couple would reach retirement with a total accumulated fund of over half a million ($506,920) in constant 1998 dollars.[25] Updated to 2010 dollars, the total would be $678,839. This would be enough to pay this low-income couple out of the continuing interest alone about one-third more than Social Security even promises them, let alone what it could pay, while still allowing them to leave over half a million dollars to their children. Or they could use the fund to buy an annuity paying them over three times what Social Security promises them. Such personal accounts would be sufficient to eliminate poverty among retirees.

This is a measure of what Social Security is costing even low-income and minority workers. The social subsidies promised to low-income workers through Social Security are simply overwhelmed by the much higher returns of real market investments. Once again, economic growth in the market is more effective than redistribution.

As a result, not only are lower-income workers—indeed, those in the bottom half of the income distribution—missing out on the additional income from capital investments enjoyed by the upper half of income earners. The one "investment" they are actually making, Social Security, is leaving them with sickeningly low returns, and huge effective losses in terms of opportunity cost.

The New Civil Rights recognizes this as a real problem for African-Americans, Hispanics, the poor, and lower-income workers. Under the agenda of the New Civil Rights, as outlined in this book, not only would these minority and lower-income workers not pay any federal or state income taxes, but ultimately, instead of payroll taxes, they would also be paying into their own personal savings, investment, and insurance accounts, building real family wealth, a personal family nest egg, over their lives.

Of course, these personal accounts would still be a choice for working people and minority families. They would be perfectly free to stay in the old Social Security system if they desire, without any benefit cuts. But remember, when the workers of Chile, lower-income by American standards, were given that choice thirty years ago, they fled to the personal account system "faster than East Germans going from East to West after the fall of the Berlin Wall."

Moreover, those workers who do choose the personal accounts would still be backed up by a social safety net equivalent to Social Security, for they would be guaranteed that they would receive at least as much as promised by Social Security under current law. As discussed in Chapter 3, long-term standard market returns are so much higher than what Social Security can even promise that the personal account system can feasibly be backed up by a guarantee that workers would receive at least that much in retirement benefits as Social Security promises. A similar safety net guarantee, proportionally equivalent to what Social Security promises average-income workers in America, has been provided in Chile for thirty years with no problem, even through the world financial crisis. As also explained in Chapter 3, the personal account system would be designed to make participation feasible for unsophisticated investors with no market knowledge or investing experience, like the working people of Chile thirty years ago.

A personal investment account alternative to the current Social Security system would provide the cornerstone for the economic liberation of those currently excluded from the American Dream. Requiring no more from these workers than what they are currently paying into Social Security, these minority and lower-income families could expect to accumulate several hundred thousand dollars in real terms, after inflation, by retirement, with just ordinary investment performance. If their employer provides an additional retirement plan on top of Social Security, those contributions would accumulate additional funds. If the worker chooses a Health Savings Account, that would add still more to their lifetime accumulation of real wealth. If they purchase a home, that would add still more to their accumulated estate. A million dollars of accumulated real wealth would consequently not be out of reach for a hardworking minority couple over a lifetime. This is why the New Civil Rights provides a newly liberating vision of lifetime prosperity for minority families and working people.

These personal savings and investment funds would provide a vital wellspring of new capital within the control of minority communities themselves, growing into a mighty river of invigorating capital investment. This capital would finance the establishment of new minority businesses hiring minority workers within minority communities. It could pay for the construction of new housing within these communities, and fund new educational opportunities for minority children. It would be a fountain of economic renaissance within minority urban communities.

This would be all the more so when combined with the newly important law enforcement in urban communities discussed in Chapter 8. This too should be recognized as a New Civil Right, neighborhoods free from the plague of crime, and gangs, and drugs. Imagine how different life would be for urban minority communities if they actually enjoyed personal security free from such depredation. But even beyond the liberation of personal security, this would be the foundation for a new explosion of economic opportunity and growth within these communities.

The greater economic growth resulting from the increased savings and investment cascading through the personal accounts would be most important for America's minorities, as they are most in need of the increased wages, jobs, and growth. Minority workers would be swimming in the sea of general economic prosperity across the entire economy, and the new, hopeful currents would carry them along to new heights of personal prosperity.

Moreover, the new lifetime of accumulated funds among minority families could be left to their children to provide a new foundation of prosperity for their lives. These funds could finance college, professional school, and graduate school educations for the grown children. They could finance the down payments on new homes purchased by the families of these grown children. They could be the seed capital for new small businesses or professional practices started by these grown children. They could be the foundation for the new lifetime savings and investment of these grown children and their families, geometrically multiplying over the years to previously unimagined heights.

Avoiding the long-term Social Security benefit cuts or tax increases that would otherwise be necessary on our current course would again be most important for lower-income workers. These workers, of course, cannot afford even higher payroll taxes. But they also can least afford cuts in the already meager benefits Social Security promises them. Moreover, delaying the retirement age hurts minority workers the most, especially African-Americans, with their lower life expectancies. Already suffering fewer years in retirement to collect benefits, African-Americans and other minorities would suffer a higher percentage cut in their retirement benefits from delaying the retirement age than other Americans. Indeed, delaying the future retirement age by more than a year would wipe out Social Security retirement benefits entirely for a typical black male born today.

With personal accounts, by contrast, workers would again each be free to choose their own retirement age. Indeed, the personal accounts would provide special opportunities to African-Americans and other minorities with lower life expectancies. Ethnic or racial organizations such as the NAACP or La Raza could offer annuities to their members limited to such ethnic or racial groups. Since the pool would then bear a lower life expectancy, the annuity could pay these members higher benefits for their fewer expected years of retirement. Legal provisions providing for this have been included in the personal accounts legislation introduced by Congressman Paul Ryan (R-WI), now chairman of the House Budget Committee. This is another way African-Americans and other minorities would benefit the most from personal accounts.

But the most obvious reason they would benefit is that, with lower incomes on average, they otherwise have little scope or opportunity to accumulate real personal savings, investment, and wealth. That is demonstrated by the real-world hard data discussed at the outset of this section. They even suffer lower home ownership rates. But with the bottom half of the income distribution accumulating substantial savings, investment, and wealth of their own for the first time through personal accounts, the overall national ownership of wealth and capital would become far more equal. As the capital accumulated through the accounts reinvigorated and rebuilt minority communities over time, wealth ownership and income would become more equal on this score as well.

Personal accounts would be the ultimate in "pension fund socialism." In other words, through these accounts the socialist dream of the nation's workers owning its business and industry would be effectively achieved. But since this ownership would be direct, rather than through the government, the result would be more appropriately called worker capitalism. With minorities and other workers all owning a share of America's business and industry, they would more vigorously support general economic freedom and prosperity for everyone.

Altogether, this is the most exciting and promising civil rights agenda since the 1964 Civil Rights Act and the 1965 Voting Rights Act. This is a true vision of a New Civil Rights of economic empowerment that minorities and the poor need today.

CHAPTER 12

THE REBIRTH OF AMERICA

More Free and Prosperous Than Ever

On our current course, America is headed for bankruptcy. The federal government's deficits, debt, unfunded liabilities, and other potential financial losses are swirling out of control. Ill-considered economic policies to address the recession have only added further to the scary outlook. The Keynesian throwback 2009 stimulus added greatly to our national deficits and debt. Runaway monetary policy at the Fed, casting aside all the hard-learned lessons of the 1970s about the impracticality of trying to guide the real economy with the monetary steering wheel, now raises the intractable threat of inflation that could be cured only with soaring interest rates and renewed recession.

Our nation is now mortally vulnerable to another recession in the shorter term, which would explode our national finances, with catastrophic consequences. America literally cannot afford the cash accounting deficits over $2 trillion and rising that would result. Indeed, the world financial markets cannot afford it, and won't even try. America reaching the dead end of Greece means we would have no means of financing half our federal budget. Who then would bail out America? Who would even have the means to try?

That would be the bankruptcy of America. We may then lose the American Dream, our national heritage of world-leading economic opportunity and prosperity that has been the hallmark of these shores for over three hundred years, attracting immigrants from every corner of the globe. Even our national defenses would then be imperiled. And that weakness would only invite especially deadly war.

But just like the eerie revelations of the Ghost of Christmas Future, this nightmarish outcome can still be avoided if we would only change. We must think anew at all levels of government, outside the box of conventional wisdom as to what is possible, and cast off the special interest chains that prevent us from following the course we know will work.

To defuse the ticking bankruptcy bomb, we must first reignite another economic boom, with the logical, proven policies that have worked before, and that we know will work again—tax rates as low as possible, government spending burdens as low as possible, government regulatory burdens as low as possible, and sound money tethered to real-world values. Then we must resize our government to fit within the means provided by those essential policies.

This book has offered a new vision to solve this otherwise intractable entitlement enigma. The solution involves not wooden tax increases and benefit cuts, but fundamental, structural reforms of our entitlement programs from the bottom up to produce a modern, 21st century social safety net ensuring that the essential needs of the poor and vulnerable regarding income support, health care, retirement, housing, and nutrition are met. If that is done right, we can achieve all of the liberal social safety net goals far better, at just a fraction of the cost of the current, outdated, old-fashioned tax and redistribution entitlement programs.

The key to that is to transform the programs to rely primarily on modern capital and labor markets to achieve the goals, with positive, pro-growth incentives, creating programs that contribute to, rather than detract from, robust economic growth and prosperity. That means replacing all unfunded retirement Ponzi schemes with new savings and investment directly owned by working people themselves, supplanting impoverishing taxes with personal engines of family wealth and prosperity. That new savings and investment will contribute to, rather than detract from, booming economic growth.

It means repealing costly socialized medicine that subtracts our rapidly developing high-tech medicine from our world-leading standard of living and replacing it with patient power reforms that unite incentives to control costs and maximize power over personal health in the patients themselves. The reduced costs from those incentives, while maintaining the best, most advanced health care system in the world, would also contribute to booming economic growth. At the same time, a comprehensive health care safety net focusing help on the truly needy, which would not be too costly, would ensure that no one would suffer without essential health care.

It means replacing our overgrown, federalized welfare state empire with a defederalized safety net that provides all assistance to the able-bodied only through a guaranteed offer of work. That reverses incentives for nonwork and family breakup that have mired the poor in long-term hopelessness and shattered America's inner cities. Instead, we can create incentives to inspire the bottom 20% of our population to work to the extent possible, contributing to, rather than detracting from, economic prosperity for all. Those incentives would also centripetally bring families together rather than split them apart. In the process, we would finally win the War on Poverty in America.

The essential insight regarding these reforms is that if we get the economy booming again, and modernize the entitlement safety net programs to ride on top of the waves of prosperity rather than underneath them, taking care of those in need will not be a difficult, costly burden. Indeed, as Charles Murray has pointed out,[1] we are already spending far more than enough to lift everyone out of poverty. The trick is how to provide that assistance in ways that would minimize costs, rather than maximize them.

With a true and complete safety net that would end poverty, deprivation, and want, it would not be desirable to go beyond that with taxation and redistribution merely to achieve more equal incomes and wealth. Such equalization policies involve counterproductive incentives that would be fatal to the booming economic growth that is essential to averting the coming bankruptcy of America.

All these pro-growth and entitlement reforms together can mean the rebirth of America, as a better and wiser country than ever, with new generations to come sharing not panic, but hard-earned prosperity and peace.

NOTES

Chapter 1: Lighting the Fuse

1. George Bush, *Decision Points* (New York: Crown Publishers, 2010).
2. Brian Riedl, Heritage Foundation, p. 91.
3. Ibid., p. 95.
4. Ibid.
5. Statement of the Acting Comptroller General of the United States, U.S. Government Accountability Office (GAO), December 21, 2010, p. 4; U.S. Department of the Treasury, 2010 Financial Report of the United States Government, Notes to the Financial Statements, December 21, 2010, p. 108.
6. U.S. Department of the Treasury, 2010 Financial Report of the United States Government, Notes to the Financial Statements, December 21, 2010, p. 65.
7. Ibid.
8. Ibid., p. 108.
9. Congressional Budget Office, The Budget and Economic Outlook: Fiscal Years 2011 to 2021, January, 2011, p. 62.
10. Steve Malanga, "America's Municipal Debt Racket," *Wall Street Journal*, June 14, 2010, p. A17.
11. Ibid.
12. Veronique de Rugy, "The Municipal Debt Bubble," *Reason*, January 2011, pp. 20–21.
13. Congressional Budget Office, The Long Term Budget Outlook, June 2010, Supplemental Data Table, Summary Data for the Alternative Fiscal Scenario; GAO, The Federal Government's Long Term Fiscal Outlook, p. 6.
14. Committee for a Responsible Federal Budget, CBO's Long Term Budget Outlook, July 1, 2010, p. 3.

Chapter 2: America's Coming Bankruptcy

1. Congressional Budget Office, The Long Term Budget Outlook, June 2010, pp. 1, 13.
2. Ibid., p. 6.
3. Ibid., p. 12.
4. U.S. Government Accountability Office (GAO), The Federal Government's Long

Term Fiscal Outlook: Fall 2010, GAO-11-201SP, December 2010. CBO projects the national debt will exceed the World War II historical peak by 2025.

5. Nicholas Eberstadt and Hans Groth, "Time for Demographic Stress Tests," *The Wall Street Journal*, November 27–28, 2010, p. A17; Stephen G. Cecchetti, M.S. Mohanty, and Fabrizio Zampolli, "The Future of Public Debt: Prospects and Implications," BIS Working Papers No. 300, Bank for International Settlements, March 2010, p. 10.

6. U.S. Department of the Treasury, 2010 Financial Report of the United States Government, December 21, 2010, p. vi.

7. Ibid., p. 1.

8. Ibid., pp. 6, 14.

9. Committee for a Responsible Federal Budget, CBO's Long Term Budget Outlook, July 1, 2010, p. 1.

10. Carmen M. Reinhart and Kenneth S. Rogoff, Growth in a Time of Debt, National Bureau of Economic Research, Working Paper 15639, January, 2010.

11. The 2009 Annual Report of the Board of Trustees of the Federal Old-Age and Survivors Insurance and Disability Insurance Trust Funds, May 12, 2009; The 2009 Annual Report of the Board of Trustees of the Federal Health Insurance and Federal Supplementary Medical Insurance Trust Funds, May 12, 2009.

12. U.S. Department of the Treasury, 2010 Financial Report of the United States Government, December 21, 2010, pp. vii, 6, 69, 71, 74, 84; Statement of the Acting Comptroller General of the United States, GAO, December 21, 2010, p. 4.

13. Ibid., p. 6.

14. Ibid., p. 71.

15. Ibid., pp. 69, 74.

16. Statement of the Acting Comptroller General of the United States, GAO, December 21, 2010, p. 4; United States Department of the Treasury, 2010 Financial Report of the United States Government, Notes to the Financial Statements, December 21, 2010, p. 84.

17. Congressional Budget Office, Federal Debt and Interest Costs, December, 2010, p. 2.

18. Statement of the Acting Comptroller General of the United States, GAO, December 21, 2010, p. 5; United States Department of the Treasury, 2010 Financial Report of the United States Government, December 21, 2010, p. 82.

19. United States Department of the Treasury, 2010 Financial Report of the United States Government, December 21, 2010, pp. vii, 14–15, 56, 83.

20. Ibid., p. 64.

21. Ibid., p. 97.

22. CBS News, "State Budgets: The Day of Reckoning," *60 Minutes*, December 19, 2010.

23. As the Bank for International Settlements explains the problem plaguing developed countries generally, "Driven by the countries' demographic profiles, the ratio of old-age population to working-age population is projected to rise sharply. . . . Added to the effects of population ageing is the problem posed by rising per capita health care costs." Cecchetti, Mohanty, and Zampolli, "The Future of Public Debt," p. 6.

24. U.S. Department of the Treasury, 2010 Financial Report of the United States Government, December 21, 2010, p. ii.

25. Ibid., p. 7.

26. Ibid., pp. 7, 8.

27. CBO, The Budget and Economic Outlook: An Update, p. 2.

28. That is because the trust fund bonds will continue to earn interest over the next twenty-five years or so, until they run out completely, and American taxpayers will have to pay that interest as well, in order to keep financing Social Security benefits.

29. U.S. Department of the Treasury, 2010 Financial Report of the United States Government, December 21, 2010, p. 11.

30. International Monetary Fund, Fiscal Monitor: Navigating the Fiscal Challenges Ahead; Glenn Beck, Broke: The Plan to Restore Our Trust, Truth, and Treasure (New York: Threshold Editions, 2010), p. 155.

31. International Monetary Fund, Fiscal Monitor: Navigating the Fiscal Challenges Ahead; Beck, Broke, p. 155.

32. International Monetary Fund, IMF Executive Board Concludes 2010 Article IV Consultation with the United States, Public Information Notice No. 10/101, July 30, 2010; International Monetary Fund, United States: Selected Issues Paper, IMF Country Report No. 10/248, July 2010.

33. Gerald Prante, Summary of Latest Federal Income Tax Data, Fiscal Fact No. 183, Tax Foundation, July 30, 2009; Scott Hodge, Tax Burden of Top 1% Now Exceeds That of the Bottom 95%, Tax Foundation, July 29, 2009.

34. See, e.g., W. Kurt Hauser, "There's No Escaping Hauser's Law," Wall Street Journal, November 26, 2010, p. A19.

35. CBO explains: "For purposes of the projections, CBO assumed stable economic conditions after 2020—in particular, a constant real (inflation-adjusted) interest rate on federal debt. . . . That approach omits the pressures that a rise in debt as a percentage of GDP would have on real interest rates and economic growth." CBO, The Long Term Budget Outlook, pp. 2–4.

36. Ibid., p. 1.

37. Douglas Holtz-Eakin, Jennifer Pollom, and Cameron Smith, A Reader's Guide to the 2012 Budget, American Action Forum, February, 2011, p. 2.

38. CBO admits that its projections "omit . . . the impact that higher effective marginal tax rates and the increasing value of government benefits would have on incentives to work and save." Ibid., p. 4.

39. CBO, The Budget and Economic Outlook: An Update, August, 2010, Table C–1, p. 78.

40. Ibid.

41. Ibid.

42. Beck, Broke, pp. 162–63.

Chapter 3: The Baby Boom's Retirement Bomb

1. The Board of Trustees, Federal Old-Age and Survivors Insurance and Federal Disability Insurance Trust Funds, The 2010 Annual Report of the Federal Old-Age and Survivors Insurance and Federal Disability Insurance Trust Funds, August 5, 2010 (hereinafter, 2010 Trustees Report), Table IV.A3, p. 43.

2. Ibid.
3. Ibid., Table IV.B3.
4. Calculated from 2010 Trustees Report, Table VI.F8.
5. 2010 Trustees Report, Table VI.F2.
6. Ibid., Table V.A3
7. Ibid.
8. Ibid.
9. Ibid.
10. Ibid.
11. Ibid.
12. Ibid., Table V.B1.
13. Ibid.
14. Ibid., Table V.B2.
15. Ibid.
16. Ibid., Table IV.B3.
17. Ibid., Table IV.B1.
18. Ibid.
19. Ibid.
20. Ibid., Table VI.F2.
21. Ibid.
22. Ibid., Table V.A1.
23. Ibid.
24. Ibid.
25. Ibid.
26. Ibid.
27. Ibid., Table IV.B2.
28. Ibid.
29. Ibid.
30. Ibid.
31. Ibid.
32. Peter J. Ferrara and Michael Tanner, *A New Deal for Social Security* (Washington, DC: Cato Institute, 1998), ch. 4.
33. Jeremy Siegel, *Stocks for the Long Run*, 3rd ed. (New York: McGraw-Hill, 2002).
34. Ibid.; *Stocks, Bonds, Bills, and Inflation 2007 Yearbook* (Chicago: Ibbotson Associates, 2007); Jeremy Siegel, *Stocks for the Long Run* (Chicago: Irwin Professional, 1994).
35. Edgar K. Browning, "The Anatomy of Social Security and Medicare," *Independent Review* 13, no. 1 (Summer 2008), p. 12. See also Siegel, *Stocks for the Long Run* (the average real return on corporate bonds over the 200 year period from 1802 to 2001 was 5%); José Piñera, "Toward A World of Worker Capitalists," *Transform the Americas*, http://www.transformamericas.org, April 2010.
36. Martin Feldstein and Andrew Samwick, "The Economics of Prefunding Social Security and Medicare Benefits," National Bureau of Economic Research Working Paper no. 6055, National Bureau of Economic Research, Cambridge, MA, June 1997.
37. Martin Feldstein, "The Missing Piece in Policy Analysis," *American Economic Review* 86, no. 2 (May 1996), p. 12. I consider that a conservative underestimate because of

the likely effects of combining booming capital investment with rapidly advancing modern technology.

38. Ibid.

39. President's Weekly Radio Address, August 14, 2010.

40. William G. Shipman and Peter Ferrara, "Private Social Security Accounts: Still a Good Idea," *Wall Street Journal*, October 27, 2010, p. A17.

41. Only the OASI portion of the payroll tax was used for the calculation.

42. Large-cap stocks are equity securities in major, large, New York Stock Exchange companies. Small-cap stocks are equity securities in smaller, riskier, midsize firms, with more growth potential and, therefore, higher average returns.

43. Ibbotson and Associates, *Stocks, Bonds, Bills, and Inflation*.

44. Capital investment returns ultimately incorporate inflation, producing the more stable real returns over time. That is why the Chilean personal account system in operation for thirty years now, as discussed in detail below, has been able to fully index all benefit amounts, and even all personal account accumulations, for inflation every year.

45. Amity Shlaes, *The Forgotten Man: A New History of the Great Depression* (New York: HarperCollins, 2007).

46. José Piñera, "The Success of Chile's Privatized Social Security," Cato Policy Report 18, no. 4, Cato Institute, Washington, DC, August 1995.

47. José Piñera, "Empowering Workers: The Privatization of Social Security in Chile," *Cato Journal* 15, nos. 2–3 (1997).

48. Piñera, "The Success of Chile's Privatized Social Security"; Piñera, "Empowering Workers."

49. José Piñera, "Empowering Workers."

50. Piñera, "The Success of Chile's Privatized Social Security."

51. Research Department, "The AFP System Myths and Realities," Chilean AFP Association, August 2004, p. 3.

52. This is possible with market investments again because inflation is reflected over time in higher capital returns, maintaining stable real returns over the long run. The Chilean system has successfully worked this way for thirty years now.

53. Piñera, "Empowering Workers"; José Piñera, "Retiring in Chile," *Transform the Americas*, http://www.transformamericas.org, 2001.

54. Piñera, "The Success of Chile's Privatized Social Security."

55. Research Department, "The AFP System: Myths and Realities," Chilean AFP Association, August 2004, p. 4.

56. José Piñera, "Retiring in Chile."

57. Piñera, "Empowering Workers"; José Piñera, "Toward a World of Worker Capitalists," *Transform the Americas*, http://www.transformamericas.org, April 2000.

58. Piñera, "Retiring in Chile."

59. Piñera, "The Success of Chile's Privatized Social Security."

60. Ibid.

61. Ibid.; José Piñera, "Toward A World of Worker Capitalists."

62. John Tierney, "The Proof Is in the Pension," *New York Times*, April 26, 2005.

63. Piñera, "The Success of Chile's Privatized Social Security."

64. José Piñera, "Empowering Workers"; José Piñera, "Toward a World of Worker Capitalists."

65. Ibid.

66. Ibid.

67. World Bank, *Averting the Old-Age Crisis* (Oxford: Oxford University Press, 1994); Peter J. Ferrara and Michael Tanner, *A New Deal for Social Security* (Washington, DC: Cato Institute, 1998), ch. 1, "The Worldwide Revolution in Social Security," pp. 1–11.

68. Testimony of Don Kibbedeaux before the Senate Committee on Finance, Subcommittee on Securities, April 30, 1996; Merrill Matthews, "No Risky Scheme: Retirement Savings Accounts That Are Personal and Safe," Institute for Policy Innovation, Policy Report No. 163, January, 2002.

69. Shipman's work showed that the personal accounts could be structured to keep administrative costs to less than one-fourth of one percent of account assets, with the cost declining further the larger the accounts grow over time. State Street Global Advisors, "Administrative Challenges Confronting Social Security Reform," March 22, 1999; William G. Shipman, Testimony Before the House Budget Committee Task Force on Social Security, April 27, 1999; U.S. Government Accountability Office, Social Security Reform: Administrative Costs for Individual Accounts Depend on System Design.

70. Once a worker age fifty-five or below started shifting funds into a personal account, the worker would be free to do so until retirement, and even beyond for postretirement work.

71. www.socialsecurity.gov/OACT/solvency/RyanSununu_20050420.pdf.

72. Estimated Financial Effects of the "Social Security Personal Savings and Prosperity Act of 2004," July 19, 2004, Office of the Chief Actuary, Social Security Administration.

73. Peter Ferrara, "A Progressive Proposal for Social Security Personal Accounts," Institute for Policy Innovation, Policy Report 176, June 2003, pp. 13–15.

74. Martin Feldstein, "Social Security and the Distribution of Wealth," *Journal of the American Statistical Association* (December 1976): 90–3.

75. This is also why those economists who have said that the personal accounts involve one generation paying twice for their retirement have misunderstood and mischaracterized the issue. The transition from a pay-as-you-go system to a fully funded system does not involve paying twice for retirement. It involves paying for the savings of the fully funded system, analogous to putting $1,000 in your savings account. Are state and local governments with unfunded pension liabilities paying twice for retirement when they build up their reserves to full funding? Once an unfunded liability is present, anything that is done to eliminate that unfunded liability could be characterized as effectively paying twice for retirement under the same logic. Paying twice for retirement is what is happening now with Social Security, as workers will have to pay for the liquidation of Social Security trust fund bonds now that the annual surpluses are being replaced with annual deficits, in addition to the payroll taxes they have paid and will continue to pay.

76. Indeed, Milton Friedman argued that the entire transition can just be financed by borrowing, as such borrowing would not, in fact, result in an increase in govern-

ment debt, but just explicit recognition of the effective government debt already existing in the unfunded liabilities of Social Security. Milton Friedman, "Speaking the Truth About Social Security Reform," Cato Institute Briefing Papers No. 46, April 12, 1999. The debt issued to finance the entire transition would just equal the unfunded liabilities of Social Security. Friedman states that "there are no transition costs to privatizing Social Security, merely the explicit recognition of current implicit debt." Ibid., p. 1. Feldstein suggests as well that just issuing government bonds to recognize all the future liabilities of Social Security would be feasible, as it would freeze the effective debt represented by the unfunded liabilities of Social Security, while the amount of net saving generated by a fully funded system to replace the current pay-as-you-go system would grow with the future growth of the economy. Feldstein, "The Missing Piece in Policy Analysis," pp. 11–12.

77. This reflects the fundamental economic reality that what is produced by the increased savings and investment from shifting from the nonsavings and noninvestment system of the current Social Security program to a fully funded savings and investment system is the before-tax real rate of return produced by that increased savings and investment. The layers of corporate and capital income taxation that would apply to that before-tax real return are what generate the increased revenues. These increased revenues are another benefit of the reform, reflecting the full gain from increased savings and investment indicated by the real, full before-tax real return to capital.

78. Feldstein, "The Missing Piece in Policy Analysis."

79. "George W. Bush 2000 On The Issues: Social Security," *4President.us*, http://www.4president.us, January 15, 2008; Governor George W. Bush, "Saving Social Security and Medicare," campaign fact sheet, May 15, 2000.

80. George W. Bush, Address to the Rancho Cucamonga Senior Citizen Center, Rancho Cucamonga, CA, May 15, 2000, pp. 3–5.

81. Ibid., p. 3.

82. Michael Tanner, Memo to George W. Bush: Social Security is a Winning Issue, http://www.socialsecurity.org, September 19, 2000.

83. Ibid.

84. Larry Kudlow, "W.'s Muscular Social Security Plan: This is 21st Century Breakthrough Stuff," *National Review Online*, May 15, 2000.

85. Jackie Calmes, "Architect of Social Security Plan Perseveres," *Wall Street Journal*, April 22, 2005, http://online.wsj.com/article/0,,SB111412410229713827,00.html.

Chapter 4: Obamacare: Death and Taxes

1. CBO Long Term Budget Outlook, p. 25; Sally C. Pipes, *The Truth About Obamacare* (Washington, DC: Regnery, 2010), p. 23.

2. Organisation for Economic Co-operation and Development.

3. International Monetary Fund, World Economic Outlook Data Base, October 2010, Table 5: Report for Selected Countries and Subjects; Gross Domestic Product (2009), World Bank, World Development Indicators Database, September 27, 2010.

4. Ibid.

5. Andrew Rettenmaier, "Health Care Spending Forecasts," Brief Analysis No. 654,
    National Center for Policy Analysis, April 23, 2009.

6. 2009 Medicare Trustees Report, Table III.B5.

7. Ibid.

8. 2009 Medicare Trustees Report, Table III.B7.

9. 2009 Annual Social Security Trustees Report, Table VI.F2

10. 2009 Medicare Trustees Report, Table III.C10.

11. 2009 Medicare Trustees Report, Table V.C2.

12. 2009 Medicare Trustees Report, Table V.C1.

13. 2009 Medicare Trustees Report, Table III.A2.

14. 2009 Medicare Trustees Report, Table III.C4.

15. 2009 Medicare Trustees Report, Table III.B10.

16. 2009 Medicare Trustees Report, Table III.C15.

17. Richard S. Foster, Chief Actuary, Centers for Medicare & Medicaid Services, Es-
    timated Financial Effects of the Patient Protection and Affordable Care Act, as
    Amended, April 22, 2010, Table 5.

18. CBO Long Term Budget Outlook, p. 28.

19. Centers for Medicare & Medicaid Services.

20. Ibid.

21. Foster, "Estimated Financial Effects of the Patient Protection and Affordable Care
    Act."

22. Ibid., p. 6, Table 2; CBO, The Budget and Economic Outlook: Fiscal Years 2011 to
    2021, January, 2011, p. 62.

23. Ibid., Table 1; Douglas Elmendorf, Congressional Budget Office, Letter to the Hon-
    orable John Boehner, February 18, 2011, pp. 9,10.

24. Douglas Holtz-Eakin and Cameron Smith, "Labor Markets and Health Care
    Reform: New Results," American Action Forum, May 2010, p. 2.

25. Ibid.

26. Douglas Elmendorf, Congressional Budget Office, Letter to the Honorable John
    Boehner, February 18, 2011, Table 2, p.5.

27. Pipes, The Truth About Obamacare, pp. 140–41.

28. Douglas Elmendorf, Congressional Budget Office, Letter to the Honorable Nancy
    Pelosi, March 20, 2011.

29. Lori Montgomery, "Proposed Long-Term Insurance Program Raises Questions,"
    Washington Post, October 27, 2009.

30. Barack Obama, Remarks by the President to a Joint Session of Congress on Health
    Care, White House, September 9, 2009.

31. Newt Gingrich, To Save America (New York: Regnery, 2010), p. 89.

32. Conrad F. Meier, Destroying Insurance Markets, Council for Affordable Health In-
    surance, Heartland Institute, 2005; Leigh Wachenheim, Principal and Consulting
    Actuary, Hans Leida, Assistant Actuary, "The Impact of Guaranteed Issue and
    Community Rating Reforms on Individual Insurance Markets," Milliman, Inc.
    (actuarial firm), July 10, 2007; Merrill Matthews, "Should We Abandon Risk As-
    sessment in Health Insurance?" Issues and Answers No. 154, Council for Afford-

able Health Insurance, May 2009; Devon Herrick, "The Folly of Health Insurance Mandates," Brief Analysis No. 652, National Center for Policy Analysis, April 9, 2009 ("In every state where guaranteed issue and community rating is in effect, health insurance premiums are two to three times the national average").

33. See also American Academy of Actuaries, Letter to The Honorable Nancy Pelosi and The Honorable Harry Reid, Re: *Patient Protection and Affordable Care Act* (H.R. 3590) and *Affordable Health Care for America Act* (H.R. 3962), January 14, 2010, pp. 2, 4. The actuaries wrote, "[T]he financial penalties associated with the bill's individual mandates are fairly weak compared to coverage costs. . . . In particular, younger individuals in states that currently allow underwriting and wider premium variations by age could see much higher premiums than they face currently (and may have chosen to forgo). The premiums for young and healthy individuals would likely be high compared to the penalty, especially in the early years, but even after fully phased in, thus likely leading to many to forgo coverage." Ibid., pp. 4–5.

34. PricewaterhouseCoopers, Potential Impact of Health Reform on the Cost of Private Health Insurance Coverage, October 2009.

35. WellPoint, Inc., Impact of Health Reform on Premiums, October 2009.

36. Matthews, "Should We Abandon Risk Assessment in Health Insurance?"

37. Congressional Budget Office, An Analysis of Health Insurance Premiums Under the Patient Protection and Affordable Care Act, Letter to the Honorable Evan Bayh, November 30, 2009;

38. Foster, Estimated Financial Effects of the Patient Protection and Affordable Care Act.

39. Grace Marie Turner and Tara Persico, "Massachusetts' Health Reform Plan: Miracle or Muddle?" Galen Institute, July 2009, p. 8.

40. Ibid., p. 3.

41. Michael Tanner, "Massachusetts Miracle or Massachusetts Miserable: What the Failure of the 'Massachusetts Model' Tells Us about Health Care Reform," Cato Institute Briefing Papers No. 112, June 9, 2009, p. 1.

42. Ibid., p. 6; Turner and Persico, p. 3.

43. Greg Scandlen, "Three Lessons from Massachusetts," National Center for Policy Analysis, Brief Analysis No. 667, July 28, 2009.

44. Ibid.; Sally C. Pipes, "Mass Health Meltdown Is Your Future," Pacific Research Institute, May 25, 2010.

45. Tanner, "Massachusetts Miracle or Massachusetts Miserable," p. 7.

46. Aaron Yelowitz and Michael F. Cannon, "The Massachusetts Health Plan: Much Pain, Little Gain," Policy Analysis No. 657, Cato Institute, January 2010, p. 10.

47. Tanner, "Massachusetts Miracle or Massachusetts Miserable," p. 4.

48. Scandlen, "Three Lessons from Massachusetts," p. 1.

49. Ibid.

50. Tanner, "Massachusetts Miracle or Massachusetts Miserable," p. 5.

51. "The Massachusetts Health Mess," *Wall Street Journal*, July 11, 2009; Kevin Wrege, "The Bay State Games," CAHI's Health Care Reform Central, Council for Affordable Health Insurance, July 16, 2009.

52. Grace Marie Turner, "The Failure of RomneyCare," *Wall Street Journal*, March 17, 2010.

53. Will Fox, FSA, MAAA, and John Pickering, FSA, MAAA, "Hospital and Physician Cost Shift: Payment Level Comparison of Medicare, Medicaid, and Commercial Payers," Milliman, Inc., December, 2008; see also, Turner, p. 10.

54. Ibid.

55. Elmendorf letter to Pelosi, Table 2.

56. Gingrich, *To Save America*, p. 93.

57. Elmendorf letter to Pelosi, Table 2.

58. Elmendorf letter to John Boehner, p. 4.

59. Pipes, *The Truth About ObamaCare*, p. 193.

60. Budget Perspective: The Real Deficit Effect of the Health Bill, Senate Budget Committee, Minority Staff, March 18, 2010.

61. Ibid.

62. Senator Barack Obama, Prepared Remarks for Obama's Event in Dover, NH, September 12, 2008; John Lott, "Obama's Health Care Bill Is Not What He Promised," *Fox Forum*, FoxNews.com, March 29, 2010.

63. Ibid.

64. Foster, Estimated Financial Effects of the Patient Protection and Affordable Care Act, p. 9.

65. Transcript, Remarks by the President to a Joint Session of Congress on Health Care, U.S. Capitol, Washington, DC, September 9, 2009.

66. Foster, Estimated Financial Effects of the Patient Protection and Affordable Care Act, Table 3, p. 8.

67. Budget Perspective: The Real Deficit Effect of the Democrats' Health Package, Senate Budget Committee, Minority Staff, March 23, 2010.

68. John D. Shatto and Kent Clemens, Projected Medicare Expenditures under an Illustrative Scenario with Alternative Payment Updates to Medicare Providers, Office of the Actuary, Centers for Medicare & Medicaid Services, August 5, 2010, p. 1.

69. Ibid., p. 5.

70. Ibid. The report from the actuaries at the government's own Centers for Medicare & Medicaid Services states, "At today's levels, Medicaid payment rates have already contributed to well-documented problems with access to physician services. For example, a 2006 survey by the Center for Studying Health System Changes found that 14.6% of physicians had no Medicaid patients and that 21.0% were not accepting new Medicaid patients."

71. U.S. Department of the Treasury, 2010 Financial Report of the United States Government, December 2010, pp. ix, 19.

72. Ibid., p. 3, Table 1 (present value of net expenditures for Medicare is shown as declining from $38.1 trillion in 2009 to $22.8 trillion in 2010, a decline of $15.3 trillion), pp. 20–21, Table 8 (net social insurance expenditures projected to decline from $46 trillion in the 2009 report to $31 trillion in the 2010 report, due to the Medicare cuts again shown in the same table), pp. 46–48; U.S. Government Statements of Social Insurance (present value of future expenditures for Medicare Part A declines from $25.8 trillion in 2009 to $17.1 trillion in 2010; present value of future expenditures for Medicare Part B declines from $23.2 trillion in 2009 to $17.7 trillion in 2010; total present values of future expenditures in

excess of future revenues for social insurance declines from $45.9 trillion to $30.9 trillion).

73. Shatto and Clemens, Projected Medicare Expenditures under an Illustrative Scenario, p. 7.

74. 2010 Financial Report of the United States Government, pp. 4, 28. This was in sharp contrast to the pre-Obamacare "Statements of Social Insurance for 2009, 2008 and 2007," which the GAO found "present fairly, in all material respects, the financial condition of the federal government's social insurance programs, in conformity with U.S. generally accepted accounting principles." Ibid., p. 28.

75. Ibid., p. 129.

76. CBO Long Term Budget Outlook, p. 36.

77. E.g., Affordable Care Act Update: Implementing Medicare Costs Savings, White House, August 2010. The president himself has directly echoed this theme in his weekly radio addresses and elsewhere.

78. Elmendorf letter to Pelosi, Table 4.

79. Ibid.; Holtz-Eakin and Smith, "Labor Markets and Health Care Reform: New Results," p. 4.

80. John Goodman, "Four Trojan Horses," Health Alert, National Center for Policy Analysis, April 15, 2010.

81. Holtz-Eakin and Smith, "Labor Markets and Health Care Reform: New Results," p. 2.

82. Ibid., pp. 2–4

83. Ibid., p. 4.

84. Stephen Moore and Phil Kerpen, "A Capital Gains Tax Cut: The Key to Economic Recovery," IPI Policy Report No. 164, October 11, 2001; Dan Clifton, "The Economic and Fiscal Impact of the 2003 Tax Cut," American Shareholders Association, April 2007.

85. Douglas Holtz-Eakin and Michael J. Ramlet, "The Fiscal Implications of the Patient Protection and Affordable Care Act," Health Affairs; Holtz-Eakin and Smith, "Labor Markets and Health Care Reform: New Results."

86. CBO Long Term Budget Outlook, pp. 29–30. See also Congressional Budget Office, "Technological Change and the Growth of Health Care Spending" (January 2008).

87. CBO Long Term Budget Outlook, Figure 2–1, p. 27.

88. Betsy McCaughey, "Ruin Your Health with the Obama Stimulus Plan," Bloomberg .com, February 9, 2009.

89. Ibid.

90. Council for Affordable Health Insurance, America's Affordable Health Reform Plan: A Common-Sense Solution, 2009.

91. Pipes, The Truth About ObamaCare, p. 150.

92. Nadeem Esmail, Dr. Michael A. Walker, and Dominika Wrona, Waiting Your Turn: Hospital Waiting Lists in Canada, 17th ed. (Vancouver, BC: Fraser Institute, 2007).

93. Matthew Young and Eamonn Butler, "Britain's Million-Year Wait," Health Care News, June 2002.

94. Gerald Anderson et al., "It's the Prices, Stupid: Why the United States Is So Different from Other Countries," Health Affairs, May/June 2002.

95. John C. Goodman, Gerald L. Musgrave, and Devon M. Herrick, Lives at Risk:

Single-Payer National Health Insurance Around the World (Lanham, MD: Rowman & Littlefield, 2004).

96. Nadeem Esmail and Dominika Wrona, "Medical Technology in Canada," *Studies in Health Care Policy*, Fraser Institute, August 2008, Table 10, p. 25.
97. Ibid.
98. Goodman, Musgrave, and Herrick, *Lives at Risk*. A 2007 study published in *Lancet Oncology* found U.S. patients fare better for 13 of 16 types of cancer studied. See David Gratzer, "American Cancer Care Beats the Rest," *Wall Street Journal*, July 22, 2008.
99. Ibid.
100. Nadeem Esmail, "'Too Old' for Hip Surgery," *Fraser Forum*, http://www.fraserinstitute.org, June 6, 2009.
101. Ibid.
102. Ibid.
103. Newt Gingrich, *To Save America* (New York: Regnery, 2010), p. 87.
104. Patient Protection and Affordable Care Act, http://www.gpo.gov/fdsys/pkg/PLAW-111pub/148/pdf/PLAW111pub/148.pdf: sections 6301, 6302, 3001, 3007, 3011–15.
105. Sections 1301, 1302, 2707, 2711, 2713, 2714.
106. Sections 2714, 2702, 2705.
107. Section 2701.
108. Section 1302.
109. Sections 1341, 1343.
110. Section 1501.
111. Sections 1511, 1513.
112. Sections 1311, 1312, 1322.
113. Section 1302.
114. Gingrich, *To Save America*, p. 94.
115. Foster, Estimated Financial Effects of the Patient Protection and Affordable Care Act, p. 10.
116. "The War on Specialists," *Wall Street Journal*, October 6, 2009.
117. Goodman, "Is Managed Competition the Answer?" in Goodman, Musgrave, and Herrick, *Lives at Risk*.
118. Ibid., p. 203.
119. Alain Enthoven, "The History and Principles of Managed Competition," *Health Affairs* (1993 Supplement), p. 35.
120. Goodman, "Is Managed Competition the Answer?" pp. 206–7.
121. Scott Gottlieb, "No, You Can't Keep Your Health Plan," *Wall Street Journal*, May 18, 2010.
122. Lloyd M. Krieger, "ObamaCare Is Already Damaging Health Care," *Wall Street Journal*, February 23, 2011, p. A15.
123. Scott Gottlieb, "No, You Can't Keep Your Health Plan."
124. Sally Pipes, "Private Practices Poor Prognosis," *Orange County Register*, December 17, 2010.
125. Krieger, "ObamaCare Is Already Damaging Health Care."
126. Scott Gottlieb, "No, You Can't Keep Your Health Plan."

127. Sally Pipes, "Private Practices Poor Prognosis."

128. Merrill Matthews, "America's Coming Health Care Oligopoly," *Forbes.com*, July 7, 2010.

129. Ibid.

130. Ibid.; Scott Gottlieb, "What Doctors and Patients Have to Lose Under Obama-Care," *Wall Street Journal*, December 23, 2009.

131. Ibid.

132. Krieger, "ObamaCare Is Already Damaging Health Care."

133. "Sebelius's Price Controls," *Wall Street Journal*, December 22, 2010, p. A18.

134. Sally C. Pipes, "Has Massachusetts Experience Put ObamaCare On A Path to Repeal?" *Investor's Business Daily*, Thursday, January 13, 2011, p. A11.

135. Betsy McCaughey, "What the Pelosi Health-Care Bill Really Says," *Wall Street Journal*, November 7, 2009.

136. "A Breast Cancer Preview," *Wall Street Journal*, November 19, 2009.

137. Dara Richardson-Heron, "Why You Should Keep Getting Mammograms," *New York Post*, November 29, 2009.

138. "A Breast Cancer Preview."

139. Patient Protection and Affordable Care Act, sections 6301, 6302.

140. Leonard A. Zwelling, " 'Comparative Effectiveness' Research Is Always Behind the Curve," *Wall Street Journal*, March 16, 2010. ("Lung, colon and breast cancer treatments are already altered by such molecular findings, and it is likely that some day all cancers will undergo molecular analysis prior to the selection of appropriate treatments.")

141. Gingrich, *To Save America*, p. 91.

142. Leonard A. Zwelling, " 'Comparative Effectiveness' Research Is Always Behind the Curve."

143. Ibid.

144. "Rethinking Comparative Effectiveness Research," Interview with Dr. Donald Berwick, *Biotechnology Healthcare*, June 2009, p. 36.

145. Gingrich, *To Save America*, p. 91.

146. Ibid., p. 90.

147. Betsy McCaughey, "Medical Privacy and Obamacare," *Wall Street Journal*, April 9, 2010, p. A19.

148. President's Council of Economic Advisors, *The Economic Case for Health Reform*, June 2, 2009.

149. Texas Physicians Hospitals, Federal Health Bill Analysis, March 23, 2010.

150. Ibid.

151. Peter Loftus, "Eli Lilly Sets Plans for Emerging Markets," *Wall Street Journal*, June 8, 2010.

152. See, e.g., Marc K. Siegel, "ObamaCare: Flight of the MDs," *New York Post*, December 10, 2010, p. 33; Sally Pipes, "The Damage Has Already Begun," *New York Post*, January 19, 2011, p. 33. ("A Physicians Foundation survey revealed that 40 percent of doctors plan to drop out of patient care in the next one to three years.") *Investor's Business Daily* reports similar survey results.

153. Milton Friedman, "How to Reform Health Care," *Hoover Digest*, no. 3 (2001).

154. Tom Daschle, *Critical: What We Can Do About the Health Care Crisis* (New York: St. Martin's Press, 2008).

155. Ibid., pp. 171–72.

156. Ibid.

157. Donald M. Berwick, MD, A Transatlantic Review of the NHS at 60, Address at the 60th Anniversary Celebration of the NHS, July 1, 2008, Wembley, England.

158. See Peter Ferrara, "The Obama Health Plan: Rationing, Higher Taxes, and Lower Quality Care," Heartland Institute Policy Study No. 123, August 2009, pp. 14–19; "Rethinking Comparative Effectiveness Research," p. 36.

159. "Rethinking Comparative Effectiveness Research," p. 36.

160. Congressional testimony quoted in "Obama's Health Cost Illusion," editorial, *Wall Street Journal*, June 8, 2009.

161. Nat Hentoff, "Health Care Rationing: The Real Death Panels Are Coming Our Way," *RealClearPolitics*, December 7, 2010.

162. "Rethinking Comparative Effectiveness Research," p. 36.

163. Grace Marie Turner, "Summit Standoff," *Health Policy Matters*, Galen Institute, February 26, 2010.

164. Marc K. Siegel, "Bill Loves American Health Care," *New York Post*, February 25, 2010.

165. David Gratzer, *The Cure: How Capitalism Can Save American Health Care* (New York: Encounter Books, 2006), p. 13.

166. Pipes, *The Truth About Obamacare*, pp. 60–61.

167. Ibid.

168. J. P. Newhouse, *Free for All? Lessons from the Rand Health Insurance Experiment* (Cambridge, MA: Harvard University Press, 1994).

169. Scandlen, "Three Lessons from Massachusetts."

170. AHIP, January 2010 Census, p. 7.

171. Ibid., pp. 8–9.

172. Greg Scandlen, "Ten Ways Consumer-Driven Health Care Is a Proven Success," Policy Study No. 125, Heartland Institute, January, 2010, p. 5.

173. Ibid.

174. America's Health Insurance Plans, January 2009 Census Shows 8 Million People Covered by HSA/High Deductible Plans, May 2009.

175. America's Health Insurance Plans, January 2010 Census Shows 10 Million People Covered by HSA/High Deductible Plans, May 2010.

176. Ibid.

177. Michael E. Martinez and Robin E. Cohen, "Health Insurance Coverage: Early Release of Estimates from the National Health Interview Survey, January–June 2009," Centers for Disease Control and Prevention, http://www.cdc.gov/nchs /data/nhis/earlyrelease/insur200912.htm.

178. Scandlen, "Ten Ways Consumer-Driven Health Care Is a Proven Success," p. 12.

179. Martinez and Cohen, "Health Insurance Coverage: Early Release of Estimates."

180. Scandlen, "Ten Ways Consumer-Driven Health Care Is a Proven Success," p. 6.

181. Laura Trueman, Health Savings Accounts: Myth v. Fact, Brief Analysis No. 479, National Center for Policy Analysis, July 19, 2004.

182. C. Hogan, J. Lynn, J. Gable, J. Lunney, A. O'Mara, A. Wilkinson, *Medicare Beneficiaries'*

Costs and Use of Care in the Last Year of Life: Final Report to the Medicare Payment Advisory Commission, (Washington, DC: Medicare Payment Advisory Commission, 2000).

183. National Institute for Health Care Management, "Understanding the Uninsured: Tailoring Policy Solutions for Different Subpopulations," NIHCM Foundation Issue Brief, April 2008; March 2007 Current Population Survey, U.S. Bureau of the Census.
184. Pipes, *The Truth About ObamaCare,* p. 50.
185. Ibid., pp. 49–50; U.S. Census Bureau, People Without Health Insurance by Selected Characteristics (Table 7).
186. NIHCM Foundation Issue Brief, p. 2, n. 71; March 2007 Current Population Survey, U.S. Bureau of the Census.
187. June E. O'Neill and Dave M. O'Neill, "Who Are the Uninsured: An Analysis of America's Uninsured Population, Their Characteristics, and Their Health," Employment Policies Institute, June, 2009, p. 14, Table 7.
188. Census Bureau, *Health Insurance Coverage: 2005,* Housing and Household Economic Statistics Division, 2007.
189. For example, see John C. Goodman, "Ten Steps to Reforming Medicaid," *Health Care News,* July 2008, and John C. Goodman et al., *Handbook on State Health Care Reform,* National Center for Policy Analysis, 2008.
190. Devon Herrick, "Exposing the Myths of Universal Health Coverage," Brief Analysis No. 651, April 9, 2009.
191. Pipes, *The Truth About ObamaCare,* p. 76.
192. Ibid., p. 86.
193. Kaiser Family Foundation, Medicaid: A Primer, January, 2009.
194. J. P. Wieske and Merrill Matthews, "Understanding the Uninsured and What to Do about Them," Council for Affordable Health Insurance, 2007; NASCHIP, *Comprehensive Health Insurance for High-Risk Individuals: A State-by-State Analysis,* 22nd ed., 2008–2009, Denver, 2008.
195. Patient Protection and Affordable Care Act, section 1101.
196. Gingrich, *To Save America,* p. 207.
197. Transcript, President Barack Obama, New Hampshire Town Hall on Health Care, Portsmouth, NH, August 11, 2009.
198. The feasibility of this result is further shown by pathbreaking studies produced over the years by the National Center for Policy Analysis. See, e.g., John C. Goodman, "A Framework for Medicare Reform," National Center for Policy Analysis, Policy Report No. 315, September, 2008.

Chapter 5: The Welfare Empire

1. William Voegeli, *Never Enough: America's Limitless Welfare State* (New York: Encounter Books, 2010), p. 3.
2. Robert Rector, Katherine Bradley, and Rachel Sheffield, "Obama to Spend $10.3 Trillion on Welfare: Uncovering the Full Cost of Means-Tested Welfare or Aid to the Poor," Heritage Foundation, Washington, DC, 2009, p. 2; Katherine Bradley and Robert Rector, "Confronting the Unsustainable Growth of Welfare Entitlements: Principles of Reform and the Next Steps," Heritage Foundation Back-

grounder No. 2427, Heritage Foundation, Washington, DC, June 24, 2010, p. 10. The estimate specifically for 2010 is $697 billion.

3. Rector, Bradley, and Sheffield, "Obama to Spend $10.3 Trillion," p. 2; Bradley and Rector, "Confronting the Unsustainable Growth of Welfare Entitlements," p. 10. The total estimate for 2010 specifically is $888 billion.

4. Rector, Bradley, and Sheffield, "Obama to Spend $10.3 Trillion," p. 1.

5. Ibid., pp. 15–16.

6. Charles Murray, *In Our Hands: A Plan to Replace the Welfare State* (Washington, DC: American Enterprise Institute, 2006).

7. Ibid., p. 20.

8. Rector, Bradley, and Sheffield, "Obama to Spend $10.3 Trillion," p. 2.

9. Edgar K. Browning, *Stealing from Each Other: How the Welfare State Robs Americans of Money and Spirit* (London: Praeger, 2008).

10. Rector, Bradley, and Sheffield, "Obama to Spend $10.3 Trillion," p. 11.

11. Ibid., p. 12.

12. Rector, Bradley, and Sheffield, "Obama to Spend $10.3 Trillion," p. 12. The amount specifically is $15.92 trillion.

13. Ibid.

14. Ibid., p. 13.

15. Ibid., pp. 7–8.

16. Robert Rector, "How Poor Are America's Poor?" Heritage Foundation Backgrounder No. 2064, Heritage Foundation, Washington, DC, August 27, 2007.

17. Ibid., p. 3

18. U.S. Bureau of the Census, Current Population Reports, Series P–60, No. 80, Income in 1970 of Families and Persons in the United States, p. 26.

19. U.S. Bureau of the Census, Current Population Reports, Series P–60, No. 180, Money Income of Households, Families, and Persons in the United States: 1991, p. 7.

20. SRI International, Final Report of the Seattle-Denver Income Maintenance Experiment, vol. 1, Design and Results (Washington, DC, February 25, 1991).

21. Arthur B. Laffer and Stephen Moore, *Return to Prosperity* (New York: Simon & Schuster, 2010), ch. 19.

22. Ibid., pp. 211–12.

23. Arthur B. Laffer, "The Tightening Grip of the Poverty Trap," A. B. Laffer Associates, April 29, 1983.

24. Laffer and Moore, *Return to Prosperity*, p. 212.

25. Linda Ginnarelli and Eugene Steuerle, "The Twice Poverty Trap: Tax Rates Faced by AFDC Recipients," Urban Institute, 1996.

26. Ibid.

27. Jeff Frankel, "Effective Marginal Tax Rates on Lower Income American Workers, *Jeff Frankel's Weblog*, February 8, 2008, http://content.ksg.harvard.edu/blog/jeff _frankels_weblog/2008/02/08/8/.

28. Nancy K. Cauthen, "When Work Doesn't Pay: What Every Policymaker Should Know," National Center for Children in Poverty, June 2006 (as quoted by Laffer and Moore in *Return to Prosperity*, pp. 214–15).

29. The illegitimacy rate is officially reported by the National Center for Health Sta-

tistics. See also, Jason L. Riley, "The State Against Blacks: The Weekend Interview with Walter Williams," *Wall Street Journal*, January 22–23, 2011, p. A13.

30. Tom Bethell, "Culture versus Economy," *The American Spectator*, February, 2011, p. 56.

31. Ibid.

32. These sources are reviewed in Peter J. Ferrara, "Welfare," in Peter J. Ferrara, ed., *Issues '94* (Washington, DC: Heritage Foundation, 1994).

33. See Nicholas Davidson, "Life Without Father," *Policy Review*, Winter 1990; Karl Zinsmeister, "Growing Up Scared," *Atlantic*, June 1990.

34. Anne Hill and June O'Neill, "Underclass Behaviors in the United States: Measurement and Analysis of Determinants," February 1992.

35. Douglas Smith and G. Roger Jarjoura, "Social Structure and Criminal Victimization," *Journal of Research in Crime and Delinquency* (February 1988), pp. 27–56.

36. Rector, Bradley, and Sheffield, "Obama to Spend $10.3 Trillion," p. 25.

37. Rector, "How Poor Are America's Poor?" p. 201.

38. As quoted in ibid., p. 204.

39. Robert B. Carleson, *Government Is the Problem: Memoirs of Ronald Reagan's Welfare Reformer* (Alexandria, VA: American Civil Rights Union, 2009), p. 78.

40. Ibid., p. 57.

41. I am not arguing here that the explosion of welfare since the War on Poverty is the sole cause of rising illegitimacy. Changing social attitudes about sexual behavior undoubtedly also have played a big role. But I am arguing that the welfare system has played a major role, perhaps the major role, based on the above incentives analysis, the data showing the heavy concentration of illegitimacy among the lower income groups most affected by welfare, the correlation between exploding welfare and exploding illegitimacy, and experiments and studies such as SIME/DIME.

42. Robert B. Carleson, *Government Is the Problem: Memoirs of Ronald Reagan's Welfare Reformer* (Alexandria, VA: American Civil Rights Union, 2009), pp. 4, 15.

43. Ibid., pp. xix, xx.

44. Ibid., pp. 104–5.

45. Ibid., pp. 138–39.

46. U.S. House of Representatives, Ways and Means Committee, 2008 Green Book, Section 7, Temporary Assistance for Needy Families, Table 7-8, p. 7-27; Gary MacDougal, Kate Campaigne, and Dane Wendell, *Welfare Reform After Ten Years: A State-by-State Analysis* (Chicago: Heartland Institute, 2009).

47. 2008 Green Book, Table 7-9, pp. 7-28–7-29.

48. Ibid.

49. Ron Haskins, *Work Over Welfare: The Inside Story of the 1996 Welfare Reform Law* (Washington, DC: Brookings Institution, 2006), p. 334.

50. 2008 Green Book, p. 7-26.

51. Ibid., p. 7-54.

52. Ibid., Table 7-4, pp. 7-13–7-14.

53. Ibid.

54. Ibid.

55. Ibid., p. 7-17.

56. Ibid., p. 335.
57. Ibid.
58. Ibid., p. 336.
59. Ibid.
60. Ibid., p. 337.
61. Kenneth Land, *Child and Youth Well-Being Index (CWI), 1975–2004 with Projections for 2005*, http://www.soc.duke.edu/~cwi/.
62. Haskins, *Work over Welfare*, p. 335.
63. Carleson, *Government Is the Problem*, p. 107.
64. Ibid., p. 112.
65. Ibid., p. 124.
66. This is only in return for work, so it is not the guaranteed national income that liberal welfare rights advocates have demanded over the years. But actually it is the true, "moral" equivalent of that demand, in that the poor morally receive that income in return for work.

Chapter 6: The End of the American Dream?

1. See, e.g., Amity Shlaes, *The Forgotten Man: A New History of the Great Depression* (New York: HarperCollins, 2007); Burton Folsom Jr., *New Deal or Raw Deal?* (New York: Threshold Editions, 2008).
2. Robert Bartley, *The Seven Fat Years* (New York: Free Press, 1992), p. 112.
3. Economic Report of the President, January 1993, Table 13-71, p. 430.
4. Ibid., Table 13-69, p. 428.
5. Ibid., Table B-28, p. 380.
6. Ibid.
7. Richard B. McKenzie, *What Went Right in the 1980s* (San Francisco: Pacific Research Institute for Public Policy, 1994), p. 102.
8. Alan Reynolds, "Upstarts and Downstarts," in "The Real Reagan Record," *National Review*, August 31, 1992, p. 26.
9. Ibid., pp. 25–26.
10. Ibid., p. 3.
11. Brian Domitrovic, *Econoclasts: The Rebels Who Sparked the Supply-Side Revolution and Restored American Prosperity* (Wilmington, DE: Intercollegiate Studies Institute, 2009).
12. Peter Ferrara, "When the Republicans Cut Spending," *American Spectator*, September 2008.
13. Ibid.
14. Ibid.
15. Ibid.
16. Bartley, *The Seven Fat Years*, pp. 135, 144.
17. Ibid.
18. Ibid., p. 4; McKenzie, *What Went Right in the 1980s*, p. 8.
19. Arthur B. Laffer, Stephen Moore, and Peter J. Tanous, *The End of Prosperity* (New York: Simon & Schuster, 2008), p. 88.
20. Economic Report of the President, January 1993, Table B-32, p. 385.

21. Ibid., Table 13-69, p. 428.
22. Bartley, *The Seven Fat Years*, p. 4.
23. McKenzie, *What Went Right in the 1980s*, p. 102.
24. Economic Report of the President, January 1993, Table B-28, p. 380.
25. Ibid., Table 13-59, p. 462.
26. Ibid.
27. Ibid., Table 13-69, p. 428.
28. Ibid.
29. McKenzie, *What Went Right in the 1980s*, pp. 7, 187.
30. Ibid., p. 183.
31. Economic Report of the President, 1993, Table B-110, p. 473.
32. Laffer, Moore, and Tanous, *The End of Prosperity*, p. 89.
33. Ibid., p. 3.
34. Steve Forbes, "How Capitalism Will Save Us," *Forbes*, November 10, 2008.
35. Dan Clifton, "The Economic and Fiscal Impact of the 2003 Tax Cut," American Shareholders Association, April 2007,
36. Ibid.
37. Ibid.
38. Ibid.
39. Ibid.
40. Ibid.
41. Ibid.
42. Laffer, Moore, and Tanous, *The End of Prosperity*, p. 9.
43. John B. Taylor, *Getting Off Track* (Stanford, CA: Hoover Institution Press, 2009).
44. Ibid., p. 1.
45. Lawrence H. White, "How Did We Get into This Financial Mess?" Cato Institute Briefing Papers No. 110, November 18, 2008, p. 3.
46. Ibid.
47. Forbes, "How Capitalism Will Save Us."
48. White, "How Did We Get into This Financial Mess?" p. 4.
49. Taylor, *Getting Off Track*, p. 4.
50. Forbes, "How Capitalism Will Save Us," sidebar: "The Importance of a Strong Dollar."
51. Ibid., sidebar: "Good as Gold?"
52. Current Inflation, Inflationdata.com, http://www.inflationdata.com, January 4, 2008.
53. Case-Shiller U.S. National Home Price Index, Standard and Poor's, http://www2.standardandpoors.com, January 4, 2008.
54. Taylor, *Getting Off Track*, p. 61.
55. Ibid.
56. Forbes, "How Capitalism Will Save Us."
57. Steve Hanke, "It's All the Fed's Fault," *Forbes*, November 10, 2008.
58. Alicia H. Munnell, Geoffrey M. B. Tootell, Lynne E. Brown, and James McEneany, "Mortgage Lending in Boston: Interpreting HMDA Data," *American Economic Review* 86 (March 1996), pp. 25–54.
59. Stan J. Liebowitz, "Anatomy of a Train Wreck: Causes of the Mortgage Meltdown,"

Independent Institute, Independent Policy Report, October 3, 2008, p. 6; Theodore Day and Stan J. Liebowitz, "Mortgage Lending to Minorities: Where's the Bias?" *Economic Inquiry* (January 1998), pp. 1–27.

60. Liebowitz, "Anatomy of a Train Wreck," pp. 16–17.

61. Ibid., p. 8.

62. Ibid., pp. 8–10.

63. Ibid., p. 10.

64. Ibid.

65. Ibid.

66. Ibid.

67. Kurtz, "Planting Seeds of Disaster," *National Review Online,* October 7, 2008.

68. Ibid.

69. Ibid.

70. Ibid.; Kurtz, "O's Dangerous Pals," *New York Post,* September 29, 2008.

71. Peter J. Wallison, "The True Origins of This Financial Crisis," *American Spectator,* February 2009, p. 23.

72. Phil Gramm, "Deregulation and the Financial Panic," *Wall Street Journal,* February 20, 2009, p. A17.

73. White, "How Did We Get into This Financial Mess?" p. 6; Thomas Sowell, "Upside Down Economics," *Washington Times,* February 22, 2009, p. B1.

74. Wallison, "The True Origins of This Financial Crisis," p. 24.

75. Ibid., p. 25.

76. Ibid., p. 26.

77. Ibid., p. 25.

78. Liebowitz, "Anatomy of a Train Wreck," p. 11.

79. Gramm, "Deregulation and the Financial Panic," p. A17.

80. As quoted in Liebowitz, "Anatomy of a Train Wreck," p. 12.

81. Liebowitz, "Anatomy of a Train Wreck," p. 12.

82. Ibid.

83. Taylor, *Getting Off Track,* p. 14.

84. Liebowitz, "Anatomy of a Train Wreck," pp. 17–18. ("The increase in foreclosures began virtually the minute housing prices stopped rising. . . . This increase in foreclosures was not due to an economic recession, since the economy was still humming along.")

85. See, e.g., Taylor, *Getting Off Track,* p. 72.

86. Forbes, "How Capitalism Will Save Us."

87. Stan Liebowitz, "House of Cards," *New York Post,* September 24, 2008, p. 27.

88. Liebowitz, "Anatomy of a Train Wreck," p. 7.

89. Peter Ferrara, "Reaganomics v. Obamanomics," *Wall Street Journal,* February 11, 2009.

90. See, e.g., Nongovernmental International Panel on Climate Change, *Climate Change Reconsidered* (Chicago: Heartland Institute, 2009); Science & Environmental Policy Project, http://www.sepp.org; Committee for a Constructive Tomorrow, http://www.cfact.org.

91. The Business Council, Business Roundtable, "Policy Burdens Inhibiting Economic Growth," June 21, 2010.

Chapter 7: The Prosperity of Freedom

1. Arthur B. Laffer, Stephen Moore, and Peter J. Tanous, *The End of Prosperity* (New York: Simon & Schuster, 2008).

2. Ibid.

3. Ibid.

4. Ibid.

5. Ibid.

6. Ibid.

7. Internal Revenue Service, Statistics of Income.

8. Ibid.

9. Ibid.

10. Ibid.

11. Ibid.; "The $31 Billion Fantasy," *Wall Street Journal*, August 28–29, 2010.

12. "The Reagan Tax Cuts: Lessons for Tax Reform," Joint Economic Committee, Congress of the United States, April 1996.

13. Congressional Budget Office; Peter Ferrara, "Federal Income Taxes: Who Pays and How Much," Americans for Tax Reform, Washington, DC, August 2008.

14. Ibid.

15. Ibid.

16. These estimates are not based on a formal econometric model, which is beyond the scope of this book. Such full formal estimates would be produced by the appropriate government agencies in the course of the legislative process. The estimated effects of these reforms are based on thirty years of experience in considering the formal and official estimates of specific reform proposals.

17. Dick Armey and Matt Kibbe, "What Congress Should Cut," *Wall Street Journal*, January 19, 2011, p. A15.

18. Emil W. Henry Jr., "How to Shut Down Fannie and Freddie," *Wall Street Journal*, November 11, 2010, p. A19.

19. Armey and Kibbe, "What Congress Should Cut," *Wall Street Journal*.

20. Stephen Power, "U.S. Weighs Funding for Renewable Energy Projects," *Wall Street Journal*, November 3, 2010; "Wind Jammers at the White House," *Wall Street Journal*, November 11, 2010.

21. Cassandra Sweet and Siobhan Hughes, "Huge Solar Plant Project Approved," *Wall Street Journal*, October 26, 2010.

22. U.S. Energy Information Agency, http://www.eia.doe.gov/oiaf/servicerpt/subsidy2/pdf/chap5.pdf.

23. Gianluca Baratti, "Job Losses From Obama Green Stimulus Foreseen in Spanish Study," Bloomberg News, March 27, 2009, http://www.bloomberg.com/apps/news?pid=newsarchive&sid=a2PHwqAs7BS0.

24. Center for Politiske Studier, "Wind Energy: The Case of Denmark," September 2009, http://www.cepos.dk/fileadmin/user_upload/Arkiv/PDF/Wind_energy_-_the_case_of_Denmark.pdf.

25. Rheinisch-Westfälisches Institut für Wirtschaftsforschung, "Economic Impacts from the Promotion of Renewable Energies: The German Experience," October 2009.

26. This is no accident. It is a direct, natural result of the fundamental science of these alternative fuels. The energy in wind and solar sources of power is vastly disbursed. In the more traditional fossil fuels, it is powerfully more concentrated. Nuclear power represents another whole universe of concentration. That is why the market has chosen these traditional energy sources. Robert Bryce, *Power Hungry: The Myths of "Green" Energy and the Real Fuels of the Future* (New York: PublicAffairs, 2010).

27. Armey and Kibbe, "What Congress Should Cut," *Wall Street Journal.*

28. Office of Personnel Management; Dennis Cauchon, "More Federal Workers' Pay Tops $150,000," *USA Today*, November 10, 2010.

29. Bureau of Economic Analysis; Dennis Cauchon, "Federal Workers Earning Double Their Private Sector Counterparts," *USA Today*, November 13, 2010.

30. Ibid.

31. Armey and Kibbe, "What Congress Should Cut," *Wall Street Journal.*

32. See, e.g., Milton Friedman and Anna Schwartz, *A Monetary History of the United States, 1867–1960* (Princeton, NJ: Princeton University Press, 1963).

33. Brian Domitrovic, *Econoclasts: The Rebels Who Sparked the Supply-Side Revolution and Restored American Prosperity* (Wilmington, DE: Intercollegiate Studies Institute, 2009).

Chapter 8: Failed States

1. Newt Gingrich, *Real Change* (Washington, DC: Regnery, 2008), p. 50.

2. U.S. Census Bureau, 2010 Census.

3. Gingrich, *Real Change.*

4. Ibid.

5. Ibid.

6. Ibid., p. 51.

7. Ibid., pp. 51–52.

8. Ibid., p. 52.

9. Arthur B. Laffer, Stephen Moore, and Jonathan Williams, *Rich States, Poor States* (Washington DC: American Legislative Exchange Council, 2010), p. 11; Joseph Henchman, "State Budget Shortfalls Present a Tax Reform Opportunity," Special Report No. 164, Tax Foundation, February 2009.

10. Gingrich, *Real Change*, p. 51.

11. Ibid., p. 48.

12. Arthur B. Laffer, Stephen Moore, and Jonathan Williams, *Rich States, Poor States* (2010), p. 47; Chris Edwards, Fiscal Policy Report Card on America's Governors: 2010, Policy Analysis No. 668, Cato Institute, Washington, DC, September 30, 2010, p. 20.

13. Edwards, Fiscal Policy Report Card, p. 20.

14. Ibid.

15. Ibid.

16. Laffer, Moore, and Williams, *Rich States, Poor States* (2010), p. 47.

17. Ibid., pp. 48, 51.

18. Ibid., p. 47.

19. Ibid.

20. Edwards, Fiscal Policy Report Card, p. 1.

21. Ibid.

22. Federal Reserve, Flow of Funds Accounts of the United States, Flows and Outstandings, Third Quarter 2010, December 9, 2010, Table L.105, p. 68.

23. Ibid.

24. 2008 Annual Surveys of State and Local Governments, U.S. Census Bureau, Table 1: State and Local Government Finances by Level of Government and by State 2007–2008.

25. United States Government Accountability Office, State and Local Governments' Fiscal Outlook: March 2010 Update, GAO-10-358, March 2010.

26. Ibid., p. 3.

27. Donald J. Boyd and Lucy Dadayan, "Sales Tax Decline in Late 2008 Was the Worst in 50 Years," Nelson A. Rockefeller Institute of Government, February 23, 2010.

28. Laffer, Moore, and Williams, *Rich States, Poor States* (2010), p. 2.

29. Ibid., p. 3.

30. Ibid.

31. Ibid., p. 3.

32. Michael Flynn and Adam B. Summers, "Failed States," *Reason*, May 2009.

33. Laffer, Moore, and Williams, *Rich States, Poor States* (2010), p. 11.

34. Flynn and Summers, "Failed States."

35. National Association of State Budget Officers, Fiscal Survey of the States, December 2009.

36. Laffer, Moore, and Williams, *Rich States, Poor States* (2010), p. 4.

37. E. J. McMahon, *Obama and America's Public Sector Plague* (New York: Encounter Books, 2010), p. 1.

38. Chris Edwards, "Employee Compensation in State and Local Governments," Cato Tax and Budget Bulletin, January 2010.

39. McMahon, *Obama and America's Public Sector Plague*, pp. 2–3.

40. Ibid.

41. Ibid., p. 7.

42. Ibid., pp. 28–29.

43. Josh Barro and E. J. McMahon, "A Tale of Two Workers: How Government Employees Are Getting Better Retirements—Paid for by Taxpayers," *New York Post*, December 19, 2010, p. 27.

44. Ibid.

45. Ibid.

46. Ibid.

47. Ibid.

48. Stephen B. Meister, "Facing the Pension Mess," *New York Post*, December 21, 2010, p. 33.

49. Ibid.

50. McMahon, *Obama and America's Public Sector Plague*, p. 40.

51. Ibid.

52. Barro and McMahon, "A Tale of Two Workers," p. 28.
53. Ibid.
54. Edwards, "Employee Compensation in State and Local Governments," p. 10.
55. Robert Novy-Marx and Joshua D. Rauh, "The Liabilities and Risks of State-Sponsored Pension Plans," *Journal of Economic Perspectives* 23, no. 4 (2009), pp. 191–210.
56. Arthur P. Hall and Barry W. Poulson, "State Pension Funds Fall Off a Cliff," American Legislative Exchange Council, January 2010.
57. Ibid.
58. Ibid.
59. Chris Edwards and Jagadeesh Gokhale, "Unfunded State and Local Health Costs: $1.4 trillion," Cato Institute Tax and Budget Bulletin No. 40, October 2006.
60. Barro and McMahon, "A Tale of Two Workers."
61. Laffer, Moore, and Williams, *Rich States, Poor States* (2010), p. 56.
62. Ibid., p. 57.
63. As quoted in Laffer, Moore, and Williams, *Rich States, Poor States* (2010), p. 57.
64. Ibid.
65. Ibid., pp. 57–58.
66. Mark Sanford, "Why South Carolina Doesn't Want Stimulus," *Wall Street Journal*, March 21, 2009.
67. Laffer, Moore, and Williams, *Rich States, Poor States* (2010), p. 3.
68. Ibid., p. 45.
69. Ibid., p. 3.
70. Ibid., p.4.
71. Ibid., p. 52.
72. CBS News, "State Budgets: The Day of Reckoning," *60 Minutes*, December 19, 2010.
73. Ibid.
74. Laffer, Moore, and Williams, *Rich States, Poor States* (2010), p. 42.
75. Ibid., p. 40.
76. Ibid., p. 45.
77. Edwards, "Employee Compensation in State and Local Governments," p. 23.
78. Ibid.
79. Ibid., p. 46.
80. Ibid., p. 44.
81. CBS News, "State Budgets: The Day of Reckoning."
82. Ibid.
83. Ibid.
84. Ibid.
85. Ibid.
86. Ibid.
87. Ibid.
88. Ibid.
89. "Maryland's Mobile Millionaires," *Wall Street Journal*, March 12, 2010.
90. "Millionaires Go Missing," *Wall Street Journal*, May 27, 2009.
91. Laffer, Moore, and Williams, *Rich States, Poor States* (2010), pp. 26–27, Table 8.
92. Ibid., pp. 28–31, Table 9.

93. Ibid., p. 31.

94. Ibid., p. 32.

95. Ibid., p. 24, Table 7.

96. Ibid., p. 29.

97. Ibid., pp. 25–27.

98. Laffer, Moore, and Williams, *Rich States, Poor States: ALEC-Laffer State Economics Competitiveness Index* (Washington, DC: American Legislative Exchange Council, 2009), p. 55.

99. Ibid., p. 56.

100. Ibid.

101. Ibid.

102. Ibid.

103. Ibid., p. 57.

104. Ibid.

105. Ibid., p.51.

106. Ibid., p.4.

107. Richard Vedder study.

108. "Interstate Migration," Center for Fiscal Accountability, Americans for Tax Reform, http://www.fiscalaccountability.org.

109. Ibid.

110. Ibid.

111. Ibid.

112. Ibid.

113. Ibid.

114. Ibid.

115. Ibid.

116. Laffer, Moore, and Williams, *Rich States, Poor States* (2010), p. 26, Table 8.

117. Ibid., pp. 15, 26.

118. Ibid.

119. Ibid.

120. Ibid., pp. 29–30, Table 9.

121. Ibid., p. 15. Economic research further supports these numbers. In 2004, a National Bureau of Economic Research study, "Do the Rich Flee High Tax States?" found that "wealthy elderly people change their state of residence to avoid high state taxes." The study concluded that states lose as much as one-third of their estate tax revenues as a result. See also Martin Feldstein and Marian Vaillant Wrobel, "Can State Taxes Redistribute Income?" *Journal of Public Economics*, vol. 68, no. 3 (June 1998); E. J. McMahon, Manhattan Institute; Laffer, Moore, and Williams, *Rich States, Poor States* (2010), p. 44.

122. Steve Stanek and Richard Vedder, State Fiscal Policy, *The Patriot's Toolbox* (Chicago: Heartland Institute), ch. 7, p. 212. See also Richard Vedder, "Taxes and Economic Growth," Taxpayers Network, 2001.

123. As reported in Moore, Analysis of the McKay Plan, pp. 5–6.

124. Arthur B. Laffer, Stephen Moore, and Jonathan Williams, *Rich States, Poor States* (2009).

125. Ibid.
126. Ibid.
127. Ibid.
128. Ibid., p. 54.
129. Ibid.
130. Ibid.
131. See, e.g., Zsolt Becsi, "Do State and Local Taxes Affect Relative State Growth?" Federal Reserve Bank of Atlanta, *Economic Review*, March/April 1996, p. 34; Charles Kadlec and Arthur B. Laffer, "Proposition 13: The Tax Terminator," Laffer Associates: June 27, 2003. Others are discussed in Arthur B. Laffer, Stephen Moore, and Jonathan Williams, *Rich States, Poor States* (2009).
132. Laffer, Moore, and Williams, *Rich States, Poor States* (2010), p. 32.
133. Ibid., p. 47.
134. Laffer, Moore, and Williams, *Rich States, Poor States* (2009).
135. J. Scott Moody and Barry W. Poulson, "Setting the Record Straight on Colorado's Bill of Rights," Maine Heritage Policy Center, October 11, 2009.
136. Laffer, Moore, and Williams, *Rich States, Poor States* (2009), p. 45.
137. Ibid.
138. Ibid., p. 51.
139. Ibid.
140. Ibid.
141. Peter Ferrara, "Phasing Out the Virginia State Income Tax," Virginia Institute for Public Policy, August 2010.
142. That investment is usually contracted out to private sector investment fund managers, but the investment is still overseen and subject to the ultimate control of the employer, which can hire and fire investment fund managers as it chooses. When the employer is the government, that means more government control over the private sector.
143. Barro and McMahon, "A Tale of Two Workers."
144. McMahon, *Obama and America's Public Sector Plague*, p. 32.
145. U.S. Government Accountability Office, "State and Local Governments Fiscal Outlook Update," March 2010.
146. E. S. Savas, *Privatization and Public-Private Partnerships* (New York: Chatham House, 2000); E. S. Savas, *Privatization in the City: Successes, Failures, Lessons* (Washington, DC: CQ Press, 2005).
147. Leonard Gilroy and Adrian Moore, "Privatization," in Joseph Bast et al., *The Patriot's Toolbox*, p. 118.
148. Ibid., pp. 120–21.
149. Ibid., p, 134.
150. Ibid., pp. 123–33.
151. Profile of Local Government Service Delivery Choices, International City-County Management Association, 2007.
152. John Hilke, "Cost Savings from Privatization: A Compilation of Findings," Reason Foundation, March 1993.
153. Gilroy and Moore, "Privatization," pp. 137–39.

154. Joseph L. Bast, "School Reform," in Bast et al., *The Patriot's Toolbox*, p. 84.
155. Ibid.
156. Ibid.
157. Ibid.
158. Caroline M. Hoxby, "How School Choice Affects the Achievement of *Public* School Students," in P. T. Hill, ed., *Choice with Equity* (Stanford, CA: Hoover Institution Press, 2002), pp. 141–78; Caroline M. Hoxby, "If Families Matter Most," in T. M. Moe, ed., *A Primer on America's Schools* (Stanford, CA: Hoover Institution Press, 2001), pp. 89–125.

Chapter 9: The Equality of Freedom

1. Kurt Vonnegut, "Harrison Bergeron," in *Welcome to the Monkey House* (New York: Dial Press, 2006).
2. Ibid., p. 7.
3. Ibid., p. 11.
4. Ibid.
5. Ibid., p. 10.
6. Ibid., p. 13.
7. Jay W. Richards, *Money, Greed, and God: Why Capitalism Is the Solution and Not the Problem* (New York: HarperCollins, 2009).
8. Robert Nozick, *Anarchy, State, and Utopia* (New York: Basic Books, 1974).
9. Ibid., p. 163.
10. Ibid., p. 160.
11. Ibid., p. 161.
12. Ibid., p. 163.
13. Sometimes, however, people do choose to make payments to others for reasons other than for production, such as in the case of charity, or gifts for friends or loved ones. But there is nothing about such exchanges that is unfair to the other. They are fully consistent with Nozick's second rationale.
14. John Rawls, *A Theory of Justice* (Cambridge, MA: Harvard University Press, 1971).
15. Ibid., p. 12.
16. Alan Reynolds, *Income and Wealth* (Westport, CT: Greenwood Press, 2006).
17. Ibid., pp. 5, 25, 26, 27.
18. U.S. Census Bureau, "Percent Distribution of Households, by Selected Characteristics within Income Quintile and Top 5 Percent in 2004," Table HINC-05, June 24, 2005, http://pubdb3.census.gov/macro/032005/hhinc/new05_000.htm; Reynolds, *Income and Wealth*, p. 26.
19. U.S. Census Bureau, "Percent Distribution of Households," Table HINC-05.
20. Ibid.
21. Ibid.
22. U.S. Census Bureau, "Historical Income Tables—Experimental Measures," Table RDI-8, May 13, 2004, http://www.census.gov/hhes/income/histinc/rdi8.html; Reynolds, *Income and Wealth*, pp. 25, 28.
23. U.S. Census Bureau, "Historical Income Tables—Experimental Measures," Table RDI-8.

24. Reynolds, *Income and Wealth*, p. 12.
25. Ibid., p. 34; *Statistical Abstract of the United States*, Table 681, U.S. Census Bureau, http://www.census.gov/prod/www/statistical-abstract.htm.
26. Reynolds, *Income and Wealth*, p. 34; *Statistical Abstract of the United States*, Table 675.
27. Reynolds, *Income and Wealth*, pp. 13, 33; *Statistical Abstract of the United States*, Table 681.
28. Reynolds, *Income and Wealth*, p. 36.
29. Griff White, "As Income Gap Widens, Uncertainty Spreads," *Washington Post*, September 20, 2004, p. A1; Robert Kuttner, "The Declining Middle," *Atlantic*, July 1983; Lester Thurow, "The Disappearance of the Middle Class," *New York Times*, February 5, 1984; David Wessel, "U.S. Rich and Poor Increase in Numbers: Middle Loses Ground," *Wall Street Journal*, September 22, 1986; Reynolds, *Income and Wealth*, p. 48.
30. Ibid.
31. Stephen Moore and Lincoln Anderson, "Great American Dream Machine," *Wall Street Journal*, December 21, 2005; Reynolds, *Income and Wealth*, p. 49.
32. Reynolds, *Income and Wealth*, pp. 49–50.
33. Ibid., p. 21.
34. Ibid., pp. 20–21.
35. Ibid., p. 54.
36. Ibid., p. 52.
37. Ibid., p. 55.
38. David Cay Johnston, *Perfectly Legal: The Cover Campaign to Rig Our Tax System to Benefit the Super Rich and Cheat Everybody Else* (New York: Portfolio, 2003), pp. 39, 307; Paul Krugman, "The Death of Horatio," *Nation*, January 5, 2004; Reynolds, *Income and Wealth*, pp. 38, 40.
39. Reynolds, *Income and Wealth*, pp. 37–38, 40; U.S. Census Bureau, http://www.census.gov/hhes/www/income/histinc/h03ar.html.
40. Reynolds, *Income and Wealth*, pp. 39–40; Congressional Budget Office, http://www.cbo.gov/ftpdoc.fm?index+7000&type=1.
41. Statistics of Income Division, Internal Revenue Service, United States Department of the Treasury, SOI Tax Stats—SOI Bulletin—Historical Tables and Appendix, Table 6, n. 3; Reynolds, *Income and Wealth*, p. 75.
42. Alan J. Auerbach, "Who Bears the Corporate Tax," National Bureau of Economic Research Working Paper 11686, October 2005, p. 4.
43. Ibid.
44. Ken B. Cyree, Scott E. Hein, and Timothy W. Koch, "Avoiding Double Taxation: The Case of Commercial Banks," Financial Management Association, October 2005.
45. Reynolds, *Income and Wealth*, p. 82.
46. Ibid., p. 84.
47. Ibid., pp. 75, 108.
48. Ibid., pp. 76, 90–94, 97.
49. Ibid., p. 99.
50. Ibid.; Investment Company Institute, Fundamentals, August 2005; Federal Reserve Board, http://www.federalreserve.gov/releases/z1/Current/data.htm.
51. Reynolds, *Income and Wealth*, p. 99.

52. Ibid.
53. Ibid., p. 79.
54. Ibid., p. 57.
55. Ibid., p. 58.
56. Ibid., p. 59.
57. Ibid., p. 62.
58. Ibid., p. 67.
59. Ibid.
60. Bureau of Economic Analysis, National Income and Products Accounts Tables, Table 7.1, http://www.bea.gov/bea/dn/nipaweb/index.asp; Reynolds, *Income and Wealth*, p. 64.
61. Bureau of Economic Analysis, National Income and Products Accounts Tables, Table 7.1; Reynolds, *Income and Wealth*, p. 66.
62. Bureau of Economic Analysis, National Income and Products Accounts, http:www .bea.gov/bea/dn/home/personalincome.htm; Reynolds, *Income and Wealth*, pp. 67–68.
63. Reynolds, *Income and Wealth*, p. 10.
64. W. Michael Cox and Richard Alm, *Myths of Rich and Poor* (New York: Basic Books, 1999), p. 10.
65. Ibid., p. 20.
66. Ibid., p. 32.
67. Ibid.
68. Ibid., p. 42.
69. Ibid.

Chapter 10: New Labor: Prosperity Unions

1. Details of this story are as reported in Randy Fitzgerald, "Murder in Logan County," *Reader's Digest*, February 1995, pp. 3–7.
2. Ibid., p. 5.
3. Ibid., p. 6.
4. Reed Larson, "Stop Coddling Big Labor Thugs!" *Human Events*, September 26, 1997, p. 6.
5. Ibid.
6. National Institute for Labor Relations Research, "Violence: Organized Labor's Unique Privilege," 1996, pp. 18–19.
7. Larson, "Stop Coddling Big Labor Thugs!"
8. National Institute for Labor Relations Research, "Violence," p. 8.
9. Ibid., p. 9.
10. Ibid., p. 11.
11. Ibid., p. 16.
12. "Judge Orders 150-foot Buffer Between Workers and Pickets," *Anchorage Times*, March 26, 1987.
13. President's Commission on Organized Crime, Record of Hearing VI, April 22–24, 1985, Chicago, Organized Crime and Labor Management Racketeering in the United States, Supt. of Docs. No. 85-603235.
14. Ibid., p. 22.

15. Ibid.
16. Alan Reynolds, *Income and Wealth* (Westport, CT: Greenwood Press, 2006), p. 193.
17. Brian Domitrovic, *Econoclasts: The Rebels Who Sparked the Supply-Side Revolution and Restored American Prosperity* (Wilmington, DE: Intercollegiate Studies Institute, 2009), p. 6.
18. Ibid.
19. Domitrovic, *Econoclasts*, p. 6.
20. Alan Reynolds, *Income and Wealth*, p. 66.
21. Ibid.
22. Stephen Moore and Julian L. Simon, *It's Getting Better All the Time: 100 Greatest Trends of the Last 100 Years* (Washington, DC: Cato Institute, 2000), p. 58.
23. Ibid., p. 98.
24. Ibid.
25. Ibid., p. 68.
26. Ibid.
27. Ibid.
28. Ibid., p. 70.
29. Ibid., p. 68.
30. Ibid., p. 120.
31. Ibid.
32. Ibid., p. 122.
33. Ibid., p. 124.
34. W. Michael Cox and Richard Alm, *Myths of Rich and Poor* (New York: Basic Books, 1999), p. 6.
35. Moore and Simon, *It's Getting Better All the Time*, p. 26.
36. Ibid.
37. Ibid.
38. Ibid., p. 28.
39. Ibid., pp. 32, 5, 7.
40. Ibid., p. 30.
41. Ibid., p. 34.
42. Ibid., pp. 34–35.
43. Ibid., p. 34.
44. Ibid., p. 52.
45. Ibid., p. 52.
46. Ibid., p. 54 (quoting the Heritage Foundation).
47. Ibid., p. 92.
48. Ibid., p. 94.
49. Ibid., p. 5.
50. 487 U.S. 735 (1988).

Chapter 11: The New Civil Rights

1. Stephen Moore and Julian L. Simon, *It's Getting Better All the Time* (Washington, DC: Cato Institute, 2000), p. 9.
2. Ibid. p. 82.

3. Ibid., p. 9.

4. As discussed in Chapter 4, the able-bodied who nevertheless choose not to work must have some other means of support, such as through family or friends, or other reasons of their own for choosing leisure. That would not be real poverty. It would be their own voluntary choice, which they should have in a free society.

5. Newt Gingrich, *Real Change* (Washington, DC: Regnery, 2008), p. 56.

6. Ibid.

7. Ibid.

8. Ibid., p. 51.

9. Ibid., p. 57.

10. Ibid.

11. Ibid., p. 53.

12. Ibid.

13. Over the past forty years, the amount spent on education per student has soared almost 4 times in constant dollars, after inflation. Total U.S. spending on education is over $700 billion, more than is spent on national defense.

14. Gingrich, *Real Change*, pp. 51–52.

15. Ibid., p. 52.

16. Joseph L. Bast, Bruno Behrend, Ben Boychuk, and Marc Oestrich, "The Parent Trigger: A Model for Transforming Education," Policy Brief, Heartland Institute, Chicago, August 2010.

17. Ben Boychuk, "Q&A: What Do Parents Need to Know About the 'Parent Trigger'?" *School Reform News*, Center for School Reform, Heartland Institute, Chicago, November 13, 2010.

18. Ben Boychuk, "Compton Parents 'Trigger' Failing Elementary School," *School Reform News*, Center for School Reform, Heartland Institute, Chicago,December 7, 2010.

19. Ibid.

20. U.S. Bureau of the Census, "Net Worth and Asset Ownership of Households: 1998 and 2000," *Current Population Reports*, May 2003.

21. Ibid.

22. Centers for Disease Control, National Center for Health Statistics, "United States Life Tables 2000," *National Vital Statistics Reports*, December 19, 2002.

23. William Beach and Gareth Davis, "Social Security's Rate of Return," Heritage Center for Data Analysis, Report No. 01-98, Heritage Foundation, Washington, DC, 1998.

24. Constantijn W. A. Panis and Lee Lillard, "Socioeconomic Differentials in the Return to Social Security," RAND Corporation Working Paper No. 96-05, 1996.

25. Peter J. Ferrara and Michael Tanner, *A New Deal for Social Security* (Washington, DC: Cato Institute, 1998), ch. 4.

Chapter 12: The Rebirth of America

1. Charles Murray, *In Our Hands, A Plan to Replace the Welfare State* (Washington, DC: American Enterprise Institute, 2006).